Success in the Stock Market
Using the Power of the Internet

Paul,

Very best wishes,

Dermod

26 July 2017

Success in the Stock Market
Using the Power of the Internet

First edition

Dermod J Sweeney

DJS Financial
Publishing
Limited

DJS FINANCIAL PUBLISHING LIMITED
Website: www.djsfinancialpublishing.com

First edition published May 2016

© DJS Financial Publishing Limited

The right of Dermod J Sweeney to be identified as the author of this work has been asserted by him in accordance with the Copyright, Design and Patents Act 1988.

DJS Financial Publishing Limited is not responsible for the content of third-party Internet sites.

ISBN: 978-0-9935561-0-4

British Library Cataloguing in Publication Data
A CIP catalogue record for this book can be obtained from the British Library.

Printed by CreateSpace, an Amazon.com Company

To my wife, Lynne, and daughters, Catherine and Natasha, who have supported me through four years of writing this book.

About the Author

Dermod Sweeney was managing director of engineering and scientific consultancy businesses for more than thirty years and began investing in 1987. He has invested in funds, listed companies, and start-up companies directly and through the Enterprise Investment Scheme and Venture Capital Trusts.

He successfully navigated the stock market crashes of 2001 and 2008.

Over the years, he has used advisory stock brokers on three occasions and has been disappointed each time. It was these experiences that prompted him to undertake his own research into the detailed operation of stock markets – which has formed the basis of this book.

He has served as a non-executive director of start-up companies.

Contents
Overview

Contents

4 About shares and how shares are valued – 47

5   Factors that influence share prices – 93

6   The market participants, facilitators, and influencers – 137

13 Fund selection methodology – 305

14 Share selection methodology – 320

15 A day in the markets – 332

18 Managing your portfolio – 368

Introduction

'Risk comes from not knowing what you are doing.'
Warren Buffett

Stock markets around the world are involved with staggering amounts of money – around US$70tn – and so they attract the attentions of a great many clever and ambitious people, many of them ruthless. Combine this with the vagaries of geopolitics and the often rapidly changing fortunes of companies – resulting in severe volatility in share prices – and the stock market becomes a frightening place for a great many people. It is important to realize that markets, as expressed through indices such as the S&P 500 (USA) and the FTSE 100 (UK), can be highly volatile, moving up and down dramatically in very short periods of time. The fluctuations in individual share prices can be even more startling. Individual share price movements of 30% or more in one day are not unusual. However, a good understanding of how the markets behave and how to manage your investment risk should enable you to succeed as an investor. An ability to cope emotionally with serious volatility is useful, but this is much easier to handle if you understand what is going on.

This book is written for people like the author – the ordinary man or woman in the street – who want to make their money work for them. He (and of course, she) is often referred to in the industry as the 'retail investor.' This is intended to be a very practical guide to successful investing. It goes into some technical depth in a few places, but this should not detract from the overall value of the book.

Most books on investment in the stock markets focus on buying and selling individual shares. This book deals fairly extensively with investing in shares through funds as well as through individual shares. This is a form of investing that will better suit many retail investors, and can be more rewarding provided you understand the drivers of the powerful financial services industry, which habitually takes advantage of the small consumer. The fund management industry is unable to distinguish in a satisfactory manner between volatility and risk and encourages the unwary retail investor to sink his money every month into large, dull funds. There are companies that offer a wealth management service that will involve investing across a range of asset classes, but the subject of this book is investing in shares – also known as equities.

There are numerous books on how stock markets work and how to make money from trading and investing in company shares. They are written from a range of perspectives and the interested investor will get something valuable out of all of them. A perspective of this book is that the unwary retail investor is at a serious disadvantage to the professionals, but if he understands the terrain of the stock markets, he can position himself to outperform a great many of those professionals. One of the advantages that the retail investor has over the larger professional investors is that he will usually have a relatively small amount of money available to invest, and it is much easier to find small areas of quality or value than large areas. This is arguably why Warren Buffett, widely acknowledged to be the world's most successful investor, doesn't beat the S&P 500 by as much as he used to through his investment company, Berkshire Hathaway – it simply has too much money to invest!

To assist you in understanding the terrain, the workings of the stock markets and how they interact globally are described, together with the forces at work that lead to often quite violent movements in share prices during the trading day – making it so problematic for the retail investor.

Investing in the US and UK markets is the main focus here. However, given the influence of the US market in particular on stock markets around the world, and the universality of factors that influence share prices, this book should be a useful addition to the bookshelf of the retail investor operating in other markets. It is based on using the Internet to support an investment strategy and many websites are referenced using search words which are underscored for clarity.

The author has been investing in the stock market for about thirty years with a fair measure of success and has endeavoured in this book to describe the investment methodology that he has developed. It is a conservative methodology with the concept of preservation of capital at its core. Nevertheless, the author cannot accept responsibility for any unsuccessful investments made by a reader.

1 The power of the Internet

Nasdaq and the Big Bang

The door is opening to the retail investor.

There have been many significant events in the evolution of 'joint stock companies' and stock exchanges around the world – 'joint' means jointly owned by a number of shareholders.

In the US, a profound change to the old order took place in 1971, when the Nasdaq Stock Market was founded by the National Association of Securities Dealers Automated Quotations. It was the world's first electronic stock market and it paved the way for easier and cheaper access to stock markets for the retail investor – as well as the introduction of automated trading systems, which has not been entirely positive.

The New York Stock Exchange (NYSE) has responded to the challenge from the Nasdaq and most of its trading is now undertaken on electronic systems. However, the traditional stock jobbers on the trading floor – matching buyers and sellers using an auction process with 'open-outcry' – still retain a place on the floor of the NYSE.

It took some time after the Nasdaq burst onto the scene for the UK to react with the 'Big Bang' on 27th October 1986. The Big Bang was centered on the deregulation of the London Stock Exchange (LSE). The exchange was privatized and became a public limited company (plc). The cozy 'club' of LSE members was opened up to outside companies and the way was paved for the introduction of automated, electronic trading systems – which has revolutionized share trading in the UK. The days of stock jobbers and open-outcry on the floor of the LSE were rapidly swept away.

Previously, private investing had been an exclusive domain, with investors paying high commissions to their stockbrokers, who advised them on investments and kept them informed by phone. The investors would hold their share certificates and receive company reports by mail. With the advent of the Big Bang, stockbroking was going to get a lot more competitive and service-orientated, to the enormous benefit of the retail investor!

The Internet opens the door wide

On 12 March 1989, Tim Berners-Lee, a British computer scientist, presented a proposal for improving the CERN (European Organization for Nuclear Research) communication system, and this laid the foundation for the World Wide Web and the boisterous rise of the Internet. Berners-Lee completed the construction of the world's first website in December 1990 and, as they say, the rest is history. The retail investor is now empowered like never before. He can buy and sell shares cheaply online, supported by virtually unlimited and easily accessible information on companies and the environments in which they operate. There is a proliferation of free websites providing advice, information flows and investor tools, and endless views and commentary, which are invaluable if you know how to filter and interpret them. Real time share price movements and trading volumes, information Level 1, can be accessed free or cheaply, and for not very much more, you can access the stock exchange automated trading systems at information Level 2. At Level 2, you can see the order book for 'buys and sells' and the stock exchange computer at work matching buy and sell orders. If you wish, you can obtain direct market access through a stockbroker and place buy and sell orders directly onto the stock exchange order book. If funds are more to your taste, there are websites that rank fund performance and provide you with invaluable information, enabling you to pick out the best funds – which have a history of spectacular performance!

With this in mind, frequent references are made throughout to Internet information sources, which should greatly enhance the value of the book – and also help to keep it up to date. As you read, you should go online if you can and access some of these sources. You will be able to interact with many of them in real time and learn to how to get the most from them. The volume of Internet data and information sources can be bewildering, but those referenced here provide a sound basis for a successful investment strategy. To succeed, you will need to build on these to develop your own portfolio of Internet data sources, newspapers, periodicals, and financial television programs that you feel comfortable with – creating your own investment management system.

The emergence of electronic trading and the birth of the Internet have changed the game for the retail investor, and while the playing field of the stock markets is not nearly level, there are some level areas, and these days the well-equipped and motivated retail investor can outperform a great many hedge funds. There are too many of them, and their size and generous fee structures handicap their performance.

Not all has been positive

Deregulation on both sides of the Atlantic sowed the seeds for the crisis that was brewing in 2007, resulting in the crash of 2008, which was the start of the global financial crisis.

You will find an informative article on the regulatory failings in the US by searching Huffington Post Robert Weissman Deregulation and the Financial Crisis.

In summary, US Federal Reserve policy sustained interest rates at too low a level, while making little attempt to contain the developing housing market bubble, which was inflated in large part by predatory lending. At the same time, financial deregulation allied with 'financial innovation' resulted in lending banks selling bad mortgages on to investment banks. In turn, the investment banks packaged them into 'Collateralized Debt Obligations' (CDOs) and sold them on to investors who thought they would provide reliable income streams. There was a complete failure by credit rating agencies, nurturing their relationships with the investment banks, to assess the true risks associated with these CDOs.

In the UK, deregulation led to wholesale restructuring of the UK financial markets, centered in London, which has had some devastating side effects. Many of the traditional City of London firms were taken over by international banks, forming the large investment banks that we see today. As you will see as you read, these organizations brought under the same roof a disparate number of activities, often with different cultures and values and with many conflicts of interest. Unfortunately, a frequently common value was greed, and the toxic mix created was a substantial ingredient in the global financial crisis – which was not in the least bit good for all but the most agile in the retail investment community. The regulatory framework was meant to develop in parallel with the rampant financial markets, but the regulators in the US, the US Securities and Exchange Commission, and in the UK, the Financial Services Authority (now the Financial Conduct Authority), found it a challenge to keep up.

Playing the game

It is common knowledge that the stock markets are gamed. The investment industry is heavily populated with people equipped with excellent information sources, using sophisticated trading algorithms and sailing very close to the wind in a number of ways. Many of the trading algorithms are capable of high-frequency trading. There are many types of trading algorithm, each designed to follow a particular trading strategy – buying and selling shares, sometimes several times a second throughout the trading day or within a millisecond of an important data release. Another section of the same industry is advising you not to get involved in the stock market unless you are prepared to think long-term, i.e., be prepared to buy some shares and then wait for many years in the hope that you might eventually see a return. These concepts are difficult to reconcile. What they have in common is that both arise from the self-centered nature of the financial industry, which pays insufficient attention to consumer needs. However, if you understand how the market participants operate and you invest intelligently, the markets can be highly rewarding.

2 Setting the scene

The market participants, facilitators, and influencers

Stock markets have participants, facilitators and influencers – and regulators. It is important to understand their roles and motivations and how they operate.

The main actors described in this book, and covered in some detail in *Chapter 6,* are:

- Dealers, brokers, and broker-dealers
- The institutional investors
- The banks
- Fund managers
- The trading desk
- Activist shareholders
- Hedge funds
- Stock exchanges
- Market makers
- Index companies
- Investment advisers
- Corporate or house stockbrokers
- Retail stockbrokers
- The analysts
- The retail market
- Private equity
- Predator companies
- Corporate interests
- Company insiders
- Founders and owners
- Short sellers
- Traders
- Futures and options traders
- High-frequency traders
- Financial information groups
- Media
- Academics
- Regulators – last, but not least!

The interplay between all of these actors creates an environment for the retail investor that is full of complexities.

Ways of investing

To offset these complexities, a strong theme of this book is that the retail investor's portfolio should be a balance between high quality funds – pooled investments – and individual company shares. If not entirely in funds! For the retail investor, the most accessible instruments for retail investing – or trading – in the stock market are the following:

- Individual company shares.
- Funds:
  - Mutual funds in the US.
  - Open-ended Investment Companies – OEICs – the UK. This is the most common form of pooled investment in the UK. OEICs have evolved from unit trusts, and most unit trusts have made the conversion to OEIC status.
  - Exchange Traded Funds (ETFs). In the context of company shares, these usually track a stock market index.
  - Investment companies/Investment trusts. Also a form of pooled investment and commonly referred to as a form of fund. These are companies traded on the stock market.
- Contracts for Difference (CFDs) in the UK. This product, where the values of shares are traded, rather than the shares themselves, is not available in the US.

For the retail investor, CFD trading overlaps with gambling. If you really know what you are doing, you can probably play with better odds with CFDs than many other forms of gambling, but for most people there are better ways to make money in the markets.

The leading stock markets

A few broad-brush comments on leading stock markets will help to set the scene.

USA

The US stock market is the most important and other stock markets around the world are strongly influenced by it. Main US stock exchanges are the New York Stock Exchange and the Nasdaq Stock Market and the most important stock market indices are the Dow Jones Industrial Average, the S&P 500, and the Nasdaq 100.

The companies of the S&P 500 have an average market capitalization – market cap – of close to US$40bn and represent a powerhouse of commercial activity that no other country comes close to. (Market cap is the value of a company based on its share price and is explained in *Chapter 3 – Stock markets*). Many of these companies operate globally, so the index is impacted by fluctuations in economic activity in many parts of the world. While the US market takes a great deal of notice of what is happening in other markets, when the US economy is powering forward it is quite capable of shrugging off perturbations in other economies.

There are ten sectors in the S&P 500. The sum of company market caps in each sector as of November 2015 is shown in Table 2.1.

Sector	Market Cap US$tn
Financials	3.7
Information Technology	3.1
Health Care	2.5
Consumer Discretionary	2.5
Consumer Staples	1.8
Industrials	1.7
Energy	1.6
Telecommunications Services	0.9
Materials	0.8
Utilities	0.6
Total	**19.2**

Table 2.1 S&P 500 sector markets caps

There is great variation in the performance of these sectors. The Financials sector, with a market cap of US$3.7tn, is larger than most stock markets around the globe. Ironically, the size of the US Financials sector was a key factor in the financial crisis, with indiscriminate lending rife across the USA.

China

A typical headline: 'Thursday sees the initial estimate of February's manufacturing PMI – Purchasing Managers' Index – published by HSBC and Markit, probably the foremost independent measure of the Chinese economy.'

Deng Xiaoping began his economic reforms in China in the 1970s, kicking off an average growth rate close to 10% year on year. Growth peaked in 2010 after touching close to 12% and then declined steadily to around 7% in 2015. Gross domestic product (GDP) grew from US$147bn in 1978 to over US$9.2tn by 2014, representing almost 15% of the world's economy and second only to the US economy with a GDP of around US$17tn. In 2009, China overtook Germany as the world's biggest exporter and became the world's largest energy user.

As the world entered the third millennium, China embarked on an unprecedented building boom. At the height of the boom in 2010, the Chinese economy was sucking in around half the resources that were being extracted from the ground around the world. This led to a boom in commodity prices and the shares of mining companies hit all-time highs.

China undertook a great deal of the heavy lifting as the world economy hauled itself back after the financial crisis, as both an importer and an exporter. It is not surprising that after the financial crisis, economic data out of China has become among the most watched by the investment community – with the ability to move major stock market indices.

As China's growth rate slowed post-building boom, it sought to transform itself into a consumer-based economy. Property prices overheated and a significant risk hanging over global stock markets was the possibility of a crash in property prices. The Chinese government has so far been able to manage this risk, though property prices have fallen.

In 2015, China's H-Shares (see *Chapter 3 – Stock markets)* had reached record levels, with the Chinese stock market indices rising faster than the technology focused Nasdaq indices before the dot.com bubble burst in 2001. In the summer of 2015, China's stock market bubble burst in spectacular fashion.

Serious retail investors should keep an eye on China.

Europe

The GDP of the European Union, at US$18.5tn, is a little higher than that of the US. Germany (US$3.9tn) and France (US$2.8tn) are the dominant continental European economies, with the UK lying in between at US$2.9tn. The travails of Europe, post–financial crisis, are well known and documented, in particular the lack of competitiveness of the southern European countries shackled by the 'one-size-doesn't-fit-all' Euro. Post–financial crisis, the UK has benefited enormously from not being a member of the Eurozone. Major European stock market indices are mentioned below.

In recent years, the UK economy has created a great many jobs, but has struggled to increase its productivity per worker. The globally focused FTSE 100's performance has been heavily hit by the number of large mining companies in the index, such as Rio Tinto and BHP Billiton, and banks, such as Royal Bank of Scotland and HSBC, which have been hit with heavy fines to compound difficult market conditions. The FTSE 250, much more reflective of the domestic UK economy, has substantially outperformed the FTSE 100.

The main German stock market index, containing 30 companies, is the DAX. Germany's economy is dominated by high quality manufacturing by household names such as BMW, Siemens, Merck, Miele, and Bayer. In recent years, it has exported strongly to the rest of the EU, and China has been a particularly important export market. The slowdown in China has had a serious impact on German's mighty exporting machine. In 2015, Volkswagen's emission problems cast a long shadow over Germany's reputation for manufacturing quality.

France has a number of world-class companies, such as LVMH, Air France, Électricité de France, Alcatel Lucent, PSA Peugeot Citroën, and Société Général. A number of these are substantially owned by the state. France has adhered strongly to socialist values and the structural reform of its economy is painfully slow. This feeds through to a lackluster performance of the stock market. France's main stock market index is the CAC 40.

Japan

Japan's economy is the third-largest in the world.

The most important Japanese stock market index is the Nikkei 225, which peaked at just short of 40,000 in December 1989 and then began a decline lasting nearly 20 years. Early in 2009, the index finally bottomed out at about 7,000. Japan's lost decade had become two lost decades. GDP collapsed and real wages fell.

Cozy relationships between banks and corporations had led to a massive asset bubble based on bad debt. The bubble burst when the bank of Japan raised interbank lending rates sharply at the end of 1989 in order to dampen inflation. Through the lost decades, the government kept 'too big to fail' institutions going through loans, with companies reluctant or unable to use the capital markets to raise money through issuing shares and bonds.

Only in the last five years has the Japanese economy begun to throw off its 20-year malaise. Shinzo Abe was elected to a second term as prime minister in December 2012 and embarked upon a 'three arrows' program of economic reform involving the fiscal stimuli of government spending and quantitative easing, monetary easing, and structural reforms. In 2015, the Nikkei 225 spent a few months over 20,000 before pulling back into a trading range between 16,000 and 20,000.

Key considerations

·It is stating the obvious to say that you need to buy cheap and sell high, but unfortunately the inexperienced retail investor has a tendency to buy high and sell cheap. You don't need to fall into this trap!

It's important to understand the great stock market crashes of the last 30 years and overall stock market valuations. You also need to understand how shares are valued and factors that influence share prices, as well as the role that Fundamentals and Technicals play in the stock market. It is important to understand risk and how to preserve your capital. You should manage your portfolio defensively and always be aware of your exposure to market risk – your percent invested (PCI). When markets appear vulnerable, you should consider taking some profit or closing positions that are not working well.

You need to develop a strategy – how will you position yourself between investing and trading; how will you allocate your investments between funds and individual shares; will you place your emphasis on investing for income – dividends – or growth in capital value; will you take a short-term or long-term perspective?

Regardless of advice from the financial services industry, the timing of your investment decisions is important. A great deal of the time, market indices are testing all-time highs, so you need to be aware of underlying sector performance as well as the fluctuating fortunes of companies. You should always try to buy on a market pullback.

You need to have some understanding of the index futures markets, which strongly influence the main cash markets, and the practice of shorting – betting on share price declines.

Methodologies for selection of funds and shares are proposed and considerable attention is paid to portfolio management with an emphasis on managing risk. There is a chapter on using a stockbroker.

Some definitions

You will notice that the book refers fairly pedantically to 'shares' traded on stock exchanges. 'Stock' and 'share' are often used interchangeably – the difference is discussed in the next chapter. Shares are often described as equities and this term is sometimes used. The book deals with buying and selling company shares directly or through funds.

It is also useful to mention that US English definitions of 'billion' and 'trillion', now broadly accepted in UK English, are used:

Million (mn): 1,000,000
Billion (bn): 1,000,000,000
Trillion (tn): 1,000,000,000,000

3 Stock markets

The Pilgrims is the name given to early settlers of the Plymouth Colony in the United States. They came from the congregations of Brownist English dissenters who had fled religious persecution in England and settled in the Netherlands. From there, they struck out for North America in the seventeenth century to establish a new colony in which they could maintain their way of life. They were financed by English investors.

Introduction

The major stock exchanges around the world, such as the New York Stock Exchange (NYSE) and the London Stock Exchange (LSE), came into existence to facilitate the activities of investors and brokers, but evolved into commercial companies operating in a competitive marketplace. Modern stock exchanges are serious businesses. In their quest for profitable business, they work closely with many market participants, including investment banks and trading houses. For example, they create special types of trade to suit major customers and they accommodate the high-frequency traders vying to co-locate their servers with those of the exchanges to create high-speed connections. And they compete vigorously among themselves for companies to list on their exchanges.

Often referred to as public exchanges, the traditional stock exchanges make up the bulk of the cash market where shares change hands for cash. Shares – or more accurately, derivatives of share prices – are also traded on the futures markets, which operate on margin – effectively, borrowed money. The futures markets are described in *Chapter 9*.

The ideal purpose of a stock market is to enable the most efficient use and allocation of capital by bringing buyers and sellers of company shares together. People or organizations that have free capital can invest in companies that they believe will do well with the expectation that they will increase their capital. If companies disappoint, investors can withdraw their capital. Especially when markets are buoyant, people and institutions will borrow heavily to invest in the markets.

A great deal of the money in the markets is invested by pension funds and insurance companies working hard, if not always effectively, for their clients. They seek to allocate capital efficiently and to reap a reward from doing so. However, there are many market participants that have no direct interest in efficient use of capital – only in making quick money. These participants have an undue influence on the markets, often creating irrationally large and rapid fluctuations in share prices – and they can do real damage to companies. You may recall Lord Turner at the World Economic Forum, Davos 2010, saying that while he recognized the need for liquidity in financial markets, 'much proprietary trading activity serves no useful social purpose.'

Notwithstanding the above, we have to deal with the markets as they are and if you want to make money, you need to understand the nature of the playing field. It will be you and perhaps one or two advisors against an army of millions that are delighted if you lose money, as it helps them to make money. The stock market is sometimes – but not always – a zero-sum game, but you should always regard it as such; i.e., your loss will be someone else's gain.

Stocks and shares

The S&P 500 accounts for close to 30% of global stock market value. 24% of the world's financial assets are in company shares.

Stock is a general term used to describe both company shares and bonds. Shares concern the ownership of companies, whereas bonds relate to a company's debt.

Stock markets allow companies to raise money to support their activities and to grow their businesses. Within a stock market, there is a primary market supporting companies coming to the stock market – listing – by issuing shares; this market also supports the raising of new capital by established companies issuing new shares. Once these new shares have been issued, they are traded on the secondary market. The secondary market is the main market.

New issues are brought to the market through initial public offerings (IPOs) on the primary market. On listing or floating on the exchange, they issue – sell – a proportion of their shares to investors at 'market value,' i.e., what investors are prepared to pay for them. Also, founder shareholders see listing as an effective way for them to convert their efforts in building their company's capital into cash.

If shareholders become dissatisfied with the performance of a company, they can sell their shares, i.e., withdraw their capital. If enough people withdraw their capital, the share price will collapse, creating serious problems for the management of the company. The managers may be major shareholders themselves, and if the company has bank debt it may well breach its loan covenants, causing the bank to call in its loans, and force the wind-up of the company. Alternatively, the bank may take over the company. The investors who have sold their shares can then opt to buy the shares of another company that they believe has a better chance of succeeding; thus reallocating their capital.

An increasing share price is a great benefit to a company – managers and staff are likely to benefit through a variety of remuneration arrangements; the company will be able to borrow money at favorable interest rates; and it has the possibility to use its shares – its 'paper' – to acquire other companies. Acquisitions are commonly made using a combination of cash and paper. The higher the share price of a company, the less likely it is to become an acquisition target itself. The senior managers in a company that is taken over are often eased out, so the last thing they want is to be taken over; but this is not always the case – it can depend on the incentivization arrangements of the senior management! See 'Acquisitions – predator or prey?' in *Chapter 5 – Factors that influence share prices*, where golden parachutes for chief executives are discussed.

Long and short

> *There is a strong strand of opinion that naked short selling – selling shares that you don't own! – was the main factor in the demise of Lehman Brothers, a highly significant event in the 2008 stock market crash.*

The focus of this book is making a profit by buying and selling shares either directly or through funds. If you buy a share that you think is going to rise in value, you are taking a long position. You can also seek to make money by taking a short position in a share by anticipating that it will fall in value. You do this by borrowing the shares (there will be a borrowing cost) and selling them – hoping to buy them back at a cheaper price. You then return the share to the lender, if things have gone to plan, having made a profit. A short position is generally regarded as more risky than a long position, mainly because with a long position the worst that can happen is that the share price drops to zero and you lose all your money; with a short position, you can lose more than your original stake. For example, you borrow an Average Inc. share worth US$100 and sell it straight away, so you have US$100 in hand. Average Inc.'s share price then goes through the roof, because it looks as though it could be taken over, tripling in value to US$300. To close your position (short covering), you have to buy the share back at US$300 and return it to the lender. You have US$100 from the original sale, so you are US$200 (plus borrowing and dealing costs) out of pocket. It's rare for a share price to triple in value in short order, but it does happen.

Shorting is described in *Chapter 8 – Short selling; Chapter 9 – Futures and options;* and in *Chapter 11 – Trading with Contracts for Difference (CFDs)*.

Market capitalization

When a company is formed, a number of shares are created, and then subject to shareholder agreement, a proportion of these are issued for ownership by founders, staff and third parties – these are known as the 'shares outstanding.'

A basic – and important – parameter for companies is their market capitalization, or market cap. This is calculated by multiplying the number of shares outstanding by the current market price of one share. When a company floats on a stock exchange, a proportion of the outstanding shares are made available for trading on the stock exchange – this is known as the company's free float. As its share price moves up and down, so does its market cap. Sometimes a proportion of a company's outstanding shares may be held by, for example, a founder shareholder or a government and not be part of the free float that is traded daily on the stock market. However, these non-free float shares will come into play if another party is looking to take over the company or take a majority stake in it. Stock exchanges have rules on the minimum size of free float – these can be complex.

Whenever you look at a company that you might invest in, you should note its market cap. This is very significant in terms of the news flow for a company. A large S&P 500 or FTSE 100 company may have a market cap of US$50bn and a constant flow of news that can have an impact on its share price. A very small company may have a market cap of just a few million dollars or pounds, and you may not get much more news than its quarterly or twice-yearly reports and perhaps an occasional press release. If these delight or disappoint the market, the accompanying percentage share price movements can be very significant.

A much-used classification system for market cap is 'large cap,' 'mid cap,' and 'small cap,' though the defining range of values will vary between stock markets and with time. Currently in the US, the convention shown in Table 3.1 is used.

Large cap	US$10bn to $200bn	e.g., Microsoft, Walmart, General Electric and IBM; the average market cap of an S&P 500 company is circa US$38bn.
Mid cap	US$2bn to $10bn	Minimum market cap for an S&P 500 company is circa US$5.3bn.
Small cap	US$300mn to $2bn	See S&P SmallCap 600 index and Russell 2000 index.

Table 3.1 US stock market capitalizations

A small number of companies with market caps above US$200bn, such as Alphabet (owner of Google), ExxonMobil, and Apple are described as mega cap.

For the UK, the convention is based on the main LSE indices, as shown in Table 3.2.

Large cap	FTSE 100	Above circa £3bn, with only a handful of companies above £50bn; only HSBC and Shell are greater than £100bn.
Mid cap	FTSE 250 and AIM 50	£500mn to £3bn; a small number of companies below £500mn.
Small cap	FTSE Small cap	Under £500mn.

Table 3.2 UK stock market capitalizations

Public stock exchanges

There are 13 traditional public stock exchanges in the US. In addition to the New York Stock Exchange (NYSE) and the Nasdaq Stock Exchange, there is the American Stock Exchange (AMEX) based in New York, specializing in small- and medium-sized companies. There are also important regional stock exchanges, such as the Philadelphia and Boston exchanges. Most share trading in the UK is undertaken on the London Stock Exchange (LSE).

Companies are 'listed' on stock exchanges for trading. The bulk of share trading still takes place on the public stock exchanges, though alternative trading venues are growing in importance. In the US, there are around 50 alternative trading systems (ATSs), many of which provide 'unlit' or dark pool trading. BATS, an electronic trading network, is the largest. Estimates put the number of dark pools at around 40. In the UK, trading also takes place on Turquoise, a multilateral trading facility (MTF) which is 60% owned by the LSE. ATSs, MTFs, and dark pools are described below.

Public stock exchanges exist around the world and are subject to strict regulation as are the shares themselves as financial instruments. In the US, the primary regulator is the US Securities and Exchange Commission (SEC). In the UK, the activities of the LSE are regulated by the Financial Conduct Authority and EU directives. In addition, the exchanges themselves strictly regulate the activities that take place on their exchanges. Shares traded on public exchanges are standardized instruments and investors are not subject to counterparty risk. This is the risk that the party you trade with does not deliver his side of the bargain, i.e., does not come up with the cash or the shares!

Each share has a unique stock ticker symbol to identify it, often simply known as the ticker. This is derived from the ticker tape, which shows movements in share prices known as ticks. For example, the symbol or ticker for ExxonMobil Corporation is XOM. Stock exchange indices also have tickers, in some cases more than one.

Trading takes place by parties bidding to buy shares or offering to sell their shares at an offer, or ask, price. Offer and ask are used interchangeably. In normal trading, the offer price is higher than the bid price because the bidder always prefers a deal below the offer price. The price difference is the bid-offer spread.

Share trading is managed through the stock exchange 'limit order book,' where 'limit' defines the highest bid and lowest offer that participants are prepared to trade at. Limit order books are described in more detail below. The major market participants arrange direct market access (DMA) to the limit order book and trade 'on the order book.' Other participants will obtain access through a broker, quite possibly on an automated trading platform. Stockbrokers can arrange DMA for retail investors.

Stock exchanges typically offer trading at two levels. Level 1, where basic bid and offer quotes are provided; and Level 2, which is the stock exchange limit order book showing buy and sell orders that will be met depending on incoming orders and share price movements. Level 2 can be viewed by retail investors who don't have DMA for a subscription, with the idea that it can support their trading activities. Levels 1 and 2 are described in more detail below and in *Chapter 10 – Trading.*

Stock markets are designed to provide liquidity in the markets. If a share has good liquidity, you will be able buy and sell it immediately in the markets while they are open at the prevailing price, i.e., for every seller there will be an immediate buyer and vice versa – but not in unlimited numbers of shares. There are various trading systems used to enable this.

The most important stock exchanges in the West are in New York and London, the home of the LSE. In the US, the largest exchanges are the NYSE and the Nasdaq Stock Market. Both are registered national stock exchanges. They operate in different ways and only a limited number of companies are listed on both exchanges. The third most important exchange is BATS – Better Alternative Trading System – which handles 11% to 12% of US share-trading volume. BATS is also a major operator in Europe through BATS Chi-X Europe, which enables pan-European share trading.

There is a great deal of information on these stock exchanges on their own websites and on the Internet, and the interested reader is referred to these sources. However, some information on the NYSE, the Nasdaq, and the LSE is provided here.

The New York Stock Exchange

At the outset of 2015, the US accounted for around 50% of global stock market capitalization.

The New York Stock Exchange is now part of NYSE Euronext, formed from a merger in 2007 between stock exchange operators on either side of the Atlantic. NYSE Euronext was bought by Intercontinental Exchange in 2013. There are about 2,800 companies listed on the NYSE with a total market cap of about US$19tn. The NYSE dominated the US capital markets for 200 years, but now has serious rivals that have introduced highly efficient, alternative trading systems making full use of rapidly developing computer technology. Competition has led to a welcome reduction in trading costs. However, the increasing complexity of market structures is an ongoing challenge for regulators. Over the past decade, the NYSE's share of US share trading has fallen from more than 70% to around 12%.

Before the revolution described in *Chapter 1,* the buying and selling of listed shares was a privilege limited to a small, inclusive group. Trading took place through stock jobbers or floor brokers on the trading floor using the 'big board' and 'open outcry' to advertise or quote their buy and sell prices – a familiar sight in many movies. As business became more sophisticated, a system evolved with trading in each share managed by a single, independent, designated market maker formerly known as a specialist. The market makers manage the opening and closing auctions on the NYSE. They are employed by a small number of firms. Floor brokers continue to operate and significant business, mainly large institutional trades, is still conducted on the trading floor of the NYSE.

A designated market maker will normally keep an inventory of each share in which he makes a market, and is obligated, if necessary, to trade from his inventory to maintain liquidity and to keep an orderly market in the share. For example, if buy orders temporarily exceed sell orders, there is the possibility of a sharp rise in price to pull in sell orders. To suppress volatility, the market maker has the option to sell from his own inventory to ensure an orderly rise in price. Though for the NYSE market maker, trading is part of the job, he must always put the public interest above his own and cannot step in front of a public order to buy or sell. A market maker can seek to stimulate the market through interaction with his major customers, keeping them in touch with the ebb and flow of the market and alerting them to opportunities for capturing value.

Market makers use a process described as an 'auction' to match buyers and sellers through the trading day. The auction functions through buyers entering competitive bids and sellers entering competitive offers on the stock exchange limit order book with the market makers looking to match and to execute orders. Additional liquidity is provided by supplemental liquidity providers.

The 1970s saw the opening up of the stock markets to wider participation through electronic systems and the increasing demand for trading was met through automation. The functions of the specialists on the NYSE were steadily automated and the stock exchange trading systems became directly accessible to many more market participants. In 1976, the NYSE established its SuperDOT (Designated Order Turnaround) electronic trading system, giving the option to bypass the floor brokers. SuperDOT operated for 33 years, until 2009 when it was replaced with the Super Display Book system (SDBK) supported by the ARCA (Archipelago Exchange) trading engine – a computer program that matches buy and sell orders. Then in 2012, the NYSE launched its Universal Trading Platform, which combined the best of its technologies with those of Euronext. Some useful information on trading on the NYSE can be found by searching markets/nyse-mkt/trading-info.

The Nasdaq Stock Market

The Nasdaq Stock Market, launched in 1971, operates in the US alongside the New York Stock Exchange and is the second largest in the world. The Nasdaq specializes in technical companies and excludes 'financials,' i.e., banks and financial services companies. There are about 3,100 companies listed on the Nasdaq with an aggregate market cap of about US$6.8tn.

The Nasdaq is an electronic communications network (ECN), linking thousands of computers – also known as a dealer network. Instead of being managed by a specialist, as on the NYSE, each traded company has a number of market makers. There are about 500 market making firms and the average number per company share is around 14. The market makers will typically be specialist firms or part of an investment bank. They compete and trade to their own accounts without the constraints imposed by the NYSE. Each market maker maintains bid and offer quotes throughout the trading day, attracting buyers and sellers to generate his trading volumes and profits. These prices are routed continuously through the Nasdaq exchange to all the market participants. The market makers maintain inventories of shares, and so are able to supplement liquidity as needed, and trade with other market makers as well as with customers. If you wish to buy a stock that trades on the Nasdaq, your broker will either call up a market maker with the information on your trade or enter your order into a Nasdaq-sponsored online execution system.

The crucial difference between the NYSE and the Nasdaq is that on the NYSE, the market maker matches buyers and sellers directly, whereas on the Nasdaq, a network of market makers competes for business around each company share. Each transaction goes through a market maker who makes money on the spread – he sells at a higher price than he buys at. The competition keeps the bid-offer spread down, the main cost of dealing. Despite claims made, there is usually not a great deal of difference in the bid-offer spreads between the NYSE and the Nasdaq.

There can be little doubt that the use of computer networks plays to the strengths of the high-frequency traders – discussed in *Chapter 10 – Trading*. The Nasdaq is an attractive trading environment for such operations, and some of the Nasdaq market makers use HF trading technology. There is an increasing body of opinion that these operators make little constructive contribution to the markets and have the potential to cause considerable harm. It is thought by regulators that HF trading created the 'flash crash' of 2010 in the US markets.

The London Stock Exchange

In 2015, foreign investment in the London stock market rose to over 50%, reflecting the international nature of London listed companies. Over the last 50 years, individual ownership has fallen from over 50% to 11% – the retail investor has been seriously put off by the great stock market crashes. Insurance and pension fund participation had fallen from a combined value of around 50% in the 1990s to just 10% by 2015 – regulatory pressure has caused the funds to switch most of their investments into safer bonds.

The London Stock Exchange (LSE) is probably the most international of all the world's stock exchanges, with around 3,000 companies from over 70 countries admitted to trading on its markets. About 1,800 companies comprise the main market, with a market cap of around £3.5tn. The LSE also operates the Alternative Investment Market (AIM), which lists small cap and start-up companies. About 1,060 companies are listed on AIM, with an aggregate market cap of about £37bn. Over 400 firms, mainly investment banks and stockbrokers, are members of the LSE.

The LSE competes for company listings with other major stock exchanges around the world, and while the LSE claims to apply stringent listing criteria, covering issues such as corporate governance and free float, there is a view that in recent years, some companies – mainly in the mining sector – have managed to get around these criteria. The LSE offers a range of trading services, described below.

SETS – Stock Exchange Trading System – is the main LSE trading system. It is described on the LSE website as its flagship electronic order book, also known as Level 2. The major market participants, such as institutional investors and investment banks, are linked electronically to SETS, and place their buy and sell orders directly onto the system using direct market access (DMA). This is known as 'on order book trading.' Some stockbrokers and trading platforms now make SETS DMA available to retail investors.

The LSE SETSqx (Stock Exchange Electronic Trading Service – quotes and crosses) is a quotation-based trading service for shares less liquid than those traded on SETS.

SEAQ is the London Stock Exchange's 'non-electronically executable quotation service' in which market makers quote prices in AIM shares that are not traded on SETS or SETSqx. They are obliged to maintain bid and offer quotes up to normal market size (NMS) continuously through the trading day. NMS, also known as Exchange Market Size (EMS), is described below.

The trading systems are supported by licensed market makers, which are an integral part of LSE stock exchange operations and take on an obligation to 'make a market' in a share. Market makers are not employees of the stock exchanges. Any member of the LSE can register to be a market maker in shares, and currently there are about 24. There are comprehensive rules for market making, which are posted on the LSE website. These require market makers to hold an inventory of each share in which they make a market, and to trade from their inventories, if necessary, to maintain liquidity when there are strong imbalances between supply and demand. The trading of highly liquid stocks – mainly the large caps – is almost fully automated with the market makers playing a minor role, e.g., facilitating trading with the retail investors through their stockbrokers. A basic requirement is for a market maker to make prices and deal either 'on the order book', placing buy or sell orders from clients directly onto the order book, or 'off the order book,' dealing with the end client through a stockbroker, or both. For smaller, less liquid shares, the market makers' role is essential and they compete for business on the buy and sell prices that they offer through the trading day. For SETSqx and SEAQ, at least two registered market makers are required for each share.

Most retail investors will work through a stockbroker who deals with retail service providers (RSPs). In turn, the RSPs interrogate the market makers, or SETS order book directly, to obtain buy and sell prices on the condition that they have to continually quote and be willing to trade the shares in which they deal up to the normal market size (NMS). Thus the system provides liquidity up to the NMS. This is a form of off order book trading. The retail investor is presented with a buy or sell price – usually valid for 15 seconds – which he can accept or decline. For off order book trading, the market maker will report the trades through the LSE reporting service in accordance with the LSE rules.

The LSE and NASDAQ market makers are traders in their own right and are in competition with other market makers as well as with market participants. From this perspective, the NYSE system, with one specialist market maker for each share and certain non-compete protocols in place, is perhaps a fairer environment for the retail investor.

All of these trading systems get the job done in their different ways.

Stock market capitalizations

Nearly all major economies have public stock exchanges and it's useful to have a glimpse of these.

The World Federation of Exchanges provides monthly data on stock exchange market cap and trading volume. 2015 data for the world's largest stock exchanges is shown in Table 3.3 in descending monthly volume.

Stock Exchange	Market Capitalization US$tn	Monthly Trade Volume US$bn
NYSE	19.2	1,520
Shanghai	4.0	1,278
The Nasdaq Stock Market	6.8	1,183
Shenzhen	2.3	800
Japan	4.5	402
Euronext	3.3	184
LSE	6.1	165
Hong Kong	3.3	155
Germany	1.8	142
India – National Stock Exchange	1.6	62.2
India – Bombay	1.7	11.8

Table 3.3 World stock markets

There is strong competition between stock exchanges, in particular to attract new listings, i.e., companies bringing their shares to the open market. Other areas of competition include liquidity, reliability, and speed.

Stock market indices

Stock market indices are run by specialist companies or by the stock exchanges themselves. Index companies are part of the indispensable natural terrain of stock markets. These companies undertake the task of tracking company share prices in real time to produce real time indices during market open hours. Indices play a very important role in the stock markets in a variety of ways, and in particular they are key indicators of sentiment.

Indices help investors to make informed investment decisions and they are broadly used for benchmarking the performance of investments and the performance of fund managers. All the major indices have sector indices and some run industry indices also. These are very helpful for traders and investors who want to specialize.

In addition, indices provide the basis for index futures trading as well as tracker funds and for many exchange traded funds (ETFs). Because of the growth in tracker funds and ETFs, indices are perhaps increasingly driving a significant amount of stock market activity, as opposed to simply reflecting it. Tracker funds are described in *Chapter 12 – About funds.*

By creating and promoting new indices, the index companies facilitate investment in new geographies and sectors – and therefore act as a catalyst for investors and the investment industry around the world.

Stock market indices are usually based either on the aggregate of the market caps of the constituent companies or a summation of the share prices of the constituent companies. Inclusion in an index will usually require companies to demonstrate certain standards – relating to such matters as sustained profitability and corporate governance. However, it is clear from the number of companies that seriously underperform their indices or even fail, that the bar is not always set very high – or that a company's fortunes can change very rapidly.

The world's largest index company is S&P Dow Jones Indices, which runs the Dow Jones Industrial Average and the S&P 500 indices. S&P Dow Jones Indices calculates over 830,000 indices each day. The Nasdaq and the NYSE run large sets of indices.

In April 2015, the LSE, owner of the FTSE Group (FTSE stands for Financial Times Stock Exchange), bought the US based Frank Russell Company, motivated by the growth in tracker funds and associated increase in demand for index products. The FTSE indices, based on LSE-listed companies, and Russell indices are now managed by FTSE Russell.

The most watched indices in the US are probably the Dow Jones Industrial Average (DJIA), the S&P 500, and the Nasdaq 100. In the UK, the most watched indices are the FTSE 100 and the FTSE 250.

YAHOO! FINANCE is a good source for main index charts.

In the US, search: usa finance.yahoo.com

In the UK, search: uk finance yahoo

For information on constituent companies:

In the US, search: S&P 500 data.okfn and DJIA CNN Money

In the UK, search: Hargreaves Lansdown – and click on Share prices & stock markets

Index companies license the use of their indices. Whenever you look at an index on a website, the provider is probably paying an index company for permission to use it. A premium will usually be paid for real time data. The index companies also provide a range of news and information services. You can check out their websites.

For the retail investor, stock market indices together with an awareness of the state of the market are more important than the mechanics of the trading systems. Some important indices are listed below.

The Dow Jones Industrial Average

The Dow Jones Industrial Average, or simply the Dow, is based on a price-weighted average share price, and not market cap, for 30 major companies. It was conceived as an index to reflect US industrial activity and excluded transport and utility companies, which have their own indices. It is calculated by adding the constituent share prices and dividing by 30.

The composition of the index is revised periodically, though rarely, by the editors of the Wall Street Journal (owned by Dow Jones & Company) and no longer comprises only industrial companies. In 2015, Apple replaced AT&T.

Anomalies in the Dow are thrown up from time to time because it is price-weighted; e.g., if a company splits its stock say, two for one, its weighting in the Dow will reduce. This is where a company wants its share price to be cheaper without affecting the value of the company; e.g., it will halve its share price while doubling the number of shares in issue. An adjustment to the index using a divisor is made to accommodate this.

The S&P 500

The S&P 500 is a market cap weighted index of 500 shares, selected by a Standard & Poor committee that applies strict criteria for inclusion – relating to a company's market cap (greater than US$5.3bn), consistent profitability, and a free float of at least 50% of its shares. The index covers around 500 large cap American companies, covering about 75% of the American share/equity market by capitalization. The constituents are periodically reviewed against established criteria, and changes are made on a regular basis. Most years see 25 to 30 changes in the index constituents.

The S&P 500 is broadly regarded as the most important stock market index globally. There is an S&P MidCap 400 for mid cap companies and an S&P SmallCap 600 for small cap companies.

The Russell Index

Russell Investments, now owned by FTSE Russell, runs a range of market indices including the important Russell 3000 Index, which comprises the largest 3,000 US companies.   These companies represent approximately 98% of US market capitalization and this Russell index is considered to be a good indicator of the overall strength of the US economy.

The Russell 2000 is an index of small cap shares with an average market cap of about US$1.9bn. Some funds use the Russell 2000 as their benchmark index rather than the S&P SmallCap 600 which has performed more strongly.

Russell adjusts its indices once a year, mainly to take account of mergers and acquisitions, and gives two weeks' notice of changes, but professional traders have already worked out likely changes and trade heavily on this information. Tracker funds have to adjust their portfolios accordingly and this leads to a great deal of front-running – high-frequency traders buying ahead of fund managers and then selling to them at a profit.

You can check out the Russell indices on <u>usa finance.yahoo.com</u> by typing the tickers ^RUA for the Russell 3000 and ^RUT 2000 in the Search box. Alternatively, you will find them on <u>Google Finance</u>.

The Nasdaq 100

The Nasdaq 100, not to be confused with the Nasdaq Composite, covers 100 large cap companies. Its composition is reviewed and adjusted annually by the exchange. Though the Nasdaq has a strong technology bias, it is interesting to note that between 2000 and the present time, the weighting of technology stocks in the index has fallen from around 60% to 40%.

Apple's market cap is so big it can give the Nasdaq 100 a bad day all by itself.

The Nasdaq Composite

The Nasdaq Stock Market specializes in growth and technology companies and includes some non-US companies. All Nasdaq-listed companies, some 3,000, are contained in the market-cap weighted Nasdaq Composite together with some American Depository Receipts (ADRs) and Real Estate Investment Trusts (REITs).

The London Stock Exchange indices

In 2014, the FTSE Group was looking into producing a version of the FTSE 100 index that excluded fossil fuel companies. These have been a substantial drag on the performance of the FTSE 100.

FTSE Russell, runs the FTSE 100 index and other indices based on LSE-listed companies. FTSE tells us that it calculates over 120,000 end-of-day and real time indices covering more than 180 countries and all major asset classes.

A FTSE 100 Fact Sheet and a FTSE 250 Fact Sheet providing interesting information can be most easily found using an Internet search.

As mentioned, LSE now has ownership of the Russell indices, giving it considerable heft in the market alongside market leaders MSCI (see below) and S&P Dow Jones Indices.

The most important LSE/FTSE indices for the retail investor are shown in Table 3.4.

Index	Number of Companies (circa)	Market Cap of Companies in Index
FTSE 100	101 Dominated by global companies	£3bn to £115bn
FTSE 250	253 Mainly UK orientated companies	£315mn to £3.7bn
FTSE 350	354 FTSE 100 plus FTSE Mid 250	£315mn to £115bn
FTSE All Share	605	
FTSE TechMARK 100	100	£5.9mn to £14.5bn
FTSE Small Cap	249	Up to £585mn
FTSE AIM 100	100	£10mn to £2.8bn

Table 3.4 LSE/FTSE indices

For detailed information on these indices, see the London Stock Exchange website. In addition, you will find useful coverage by searching Hargreaves Lansdown Share prices & stock markets and Daily Telegraph Markets Shares and many other websites. For the FTSE AIM 100 companies, search DigitalLook AIM 100.

The FTSE Group undertakes a quarterly review of the market caps of the companies making up its indices and companies are promoted or relegated accordingly. As a review date approaches, share prices of companies that are candidates for promotion or relegation can experience significant movements – not just from gaming and sentiment, but because index-tracker funds and Exchange Traded Funds (ETFs) based on an index have to adjust their holdings to reflect the modified index.

China

In May 2015, daily trading volume in Shanghai and Shenzhen peaked at around US$300bn. On the same trading day, the LSE volume was about US$8bn.

China has three important stock exchanges:

- Shanghai Stock Exchange (SSE), which runs a Composite Index.
- Shenzhen Stock Exchange, which also runs a Composite Index.
- Hong Kong Stock Exchange, which runs the Hang Seng Index.

The Shenzhen exchange has a strong emphasis on technology companies.

The SSE and Shenzhen Stock Exchange, which trade China's A-shares, are not fully open to foreign investors and contain companies that are state-owned and controlled. The Hong Kong Stock Exchange is home to China's H-shares, which are freely available.

It is often reported that the Chinese people tend not to trust the stock market very much and prefer property and precious metals. For this and no doubt other reasons, the Shanghai and Shenzhen stock markets are not as strongly in sync with the other main markets around the world as Hong Kong perhaps is.

Japan

The Tokyo Stock Exchange, part of the Japanese Exchange Group, is the fourth-largest stock exchange in the world, with an aggregate market capitalization of around US$4.5tn for its approximately 3,000 listed companies.

There are a number of indices for the Tokyo Stock Exchange. The most important are:

- Nikkei 225 – comprising major companies across a range of key sectors. This is a price-weighted index.
- Topix – includes about 1,670 companies, which comprise the Tokyo Stock Exchange's First Section. This is a market cap weighted index.

France

The main French stock market index is the CAC 40, where CAC stands for Cotation Assistée en Continu (Continuous Assisted Quotation). It is based on the market caps of 40 companies selected from the 100 highest market caps on the Euronext Paris stock exchange. The constituent companies are considered to be most reflective of the French economy, and are reviewed quarterly by an independent index steering group. The historic Paris Bourse was taken over by Euronext in 2000.

Germany

The most important German stock exchange is Deutsche Börse and its main index is the Xetra DAX 30, named for the Xetra electronic trading system. DAX stands for Deutscher Aktienindex. It comprises the 30 largest German companies in terms of market cap and takes account of stock exchange order book volume. Containing just 30 companies, it is not a broad indicator of the state of the German economy. Unlike other major indices, the DAX 30 takes account of dividend income in order to reflect each share's total return.

The German and French markets are quite a lot smaller than that of the UK, to some extent because these countries have more companies that are privately or government owned, and because historically they have adopted a different attitude towards finance.

Some global indices

MSCI

MSCI is a leading provider of index products across a range of asset classes. In 1968, Morgan Stanley licensed the rights to a set of indices from Capital International to create the brand MSCI. It runs indices for 23 'developed' countries as well as a composite MSCI World Index based on more than 1,600 companies from these countries. It also runs the MSCI EAFE index covering important developed market economies around the world and widely used to benchmark fund and asset class performances as well as that of many ETFs.

Another much-used set of indices is the MSCI Emerging Market Index family, comprising 23 indices. In June 2015, MSCI deferred the inclusion of Chinese A-shares, which trade on the Shanghai and Shenzhen stock exchanges, in the main MSCI Emerging Markets Index. The concern was over market access to these shares by overseas investors. This was considered to be significant in respect of global investor confidence. The inclusion of the A-shares would affect all index products based on the

MSCI index, as they would need to buy A-shares in large quantities. If you are interested in some international exposure, then the MSCI website is worth a look.

STOXX

Deutsche Börse owns STOXX, which runs about 7,500 indices around the world including a wide range of European Indices. It is the preeminent index provider in Europe but now operates globally. The STOXX indices are quite diverse, with, for example, indices focused on dividends, strategy, faith, and more. They also provide customized indices for clients. Many of their indices are provided on a fee basis. Again, the STOXX website is worth a look.

Private exchanges – alternative trading venues

There are now around 70 trading venues, including about 40 dark pools in the US. It is estimated that something like 40% of US equity trading takes place away from the public stock exchanges.

The development of financial markets has seen the introduction in recent times of many private exchanges, particularly in the US, UK, and Europe. They create venues for trading a wide range of asset classes, including shares. These are known in the US as alternative trading systems (ATSs) or venues and are regulated as broker-dealers. In Europe they are known as multilateral trading facilities (MTFs) – a regulatory name. MTFs are enabled by MiFID – the pan-European Markets in Financial Instruments Directive. In the UK, regulation is also provided by the Financial Conduct Authority. These exchanges are run by independent specialist operators, by investment banks, and sometimes by public exchanges. Significant volumes are now traded in these specialist venues. They compete with the public exchanges on range of products, service level, and trading fees. The proliferation of private exchanges has led to fragmentation in the share trading market, and meaningful tracking of trading volumes in real time is now problematic.

The largest alternative stock exchange is BATS which began in 2005 seeking competitive advantage through innovation. BATS is regulated by the US SEC and is also an SRO – a self-regulatory organization.

BATS has increased competition in the US market and captured more than 10% market share. Like the Nasdaq Stock Market, BATS is an electronic communications network (ECN) and has grown organically and by acquisition. It acquired Chi-X Europe in 2011 to form BATS Chi-X, now a major pan-European trading venue. In the UK, Turquoise (TQ), which is 50% owned by LSE, is an important MTF. Both BATS Chi-X and TQ facilitate trading of LSE shares.

Most share trading in these venues takes place in 'lit' conditions where offer and bid prices together with the limit order book are visible to the markets. Trades, time of trade, and volume are available to the market at large in real time. However, some trading also takes place in off-exchange venues known as dark pools, where there is less transparency in trading and considerably less regulation compared with the main exchanges. Dark pools are discussed in more detail below.

A proliferation of trading venues offers arbitrage opportunities, where traders will seek out price discrepancies between venues and seek to turn these into profit. For example, buy shares at one venue and sell them immediately on another for a slim but useful profit margin, especially if some good volume in the trade can be achieved. Arbitrage helps to keep share prices more or less in line across all the trading venues, which is a regulatory requirement of the venue operators, but results in the arbitragers taking money out of the markets without adding much value to the process. A commonly held view is that a much smaller number of venues would help with the integrity of the market structure and reduce the need for endless arbitrage.

The dark pools

Large trades have always taken place off-exchange, but now there are too many specialist dark pool trading venues. Surveys have shown that most institutional investors now regard dark pools as negative in that they distort price discovery as well as taking liquidity from the public exchanges. Share trading volume in dark pools now exceeds that of the NYSE.

What are they?

Dark pools are off-exchange, over-the-counter (OTC) trading networks created to enable large blocks of shares to change hands anonymously with minimal disturbance to price. OTC is a term used to describe trades in a somewhat unregulated trading venue. Dark pools were created to meet the needs of institutional investors and are described as 'unlit' trading venues. In dark pool trading, the limit order book is not visible and the identity of the traders, the size of the trades, and the pre-trade prices are not revealed until sometime after the trades are complete. Dark pools are operated by some public stock exchanges, alternative trading venues, broker-dealers, investment banks as well as some independent companies. They take business away from the public exchanges.

There are now dozens of dark pool trading venues operating across the US and Europe. Unsurprisingly, accurate dark pool share trading volume as a proportion of total trading volume is not readily available, but in 2015, estimates were around 15% in the US and 8% in the UK.

In the US, most of the major investment banks operate dark pools. They send most of their share trading orders to their dark pools. However, best execution regulations then result in orders being sent on to rival exchanges. This leads to further fragmentation of trading volume and enhances the risk of leakage of sensitive client information and gaming. In Europe, the largest dark order book is provided by BATS Chi-X Europe. Also significant are Turquoise, UBS MTF, ITG Posit, and Liquidnet.

Because dark pools are not subject to the stringent regulation of the public stock exchanges, the counter-party risk is greater, i.e., the risk of a party to a trade not being able to settle the contract by delivery of cash or shares. Fast-moving technology has supported the development and proliferation of dark pools and this has created a challenge for regulators in staying abreast of their activities. For example, the priority of an investment bank running a dark pool is to maximize its profits and there is scope for conflict of interest with its clients. An undeveloped and weak regulatory framework is not helpful, and *caveat emptor* – buyer beware – applies perhaps more than usual. However, dark pools are now subject to increased regulatory scrutiny and a strengthening of regulatory frameworks.

Dark pool exchanges are not generally open to retail investors, though this is slowly changing.

Impact on price discovery

Opponents of dark pools, notably the public exchanges, maintain that they are self-serving and that by hindering broad price discovery, a fundamental mechanism in a fair market, they degrade the integrity and structure of the market.

In a real sense, the 'lit' public stock exchanges comprise the cauldron in which share prices are determined, with every bargain a part of the price discovery process. Most bids for shares or offers of shares are transparent in real time, and anyone can get on the other side of the deal if they have the wherewithal and are quick enough. However, large late trades are regularly reported by the public exchanges that have no discernible effect on the traded share prices. Stock exchange rules can permit late reporting of transactions as well as types of order, such as the iceberg, which buys or sells in tranches to conceal the ultimate size of the order. So price discovery is hampered to a degree on the public exchanges.

In contrast, the *raison d'être* of dark pools is to hinder price discovery. An institutional investor who has invested in research in a particular company and wants to dramatically reduce his holding, believes that he should be able to legitimately do so without revealing his intent or rationale in real time. It is hard to argue against this. However, an institutional investor shifting a large block of shares should be a market-moving occurrence even if his motivation is unknown. When these transactions are reported late, the markets are being denied market-moving information in real time.

There is no right answer to this dilemma, though the forces in the marketplace and regulatory pressures are likely to diminish the differences between the lit and unlit venues over time. During 2015, the NYSE was contemplating a price war with the dark pools, and the LSE was planning to introduce a midday auction to accommodate discrete trading of large blocks of shares in an effort to win back business from dark pools.

The emergence of dark pools has resulted in two classes of investor trading to different sets of rules. Retail investors should probably not be too concerned about this, as dark pool trading should reduce share price volatility. Traders, who thrive on volatility, will be less impressed. Also, the proliferation of stock exchanges is not helpful to the retail trader, as it becomes increasingly difficult to interpret trading patterns.

Dark pools and high-frequency trading

A proclaimed benefit of dark pools is that they provide some protection for the large institutional investors from the activities of the professional traders, in particular the high-frequency traders who will seek to manipulate share prices to their advantage – and so to the disadvantage of the institutional investors. However, the catch is that the dark pools allow some access to high-frequency trading firms to boost liquidity. There is then a need to set rules that will keep the activities of the HF traders net positive. It's a bit like asking foxes to behave in a chicken coop.

Some people spring to the defence of the HF traders on the basis that when they trade in a particular venue, they will simply work within the rules of the venue and it is up to the venue operator to set and enforce the rules. The law of unintended consequences has perhaps come into play and many of the large block trades, the original business of the dark pools, are now broken down into much smaller packages of perhaps a few hundred shares in an effort to combat the HF traders. The result is further fragmentation in the market, adding to the challenge of meaningful tracking of volume, and weakening of the price discovery process. As a result, many people maintain that these private venues are simply becoming less-regulated versions of traditional exchanges.

Barclay's dark pool found itself in serious difficulty when it was alleged by regulators that it had allowed high-frequency trading firms into its trading environment without informing its institutional clients.

HF trading is discussed in more detail in *Chapter 10 – Trading.*

Reporting

In a dark pool trading, buyers and sellers have effectively taken a view on the value of a company share and do not want to share this with the market until the trade is complete. Some dark pools have quick post-trade transparency regimes and sell this as a win-win. This is better than having to wait until the trade is finally reported and has to be identified from statutory reporting.

Dark pool executed trades are recorded to the main exchange's consolidated tape as over-the-counter transactions. Dark pools can provide detailed information about the volumes and types of transactions to clients on request.

Buying and selling shares on the public exchanges

The trading of highly liquid stocks – mainly the large and mid caps – is now almost fully automated with the major players, such as institutions, investment banks, and hedge funds working with computerized trading systems and sophisticated support teams. Their computers access the stock exchange computerized trading systems directly through DMA to the limit order book, which is described below.

No two stock exchanges work in exactly the same way, and the following description of share trading will not fit every stock exchange trading system exactly, but it should convey the main principles.

First, we'll take a look at the bid-offer spread.

The bid-offer spread

Buyers are bidding to buy shares and want to get them as cheaply as possible, while sellers are offering to sell their shares and want as much as they can get for them. At any point in time, there will be a 'best bid' and 'best offer' price available. Absent trading anomalies, the best offer price will be higher than the best bid price and the difference is referred to as the bid-offer spread.

In a trading system, provided the share has strong liquidity, you can buy or sell in real time. The system will hold the price for you – buy or sell – for typically 15 seconds.

For a large cap company, the spread will usually be quite small. It can be as low as 0.01%. For mid cap companies it will more likely lie in the range 0.05% to 0.15%. For a small cap company, where there may be only two market makers involved, it can be much larger, even up around 5% or 6%, as the market makers seek to balance supply and demand in a less liquid share. As a practical matter, the wider spread will compensate the market makers for the additional risk involved in making a market in small cap shares.

Normal market size/Exchange market size

Each share traded on a stock exchange will have a normal market size (NMS), also known as exchange market size (EMS). Stock exchanges and market makers have an obligation to provide liquidity at all times up to NMS, i.e., be able to immediately execute trades up to NMS.

The calculation of NMS is set by the stock exchange, and will usually be based on average daily turnover in the previous year. NMS is unlikely to be an issue for a retail investor trading in large cap companies. For a small cap company, there may sometimes be a need to drop order size in relation to both buying and selling to achieve execution, i.e., completion of the trade.

Trading levels

As mentioned above, stock markets have 'trading levels.'

Level 1

At Level 1, the trader sees real time bid and offer prices, but does not see the depth of the market or the individual market makers. He will see trading volumes and there will probably be a sophisticated charting capability on his trading platform.

Level 2

Level 2 provides a much greater level of detail. It shows the stock exchange limit order book and the trader can see the quotes offered by various stock exchanges and market makers dealing in each share, as well as the depth of the limit order book.

Level 3

The Nasdaq stock exchange has a Level 3. All trades take place through market makers who access the order book directly at Nasdaq Level 3, to which they have exclusive access.

The stock exchange limit order book

Stock exchange trading takes place in two main ways – through the limit order book and through market orders, which may be 'aggressive.'

Many market participants place buy and sell limit orders on the stock exchange limit order book, indicating the volumes and price limits at which they are prepared to trade. These are also known as persistent or passive orders. The limit order book operates at the stock exchange Level 2. An example of a Level 2 screen is shown in Table 3.5. This is a snapshot of a rapidly changing situation.

			Best bid	Best offer			
4	1,196,511		158.5	158.6		1,574,964	5
Bid Vol	36,239,748	383,295	158.5	158.6	215,605	45,672,919	Offer Vol
Depth	156	235,197	158.5	158.6	654,953	208	Depth
		346,121	158.5	158.6	234,987		
		231,898	158.5	158.6	345,765		
		354,785	158.4	158.6	123,654		
		79,987	158.3	158.7	79,968		
		234,567	158.3	158.7	232,656		
		36,892	158.3	158.8	45,328		
		162,985	158.2	158.8	564,324		
		245,987	158.2	158.8	89,562		

Table 3.5 Stock exchange Level 2 screen

The stock exchange trading system stacks these orders as shown in the table, with best bid (buy) and best offer (sell) on a yellow bar (shown shaded) in the middle of the screen – the 'touch bar.' The touch bar also shows the number and volumes of limit orders at best bid and at best offer. Limit orders sit passively on the order book and may or may not get filled. Participants place orders at prices above best offer and below best bid current prices, in the hope of making a trade above or below current price, based on a favorable price movement.

The depth, or liquidity, of the order book is defined in terms of the number and sizes of limit orders. A healthy order book will have good depth supporting the liquidity of the share.

If the best bid is US$10.50 and the best offer is US$10.60 on the limit order book, the bid-offer spread is US$0.10. However, the trades are not exactly matched, so the trading system is at an impasse. This is resolved by incoming limit orders and market orders, explained below, that can be matched from the limit order book. This real time flow of orders is the mechanism for shifting the share price either up or down, and allows some of the limit orders to be filled, i.e., cleared. Limit orders don't necessarily get filled.

The trading computer – matching engine – works at high speed, matching buys and sells as they hit the touch. A great many orders are cleared without appearing on the limit order book.

Many retail traders monitor Level 2 in the belief that seeing the levels and quantities of orders can give them insights into future share price movements. Keep in mind that the professional traders will be using computers to do this for them and are likely to be trading directly on the order book through DMA. Another important use is to obtain insights into where 'support levels' for a share might lie – and where there might be some buying interest when a trader is assessing where to place a stop-loss (see below).

But keep in mind that the buying interest may be cancelled if a share price is falling precipitously.

The primary trading venue for a share will report volume from other exchanges, but at Level 1 the other exchanges will probably not be identified. Level 2 provides more information, identifying activity on other exchanges and the individual market makers. However, even on Level 2, you will not see all the trading volume in real time. This is because stock exchanges permit late reporting of trades in some circumstances, e.g., trades above normal/exchange market size. Also, significant trades are likely to be taking place in dark pools – unlit – with the express intention of concealing this from the market at large for as long as possible. Dark pool trades should ultimately be reported to the consolidated tape as OTC transactions.

You can find detailed explanations of Level 2 on the Internet. If you search the Internet, using a <u>stock exchange name</u> and <u>Level 2</u>, you should find a great deal of interesting information on the workings of that stock exchange.

Retail traders can place limit orders through their stockbrokers but need to be aware that the algorithmic traders may well be executing complex buy and sell strategies, using both limit orders and market orders, and this can make it difficult for the retail trader in particular to obtain the best prices.

Best execution

Brokers have professional responsibility to 'execute at best' for their customers. This is regulated by the Security & Exchange Commission in the US and through the Markets in Financial Instruments Directive (MiFID) in the UK. For example, under MiFID Article 21, a firm must take all reasonable steps to obtain the best possible result, taking account of the following:

- Price,
- Costs,
- Speed,
- Likelihood of execution,
- Settlement size,
- Nature of the execution,
- Or any other consideration relative to the execution of the order.

In brief, the broker is required to get the best price in the shortest time frame. However, he will work to his client's instructions with respect to type of order, which we have just discussed. There is a great deal of competition in the markets, through trading algorithms in particular, to pick up best value as offers to buy and sell shares appear on the order book.

A useful description of order execution can be found by searching <u>TD Ameritrade order execution FAQ</u>.

Market orders and aggressive orders

Market orders are made through a broker to buy or sell a share at best available price – execute at best. They will not normally make restrictions on price or timeframe and are therefore likely to be filled. The broker has an obligation to achieve best execution, so will sweep stock exchanges and market makers for the best price for his client.

Aggressive orders will often execute at a specific price and in order to do so, may cross the bid-offer spread. An aggressive buy order will be priced on the offer or higher while an aggressive sell order will be priced on the bid or lower. So aggressive orders will always be filled, subject to quantities of shares posted on the order book – and provided the trader is not beaten to the trade. Aggressive orders will usually execute immediately and they are regarded as removing liquidity from the order book.

There is considerable complexity around aggressive orders. A common order type is 'execute and eliminate,' i.e., execute that part of the order that can be filled and cancel the rest - or post it on the limit order book. An aggressive order may or may not have a limit price and there may be a condition attached that they must be executed in full or not at all. This is known as 'fill or kill' and is used by traders seeking to execute a particular strategy.

As we have mentioned above, market orders and aggressive orders are an important stimulator of price movements, interacting with the limit order book, which will tend to reflect market sentiment.

Trading volume

Market participants follow trading volumes closely as an indicator of likely share price movements. Trading volume is the sum of transactions in the day. Volume can be expressed as both numbers of shares traded and value of shares traded. Large cap companies are traded actively every day. Trading volume will increase on share price moving news. Smaller cap companies will be less actively traded, but again, trading volumes will increase on news.

While a great deal of share trading takes place on public stock exchanges, an increasing amount takes place 'off-exchange' in alternative trading venues. This proliferation of share trading venues in the US and UK, including the dark pools, has led to fragmentation of volume data making it difficult to track share trading volumes in real time or even at the end of the trading day. Consequently, the value to the retail investor of using volume as a guide to strong buying or selling activity in a particular share has diminished. Now, to a significant degree, this is the domain of well-resourced professional teams.

The US Consolidated Tape Association (CTA) seeks to draw together, in real time, trading volume and price for all exchange-traded shares – on the US national consolidated tape. However, it does not always get full cooperation from all the US exchanges. Dark pool transactions are at some point recorded to the consolidated tape, but they are recorded as OTC transactions and reporting can be incomplete and lacking in detail. Real time volume information is accessible from the CTA on a subscription basis.

In Europe, establishing a consolidated tape is a work in progress. Thompson Reuters is taking a lead on this and now provides data for most European equities on the Thompson Reuter Eikon desktop system.

The pan-European Markets in Financial Instruments Directive (MiFID), which sets best-execution requirements for trades, mandates that financial firms submit to their local regulators detailed end-of-day reports, including the time and price of a trade and the counterparties involved. Firms must either become so-called accredited regulatory mechanisms (ARMs), or use one of the accredited service providers. In most cases, both the fund manager and its executing broker-dealer or bank must include the same details of each trade on their respective transaction reports.

Each day, BATS Pan-European Stock Market summarizes trading volumes on Europe's major stock exchanges, undertaken on a range of trading platforms, both lit and unlit.

You will sometimes be able to find the daily volume for an index, but this can take a bit of digging. Stock exchange and other websites provide daily volumes for individual shares. Aggregate daily trading volume from all the public stock exchanges that trade the share can be found, at a fee, on a Level 2 platform.

Market information company FactSet provides a sophisticated volume tracking service on a fee basis.

Platforms

Since the big bang in 1986, there has been a dramatic reduction in the cost of buying and selling shares, and a proliferation of website platforms offering competitive commissions and arranging discounts for more active users. Also, there is no shortage of stockbrokers vying for retail business. Selection of platforms is discussed in *Chapter 12 – About funds* and *Chapter 18 – Managing your portfolio.* Use of stockbrokers is covered in *Chapter 17.*

Types of order

There are a great many types of order, which highlights the complexity of modern share trading.

In 2014, the CEO of Intercontinental Exchange, which had recently taken over NYSE Euronext, undertook to drop a number of order types in order to reduce market complexity and to rebuild public confidence in the markets. Many types of order had been introduced that accommodated traders, and were well-suited to exploitation by high-frequency traders.

For types of order, search, for example:

NYSE Trading Information
Nasdaq Order Types and Modifiers
London Stock Exchange SETS

Examples of common types of trade on US exchanges are Form T, signifying a trade outside normal market hours; or basket trades where a major investor wishes to trade a number of shares simultaneously. In the UK, common types of trade include:

- OT   Ordinary Trade
- AT   Automatic Trade
- NT   Negotiated Trade
- UT   Uncrossing Trade – a technical transaction at the end of an electronic auction – the computer matches as many buy and sell orders as possible.

You can place an order for shares based on the concept of 'partial fulfilment,' where your order may eventually be filled by tranches at slightly different prices. Alternatively, you also have the option to place a 'fill or kill' order – if your order cannot be immediately filled in full, it will simply cancel.

Automatic trades

There are a number of automatic trading devices readily available to the retail investor. Some of these are described briefly below. Before using them, you should check out on the exact details of how they will work with your chosen platform or stockbroker.

Limit order

Limit orders have been described above. You place your buy or sell order in advance, e.g., you are prepared to buy 100 shares in Desirable Inc. at 230 cents. If the share price drops to 230 cents, your order will be filled. Or you can set a limit order to sell, e.g., if you are prepared to sell 100 shares in Takeprofit plc at 250 pence, you set your limit accordingly and if the price reaches 250 pence, your shares will be automatically sold.

You can simply let a limit order expire at the end of the trading day, or you can set an expiry date. Typically, you will be offered somewhere between 30 and 90 days. A common instruction is 'good till cancelled' (GTC), but stockbrokers will not keep orders open indefinitely.

Rising buy order

A rising buy order, also known as a 'stop buy order,' is an order to buy shares that have risen to a price above the current price. It is triggered when the market price touches or goes through the lower limit set. This type of order is used by investors looking to gain on the momentum of a share price rise.

Stop-loss

With a stop-loss, you in effect place a sell order in advance, to mitigate a loss on a holding. You place an instruction with your stockbroker to sell the holding if the price falls to a level that you specify. Usually this will be defined in terms of a percentage below your buy price or current price.

An issue with stop-losses is that if a share price 'gaps' below your stop level on market opening, it won't be filled. Also, if the share is not very liquid, there simply might not be anyone to match your sell order and your stop-loss will fail to execute or may execute at the first matching order below your stop-loss level. To overcome this problem, you can opt to pay for a guaranteed stop-loss.

Stop-losses are discussed in some detail in *Chapter 10 – Trading* and *in Chapter 18 – Managing your portfolio.*

Trailing stop-loss

A trailing stop-loss is one that follows the share price upwards (hopefully) at a constant percentage below it. If the share price falls by the defined percentage, the share will be automatically sold.

Stock market sectors

Economies have sectors and stock markets and indices reflect these through sub-indices, which can put in quite disparate performances. These are watched carefully by the markets with professional traders and investors seeking to rotate from sector to sector depending on where we are in the economic cycle. At least that's the theory – in reality it's not that easy to do!

The S&P 500 recognizes ten sectors, as shown below:

- Consumer Discretionary
- Consumer Staples
- Energy
- Financials
- Health Care
- Industrials
- Materials
- Technology
- Telecommunications Services
- Utilities

Each sector has a number of Sub Industries. Sector and Sub Industries use the Global Industry Classification Standard (GICS). For a breakdown of S&P 500 subsectors, search S&P 500 GICS Sector Scorecards. The Dow Jones Transportation Average (insert ^DJT into the YAHOO! FINANCE Look Up box) is regarded as particularly important, as it's a strong indicator of economic activity.

There are 41 LSE sectors to accommodate the circa 3,000 companies listed on the exchange. These are shown in Table 3.6.

Aerospace & Defence	Industrial Metals & Mining
Alternative Energy	Industrial Transportation
Automobiles & Parts	Leisure Goods
Banks	Life Insurance/Assurance
Beverages	Media
Chemicals	Mining
Construction & Materials	Real Estate Investment & Services
Electricity	Real Estate Investment Trusts
Electronics & Electrical Equipment	Mobile Telecommunications
Equity Investment Instruments	Nonequity Investment Instruments
Financial Services	Nonlife Insurance
Fixed Line Telecommunications	Oil & Gas Producers
Food & Drug Retailers	Oil Equip. & Services & Distribution
Food Producers	Pharmaceuticals & Biotechnology
Forestry and Paper	Real Estate Investment & Services
Gas, Water, and Multiutilities	Travel & Leisure
General Industrials	Software & Computer Services
General Retailers	Support Services
Health Care Equipment & Services	Technology Hardware & Equipment
Household Goods & Home Construction	Tobacco
Industrial Engineering	

Table 3.6 LSE sectors

A useful website for monitoring the performance of LSE sectors is shareprices.com which provides sector performance during the trading day with a 15-minute delay. This site also provides sector charts going back up to three years.

In recent years, the mining and banking sectors have depressed the performance of the FTSE 100, which has underperformed the FTSE 250.

Stock market correlations

The US is the world's dominant economy and will continue to be into the foreseeable future.   Most important economies around the world have some degree of interconnection with the US economy and, as a consequence of this, their stock market indices will often move roughly in sync with the main US indices – this phenomenon is referred to as correlation. There can also be correlation at sector level and within an index. Correlations between markets tend to be strongest when macro events are to the fore, e.g., correlations were strong in the aftermath of the global financial crisis, which got underway in 2008, as share prices since then have been reacting to a series of crises. When macro events die down, the fundamentals tend to re-emerge and correlations weaken.

Probably the strongest correlation in stock market behavior is between New York and London. The main indices comprise major companies, and tend to move up and down together – but not by the same amount, especially over significant periods of time. This is not too surprising, as global companies dominate the indices and the big investment players operate in an integrated way across the markets.   Currency fluctuations are an important consideration when examining correlative behaviors.

You will find it difficult to successfully invest in individual shares listed in London without keeping up with the US as well as the London stock market indices.

The French and German stock markets are somewhat correlated with New York, but during the European debt crisis, their performance has not been as strong. Both Japan and China have gone their own way for some time.

The MSCI emerging markets index had recovered its pre-financial crisis highs by the end of 2010 but then tracked sideways, albeit with considerable volatility while the US and UK indices were rising.   Early in 2011, the index broke ranks and decoupled. Money was flowing out of the developing world as confidence in the economic outlook for the developed world strengthened. At the same time, the pace of 'globalization' slowed, accompanied by a reduction of capital flows within the global economy. In May of 2015, the MSCI Emerging Markets Index went into a steep decline.

A good website for studying correlations between various stock markets indices is, as mentioned above, YAHOO! FINANCE.

The trading day

In the US, a great deal of activity goes on before and after normal market open hours through extended-hours trading, both pre-market and after-market. Whereas many retail investors will not involve themselves outside normal hours, some background knowledge is useful.

The NYSE, the Nasdaq, and the LSE all hold opening and closing auctions to determine opening and closing prices. Opening auction bidding will be informed by all the overnight news and in particular by company reports, and participants have the opportunity to get better buy or sell prices than they would obtain immediately after the market opens. Share prices often gap up or down on opening, i.e., they can open above or below the previous day's closing price.

The out of hours trading on the US exchanges, i.e., the pre-market and after-market, has an important read over into other markets around the globe.

Opening and closing auctions are the domain of the public exchanges and are not used by the alternative trading venues. A benefit to those not equipped with high-frequency trading capability is that the auctions are a level playing field with respect to speed of trading.

The schedules for the major US and UK markets are shown below.

NYSE

A brief summary of the NYSE daily schedule is shown in Table 3.7. For a detailed description of the NYSE opening and closing auctions, search <u>NYSE Open and Closing Auctions</u>.

Eastern Time

4:00 am to 9:30 am	Pre-market trading
7:30 am to 8:30 am	Common Customer Gateway (CCG) opens for order entry
8:30 am to 9:35 am	Imbalance and paired-off information is disseminated with increasing frequency
9:28 am	Indicative opening price information is provided
9:30 am	Designated Market Makers begin to open each share
9:30 am to 4:00 pm	**Market hours**
4:00 pm	Closing auction/Closing prices disseminated
4:00pm to 8:00 pm	After-hours trading

Table 3.7 NYSE daily schedule

Only NYSE and NYSE MKT-listed names can participate in the opening auction.

Leading up to 9:28 am, the stock exchange provides information on the current imbalance between buy and sell orders, giving traders the opportunity to trade buy and sell orders into equilibrium. This will usually be around the previous day's closing price. At 9:28 am, the exchange begins to announce the likely opening price of each share. Orders placed between 9:28 am and 9:35 am cannot be cancelled. If there has been some significant overnight news affecting a particular share, the designated market maker can make a significant adjustment to the opening price, and possibly delay opening in order to maintain an orderly market in the share.

The Nasdaq

The Nasdaq daily schedule is shown in Table 3.8.

Eastern Time

4:00 am to 8:00 am	Quote and order entry
9:25 am to 9:28 am	Nasdaq opens/enters quotes for participants with no open interest
9:28 am to 9:30 am	Dissemination of imbalance information begins
9:30 am	The opening cross occurs
4:00 am to 9:30 am	Pre-market trading
9:30 am to 4:00 pm	**Market hours**
4:00 pm to 8:00 pm	After-market trading

Table 3.8 The Nasdaq daily schedule

Traders on the Nasdaq stock exchange can place buy and sell orders through their broker onto the stock exchange order book while the market is closed. Just before market opening, a stock exchange computer analyzes all the orders received, and selects a tentative opening price for each share. The exchange then communicates this information to its dealer network, which will react to any significant imbalance between buy and sell orders with additional orders, and the final opening price is determined.

This auction process is known as the 'opening cross' and takes place in just a couple of minutes. This is the price at which the maximum volume of trades can be executed and largely determines the opening price of each share. A closing cross is made to determine the closing price of each share.

In earlier days, the main participants in these extended hours were the institutional investors, but now many professional investors within the investment banks and hedge funds participate. Also, technology is now enabling retail investors, working through their brokers, to participate.

LSE

The LSE daily schedule is shown in Table 3.9.

GMT or BST

7:50 am to 8:00 am	Opening auction
8:00 am to 4:20 pm	**Continuous trading**
4:20 pm to 4:30 pm	**Calculation of Volume Weighted Average Price**
4:30 pm to 4:35 pm	Closing auction

Table 3.9 The LSE daily schedule

In the opening auction, market participants place limit or market orders to buy and sell shares based on their assessment of overnight developments. The stock exchange trading computer then calculates the uncrossing price.

The closing price for a share will be based on the results of the closing auction or the mid price of the best bid and offer prices at the time the market closes.

Cross-listing and American depositary receipts

Many companies are cross-listed, i.e., they are traded on more than one stock exchange in different time zones and in different currencies.

In the US, most foreign companies cross-list as American depositary receipts (ADRs) which are traded on the US stock exchanges. These were established to simplify the process for US investors wishing to invest overseas and are issued by banks or brokerages. Each ADR will consist of a bundle of shares in a foreign company.

US pre-market trading starts at 9:00 am London time and after-hours trading finishes at 01:00 am London time the next day. So UK company shares, in the form of ADRs, are being traded in New York for 16 hours a day. ADR daily traded volume for a particular share can compare with LSE daily traded volume.

The futures and options markets

The futures and options markets are a large and integral part of stock market activity. They are covered briefly in *Chapter 9 - Futures and options.*

They are of interest to the retail investor in that they are part of the pricing mechanism – price discovery – for shares, and they give an indication of sentiment before the markets open. Of most interest to the retail investor is the trading that takes place in index futures. On the financial TV channels, you will see Dow, S&P 500, Nasdaq, FTSE 100, DAX, and CAC futures indices fluctuating throughout the day as futures contracts in these indices are traded. While the main markets are open, there is a small 'fair value' difference between the cash indices and the futures indices. They converge on contract expiration date. Fair value is explained in *Chapter 9.*

The main US futures exchange is the <u>Chicago Mercantile Exchange</u>, which operates Sunday to Friday, from 5:00 pm the previous day to 4:15 pm with a halt from 3:15 pm to 3:30 pm, US Central time. So from Sunday afternoon to Friday evening trading is nearly continuous, though the main volume of trading takes place when the main New York stock exchanges are open.

FTSE 100 index futures are traded on the London Stock Exchange from 8:00 am to 4:30 pm. They are traded on the US <u>Intercontinental Exchange</u> from 1:00 am to 9:00 pm London time.

Because of their long opening hours, especially in Chicago, the futures trading exchanges will take into account information flows on a global basis, virtually around the clock.

Traders pay a great deal of attention to the behavior of the futures markets, and the retail investor looking to time his buys and sells can derive useful guidance from them. Even when taking a longer-term perspective, he won't want to be down 2% or 3% at the end of the day when he has bought a tranche of shares and misjudged market sentiment.

There are specialist exchanges where you can trade futures and options on individual shares, e.g., OneChicago, which has a specialization in single stock futures (SSFs).

Stock transfer and registrar services

All listed companies use specialist service providers to keep a register of current shareholders and to act as agent for transfer of shares from one registration to another. Clearly, this is a massive data management project. The registers also support the payment of dividends and issue of proxies for shareholder voting.

These days there is no need to hold physical share certificates. In the US, holding shares in electronic format is enabled by the <u>Depositary Trust & Clearing Corporation</u> (DTTC). In the UK, an equivalent service is provided by the <u>Certificateless Registry for Electronic Share Transfer</u> (CREST). When you buy or sell a share electronically, your shares will be held by a registrar, who will report your transactions to the DTTC or CREST (now owned by Euroclear).

Users of the DTTC or CREST will not automatically receive annual reports or invitations to Annual General Meetings (AGMs). However, annual reports can be readily downloaded from the Internet and your investment manager/stockbroker can arrange an invitation to AGMs, though there is likely to be a fee for this.

If you hold any physical share certificates, you could consider sending them to your investment platform/stockbroker, which will hold them electronically through a registrar. You can then sell them readily if you wish.

Settlement

When you buy or sell a share, the transaction (T), normally has to be settled within three days – T+3, i.e., you come up with the cash if you are buying or you come up with the share if you are selling. This is all done for you by your investment platform/stockbroker. You can agree to longer settlement times with a stockbroker, e.g., T+5, T+10 or T+20, but there is likely to be an administrative charge. This would allow you to buy and sell a share – making a profit or a loss – without actually handing over any cash, except for commissions (and in the UK, stamp duty). If your transaction makes a loss, you will have to come up with the cash to cover this.

4 About shares and how shares are valued

Introduction

> *'The market can stay irrational longer than you can stay solvent.'*
> **John Maynard Keynes**

How are shares valued? There are probably as many views on this as there are people working in the investment industry. But central to the art or science of valuing shares is forecasting a company's earnings (defined below), which are conventionally expressed as earnings per share (EPS). Some companies pay out a portion of EPS to shareholders as a dividend. At a basic level, the price of a company share is what investors are prepared to pay at any particular moment in time for the forecast earnings stream of the company. This is expressed simply as the price/earnings ratio – P/E – where P is the price per share and E is the EPS. The level of confidence in and risks to the forecasts will be built into the price. Based on this assessment, investors will buy the share, increase or reduce their holding, possibly sell it in its entirety – or maintain their position.

Forecasting EPS is difficult enough even for the best companies with strong track records. Once you have taken a view on the likely EPS for a company, looking many years ahead, you then endeavor to foresee all the possible factors that could have an impact on this and the probability of them occurring. Strong, reliable earnings growth should be rewarded with a favorable company analysts' rating, for example 'buy' or 'strong buy' or even 'conviction buy' – and a healthy valuation in terms of P/E ratio.

A company's assets, including its intellectual property, also have a bearing, sometimes very strong, on its share price. Analysts take a view on these factors and exert a strong influence in the market. Their activities are discussed in some detail in *Chapter 5 – Factors that influence share prices* and *Chapter 6 – The Market participants, facilitators, and influencers.*

The global economic context is crucial – most companies benefit from strong global growth, or from strong growth in their regional or sector context. These factors affect both market sentiment and the realities of company earnings. Interest rates also have an important bearing on share valuations. If interest rates, which can provide a risk-free return, are on the rise, funds will flow from company shares to fixed interest instruments, causing a drag on share prices.

There is competition between asset classes, and relative value between asset classes has a significant bearing on share prices. The influence of interest rates is discussed in *Chapter 5 – Factors that influence share prices.*

If you are serious about investing in individual companies, you should spend some time looking through company reports and become familiar with income statements, cash flow statements, and balance sheets.

Total return on investment

Total return on investment (TRI) is the definitive measure of a company share's performance. It is simply the return based on capital appreciation as the share price rises (hopefully) and dividend payments, if made, are reinvested in the company. TRI is also the definitive measure of a fund's performance.

An individual using TRI to assess the merits of investing in particular companies should take account of the tax treatment of capital gains and dividends, which will depend on his tax situation. His real TRI will be impacted by these tax liabilities.

Capital structure

Companies need money to operate and to grow, and the classes of funding that a company uses make up its capital structure. In most cases, capital structure will be made up of some or all of the following liabilities:

- Short-term debt; typically bank loans.
- Long-term debt; typically bond issues by the company.
- Preference shares; issuance of 'preferred stock' is a specialized way for a company to raise finance. Their value is related to interest rates (as with bonds) and they are traded. Preference shares pay a fixed dividend, which has priority below payouts on bonds but above dividends to owners of shares. The use of preference shares as an instrument for raising finance is declining.
- Capital account; shares issued at par value to establish a company.
- Share premium account; shares issued to investors at a premium to par value.

'Par value,' 'capital account,' and 'share premium account' are described below.

A company operating with a high level of debt is regarded as highly leveraged and can be more vulnerable than a company with little or no debt – for example to rising interest rates; an economic downturn, during which it may struggle to service its debt; or to being hit hard by aggressive competitor activity, when it may struggle to lower its prices.

If a company fails and goes into administration, to the extent that monies are available, bank debt will be paid first with the holders of bonds and preference shares next in line. The holders of shares will be last in line. Companies sometimes survive by reorganizing their capital structure – commonly through the banks swapping their debt assets for equity, i.e., shares in the company. This can involve wiping out the original shareholders.

This is only a very basic outline of a highly complex subject; if you are interested in capital structure, you will find a great deal of information on the Internet.

Shares in issue

The concept of company shares and how they are traded on the stock markets has been covered from a practical standpoint in the previous chapter. However, it is useful to take a step back to look at the process of issuing shares.

There are many types or class of share which you can research on the Internet. However, the main class is common stock (US usage) or ordinary shares (UK usage). These are usually what you purchase when you buy company shares on a stock exchange.

When a company is established, a fixed number of shares is created and a number will be issued (becoming shares outstanding), say to the founders, at par value – a nominal value of perhaps one cent or one penny per share. The balance is held in reserve. Funds raised are recorded in the company's capital account. Then, if the company needs to raise more money, it will issue/sell another tranche of shares at a value greater than par, i.e., at a premium to par. These funds are recorded in the company's share premium account.

The owners of common stock/ordinary shares carry greater risk than lenders, but also have an opportunity for attractive returns if the price of the shares they hold rises. Conceptually, the shareholders own the 'shareholders' equity' equal to 'total assets less total liabilities'; also known as 'book value'; or 'net asset value' of the company.

The market capitalization of a company is the number of shares 'in issue' multiplied by the share price. Holders of shares want the market capitalization of the company to rise above book value. If it doesn't, the company management is failing to make the company's assets work for the investors.

The number of shares that there are in a company is usually fixed, and specified in the company's articles of association. The shareholders of a company determine how many may be issued for other investors to buy, or, depending on the jurisdiction and the articles of association, directors' approval may be sufficient. The balance is held in reserve. So when you buy some shares in a company, you can calculate what percentage of the company you own and this will determine your voting rights. You then receive the benefit of the EPS and dividends paid out of EPS, if the company pays a dividend. Not all do. Strong and growing EPS should cause the share price to rise. If the company has a good record of increasing its dividend payout each year, this should also have a beneficial effect on the share price.

It is important to be aware that from time to time companies issue more shares from their reserve in order to raise money, usually because either they are running out of cash, or they want to invest in the business over and above the level that their normal operating cash flow will allow. This process is known as a rights issue. The existing shareholders are given the right, without obligation, to buy the new shares in proportion to their holdings, usually at a discount.

On the downside, the EPS will fall because there are additional shares in issue to which a proportion of earnings have to be assigned. This is known as dilution. Investors tend not to like rights issues and the announcement of a rights issue will more often than not cause the share price to fall, usually to reflect the proportion of additional shares to be issued.

The other side of the coin is that companies sometimes buy back their shares and then cancel them. This causes EPS to rise, because there are less shares in issue, and this means that earnings have to be allocated over fewer share. This should benefit the share price. The buybacks are usually done either by a tender process, most likely involving the investment banks, or simply by the company buying back its shares on the open market.

The markets have mixed feelings about share buybacks. On the one hand, they increase EPS, all other things being equal. On the other hand, it could be an indication that management has run out of investment ideas.

Income statement and earnings per share

As indicated above, company shares have value when the companies generate cash through profitable activities. Shareholders receive the benefit of this through EPS.

It's important to understand definitions around profits, earnings, and dividends. Current practice is to provide considerable detail on the determination of profit on a profit and loss account and to refer to it as an income statement.

Table 4.1, using fictitious numbers, shows how an income statement treats profit and how EPS is derived.

Company, Inc. Income statement:

US$1million

Revenue	6,050	A company's top line income
Operating costs	-5,200	Normal costs of running the business
Exceptional items	-50	Non-recurring items
Operating profit	800	Revenue less operating costs and exceptional items
Interest on cash in hand	+20	
Interest on debt	-30	
Profit before tax	790	
Corporation tax	-60	
Profit for the financial year	730	
Dividends on preference shares	-10	
Profit after preference share dividends - Net profit or earnings	720	Used for earnings per share
Allocation to dividend	240	
Dividend payment ratio	0.33	Allocation to dividend/Earnings
Dividend cover	3	Earnings/Allocation to dividend
Shares in issue	1000,000,000	
Earnings per share	72 cents	Net profit/Shares in issue
Dividend per share	24 cents	Cash paid to shareholders
Share price	1,080 cents	Based on P/E ratio of 15 (72 x 15)
Price/Earnings ratio	15	1,080/72
Dividend yield	2.2%	24/1,080

Table 4.1 Company income statement

Price/earnings ratio is a key metric for share valuation and is discussed later in this chapter. The P/E ratio used in the table is just a typical value.

Share prices are very largely based on EPS and EPS growth, so we should explore some of the important aspects of net profit, or earnings, and EPS.

Exceptional items

There is turbulence in the affairs of every company and this can lead to exceptional cost items arising from time to time. These are subtracted from company revenue along with operating costs to derive operating profit. Happily, exceptional revenues also occur from time to time and are added to normal revenues. An exceptional item should be associated with normal business operations. If a cost arises from an abnormal event – perhaps an extreme weather event – then it will be classified as an extraordinary item.

A common exceptional item is a restructuring cost, e.g., where a company decides to discontinue one of its operations. It will incur many expenses, such as redundancy costs and the buy-out of leases. The logic is that these costs are regarded as unusual, not reflective of the quality of the ongoing operations, and they should be identified as such. However, the need to close an operation could be the result of poor management – in setting up the operation in the first place, followed by ineffective management. Prudent investors will look closely at the background to significant exceptional items, and make their own judgment on whether there might be implications for the ongoing performance of the company. Explanations for exceptional items will be found in company reports.

Interest

Companies pay interest on their debt and on any bond issues that they have made and will receive interest from cash in hand in the bank. The net figure is taken from operating profit to give 'profit before tax.'

Tax

> *March 2014: according to an official report, one in five of Britain's largest businesses paid no corporation tax in 2013, while more than half paid less than £10m.*

Companies are liable for corporation tax, and will usually seek to limit their tax liability within the law. It is not unusual for a company to minimize taxes by offsetting prior year losses against current profits. Deduction or addition of taxes leads to the profit for the financial year.

Dividends on preference shares

When dividends on preference shares have been paid, we are finally left with net profit, or earnings.

Earnings per share and P/E ratio

The very important EPS is calculated by dividing earnings by the average number of shares in issue in any particular period. Companies are able to report an adjusted EPS by adding back exceptional items. On the other hand, EPS may be diluted to take account of obligations to issue further shares, for example through an employee share option scheme.

Finally, out of EPS, the directors of a company may decide to pay a dividend to holders of common stock/ordinary shares.

P/E ratio is usually expressed as the current share price divided by the latest reported annual EPS. More precisely, it is referred to as trailing 12 month P/E ratio. It is a measure of how much the market is prepared to pay for a company's earnings stream.

A forward 12 month P/E ratio is also calculated from analyst forecasts as a means of forecasting share price movements. P/E is discussed in more detail below.

Smoothing EPS

The markets look for reliable and rising EPS streams - they do not like surprises, and profit warnings are detested. As are cuts in dividends arising from flagging EPS - this can be a serious headache for pension funds. Companies will go to a great deal of trouble to deliver what the markets want.

There is an unlimited number of factors that can set back a company, creating an adverse impact on EPS. A company with a healthy profit margin is in a better position to manage its EPS than a company with a thin profit margin, for example by using adequate contingencies in its project accounts or by judicious allocation of costs and profits between one financial year and the next.

The treatment of exceptional items provides some scope for creativity. While staying within a legal accountancy framework, companies seek to manage their EPS stream in accordance with market expectations. Or if things are going particularly well, they may 'beat expectations.'

Underlying profit

Companies must prepare statutory accounts according to accountancy rules, and are assessed for corporation tax based on these. Companies also work with management accounts, which may be more reflective of underlying business performance and therefore more useful to management.

If a company's management judges that the statutory accounts do not result in a fair indication of the underlying profitability of the business, then it may report in addition their assessment of underlying profit. Professional investors will look carefully at this assessment and form their own view.

Balance sheet

An example of a company balance sheet is shown in Table 4.2.

Company, Inc. Balance sheet:

US$

Assets		Liabilities	
Current Assets		Current Liabilities	
Cash	35,000	Accounts Payable	145,000
Accounts Receivable	45,000	Accrued Expenses	2,500
Inventory	6,000	Notes Payable	110,000
Short-Term Investments	3,000		
Pre-paid Expenses	650		
Total Current Assets	89,650	Total Current Liabilities	257,500
Fixed Assets		Long-Term Liabilities	
Office Building	650,000	Long-Term Debt	580,000
Factory Building	350,000		
Plant and Equipment	225,000		
Total Non-Current Assets	1,225,000		
		Total Liabilities	**837,500**
		Shareholders' Equity	**477,150**
Total Assets	**1,314,650**	**Total Liabilities + Equity**	**1,314,650**

Table 4.2 Company balance sheet

You will see that Shareholders' Equity is the difference between Total Assets and Total Liabilities.

A common way of manipulating cash is to delay payments to suppliers. This behaviour has run at particularly high levels since the financial crisis and is damaging for supply chain companies.

EBITDA and gross margin

EBITDA stands for Earnings Before Interest Tax Depreciation and Amortization. Opinions as to its usefulness in assessing the quality of a company are varied because interest, tax, depreciation, and amortization all effect EPS. It is commonly used to value start-up companies using a simple multiplier on EBITDA.

Gross margin is revenue less the direct cost of producing a company's products or services. So it is a good indication of the how much value customers attribute to its products or services. Other operating expenses or overheads are then subtracted from gross margin, to give operating profit.

Dividends and cover

As illustrated in the table above, annual dividend payout comes out of EPS, and is expressed as a percentage of share price and referred to as dividend yield. Yield will vary as a share price fluctuates.

In the US, quarterly dividend payments are the norm for most companies. In the UK, dividends are usually paid twice yearly – an interim dividend and then a final dividend, with the final dividend being the larger component, typically around twice the interim.

Some UK companies pay a quarterly dividend. This is limited to about ten FTSE 100 companies (e.g., Royal Dutch Shell, HSBC, GlaxoSmithKline) to keep their US shareholders happy.

From time to time, if a company generates cash in excess of its operational needs, it may pay out a special dividend.

You can research a company's dividend payment record, for example, in the US using the Nasdaq website. Search Nasdaq dividend history – insert the company name or ticker. And in the UK, search ADVFN – insert the company name or ticker and click on the Financial tab.

You can readily see the size of the dividend and the company's track record in increasing the dividend over a long period of time. In looking at a company's historical dividend stream, it is worth bearing in mind that the dividend payout of many companies was severely disrupted by the global financial crisis, and you may decide to give them the benefit of the doubt based on a shorter track record.

Dividend cover is the ratio of profit at EPS level to annual dividend payout. Dividend paying companies need to be generating enough earnings to be able to comfortably pay out the dividend expected by the market. Investors will look for dividend cover to be over two and will worry that if it is much lower than this, the company may have difficulty in paying the dividend. The market will become nervous and quite likely will mark the share price down. This causes the dividend yield to go up and the market may eventually take a view that a dividend cut is in the pipeline. The market is often right on this.

During 2013 through 2015, some companies were even borrowing to keep their dividend payouts on track, no doubt anticipating better cash flow ahead. On the face of it, not impressive, but viable in a low interest rate environment.

Enterprise value

Enterprise value (EV) is the market capitalization of a company adjusted for debt (added) and cash/cash equivalents (subtracted). Debt is added because it is a liability in the company's capital structure. To own 100% of a company, a buyer would have to take on the debt as well as buying the equity, i.e., acquiring all the outstanding shares for the value of the market cap. The buyer would then own all the company's cash, so you could think in terms of the buyer taking on the net debt, i.e., the total debt less the company's cash.

EV is considered to be a more reliable assessment of the value of a business than market capitalization and is often used for assessing takeover value.

Analysts sometimes use a company's EV in assessing share value.

The difference between income and growth shares

Investors have different perceptions of what a share is worth to them. A useful precursor to looking at how shares are valued is to understand the difference between income shares and growth shares, though in reality, companies sit across a spectrum in relation to this.

Income shares

At one end of the spectrum are steadily performing dividend payers – sometimes known as 'blue chips' – paying out quite a high proportion of their earnings each year as dividends, expressed as a percentage of the share price. Many large cap companies yield 2% to 4% and these are attractive levels of yield to many investors. Some companies yield quite a bit more than this, sometimes because the share price has fallen, which may indicate that the company is experiencing some difficulties, and the share price may fall further or drift sideways. Such companies may be facing ever-increasing competition through globalization, disruptive technologies, changing consumer behavior, and many other factors.

These companies should be generating sufficient cash to meet their internal investment needs, as well as paying out a dividend to their shareholders. A good company will achieve some growth, and perhaps substantial growth. If the company is short of investment opportunities, their major shareholders may press them to return cash to shareholders by increasing the dividend payout or even to pay a special dividend; or, to buy back a proportion of their shares and cancel them, which increases the EPS and has the potential to increase the dividend per share.

Dividends from large cap companies make a vital contribution to US and UK pensions. It makes the most sense to buy into a dividend stream with a long-term view, so the reliability of the dividend stream is crucial. Pension funds value dividend streams because they have to make monthly payments to pensioners, and reliable income from dividends is preferable to regular selling of a batch of shares as markets go up and down. The pension funds will analyze company performance in great depth to satisfy themselves that the dividend stream is robust – and ideally steadily rising, at least in line with inflation – and they will tolerate (unhappily, and increasingly in 'activist' mode) significant drops in share price provided that they can rely on the dividends.

Calculations show that the effect of reinvesting dividends over a long period of time, say for five to ten years or longer, can produce excellent returns from the effect of compounding. However, entry price level has a strong bearing on this (see *Chapter 18 – Managing your portfolio*) and the quality of the company is crucial. Another factor is the fees or commissions you will pay on reinvesting a dividend. These could erode the value of a smaller dividend and impair the effectiveness of the compounding.

Growth shares

At the other end of the spectrum are companies that seek to grow their businesses vigorously and choose to reinvest a high proportion of their profits, rather than pay a dividend; or they may pay a small dividend, perhaps between 0.5% and 2.0%. A good growth company will increase its revenue and its earnings per share significantly year on year, and its share price is likely to rise nicely. Companies can grow EPS at perhaps 30% per annum and upwards, and this will cause their share price to rise strongly. However, a substantial gain in share price can disappear quickly on a profit warning.

Investing in growth companies can be more rewarding than investing in income companies, but it is frequently advised that the risks are greater. It's not as simple as that. If you look at the fluctuations in the share prices of a great many 'blue chip,' big-dividend payers, you will observe some extraordinary volatility. The dividend yield can be high simply because the share price is low – and the share price may be low because the markets don't like the company's fundamentals. The company may be poorly managed, running out of ideas, and being slaughtered by its competitors. Companies like this tend to be gamed by the markets that look to exploit the significant share price fluctuations that frequently occur before and after a share goes ex-dividend. See *Chapter 5 – Factors that influence share prices.*

A useful approach is to select companies that are somewhere in between – growing nicely, and paying a 2% or 3% dividend that the company is steadily increasing year on year. Young companies sometimes grow EPS at an astonishing rate, say, 40% or 50% a year for several years, but growth inevitably slows as the company matures, and the company may seek to maintain its attraction to the market by developing a dividend program.

Global economic context – some key indicators

The dominance of the US stock markets is a strong theme of this book – keep in mind that they account for close to 50% of total global stock market capitalization. Due to this, there is always a great deal of focus on whether US indices are overvalued or undervalued while not neglecting other major indices. A number of indicative factors are carefully watched – these affect market sentiment and therefore share prices. These include:

- Historical P/E ratio – index average.
- CASE – Robert Shiller's Cyclically Adjusted P/E ratio – index average.
- Forward P/E ratio – index average.
- Tobin's Q ratio.
- Relative Strength Index (RSI) for the major indices.
- Moving averages for the major indices.

These factors are described in *Chapter 5 – Factors that influence share prices*.

Another important factor that affects share valuations is 'correlation,' which has been described in the previous chapter. When 'macro events' are dominating the markets, share prices tend to move together, e.g., most share prices will move down if there is a major shock to the markets; or vice versa if, for example, a major central bank governor makes an upbeat statement.

Fundamentals or Technicals?

How do you judge whether a share price is undervalued or overvalued? The right answer ought to be by fundamental analysis. However, you can carry out the most thorough fundamental analysis, and determine that a particular share is seriously undervalued. And then watch the share price fall relentlessly, before it eventually bottoms out and begins to recover. By which time, if you had invested in the share, you would have suffered an unpleasant loss.

So what is going on? A great many market participants will be guided by technical analysis of the actual share price movements and associated trading volumes in their buy and sell decisions, and their activities are influential on share prices. So to trade or invest successfully, it is important to understand both fundamental and technical analysis.

There are many people who just concentrate on the fundamental characteristics of a company and will invest in it for the long term, believing that it will overcome any short-term difficulties and temporary market perturbations. Warren Buffet is such an investor and has enjoyed great success over decades. At the other end of the spectrum are the technical traders who believe that the fundamentals of a company are less important than the day-to-day realities of share price movements, which can be predicted by following charts and a myriad of other metrics – together with all-important news flow. So technical trading tends to be the domain of the traders and short-term investors. However, it is also important for the long-term investor, as he needs to invest in a particular share ideally when it is cheap and the Technicals will inform his judgement with respect to entry point. Similarly, the Technicals can be helpful in informing sell decisions.

In reality, when addressing the question of 'Fundamental or Technical?' it is useful to think in terms of a spectrum of approaches with Fundamental and Technical at either end and some combination of both occupying the middle ground. No sensible market participant would operate only on Fundamentals or only on Technicals and a good blend is the key to success. There is an exception to every rule, and in this case it is the high-frequency traders, whose activities are described in *Chapter 10 – Trading.* Some of their trading strategies will be based only on Technicals.

Fundamentals

> *'Your premium brand better be delivering something special, or it's not going to get the business.'*
> **Warren Buffett**

Fundamental analysis is based on a deep understanding of a company and does not accept that the markets always get it right. A 'fundamental investor' will make his analysis, and may conclude that for a particular company the market has simply got it wrong. The traders may have taken the share price far too high or far too low – overbought or oversold; the share price may be languishing because the company is out of fashion or unloved; the investor may judge that the company has much better longer term prospects than the market is recognizing; a small company may have little or no analyst coverage, and the fundamental investor may have done his own detailed research. This is described as value investing and is discussed in some detail below.

A full fundamental analysis entails a great deal of hard work and for a company will address, inter alia:

- Financials: income statement, cash flow statement, balance sheet.
- Free cash flow and conversion of profit to cash.
- Dividend policy and in particular dividend cover.
- Price to book ratio.
- Capital ratios for banks.
- Capital structure.
- The quality of the management team and succession planning.
- Whether the company is defensive or cyclical.
- Sector factors.
- Competition.

- Pricing power.
- Its regulatory environment.
- Its legal environment.
- Tax rate and tax position.
- The quality of its products and services.
- Its new product pipeline.
- Patents held, pending, or expiring.
- Profit margin.
- Exposure to currency fluctuations.
- Approach to profit recognition – is it aggressive or conservative?
- Depreciation and amortization – management has some discretion which can be abused.
- Provisions and their adequacy.
- Opportunities for profitable growth.
- Scalability, e.g., does the company have a good product and can potentially increase sales volume strongly with a relatively small increase in overheads?
- Mergers & Acquisitions activity – is the company potentially a predator or a target?
- Goodwill on the balance sheet.
- Debt.
- Any defined benefit pension liability.
- ROCE – Return on Capital Employed.
- Investment performance which bears on ROCE – does the company manage its investments well using good processes, e.g., in: capital equipment; new facilities such as factories, process plants, mines, and stores; R&D; IT?
- For companies that hold a lot of money, e.g., insurers and banks, is their investment performance in managing these monies good?
- Project risk profile – poorly priced or executed projects can hit the bottom line severely.
- Political risk, e.g., vulnerability to changes in government policy or strike action.
- Threats.
- Quality and competitiveness of supply chain.
- Commodity prices where the company's profitability is dependent on these.
- Is the company in a supply chain with commodity companies at the top of it?
- Shareholder register: is this dominated by solid long-term investors or by short-term speculators, such as hedge funds; does it contain activist investors – these have a mixed track record in boosting company performance?
- And so on.

A great many of these factors are expressed in terms of standard metrics and ratios by analysts and can be found on numerous financial websites. In the US, search and enter company name or ticker: usa finance.yahoo.com – under Key Statistics; CNN Money – under Financials. In the UK, search and enter company name or ticker: uk finance yahoo – under Key Statistics; ADVFN – under Financials; Hargreaves Lansdown – under Share prices & stock markets.

The importance of various metrics will vary from sector to sector and also each analyst will have his preferences or even idiosyncrasies.

The analysts will also seek to glean additional information on a company by seeking out meetings with the company management, and sometimes by visiting company facilities.

All of the above (and quite a lot more) has to be assessed within the context of global and regional economic outlook and then fed or synthesised into an assessment of:

- The extent to which the company will be able grow its EPS in the years ahead.
- The company's ability to also grow its top line, i.e., its revenue or turnover. It can be difficult for a company to grow EPS if it is not also growing turnover.
- The company's dividend program, if they have one, and projections.
- The risks that may have an impact on the company's ability to achieve EPS growth and dividend growth.
- And the level of confidence that can be mustered in these projections.

For a company with a substantial asset base, such as a property company, the performance of these assets in contributing to earnings will be an additional important consideration.

Based on their assessments, the sell-side analysts will produce their target prices – which may be above or below the current share price. The projection will usually only be for a few months ahead. It is important to recognize the difference between the sell-side analysts, who want clients to buy the shares – and pay brokerage commissions – and therefore may take an overly upbeat view of a company's prospects; and the buy-side analysts working directly for, say, fund managers, who are motivated to make a more measured assessment.

For large cap companies, the retail investor could spend weeks pouring through information. For a small cap company, he may simply not be able to get his hands on very much. So the retail investor may well ask, 'Well what's the point, then?' To a considerable degree, you need to let the analysts, commentators, and Internet sources do much of the work for you – or you will never get around to an informed decision to buy company shares. However, you should be able to find your way around a company report and to know the key issues to look for.

The fundamental investor will also look closely at and take account of Technicals, but will always place the Fundamentals at the center of his investment strategy. Clues to value opportunities could include companies that have good dividend yields without there being much wrong with the company; unusually low P/E or Price to book ratios; or strong (believable?) growth forecasts not reflected in the current share price.

Technicals

Technicals play an important role in investment and trading decisions. They have considerable validity to some extent because a great many market participants use them as a guide. They also have considerable historical significance. They no doubt make a substantial contribution to 'group think' and herd behavior in the markets. Traders in particular like the signals that they give – they can all buy or sell on a clear signal that they all recognize. If the S&P 500 index futures traders believe that the S&P 500 is 'toppy' when it rises to 6% to 8% above its 200 day moving average, you have to take that seriously.

To avoid repetition, the book's main coverage of Technicals is to be found in *Chapter 10 – Trading*. Some of the most important metrics and devices covered there are:

- Volume
- Beta
- Relative strength index – RSI
- Chart patterns
- Moving averages
- Bolinger bands
- Keltner channels
- Candlestick charts – price action
- Support levels and resistance levels
- Accumulation and distribution
- VIX – volatility index
- Slippage

Efficient markets, price discovery, and value

In this chapter, we look at the inherent uncertainty in valuing shares, and then in *Chapter 5*, we look at a wide range of factors that influence share prices. In *Chapter 6* we take a look at the wide ranges of market participants, all with different agendas.

Efficient markets

Professor Eugene Fama, an American economist and Nobel Laureate, is an original proponent of the efficient market hypothesis, the basis of his 1965 paper 'Random Walks in Stock Market Prices', which has received considerable attention over the years. The proposition is that markets are 'informationally efficient,' in that investors immediately incorporate any new information into the price of a share. So shares are always 'priced to perfection.' This is something of a circular argument, and the theory doesn't make a great deal of distinction between share price and share value – it assumes, somewhat controversially, that they are more or less the same thing. In which case, is difficult to see that the efficient market theory does anything other than state the obvious. The theory is sometimes used to make the case that it is impossible for a fund manager to consistently outperform the market through expert share selection, combined with astute market timing. As a majority of fund managers fail to outperform the market, i.e., 'beat the index,' it is perhaps not surprising that the theory has many adherents. Another problem with the efficient market theory is that stock markets are not always particularly efficient.

You will find many articles on the Internet addressing the efficient market theory and they make interesting background reading.

Price discovery

Price discovery is a continuous process for determining the price for an asset, such as a company share or a commodity, at which supply and demand come into balance. Particularly important are the agendas of market participants, the interplay between them, and the availability of trading information in real time.

Stock markets require companies to update the market regularly. This will be a combination of formal reporting and news releases, e.g., reporting the departure of the chief executive or announcing an important contract award. This is central to the price discovery process.

Considering the complexities around share valuation, the level of short-term trading that takes place in the modern markets, and the influence of sell-side analysts who create a measure of upside bias, price discovery is bound to be an unreliable process. Information that has a significant bearing on 'market expectations' in relation to forecast earnings will trigger either heavy buying or selling of the share – often with considerable volatility. The traders will seek to amplify the volatility, which may continue for quite some time. The share price may eventually settle into a new trading range, awaiting further news or it could move into an upwards or downwards trend. The trend will be clear enough in hindsight but not so easy to identify in real time. In real time the movement may look like Professor Fama's random walk as more and more market participants form a view on the company and where its share price is trending.

Value

An analyst reported in March 2014 that Smith & Nephew would be worth 15% more if split into three companies.

Notionally, the market's assessment of share price is based on publicly available information on the company and its trading environment. However, there is never 'enough' information and also the future trading environment is a matter of conjecture. This leads into the concept of value investing, which has already been touched upon. At any point in time, the price of a company share may or may not be the same as its 'fair' or 'intrinsic' value. (In the futures markets, fair value has a different meaning – see *Chapter 9 – Futures and options*.) The company could be doing a lot better or worse than the market expects; there may be a predator that believes it can improve its efficiency or strip its assets; frenetic trading may have driven the price way above or below fair value; for a resource company, the markets may be taking a very short-term view on commodity prices and marking the share price below value assessed over the longer term – and so on.

Value investors believe that the market sometimes gets it wrong and dedicate their research to the identification of companies that are under-valued due to weaknesses in the price discovery process. They will then invest in the company in the belief that the share price will eventually rise to their assessment of fair value. For a value investor, the difference between price and fair value is his margin of safety, should he decide to invest in the share. An acceptable level of margin of safety – with respect to preservation of capital - will vary from investor to investor, and should take account of the risk factors that pertain to any particular company. Of course, it can also work the other way, and the shrewd value investor may decide to short a company that he judges to be overvalued.

Short selling

Short selling plays a significant role in price discovery and, intriguingly, this is a common justification for it. It is probably not too cynical to suggest that the main justification is that traders and hedge funds like to be able to make money when markets are falling as well as when they are rising – and they can exploit the induced volatility. See *Chapter 8 – Short selling*. However, situations arise from time to time where an obdurate and entrenched management can be driving a company into the ground, even operating illegally, and aggressive short selling can bring management to its senses, or result in needed management changes. There is a credible view that the research undertaken by specialist short sellers can be of particularly high quality. In periods of financial crisis, regulators will from time to time ban the short selling of the shares of banks and other key financial companies.

Reporting day

The moments of truth for a company are its reporting days. US companies and major UK companies report earnings four times a year. Reporting dates for all but the smallest listed companies will be provided well in advance on company financial calendars, and conveniently listed on a number of websites. Many companies upload their reports onto their websites an hour before market opening. Some will issue their reports after the markets have closed for the day. Whenever they are issued, they will be voraciously devoured by a swath of market participants, some of whom will make a very rapid assessment and participate in the pre-opening auctions. Sell-side analysts will also be quickly onto each report, seeking to drum up business, and some will issue their recommendations before market opening, and will sometimes call an opening share price up or down by an estimated percentage. The best informed participants will have a view on which are the most authoritative analysts for each company, and this knowledge will come into play. For a large cap company, there will be a succession of analyst reports emerging as the day progresses, and into the next day.

The aftermath of reporting day is when price and value are most likely to converge. If the company's results meet market expectations, then there may not be much change in share price. However, if the company beats or misses expectations, the market will reset the price to its perception of value – it re-rates the company. But as we have discussed, the market may still be getting it wrong, leaving some unrecognized value for the value investors to exploit.

If a company beats or misses 'analyst expectations' by a substantial amount, share prices movements on or immediately after opening can be dramatic – 20% to 30% or even more. If the movement is sharply downwards, the sound of stock brokers telling their clients that it's been 'overdone' can be deafening. The stock exchange computers and market makers will be in overdrive trying to match buys and sells and to achieve some stability. Quite often the movement is overdone but by no means always.

News flow

In the context of the stock market, news flow is any emerging information that can bear on the performance of an index, sector, or individual share price. The amount of news flow pertaining to a company is an important factor in the price discovery process. Large cap companies are heavily traded and followed by many analysts, resulting in continuous and dynamic price discovery and a moderately efficient market. Also, management works hard to manage company earnings, not wanting to surprise the markets. So there should be less surprises than there are for smaller cap companies. Probably there are more surprises with the large caps than there used to be due to globalization, increasing competition (often disruptive) and many other factors, and it has become impossible any longer to think there are such things as reliable 'blue chip' companies.

For small cap companies, the information flow will be much less and trading may be light and intermittent – there will be a somewhat illiquid market in these shares. In addition, there may be very little news between reporting dates. The directors of small cap companies often find it a challenge to strike the right balance between too much news – some of it hot air – and too little news. The market struggles to be efficient in these circumstances. So there is a great deal of scope for price and value to become seriously misaligned. This can lead to very large share price movements on reporting day, as the market trades price back into line with the market's new assessment of value. The small number of market makers in a small cap share will be significant traders with their own agendas.

Company management does not want to see volatility in its share price on reporting day. It wants to convince the markets that the company is well managed and consistently beats expectations – though not by too much! It is increasingly common for companies to 'manage shareholder expectations' to make it a little easier to beat them. In the US, it is now accepted practice that companies make pre-announcements to the markets a month or so before they report, if they feel the need to prepare the market for disappointment.

Macroeconomic events

A company's reporting day may be overshadowed by macroeconomic events, tail risks and black swans which are explained in *Chapter 5 – Factors that influence share prices.* Even a company beating expectations strongly may be heavily sold off, while the market evaluates the implications of the event on the fortunes of the company and its sector. There is much scope for difference in view among analysts and if, for example, an important macroeconomic event is unfolding, the way it could affect the fortunes of a particular company or sector may be no more than guesswork – this is fertile ground for volatility. As the fundamental investors are running sensitivity analyses on their spreadsheets, the traders will be trading the volatility and the more the better. Traders can't make good money unless share prices are moving!

The analysts

As already mentioned, there are two kinds of company analyst. Sell-side analysts work for brokerages, investment banks, and research houses and they seek to identify good investment opportunities to promote, i.e., sell, mainly to fund managers and other large investors – buyers – thus earning a commission or fee. The buy-side analysts are employed by the buyers to provide internal investment advice. They assess the recommendations of the sell-side analysts as well as making their own assessments. Company analysts exert a significant influence on share prices. They use a variety of approaches for valuing shares and for disseminating their recommendations. Their role and the influence of sell-side analysts is described in some detail in subsequent chapters.

Let's look at some charts

It's worth spending time looking at some charts. Before investing in a company, it's useful to see how it is performing within its sector as well as over various time frames.

This is a useful first look at a company's performance. Keep in mind that many individual company charts will not reflect the dividend contribution so they will not show total return. For a good charting service, search: <u>Google Finance</u>. It includes a 10-year time frame, which not all charting services do. Especially if you are unfamiliar with share price movements, it's worth spending a little time comparing some sector performances with a major index, and then overlaying some individual share price performances – and looking at various time frames, e.g., 6 months, 10 years, All. 'All' should take you back through the two great crashes of recent years.

US

Table 4.3 gives tickers for some of the major US indices, the ten S&P 500 sector tickers, and a couple of companies and tickers from each sector. Spend a few minutes looking at a sector performance against a major index and the performance of one or two companies within the sector.

Index or sector	Ticker	Companies in the sector	Company ticker
S&P 500	.INX		
Dow	.DJI		
Consumer Discretionary	SP500-25	Starbucks	SBUX
		Whirlpool Corp	WHR
Consumer Staples	SP500-30	Proctor and Gamble	PG
		Wal-Mart Stores	WMT
Energy	SP500-10	Marathon Oil Corp	MRO
		Chevron Corporation	CVX
Financials	SP500-40	Citigroup Inc.	C
		McGraw Hill Financial	MHFI
Healthcare	SP500-35	Johnson & Johnson	JNJ
		Pfizer Inc.	PFE
Industrials	SP500-20	Caterpillar Inc.	CAT
		Lockheed Martin	LMT
Information Technology	SP500-45	Facebook Inc.	FB
		Altera Corp	ALTR
Materials	SP500-15	Alcoa Inc.	AA
		Sealed Air Corp	SEE
Telecommunication Services	SP500-50	Frontier Communications	FTR
		Verizon	VZ
Utilities	SP500-55	NRG Energy	NRG
		Edison International	EIX

Table 4.3 US index and sector tickers

You can a find a useful site for exploring sector performance by searching <u>Sector Tracker spdr</u>.

SPDR is the name given to a family of funds run by State Street Global Advisors. The site specializes in ETFs that track the S&P 500 sectors.

If you look, say, over a ten year time frame, you will see why the market professionals seek to rotate through the sectors.

UK

In the UK, sector tickers are a little difficult to find on the Internet, so they are shown here in Table 4.4, together with main index tickers that work on <u>Google Finance</u>.

Index or sector	Ticker	A company in the sector	Company ticker
FTSE 100	UKX		
FTSE 250	MCX		
Aerospace & Defence	NMX2710	Cobham	COB
Alternative Energy	NMX0580	Ceres Power Holdings	CWR
Automobiles & Parts	NMX3350	GKN	GKN
Banks	NMX8350	Barclays	BARC
Beverages	NMX3530	Diageo	DGE
Chemicals	NMX1350	Carclo	CAR
Construction & Material	NMX2350	Galliford Try	GFRD
Electricity	NMX7530	Drax Group	DRX
Electronic & Electrical Equipment	NMX2730	Oxford Instruments	OXIG
Equity Investments Instruments	NMX8980	Alliance Trust	ATST
Financial Services	NMX8770	ADVFN	AFN
Fixed Line Telecommunications	NMX6530	BT Group	BT.A
Food & Drug Retailers	NMX5330	Ocado Group	OCDO
Food Producers & Processors	NMX3570	Premier Foods	PFD
Forestry & Paper	NMX1730	Mondi	MNDI
Gas, Water & Multiutilities	NMX7570	Centrica	CAN
General Industrials	NMX2720	Rexam	REX
General Retailers	NMX5370	Mothercare	MTC
Health Care Equipment & Services	NMX4530	Smith & Nephew	SN.
Household Goods & Home Construction	NMX3720	Taylor Wimpey	TW.
Industrial Engineering	NMX2750	Rotork	ROR
Industrial Metals & Mining	NMX1750	Ferrexpo	FXPO
Industrial Transportation	NMX2770	BBA Aviation	BBA
Leisure Goods	NMX3740	Fishing Republic	FISH
Life Insurance/Assurance	NMX8570	Old Mutual	OML
Media	NMX5550	ITV	ITV
Mining	NMX1770	Anglo American	AAL
Real Estate Investment & Services	NMX8630	St Modwen Properties	SMP
Real Estate Investment Trusts	NMX8670	Great Portland Estates	GPOR

Index or sector	Ticker	A company in the sector	Company ticker
Mobile Telecommunication	NMX6570	Inmarsat	ISAT
Nonequity Investment Instruments	NMX8990	World Trust Fund	WTR
Nonlife Insurance	NMX8530	Hiscox	HSX
Oil & Gas Producers	NMX0530	Cairn Energy	CNE
Oil Equipment Services & Distribution	NMX0570	Petrofac	PFC
Pharmaceuticals & Biotechnology	NMX4570	BTG	BTG
Real Estate Investment & Services	NMX8630	Countrywide	CWD
Software & Computer Services	NMX9530	Computacenter	CCC
Support Services	NMX2790	Atkins (WS)	ATK
Technology Hardware & Equipment	NMX9570	Nanoco Group	NANO
Tobacco	NMX3780	Imperial Tobacco	IMT
Travel & Leisure	NMX5750	Easyjet	EZJ

Table 4.4 UK index and sector tickers

Intrinsic share valuation – value investing

'Beware of geeks bearing formula.'
Warren Buffett

Intrinsic share valuation methodologies are widely used across the markets, so it's worth having a close look at the underlying concepts. There are many proprietary models developed by analysts in particular who will closely guard their methodologies, though great complexity in modelling is hard to justify given the uncertainty in forecasting earnings.

Share valuations in the 1920s

It was in the 1920s that the modern approach to valuing shares began to emerge. We need to start with earnings yield, which is the inverse of P/E ratio, i.e., E/P. Take a company trading at a P/E of 15 (not far off the long-term average of the S&P 500 companies). Its earnings yield will be 1/15 = 0.0666, i.e., approximately 7%. In other words, a share priced at US$100 will give you US$7 of earnings each year. A P/E of 40 will give an earnings yield of 2.5%. As the share price goes up or down, the earnings yield will fluctuate.

In the 1920s, New York with its burgeoning financial markets was overtaking London as the world's leading financial center. The convention that had developed is that people invested in companies for their dividends – not for growth in profits. Take a company earning 50 cents per share and paying out 30 cents per share in dividend – a dividend cover of circa 1.8, which was something of a norm for the era. With a P/E ratio of 10, the company's share price would be 10 x 50 cents = 500 cents or US$5 and the dividend yield would be 30/500 = 0.06 = 6%. This was fairly typical for large industrial companies, paying a good dividend, which were quite simply valued at a P/E of around about 10 – corresponding to an earnings yield of 10%.

What has happened to share valuations since those early days?

A plausible dataset from 1929 to 2014 is provided by Seeking Alpha and Bespoke Investment Group and can be found by searching: <u>Seeking Alpha S and P 500 historical p-e ratio</u>.

The S&P 500 chart provides less than compelling evidence that valuations have increased systematically over the years, though considerable volatility is evident. However, the current average P/E of about 20 is significantly above the long-term average of around 16. Over the years, companies have come and gone. Some have continued to be steady dividend payers and others have exhibited spectacular growth. The stock markets have been through cycles, bubbles, and crashes, so it's not surprising that we cannot observe a systematic increase in valuations.

Table 4.5 shows some historical data on share valuations and interest rates.

Era	P/E	Earnings yield	Dividend		Dividend cover	10 Year Treasury Rate	AAA rated corporate bond yield
			Yield	Payment ratio			
1920s	15	10%	6%	60%	1.7	5% to 3.3%	6% to 5%
1930s	15	6.7%	5%	75%	1.3	3.3% to 2.2%	5% to 3%
1960s and 70s	15	6.7%	3%	45%	2.2	4.7% rising to 10.8%	5% rising to 13%
1990s	20 to 25	4% to 6%	2%	47%	2.1	8% falling to 5%	9.5% falling to 7.5%
2010s	20 to 25	4% to 6%	2%	47%	2.1	3.7% to 2.6%	3.6%

Table 4.5 Historical share valuations and interest rates

You can see that in the 1920s and 1930s, both earnings yield and dividend yield were above the AAA rated corporate bond yield and the 10 Year Treasury Rate. This is what you would expect because the markets at large would prefer the safe yield from bonds and treasuries, unless they were likely to do better in shares. This was not the case in the 1960s and 1970s, when the stock market performance was somewhat lackluster, and yield from interest-paying instruments reached very high levels.

The table shows that dividend yields have fallen since the 1920s, as companies were investing more of their profits to generate growth. Then from around the mid-1990s, you can see from the S&P 500 charts, evidence of the markets paying for earnings growth, through elevated P/E ratios – though leading up to the bursting of the dot.com bubble in 2001 the markets were clearly paying too much!

The last 20 years or so have seen the emergence of companies, often Internet-based, exhibiting spectacular rates of growth and attracting stellar valuations.

Benjamin Graham's Intrinsic Value formula

Benjamin Graham, acknowledged by Warren Buffett as his early mentor, was influential in developing the concept of value investing, in which you look for undervalued shares to achieve a margin of safety in your investments. You assess if a share is undervalued by calculating its intrinsic value (IV) based to a large extent on forecasts of future earnings. Though this approach does not lend itself to accurate calculation, it is nonetheless a useful concept. IV and fair value tend to be used synonymously.

Graham produced his intrinsic value formula in 1934 and modified it in 1974 to take account of interest rates. His purpose was to provide a quick and easy way for an investor to make an initial assessment of the intrinsic value of a share – if the share passes the test, then it would be worth researching further. Graham used an earnings yield of 11.7% corresponding to a P/E ratio of 8.5, which was more or less in line with the prevalent approach to share valuation – and he added an empirical component, g, to take account of potential growth in earnings per share.

IV, according to Graham, can be calculated approximately as follows:

$$IV = \frac{EPS \times (8.5 + 2g) \times 4.4}{Y}$$

Where:

- IV = Intrinsic value.
- EPS = Diluted* earnings per share.
- 8.5 = Price/Earnings ratio for a 'no growth' company (implies an 11.7% earnings yield).
- g = Conservatively estimated percentage growth in EPS for the next 7 to 10 years.
- 4.4 = The average percentage yield for high grade corporate bonds in 1962, when the model was introduced.
- Y= The current yield on AAA Rated corporate bonds**.

*Diluted to take account of 'convertible securities' such as preference shares and employee share option schemes.
**Currently around 3.6%; in the UK context, this would most likely be the yield on 10 year gilts, currently about 2%.

Graham conceived his interest rate modifier in 1974, a period when interest rates were rising to extraordinarily high levels, well above 4.4%. So he was anticipating that the attraction of interest-paying instruments would depress share prices. In the current era of extraordinarily low interest rates, the modifier has the opposite effect and would lead to an enhancement of an IV by a factor something like 4.4/3.6 or 22%.

Even though low interest rates are usually good for share prices, the formula currently appears to work better without this adjustment. The formula then reduces very simply to:

IV = EPS (8.5+2g)

The crucial aspect to the formula is 'g', the growth rate. Graham would have based his treatment of growth on experience and observation and on the proposition that in the future, growth potential would play an increasing role in share valuations. Note that Graham concentrates on a time frame of 7 to 10 years ahead – introducing an element of convention as opposed to logic into his concept.

Discounted cash flow (DCF) methods

Markets are discounters of the future.

Graham's initiative has led to a proliferation in methods for determining intrinsic share value, predominantly based on the concept that a share is worth the amount of cash that it will deliver to an investor over time. The present value of future cash is determined by discounting as described below.

Net present value (NPV)

As indicated above, the IV of a share is assessed by looking at the 'present value' of cash that will accrue to it over time. The aim, then, is to forecast annual cash produced many years ahead, then to determine its aggregate present value using net present value (NPV) calculations.

As we are only concerned with 'cash in' and not 'cash out,' we can forget about the 'net,' and just consider present value (PV) which takes account of the 'time value of money' and risk.

If you have a sum of money in hand, you may be able to invest it opportunistically at an attractive rate of return, albeit with some risk attached. Imagine you are considering buying a share in Vanilla plc and that it is forecasting that it will achieve for you an EPS – a measure of cash – of 100 pence a year from now. 100 pence then is worth about 98 pence now, because you could invest it for a fixed and guaranteed return of, say, 2% per annum (this will vary with prevailing interest rates). You believe there is some upside potential and that you might get more than 100 pence a year from now, perhaps 103 pence, but also that there is some downside risk. You might only get 95 pence, but you regard this as a worst plausible case and accept this as the 'present value' that you will use in judging the value of the share. So you are discounting the one-year forecast EPS back to the present by 5%.

You then look at the forecast EPS of Vanilla plc several years into the future and apply an appropriate rate of discount to each year's EPS, to take each amount back to PV. Then you aggregate these to arrive at the IV of the share. But what discount rate should you assume, and how many years do you use? These crucial questions are addressed below, but first let's consider how cash is assessed.

Assessing cash

Predicting the amount of cash that will accrue to a share is fraught with difficulty. A company may simply accrue surplus – free – cash to its balance sheet as retained earnings or it may invest it in 'assets' with a view to generating more cash in the future. It may pay out some of its free cash as dividends to shareholders. An investor in a non-dividend paying company will only receive the benefit of cash accrued or new assets when he sells his shares. An investor in a dividend paying company will receive some real cash dividends on a regular basis.

A pension fund investing for dividend income to support regular payments to pensioners may analyze the strength of the dividend stream using a dividend discount model – search Investopedia DDM. A DDM will use assumptions on dividend growth and discount rate to assess the PV of the future dividend stream. It will take account of interest rates by using risk free returns as a benchmark. In terms of share price, the pension fund is likely to be content if this keeps pace with inflation – then it will not suffer a capital loss. A pension fund will pay a premium for a company share that delivers a robust dividend stream – one that allows the pension fund manager to sleep well in his bed at night. The size of the premium will bear on share price.

For companies that pay little or no dividend, there are two strands of thought for assessing cash. One is based on free cash flow, and uses models such as free cash flow to equity – search Investopedia FCFE. The other is based on EPS as a proxy for cash delivered.

EPS is widely regarded as a good proxy for cash flow, but many analysts prefer to work with free cash flow, which is cash from normal operations less capital expenditure. They believe that cash is a better indicator of performance than earnings, which are more readily manipulated. Free cash flow is impacted by capital expenditure and, as many companies are able to invest effectively, an approach based solely on free cash can give misleading results.   Analysts with the time and the money may well use a range of approaches in taking a view.

For companies at either end of the income-growth spectrum, the modelling will not be too difficult, but the selection of input parameters will be. It is worth noting that for an income company, the DDM will be relatively stable because it will usually not have to deal with the compounding of high growth rates; it is likely to use smaller discount factors, as in general there will be less risk around a dividend stream than a high EPS growth rate.

Companies combining growth and dividend yield are the most problematic in applying DCF to assess intrinsic value, but simply using EPS as a measure of cash generated works quite well. An advantage of using EPS is that it is a measure of a company's earnings before dividends are paid and therefore it reflects cash available for dividends. In the spirit of Benjamin Graham, EPS rather than free cash flow is used in the treatment that follows.

Before undertaking some analyses, it is worth noting that the mechanics of a DCF model don't have to be complicated, but the process of selecting input parameters to forecast EPS streams is complex and uncertain, and really the realm of the professional who has the time to spend and good research support. The key variables in the following DCF IV calculations are EPS growth, discount rate, and time frame.

EPS growth

In taking a view on the EPS growth rate to use in a PV calculation, it is necessary to take a view on the revenue or 'top-line' growth potential of the company. For assessing top-line growth, analysts use compound average growth rate (CAGR). Usually a company will find it difficult to grow EPS strongly over several years, unless it is also achieving strong top-line growth. Its possibilities may be limited to cost cutting and trying to push through price rises, and both can be difficult to achieve. If it operates only in the UK, this might limit just how big the company can get. In the much larger US market, this is less of a problem. If its product differentiation is not exceptional, fierce competition may limit its growth potential. The concept of 'scalability' is useful here – does the company have a range of products and services that have good differentiation, and will its business model work in China, Brazil, or India just as well as it works in the US or UK? If the answer to this is 'yes,' then the company may be able to keep up strong EPS growth for quite some time.

The first things to look at before attempting a forecast are past performance in terms of CAGR and EPS growth – both recent and longer term history will give insights into the strength and nature of the company. You will then need to be quite familiar with the fundamentals of a company, and from the discussion above you will see that this is no easy task – particularly for large, complex companies. You may take the view that the company has a great business model, and a strong and highly motivated management team that will keep strong earnings growth going for many years. The company's reports will give guidance on outlook and future earnings prospects. CAGR and EPS growth forecasts can be obtained from Nasdaq, CNN Money and DigitalLook.

You can have much greater confidence in EPS growth projections over just a few years than over ten years or longer. Also, it is helpful if the global economic outlook is set fair. It is very difficult for a company to keep a strong rate of growth, say 20%, 30%, or even 50% per annum, going indefinitely. So in a DCF model, it would make sense to ease growth rate down as you project further into the future. You could, for example, switch to rate of inflation after five years, as some experts recommend, but that would be a fairly arbitrary call.

You then have to take account of the real world – risks, threats and opportunities to your projections. Macroeconomic factors, sector and competition factors, management issues, politics and regulation, and much more will all have a bearing. See *Chapter 5 – Factors that influence share prices.*

Discount rate

Factors that will affect the discount rate used will include interest rates and risks. If you judge that interest rates will rise – so you could get a safer return on your money in government bonds – and that the company is particularly vulnerable to external influences, you could reflect this by using higher discount rates in years that are further into the future. Just about any company could be struggling to make a profit seven or eight years from now. Think of disruptive business models and technologies, black swans and market crashes. You might see fit to discount distant cash flows dramatically.

A discount rate of 5% is used in the treatment that follows. This is a reasonable value to use, taking account of economic conditions, current low interest rates, and the state of equity markets.

Time frame

Shaftesbury plc owns around 500 properties in London's West End.

DCF analysis runs into very serious difficulty when it comes to determining the time frame to use. It is simply not possible to make a rational determination of this.

Technically, the purest way to undertake a DCF calculation for IV is to reduce the EPS growth rate fairly strongly after, say, ten years, and to increase the discount factor year on year – both actions can be said to reflect increasing uncertainty into the future. Then, in something like 20 or 30 years, the yearly EPS arising from the calculation will become small and immaterial. Despite this being an intuitively satisfying approach, it is unlikely to be any more useful than the terminal or disposal value approach. This involves running an analysis to obtain the aggregate of 10 years of EPS at present value and then adding a terminal value or disposal value for the company – you assume that you will simply sell the company, or your shares in it, after 10 years. In many cases the disposal value may be of similar magnitude to the ten years' worth of EPS, so the assessment of disposal value is very significant. Of course it is not possible to know in what shape a company will be in ten years' time. It could have failed or be going from strength to strength. It might have been taken over. A reasonable base case is to assess the disposal value at a P/E of around 10 – so to obtain IV, you simply multiply the year ten EPS by 10, discount back to the present and add the result to the ten years' worth of EPS.

If you are considering investing, say, US$50mn in a company, a good use of time would be to expend considerable effort in assessing terminal or disposal value – this would be over the top for a US$3,000 investment. Pertinent factors will include:

- The strength of the company's brand
- Balance sheet strength
- Tangible assets
- Strength of management and succession management processes
- The quality of its products and innovation
- Scalability – especially in a global context
- Intellectual property
- Barriers to entry to its markets – keeping competition out
- Vulnerability to disruptive business models and technologies
- Break-up value – could be an added incentive to invest
- Take-over potential – another positive factor
- Gearing (through debt) and interest rate trends
- Etc.

You might take the view that a property company with several hundred prime properties in Manhattan or the West End of London is more likely to have a high value 10 years from now than a microchip company which operates in a ferociously competitive market. Of course the key word in this proposition is 'likely.'

The above approach seems quite reasonable, but the logical case for it is not all that strong, so again we are looking at convention.

Some calculations

Consider a company with the following characteristics:

- Trailing 12-month P/E of 25.
- Current EPS of 120 cents, so current share price will be 25x120 = 3,000 cents or US$30.
- Average earnings growth forecast 8% per annum.
- Forecast EPS a year from now of 129.6 cents (120 x 1.08).

Apply a discount factor of 5% and take terminal value at 10 times discounted EPS from ten years ahead, and you get the intrinsic value calculation shown in Table 4.6.

End of year	EPS – 8% annual Growth	Discount rate 5% compounding	Discounted EPS	Share Price
0	120			**3,000**
1	129.6	1.05	123.4	
2	140.0	1.10	127.0	
3	151.2	1.16	130.6	
4	163.3	1.22	134.3	
5	176.3	1.28	138.1	
6	190.4	1.34	142.1	
7	205.7	1.41	146.2	
8	222.1	1.48	150.3	
9	239.9	1.55	154.6	
10	259.1	1.63	159.0	
		Total	1,406	
		Terminal value		
		10 x 159	1,590	
		Intrinsic Value	**2,996**	

Table 4.6 Intrinsic value calculation

You can see that this calculation has worked quite well with IV close to current share price. However, you will also see that you can get virtually any answer that you want, by adjusting the growth and discount rates as well as the P/E ratio and by applying a different multiplier to obtain terminal value. Nevertheless, a P/E ratio of 25 for a company growing at 8% per annum is not inappropriate and nor are the other metrics used.

But why use ten years? Well, convention!

Now let's look at some calculations on specific companies. The vagaries of dealing with the accrual of cash have already been discussed but it is nevertheless useful to apply a simple approach and to see what emerges. The following treatment covers a range of companies across the growth-income spectrum and uses EPS as the proxy for cash accrual – consistent with Graham's simple approach.

US

The data in Table 4.7 has been calculated using the above format and taking terminal value as 10 times the discounted 10-year EPS. The EPS in the table is the forecast EPS in one year's time from March 2016. A discount rate of 5% has been used throughout. The average EPS growth rate over ten years has been taken as half of the next 5 years' earnings growth forecasts obtained from the Nasdaq and CNN Money websites. Search: Nasdaq Revenue and EPS Summary – insert company name or ticker; CNN Money – insert company name or ticker. This is just a reasonable assumption. In a number of instances the forecast data is erratic and 'best estimates' have been made. Only companies forecasting growth in earnings are included.

Sector Company	Market Cap US\$bn	10 yr Growth rate %	Share Price US\$	EPS cents	Discount rate %	EPS(8.5+2g)* US\$	Intrinsic Value IV US\$	SP/IV	P/E Ratio
Consumer Discretionary									
Starbucks	85	10	57	220	5	62.7	58	0.98	36
Nike Inc.	102	7.5	58	215	5	50.5	47	1.23	32
Consumer Staples									
Proctor & Gamble	224	3.6	83	400	5	63	70	1.18	20.7
Wal-Mart	218	2.7	68	470	5	65	72	0.94	14.8
Financials									
McGraw Hill Financial	25	6	93	480	5	98	97	0.96	21
Berkshire Hathaway	173	3.3	138	732	5	110	126	1.1	14.2
Health Care									
Johnson & Johnson	293	3	106	680	5	99	113	0.94	17
Gilead Sciences	121	1.5	88	1,150	5	132	175	0.5	7.1
Merck & Co	145	3.1	52	350	5	51	59	0.88	14.7
Industrials									
Caterpillar	42	2.5	72	360	5	49	57	1.26	15.5
Lockheed Martin	66	3.1	216	1,280	5	188	216	1	18.7
Materials									
Monsanto Co	39	6	87	450	5	92	91	0.96	19.5
Alcoa Inc.	12.3	3.5	9.4	40	5	6.2	8.7	1.08	16.7
Sealed Air	8.9	3.2	46	230	5	34	39	1.18	17.5
Technology									
Apple	561	5.5	102	900	5	175	177	0.58	11
Facebook	306	15	108	250	5	96	91	1.28	71
Telecommunications									
Verizon	213	4.6	52	100	5	18	19	2.74	13
AT&T	201	2.2	38	280	5	36	44	0.86	14
Utilities									
Edison Intl	22.7	2.7	69	360	5	50	59	1.17	17
Duke Energy	53	2.2	77	440	5	57	70	1.1	17
							Average	**1.09**	

*Benjamin Graham IV = EPS (8.5+2g)

Table 4.7 US shares intrinsic value calculations

The average ratio of Share Price/Intrinsic Value is 1.09 (0.98 without Verizon) indicating that the calculation model has worked reasonably well. There is strong evidence in the table that companies with high forecast growth rates enjoy higher P/E ratios, but there are a few anomalies.

Both Gilead, a biotech company, and Apple have share prices well below IV – they would require discount rates of 15% and 13% respectively to bring IV down to their share price levels. This suggests that the investment community does not have much confidence in the analyst forecasts of earnings growth rates, or that there are concerns about terminal value – or both. P/E ratios for these companies are on the low side at 7 and 11 respectively.

Verizon, a large telecommunications company, has a very high ratio of SP/IV at 2.74, indicating the premium that the market is prepared to pay for a presumably reliable dividend stream of more than 4%.

Facebook enjoys a particularly high P/E ratio, indicating that for now the market has confidence in the high growth forecasts.

UK

The data in Table 4.8 has been calculated using the above format and taking terminal value as 10 times the discounted 10-year EPS. The EPS in the table is the forecast EPS in one year's time from March 2016. A discount rate of 8% has been used throughout.

In the table below, the average EPS growth rate over ten years has been conservatively estimated using data from the DigitalLook website coupled with the author's knowledge of the companies and their sectors.   You can make your own assessment using DigitalLook – search by company name or ticker.

Sector Company	Market Cap £bn	10yr Growth rate %	Share Price pence	EPS pence	Discount rate %	EPS(8.5+2g)* pence	Intrinsic Value pence	SP/IV	P/E Ratio
Aero & Defence Cobham	2.7	2	213	20	8	250	256	0.83	12.3
Autos & Parts GKN	5	2	280	27	8	337	345	0.82	8.7
Banks OSB Barclays	0.7 29.3	4 7	249 166	37 20	8 8	610 450	535 348	0.47 0.48	8.2 13
Beverages Diageo	47.2	5	1,873	91	8	1,683	1,398	1.33	21
Chemicals Carclo	0.09	8	134	11	8	269	204	0.66	9.4
Construction & Mats Galliford Try	1.2	7	1,361	130	8	2,925	2,262	0.6	11.2
E&E Equipment Oxford Instruments	0.41	4	696	50	8	825	723	0.96	15
Financial Services Hargreaves Lansdown	6	10	1,273	39	8	1,111	861	1.48	34

Sector Company	Market Cap £bn	10yr Growth rate %	Share Price pence	EPS pence	Discount rate %	EPS(8.5+2g)* pence	Intrinsic Value pence	SP/IV	P/E Ratio
Telecommunications									
BT Group	46.8	4	459	32	8	528	462	0.99	14.5
Vodafone	58.8	12	217	6	8	195	143	1.52	46
Food and Drug									
Ocado	1.7	30	259	2.6	8	178	191	1.35	140
Food Production									
Cranswick	0.99	4	1,993	110	8	1,815	1,691	1.18	17.1
Forestry									
Mondi	5	5	1,334	110	8	2,035	1,691	0.79	12
General Industry									
Rexam	4.3	5	612	40	8	740	615	0.99	15.3
General Retailing									
Mothercare	0.33	12	186	11	8	357	262	0.71	20
Healthcare									
Smith & Nephew	10.3	4	1,121	60	8	990	867	1.29	19
House & Home									
Taylor Wimpey	5.8	5	178	17	8	314	261	0.68	13
Industrial Engineering									
Spirax-Sarco	2.5	5	3,445	154	8	2,849	2,244	1.54	24
Industrial Transport									
BBA Aviation	2.1	3	194	13.4	8	194	182	1.06	14
Leisure Goods									
Photo-Me	0.7	7	174	7.3	8	164	148	1.17	24
Life Insurance									
Old Mutual	8.9	3	182	19	8	275	258	0.7	9.9
Media									
ITV	9.3	6	234	18	8	261	294	0.80	14
Real Estate									
Foxtons	0.43	4	159	13	8	214	188	0.85	13
Mobile Telephones									
Inmarsat	4.2	7	918	35	8	787	609	1.51	27
Nonlife Insurance									
RSA	4.6	8	454	32	8	784	593	0.77	17
Pharma/Biotech									
BTG	2.4	15	617	18.6	8	716	535	1.15	34
Real Estate									
Countrywide	0.84	5	354	36	8	666	553	0.64	11
Software & Comput Svc									
Computa-center	1.0	3	820	54	8	783	734	1.12	15.5
Support Services									
Atkins	1.3	3	1,285	110	8	1,595	1,495	0.86	12.9
Tech Harware									
Arm	14.3	15	983	35	8	1,347	1,007	0.98	40

Sector Company	Market Cap £bn	10yr Growth rate %	Share Price pence	EPS pence	Discount rate %	EPS(8.5+2g)* pence	Intrinsic Value pence	SP/IV	P/E Ratio
Tobacco									
Imperial Brands	35.2	5	3,752	237	8	4,384	3,642	1.03	15.5
Travel & Leisure									
EasyJet	6.2	5	1,521	150	8	4,275	2,305	0.66	13.3
Real Estate Inv Trust									
Gt Portland Estates	2.5	20	702	13.4	8	650	529	1.33	53
Land Securities	8.4	5	1,051	46	8	851	707	1.49	25
							Average	0.98	

*Benjamin Graham IV = EPS(8.5+2g)

Table 4.8 UK intrinsic value calculations

The selected discount rate of 8% has been used throughout to give an average value for SP/IV of approximately one (0.98). Leaving out the banks, which have a ratio below 0.5, SP/IV ranges between 0.6 and 1.54, which is perhaps quite a narrow range, given the disparate nature of the companies and their sectors. There is some evidence of companies with high growth rates enjoying high P/E ratios, but not in a strongly systematic way. A little more than half the companies in the sample have a forecast growth rate between 3% and 8% and a P/E between 12 and 18.

Where the SP is significantly higher than IV, 8% discount rate may be too high and the estimate of terminal value may be too low. You could infer that the market has considerable confidence in the company's long-term prospects.

Where SP is significantly below IV, you could infer that the market has a lack of confidence in the company, or simply little interest in it. You could reduce IV to the SP by using a higher discount factor or smaller terminal value. A higher discount factor would indicate uncertainty particularly in growth forecasts.

It can perhaps be inferred from the discounts used in Tables 4.7 and 4.8, 5% in the US and 8% in the UK, that the US markets have more confidence in the analyst EPS forecasts than the UK markets.

It's interesting to note that the two real estate investment trusts have high ratios of SP/IV – Great Portland Estates at 1.33 and Land Securities at 1.49. This could imply a greater terminal value than the norm which you would expect with holders of high quality rental properties. As a point of detail, Great Portland Estates' high P/E of 53 is based on past exceptionally strong growth – forecast growth is weak. The company has strong institutional shareholders who presumably have faith in the long-term performance of the company.

Vodafone (VOD Telecomms sector) is an interesting case and is included in Table 4.8. Take a more detailed look at Vodafone on the DigitalLook website. You will see that since 2011, Vodafone's EPS has collapsed, reducing by about 60% – yet the share price has not collapsed, with P/E increasing dramatically from about 11 to well over 40! Yield is attractive at over 5% but this is not enough to justify such a high valuation. Vodafone's market cap is £58bn. You can see from DigitalLook that analysts are forecasting a dramatic increase in earnings in 2017. Vodafone is so important to UK pension funds that investors are hanging in there.

Non-life Insurance has not been represented in Table 4.8 because there are no companies in this sector forecasting growth. However, the sector has soared in the second half of 2015 compared with the FTSE 250. This is against a backdrop of gloomy analyst assessments across the sector. So what is going on? Anticipation of consolidation within the sector, with traders and investors speculating that there will be takeover bids for these companies, which are struggling to grow their profits. In September 2015, Amlin, a Lloyds of London insurer, received a £3.47bn cash bid from Mitsui Sumitomo Insurance. This represented a 36% premium to the share price, which rose by about a third.

Benjamin Graham formula

Graham's IV has been included in the tables above. For US companies Graham's IV is on average 0.9 x IV, indicating that Graham's formula discounts at about 5%, the value used in Table 4.7.

However, for UK companies, Graham's IV is on average 1.18 x IV – unsurprising because a discount of 8% has been used in Table 4.8, which has suppressed IV.

Notwithstanding the difference between US and UK shares, a quick way of assessing market confidence in analyst forecasts, which are informed by companies' outlooks and guidance, is to calculate Graham's IV, which can be done in just a few minutes. If it is significantly higher than the current share price, then this suggests that the market is heavily discounting the EPS growth forecasts for the share. This could indicate value in the share not recognized by the market – or the market could be right to doubt the forecasts!

Use of DCF

What emerges from these considerations is that DCF IV is not a predictive tool. It is an analysis tool that allows you to set up a useful financial model for a company, and then to explore how it responds to variation of key variables. This process can address a range of future scenarios – based on expert economic forecasting. In other words, sensitivity analysis. IV analysis may play a role in the toolkit of the retail investor, but it is not essential. However, a large institutional investor investing substantial sums in a company is more likely to regard this as an essential tool to support sound investment management decisions. It is a valuable tool to explore the range of long-term performances of a share that might be anticipated.

Under Fundamentals above, there is a long (and no doubt incomplete) list of factors that an analyst may need to take into account. Whatever assumptions he makes in his model, the further he probes into the future, the more the uncertainty around those assumptions will increase. He can apply risk analysis to key parameters and run extensive sensitivity analyses, but will still be dealing with a great deal of uncertainty.

Empirical share valuation

> *The Keynsian beauty parade: based on a 1930s newspaper beauty competition asking people to judge not who they think the five most beautiful women are, but who other contestants will judge the most beautiful to be. Keynes believed that the same concept is at work in the stock market. So concentrate on demand for shares rather than their intrinsic value. Keynes believed that investors exhibit herd-like behavior – 'animal spirits.' It's a point of view!*

We have explored the concept of intrinsic share valuation in some detail and assessed its uses and limitations. The other main approach to share valuation is empirically based with convention playing a central role.

Convention

Convention has already been mentioned a number of times.

According to John Maynard Keynes, share valuation is *'not a prediction but a convention which serves to facilitate investment and ensure that shares are liquid, despite being underpinned by an illiquid business and its illiquid investments, such as factories.'* What it boils down to is that after all the intrinsic analysis has been done, a share is worth what the market will pay for it – supply and demand. Price discovery is a continuous dynamic process, and both share value and share price can change in an instant. Experienced and savvy market participants will have a subliminally shared view on what the conventions are and therefore what a share is worth at any particular point in time.

We have seen elements of convention in Graham's IV formula and also in the more detailed approach to DCF IV calculations.

The surprisingly high valuations sometimes attached to companies growing very rapidly could be attributed to a combination of convention and over-optimistic groupthink, producing a long, momentum-driven rise in share price. Quite often the market assigns extraordinarily high P/E ratios to companies exhibiting relatively short bursts of exceptionally strong growth – perhaps lasting a few years. Facebook, with a P/E ratio of close to 100, and Ocado, whose P/E ratio flirted with 150, are good examples. Logic and history tell us that stellar growth rates are always unsustainable.

Price/earnings ratio

The price/earnings ratio, P/E, tells you how much you are paying for a company's annual earnings. It is one of the most used parameters in assessing share prices. Price is current share price. Earnings are net profit after tax and dividends on preference shares but before dividends on common stock/ordinary shares (see Table 4.1). P/E ratio can be trailing or forward – trailing P/E is based on the last 12 months' earnings; forward or prospective P/E is based on the forecast of the next 12 months' earnings. For a company that reports half-yearly, the trailing P/E ratio will be updated twice yearly. If the company reports quarterly, it will be updated quarterly.

So if Ace plc's current share price is 135p and its trailing EPS is 8p, then its trailing P/E ratio will be 135/8 = 16.9.

P/E will vary in real time with share price.

A very rough guide to P/E ratio is provided in Table 4.9.

P/E	Company characteristics
3 or 4	The company is in difficulty and may not survive – or it may be a good recovery play.
8 to 12	A fairly dull company – some small growth forecast and may pay a modest dividend which has been erratic in the past and is possibly not reliable. Or, an undervalued company.
12 to 20	A company growing steadily but modestly, perhaps EPS growth of 4% to 6% per annum and a fairly reliable dividend yield between 2% and 4%.
20 to 30	Growing strongly – perhaps EPS growth of over 10% for the last three or four years, and likely to continue in that vein; dividend yield around 2%; well-liked by investors at large, so some momentum.
30 and above	Stellar performance, with EPS growing at over 15% per annum. Well-liked and new investors rushing to get on board; could be quite risky if there is a hint of a slowdown in EPS growth – e.g., presaged by an aggressive competitor move.

Table 4.9 Guide to P/E ratio

The markets pay for growth, and it is a reasonable proposition that there is more risk inherent in growth companies than steady dividend payers. At some point the growth will falter. Risk is not built into P/E in a systematic way. It can only be assessed on an individual company basis. It's important to be aware that a P/E ratio can be very high because a company's earnings have collapsed, as with Vodafone, mentioned above. Eventually the share price will move down, or earnings will move up, until the P/E ratio becomes more reflective of the value of the company.

The role that P/E plays in share valuation is based to a significant degree on convention. For example, there will be a fairly widely held view on what the average P/E of each sector should be. This will take account of a range of factors, in particular the growth potential in the sector and the risks associated with that sector at any point in time. There will also be conventional wisdom, e.g., that the P/E for a fast-growing retailer should be in the range to 15 to 20. Awkwardly, if you look at a number of companies in a particular sector, you are likely to find a wide range of P/E ratios without the reasons for this being very evident.

An important tool of analysts and media commentators is to compare P/E ratios between sectors. They then compare companies in the same sector, and attempt to judge if a company is overrated compared with its peers or perhaps underrated; in other words, at a premium or at a discount to its sector average. If a company outperforms or underperforms analyst expectations, it is likely to be 're-rated.' The market will vote and its P/E ratio may move towards the top of its sector range or towards the bottom.

In its early stages, a company might achieve 30% or 40% – or even more – EPS growth for several years, but this will eventually ease down. After a very strong growth spurt, say 30% to 40% EPS growth over four or five years, a company can reach a very high P/E ratio, 40 to 50 or even considerably more. As the rate of EPS growth declines, the P/E will probably also decline, though the share price may well continue to gain year on year. This can be regarded as a maturing process for the company.

US growth companies that have achieved very high P/E ratios during their very strong growth phases include Amazon (AMZN) and Netflix (NFLX). UK companies that have reached very high levels of P/E include ARM Holdings (ARM), Asos (ASC) and Ocado (OCDO), touched on above. You can take a look at their P/E journeys on DigitalLook.

When a high-flying company's earnings have fallen sharply, it can take some time for the P/E ratio to fully reflect this – quite possibly the market is expecting a recovery as management responds to the challenge. Both Amazon and Netflix wobbled but managed to get their EPS growth back on track.

During 2013 and 2014, average US and UK P/E values rose significantly, based not on strong growth in revenues – top line – and EPS, but on a favorable global economic outlook. Higher earnings were anticipated, emphasizing the role that market sentiment plays in the determination of P/E values.

PEG

As mentioned in the introduction to this chapter, central to the art or science of valuing shares is forecasting EPS. PEG is an important metric dealing with growth in earnings, and you should not invest in individual shares unless you understand it. It is a particularly valuable metric for a growth company. Fortunately, it is easy to understand. Somewhat perversely, the lower the PEG, the better!

PEG is the ratio of P/E ratio to rate of growth expressed as a percentage. For example, if a company has a P/E ratio in a particular year of 20 and grows EPS by 10% in that year, its PEG is 20/10 = 2. This is not very punchy. If a company has a P/E of 10 and an EPS growth rate of 40%, its PEG will be 0.25 which is very punchy, but the burning question is 'are the EPS projections believable?' and, 'can the company sustain this rate of growth for the next three or four years?' If the market believes that the answer to both questions is 'yes,' and this view is reinforced by a recent set of results, then the share is likely to be in demand and on the rise. For current PEG values, search Nasdaq PEG or DigitalLook – insert company name or ticker.

Both historical and forecast data is shown. The forecasts are a consolidation of the forecasts of the analysts that cover the share. For a large cap company, this can be a couple of dozen analysts. For a small cap company, there may be only one analyst who made his forecast six months ago. Also, many companies will summarize the most recent analyst forecasts for their share prices on their websites.

Good growth companies will have a strong track record in terms of both top-line growth and EPS growth – and forecasts reflecting more of the same. Low PEG from forecasts is a good indicator of where value may be found and where time on more detailed research could be time well spent. For smaller cap companies, there may be insufficient confidence in forecasts by only one or two analysts and the markets may be tentative in re-rating such shares.

Price/sales ratio

The simplest way to calculate a company's price/sales ratio is to divide its market cap by its most recent one year's sales. This metric is most useful in comparing companies in the same sector.

Enterprise value/EBITDA

Where a company has high levels of debt or depreciation, enterprise value/EBITDA is regarded by some as a good valuation tool. It is another, albeit complicated, way of looking at P/E. If enough analysts make us of it, EV/EBITDA will play a role in share valuations.

Momentum investing

In April 2014 it was reported that declines in momentum shares – fast-growing companies which have outperformed the market recently – have left investors anxious about how much further they may fall.

Momentum investing contains a significant empirical component. A concept behind momentum investing is that you are more likely to succeed by backing consistent winners than consistent losers – or alternatively, shorting the consistent losers. A risk of this approach is that shares that have risen substantially above fair value are likely to be more susceptible to shock from bad news or maybe a tail risk materializing.

Share prices very often surprise both on the upside and downside. Just when you figure that a share price can't go any higher, that is exactly what it does. On the downside, a share that looks as though it can't possibly go any lower begins to look seductive as a recovery play, and then either plunges again or goes nowhere for years.

Good recovery plays are often difficult to spot. Hindsight is 20/20 – it's easy to look back and see the good momentum plays but not so easy to see them in advance and get on board. Reliance on charts only is not a recipe for success. If you look into the rationale of successful momentum players, you will find that they are in reality traders or they are savvy investors who look for possible momentum movers and then take quite a deep look at fundamentals before they invest.

An interesting website for US investors is Optimal Momentum Investing, which has published an award-winning book on the subject. UK investors could take a look at the Momentum Investor Newsletter.

How does momentum investing bear on price discovery? Critics would say that it doesn't – it leads to mispricing of shares, albeit perhaps only temporary. Research shows that many active fund managers are using shorter holding periods for shares. Possibly fund managers are becoming more astute but also perhaps are increasingly playing the momentum game, in an effort to enhance their portfolio performance – which would perhaps render them complicit in mispricing.

Mispricing will inevitably exacerbate volatility to the liking of traders – the more the better – but may be less helpful to retail investors. On the one hand, they may be panicked into selling on a sharp plunge in price or tempted into buying when a share has gone too high – not wanting to miss out. On the other hand, for those ahead of the game, it can provide good buying opportunities or the possibility to lock in a decent profit.

Goodwill

The difference between a company's value in a takeover situation and its book value is the company's goodwill. Typical items of goodwill are brand value, loyal customer base, a stable and skilled work force, intellectual property, and patents.

Usually in acquiring a company, the buyer will pay a premium over book value which will reflect the goodwill. If a company becomes a takeover target, its share price and therefore the value of its goodwill is likely to rise sharply. The buying company will recognize the acquired goodwill on its balance sheet as an intangible asset. Under current accountancy rules in both the US and UK, companies have to reassess the fair value of their goodwill each year. If a reduction in value is deemed to have taken place, then a charge or 'impairment of goodwill' is made to the balance sheet. However, if the fair value of the goodwill rises, an upwards adjustment is not made.

Price to book ratio (P/B)

In March 2014, British Land and Land Securities were cut from the buy list of an important analyst who said: 'with both stocks trading around where we think their 2013 NAV will come in, we aren't prepared to pay for growth any further forward as the world gets a riskier place to invest in.'

Book value is a company's net asset value (NAV) – from its balance sheet also known as shareholders' equity or shareholders' funds. Theoretically, the NAV is the amount of cash that would be realized if the company were to be wound up. In reality, there would be substantial costs in winding up a company, which would diminish the cash realized.

Price to book ratio (P/B) is the ratio of a company's share price to its book value. If a company's share price is equal to its book value, then its P/B ratio is 1. Some companies trade below 1, others trade with much higher ratios. Analysts and commentators often discuss P/B ratio, so it is useful to understand its limitations as an indicator of value and how it can be helpful.

P/B as a metric is most useful for assessing the value of companies with substantial asset bases, e.g., capital-intensive companies such as oil and gas producers and miners, real estate companies and financial businesses such as banks. Such companies tend to have quite low P/B ratios, sometimes as low as 0.6 or 0.7. A low P/B does not necessarily mean that a company is performing poorly. The market will take a view on whether the company could achieve a better return on its assets, or they could judge that the assets are overvalued. Currently some major banks have P/B ratios significantly below 1, which could indicate that the market believes that their loan books are overvalued.

On the other hand, a low P/B ratio could indicate that a company is undervalued by the markets and is worth a closer look. If its assets possibly have good liquidity, i.e., could be easily sold off, it could attract attention for its breakup value.

For growth companies, P/B ratio has some particular limitations. The ratio will depend on whether you include intellectual property in book value – analysts vary on this – and if a company is strongly leveraged through debt, not necessarily bad, this will reduce the book value and increase the P/B ratio.

P/B ratio is perhaps most useful in making comparisons between companies in the same sector. Average P/B across a sector, or even a country, is often used by asset managers to make a general assessment of value. This should have the effect of averaging out the anomalies, if there are as many overstated P/B ratios as there are understated. For example, as a generalization, P/B ratios in emerging markets tend to range between about 1.5 and 3, so below 1.5 there is likely to be value to be found and above 3 might signal a time to sell.

Another metric that analysts use to compare companies is NAV per share.

Return on capital employed (ROCE)

Capital Employed is the value of the assets that enable a company to generate revenue and create profit. There is not a consistent approach to assessing capital employed from a company's balance sheet but there is some consensus that the following works reasonably well.

Capital Employed = Total Assets – Current Liabilities

Or from the balance sheet in Table 4.2:

Capital Employed = Total Liabilities + Shareholder Equity – Current Liabilities

In other words, the company is run on long-term debt plus the shareholder's stake less current liabilities. But why are current liabilities subtracted? Because this is likely to be money owed to employees and suppliers on which no interest is incurred. It is, in effect, free finance. Return is taken as profit including adjustments for exceptional items before interest and tax – in other words, operating profit. So:

ROCE = Operating Profit/Capital Employed

Capital Employed can be assessed at year end or an average through a year can be assessed and used.

ROCE is a measure of the efficiency with which capital is being used to generate operating profit but as it takes no account of tax or interest paid, it does not feed readily into share valuation methodologies. Nevertheless, analysts pay close attention to it, so it's worth considering in an assessment of the value of a share. Greater than 15 is reasonably healthy. Companies with low levels of debt will tend to have higher ROCE.

Perhaps more usefully, ROCE can be used to make comparisons between sectors and between companies in the same sector – with respect to efficient use of capital.

Return on equity (ROE)

In 2006, Goldman Sachs' ROE reached almost 40%; by 2016, it had fallen to 6.4% against a sector average of 10.3%.

This is a measure of the return achieved on shareholders' equity, i.e., the current value of the shareholders' investment in the company. The return is based on net profit or earnings as defined above.

ROE = Net profit/Shareholders' Equity

As with ROCE, ROE does not feed readily into share valuation methodologies, but it is an important metric in an overall assessment of value. It features strongly in the assessment of the state of health of banks' financials.

Another measure used by analysts searching for value is CROCI – cash returned on capital invested – which you can research on the Internet.

Debt

Companies take on debt for various reasons. For example, for capital investment or to finance their operations as most companies incur costs in advance of receiving their revenues. In recent times, many companies have taken on debt to buy back their own shares or even to support their dividend programs. Companies with high levels of debt are referred to as highly leveraged. In a healthy corporate situation, profit margins will be high enough to cover interest payments with some degree of comfort and to be able to cope with rises in interest rates.

During 2014 and 2015, interest rates continued to run at historically low levels with the markets becoming increasingly nervous about what would be the effect on corporate earnings when interest rates eventually rose. If rising interest rates would be accompanied by steadily improving market conditions, then the better companies would be able to absorb these extra costs without impairment to earnings. But if central banks put up interest rates too soon, then a great many companies would struggle with earnings growth. There was a widely held view that many poor companies were only surviving as a result of abnormally low interest rates. Pressure on earnings applies downwards pressure on share prices, and the markets would mark down the share prices of companies sensitive to interest rate rises.

Cash flow

'Cash is king' is one of the most well-worn clichés in the markets, but then cash is important. There is plenty of scope for companies to make their profit look better than it really is. It's more difficult to manipulate cash in the bank, though certainly not impossible for a company to create a false impression, e.g., by slowing payments to its supply chain or firing up its receivables team close to financial year end. This won't affect shareholder funds or equity because the company is just converting a receivables asset to a cash asset – but the cash in the bank is enhanced.

Analysts like to see profits backed by cash and if they see a profit of, for example, US$15mn declared at year end but not much improvement in cash, they will investigate.

Some analysts prefer the ratio of cash flow per share over P/E because they believe that cash generated is less susceptible to manipulation than profit. A further refinement is to look at free cash flow, which is operating cash flow less capital expenditure. This is a measure of the cash available for investment or, perhaps, return to shareholders. The markets like companies with strong free cash flow.

Pension fund liability

Companies that have obligations to defined benefit pension schemes can struggle if the scheme is in deficit, and this has to be addressed out of earnings. This can be a significant drag on share price. A company's annual report will provide information on its pension arrangements. Worrying situations will be reported by the media from time to time, especially for larger cap companies.

More than two-thirds of S&P 500 companies have defined benefit pension plans and only a handful are fully funded.

In the UK, companies with notable pension fund deficits include BT Group, BAE Systems, and International Airlines Group – all once owned by the UK Government. Energy companies Royal Dutch Shell and BP also have sizeable pension deficits.

Addressing a substantial deficit can have a serious impact on a company's earnings.

Predator or target

In March 2014, fears that Vodafone might take a 'poison pill' knocked 7% off its share price. The possible poison pill was Ono, Spain's largest cable company, the proposition being that if Vodafone acquired Ono, this would make Vodafone less attractive as a takeover target for AT&T.

Over many years, analysts have become skeptical about the ability of management teams to deliver successful acquisitions, and may well mark share prices down for companies announcing takeovers. On the other hand, target companies can experience a sharp rise in share price. This is because the markets assume that the predator company will be prepared to pay a premium over current share price. Companies will pay a premium, e.g., to increase their market share and pricing power; or to obtain some key technology or perhaps to increase their global coverage; or simply to massage the egos of the chief executive and finance director.

During 2013 and 2014, there was a gradual shift in sentiment with respect to takeovers. As cash piles built in many companies, and top-line growth was stalling, analysts began to look more favorably on acquisitions as a means to kick-start growth.

Many companies are regarded perennially as potential takeover targets and some analysts will figure this into their equity valuation models. Hedge funds are prolific speculators in companies judged to be takeover targets.

5 Factors that influence share prices

Introduction

'We simply attempt to be fearful when others are greedy and greedy when others are fearful.'
Warren Buffett

The list of factors that influences share prices is more or less endless, and a great many of them may be unknown to the retail investor who struggles to make sense of it all. An understanding of these factors should help the investor to operate successfully in the world's complex markets.

In an attempt to bring some order to a diverse range of factors, a classification system is used with the following main headings:

- Macroeconomic factors
- Company factors
- Market factors – general
- Market factors – technical

It would be impossible to list all factors that influence share prices, but even an incomplete list should be helpful.

After the financial crisis, the US stock market began, in 2009, a great bull run; however, by 2015 world economic growth had become sluggish, especially in the emerging markets, and there was a dearth of investment opportunities for many US companies. This resulted in an unprecedented run of share buybacks – companies buying their own shares – as discussed below.

Macroeconomic factors

Gross domestic product

The 28 EU member states now make up 19% of global GDP.

Gross domestic product (GDP) is the market value of goods and services produced within a country each year, so in effect it is the aggregate of all companies' revenues each year. Therefore, GDP is an important number for all market participants and is highly anticipated. A good number will likely cause stock markets to rise and a poor number will cause them to fall. If GDP is rising, it does not mean that all companies will be enjoying an increase in revenues, but many will. Rising revenues should lead to increasing profits and earnings per share (EPS).

The most important GDP numbers are for the US, Japan, and China, together with Europe as the world's largest trading bloc. All the major European economies are watched keenly on an individual basis. GDP for the world's ten largest economies are shown in Table 5.1.

Country	GDP US$tn
United States	17.4
China	10.4
Japan	4.6
Germany	3.9
United Kingdom	2.9
France	2.8
Brazil	2.4
Italy	2.1
India	2.0
Russia	1.9

2014 figures

Table 5.1 GDP by country

GDP figures are typically published quarterly and revised monthly.

Correlation

Correlation in the S&P 500 sectors was running at over 90% in the summer of 2015, i.e., the sectors were tracking the S&P 500 closely. In the final quarter of 2015, Consumer Discretionary and Information Technology broke sharply to the upside while Energy, Materials, and Telecommunications broke sharply to the downside.

The concept of stock market correlations has been introduced in *Chapter 3,* in the context of stock market indices sometimes moving in some degree of synchrony. The concept of correlation is also useful in looking at the degree of synchrony in share price movements within an index.

When the prices of two assets move exactly together, the correlation is +1. When they move in the opposite direction, the correlation is -1. For an index, it is useful to look at average correlation between individual share prices and the index. A correlation of 75% would mean that on average 75% of the movement of each share price could be put down to the movement of the index and only 25% to company-specific issues.

Correlation within an index for a period of time is obtained by determining the correlation between each share price and the index and calculating the average.

Detailed correlation data of this nature is not readily available, but if you search S&P 500 correlation and BARRON'S S&P 500 correlation you will find some data starting around 1980. You can see from this data that correlation shot up after the 1987 crash to over 80%, and again was high through the 2001 crash, reaching over 60%, and through the 2008 crash, reaching over 80%. If you take out the extreme peaks and troughs, from 1980 to 2000 correlation ranged between about 25% and 50%; from 2001 to the present it has ranged between about 40% and 65%.

The argument is often made that when correlation within an index is high, it is more difficult for fund managers to beat the index. Strong flows of money into the market through tracker funds – funds that replicate the constituents of an index – will tend to increase correlation. So we are getting into the realm of self-fulfilling prophecy with the tracker fund managers pumping money into good shares and bad shares!

A closely related metric to correlation is dispersion. When all the share prices in an index move roughly together, dispersion is low and vice versa.

Key economic data

During 2013, the Thomas Reuters/University of Michigan monthly Consumer Sentiment Survey came under a great deal of pressure from the New York Attorney General, as it was releasing its data two seconds early for a fee to a select group of trading clients. The practice was stopped and trading around this release subsequently collapsed.

The feed of key economic data is near continuous. Search the Internet for economic calendar and you will be presented with a range of options. MarketWatch, Nasdaq, Financial Times, YAHOO! FINANCE, Bloomberg, Hargreaves Lansdown, and many other websites provide calendars showing data releases and times.

The financial TV channels will sometimes announce important data releases and times for the day ahead. Many of these data releases are significant events for the markets and move share prices both at individual company and sector level. The biggest events can create highly correlated share price movements, moving a whole index.

Successful trading is not really possible without close to attention to the financial calendar, and all good trading platforms used by day traders provide their own economic calendars.

Examples of some key events that come out on a country basis are:

- US Nonfarm Payrolls

- US Institute for Supply Management's Index of Non-manufacturing Activity
- Jobless Claims
- Purchasing Managers' Index
- Trade Balance
- Industrial Production
- Manufacturing Orders
- Employment Cost Index
- Retail Sales
- Housing Starts
- Existing Home Sales
- New Home Sales
- Defence Spending

The US economy is the engine room of the world! Probably the most important data event is the US nonfarm payrolls, usually out on the first Friday of each month. If the reported data is substantially different from consensus expectation, the US stock market indices will move fast either up or down – and just about all the other major world markets will follow. During 2013, there was a curious reversal of this effect. The markets were nervous that if the payroll numbers were too strong, the US Federal Reserve would assume that the economy was strengthening, and get underway with tapering their quantitative easing (QE) program. This would mean less money to find its way into the markets. For a great deal of the time, 'good news' was 'bad news' for the markets, which threw a series of 'taper tantrums' through the year, whenever Fed chairman, Ben Bernanke, hinted at the start of tapering. In retrospect it can be seen that the taper tantrum perturbations in the stock markets were in reality quite small, in the region of 5% falls in the S&P 500, with the market recovering quickly. In December 2013, the Fed finally began its taper and the markets took this with some equanimity.

In the US, consumption accounts for around 70% of US GDP and 15% of global demand. As consumer spending is such an important driver of the US economy, data reports related to consumer sentiment and activity are particularly important. Another important US data release is the US Institute for Supply Management's index of non-manufacturing activity, which accounts for more than 80% of private sector jobs.

In Europe, the strength of the German economy, and in particular its manufacturing base, is closely watched by the markets.

Currency movements

In May 2014, a Rolls-Royce trading statement reported that sterling's rise against the US dollar and Euro would reduce its revenues by £300mn and profits by £40mn in the full year.

Currency movements affect whole economies as well as sectors and individual companies. One of the most significant recent examples of this was the sharp drop in the Japanese yen in the first half of 2013. This made Japanese exporters such as Toyota and Sony much more profitable, and the Japanese stock market rose strongly. Foreign investors benefited from rising share prices, but this had to be set against the fall in value of the yen against their home currencies.

Currency fluctuations affect companies in different ways. Where a US company makes a substantial portion of its profits in, say, Europe, and the Euro falls against the dollar, its European profits when reported in dollars will be reduced. A rising dollar will make US exports more expensive, but overseas supply chain costs will reduce.

When investing overseas, you should look into long-term currency trends against the US dollar or sterling, whichever you regard as your home currency. There is no certainty in this, but you should always look. Conversely, if your home currency appears to be in a downwards trend against other major currencies, you could take a keener look at overseas investment opportunities.

Politics – elections and political unrest

Elections often influence market sentiment because they create uncertainty. A change in government will usually lead to a change in spending policy – from which some sectors and companies will benefit, while others will not. Company analysts will continually reassess company outlooks depending on various election outcome scenarios, and this will influence share price movements leading up to the election. After the election, there will usually be a spending review, and the uncertainty can continue for quite some time. Some sectors and companies, e.g., healthcare or construction, may be more sensitive to the range of possible political outcomes than others.

Some examples of political factors that have influenced markets are:

- The US quantitative easing program, which ran from post–financial crisis to October 2014, and involved the purchase by the US Federal Reserve of over US$6tn of bonds.
- China's devaluation of the renminbi in August 2015 threw world stock markets into turmoil. This was coupled with the Chinese government encouraging investment in the Chinese stock market and then trying to prop it up when it collapsed.
- The introduction of ObamaCare in 2010 – helping healthcare shares.
- The threat of automatic budget cuts by the US Federal Government in 2013 and their implications for defence spending. Many US- and UK-listed companies were affected by these considerations.
- The economic saga in Greece has been unsettling markets since 2011, creating a tail risk – that of Greece quitting the Euro. Tail risks are described below.

- The Ukraine crisis pushed markets, already jittery at the start of the US earnings season, down by several percent – creating good buying opportunities. In Russia, sanctions and threats of further sanctions caused an already cheap market to crash. Multiples, i.e., P/E ratios, were down around 4 with Gazprom on a P/E in the region of 2, but investors were wary at even these price levels.
- Governments impose windfall profit taxes from time to time. In the UK, Tony Blair's Labour government imposed such a tax on utility companies in 1997. In 2013, Ed Miliband's pledge to freeze energy prices did not help share prices in the sector.
- The mining industry is regularly impacted by political unrest, e.g., in the platinum mines in South Africa in 2012/13. Worker demands for higher wages, supported by strike action, were threatening the viability of a number of mines.
- The flare-up between Saudi Arabia and Iran at the outset of 2016 unsettled markets.

A war involving any of the world's major economies would almost certainly have a devastating effect on stock markets. Other wars between nations or civil wars will be assessed for their impact on factors such as supply routes, availability of important commodities, and implications for the financial sector.

Law and regulation

This is an extensive subject. Some examples of how changes in laws and regulation, or the anticipation of such, can influence sectors and individual companies are given below.

- Environmental regulation has had a massive influence on the automotive industry, with a conflict between global warming concerns and health concerns. Global warming concerns have led to the proliferation of diesel engines in Europe, but these produce deadly nitrous dioxide emissions, and recently health concerns have come to the fore. In 2015, Volkswagen's travails over emission levels gripped the world, and the company's share price lost around half of its value.
- The tobacco industry is continually threatened, country-by-country, with regulations that are negative for their business, such as bans on smoking in certain places, compulsion to use plain packaging and regular anti-smoking campaigns. Nonetheless, 'big tobacco' continues to outperform the markets.
- Extension of patent validity durations would benefit the pharmaceutical industry.
- In 2011, North Sea oil and gas producers were hit with a significant tax increase on their profits. This exerted downwards pressure on share prices in the sector.

- Undeveloped contract law in major economies such as China and India adds an additional dimension of risk for companies' overseas operations.
- The investment community tends to avoid countries with poor corporate governance regimes.
- Governments around the world want a greater take from mining companies extracting their valuable mineral resources, and achieve this through legislation and tough negotiation. Increasingly stringent environmental regimes put additional pressure on the performance of these companies.
- Gambling companies are under endless legislative attack, as their products can be addictive and socially damaging.

Tail risks and black swans

Tail risks are visible, while black swans emerge without warning.

Tail risks

Market professionals pay a great deal of attention to tail risks. The concept is derived from the shape of the normal distribution curve or 'bell curve' in statistics. For an excellent explanation of the concept, search <u>PIMCO Understanding tail risk</u>.

The bell curve concept arises from portfolio management theory. Risk of loss is to the left of center of the bell curve and a fattening of the tail of the curve in this area indicates a higher probability of big losses. In common market usage, a tail risk is simply an identifiable and significant threat to asset prices – that may or may not occur. Good examples of tail risks are the implications of the UK leaving the European Union and the threat of Greece leaving the Euro. Risk is probability times consequence. The consequence of Greece leaving the Euro has been constantly severe, but the probability has fluctuated a great deal, so the tail risk has been coming to the fore and receding since around 2011.

It is not all that obvious how this concept helps a fund manager to manage his portfolio risk, as his capacity to go into cash is quite limited. He can select less volatile shares in his portfolio or he can hedge in various ways. The concept is certainly important for the more agile market participants. Tail risks hang over the market on a regular basis, and sometimes there will be several at the same time. Some crystallize or 'happen,' some go away. At any particular time the air may be thick with tail risks, or there may be few around – dark clouds that may or may not burst. Some examples of recent and current tail risks are:

- Faltering global growth was concerning the markets throughout 2015.
- Following the end of QE by the US Federal Reserve, there is reduced liquidity in both equity and bond markets, making them liable to disproportionate falls on bad news.

- Every quarter, the US corporate earnings season. Weakness will impact the market.
- In 2015, the timing of the first interest rate rise by the Fed since the financial crisis. This took place in December 2015, with the Fed raising its key interest rate by 0.25%.
- In 2013, the possibility of US Federal Reserve announcing that it is going to accelerate the tapering of its QE – quantitative easing – program; the issue was the timing.
- The Eurozone debt crisis, at its most intense in 2011 and 2012.
- Greece has provided the markets with a series of tail risks around its level of debt, most intense during 2012 around a series of Greek elections, the outcome of which could have led to the breakup of the Eurozone. This could have caused the markets to lose half their value once again – or perhaps even more. The risk came to the fore again in 2015, i.e., of Greece leaving the Eurozone, but the integrity of the Eurozone was less threatened.
- China slow down – the failure of China to achieve a 'soft landing' following its infrastructure boom, i.e., avoiding recession.
- The China property bubble bursting in 2015, together with the possible collapse of the housing market in China.
- Civil war in the Ukraine.
- The US election of 2012 – how would sectors such as defence and healthcare be impacted by the outcome?

Sometimes it is hard to avoid the impression that markets focus on one issue at a time. A particular tail risk can consume the markets for a spell, and then simply move into the background while the market becomes preoccupied with a new issue.

Black swans

In 2007, Nicholas Taleb wrote *The Black Swan – The Impact of the Highly Improbable*. The term 'black swan' has entered the language of the financial industry to mean a highly significant, negative event coming out of nowhere that has a severe impact on the markets. Clearly, black swans are unwelcome visitors to the investment community – but not to the best players in the trading community, who thrive on volatility.

Some significant black swan events were:

- The Russian financial crisis of August 1998, when Russia defaulted on its debts. As well as a collapse in the rouble, this led to a 17% fall in the S&P 500. Summer can worsen falls due to low trading volumes and poor liquidity. This event merits black swan status, as nobody really saw it coming. Stock markets around the world lost up to 16% in value but had recovered within a year.
- Iraq's invasion of Kuwait in 1990 led to a 15% fall in the S&P 500.

- The September 11, 2001 terrorist attacks on the World Trade Centre and the Pentagon, which led to the second leg down of the 2001 crash, are a shocking example a black swan event.
- The world financial crisis commencing in 2007 can also be regarded as a black swan event, because so few people – politicians, central bankers, regulators, market participants, and commentators – saw it coming. Groupthink has been cited as a substantial factor in this huge failure of foresight. Even though the collapse was in reality a slow burn, the unexpectedness and scale of the collapse certainly puts it into the black swan category.
- The Fukushima nuclear power plant incident in March 2011 in Japan hit the Tokyo stock markets hard, but the perturbations around the world were short-lived. The FTSE 100 fell about 6% but recovered quickly. It gave investors a nasty turn, but many traders would have done very well – especially the high-frequency traders, who would have been trading within microseconds of the news.
- The fall in oil price in 2014 to under US$60 per barrel had been unanticipated and oil sector shares were badly hit. Companies that benefited strongly from the fall enjoyed a boost in their share prices, e.g., by 2015, General Motors was enjoying a strong and profitable sales run as a result of the sharp fall in gasoline prices.

Commodity prices

A great many companies are affected by commodity prices in one way or another. Hard commodities include oil, gas, iron ore, copper, silver, platinum, palladium, and nickel and soft commodities include such as corn, wheat, fiber, pork bellies, and chicken wings.

The profitability of resource companies that explore for, extract or farm, and sell commodities is directly affected by commodity prices, and there is strong correlation between their share price movements and commodity prices. Resource company share prices are often volatile. Share prices of companies in the resource company supply chains will also be affected by fluctuations in commodity prices.

Companies with high costs of production will be viable when the price of the commodity that they extract is high, but if the price falls they could become unviable or only marginally viable. Companies with lower production costs will fare better and will seek to increase their market share at the expense of their less competitive rivals.

While high commodity prices are good for the producers, such as miners and farmers, they are bad for companies that have to buy the commodities to use in their products and operations. For example, airline profitability is sensitive to the price of jet fuel, which is derived from oil. Copper is the most widely used commodity in industry, and the price of copper is seen as a useful barometer of industrial activity.

Commodities are traded extensively on the futures markets and this feeds into the share prices of a great many companies on a continuous basis. Successful traders and investors will understand the interplay between commodity prices and company fortunes in some detail.

Company factors

> *On May 8, 2014, Barclays announced 20,000 job losses – its share price rose by 6%.*

Listed companies report their activities to the markets in a number of ways. Corporate communications are keenly anticipated by market participants.

Company communications

Financial calendars

The publication dates for most company earnings reports are posted well in advance, and there are many market information websites providing financial reporting calendars.

There will be some companies reporting on most market open days. During the reporting season, there can be a dozen or so of the larger cap companies reporting every day. They are posted on company websites before, during and after normal trading hours. Some financial websites post the reports on their websites as a service to their users. The markets will be absorbing these from the second that they appear.

For the retail investor with a number of individual holdings, it is quite challenging to keep on top of all the reporting dates, to rapidly digest the information, and to take a view on whether to buy, sell, or hold. Very often a company share price will move quite a lot in the days leading up to a reporting date – based on the rumor mill, sector factors, etc. And you can't rule out some insider trading from time to time.

Company financial calendars

All listed companies will post their own financial calendars on their websites, setting out their reporting dates and ex-dividend dates, giving notice of events of interest to investors and possibly providing key economic data. For example, an airline may publish monthly passenger information. Information on upcoming company roadshows will be posted.

Statutory financial reporting

Publication of an earnings report is the moment of truth for any company when revenues, earnings, and much more are compared with consensus expectations or forecasts in very short order. Consensus forecasts are discussed below.

US

There is always great focus on the US reporting season, when companies report their earnings. US-listed companies are obliged to report quarterly, and most of them are geared to quarters ending at the end of March, June, September, and December. The quarterly reporting season gets going two or three weeks after the month end. The most important season is following the full year close at the end of the calendar year, and runs from around the middle of January until around the end of February – so, for five or six weeks.

Traditionally, Alcoa (formerly a Dow 30 constituent!) is the first major US company to report, and this is regarded by the market as the start of each quarterly reporting period. The US earnings season is a very busy season for market participants, not just in the US but around the world. Many US companies are a barometer for the global economy, as well as proxies for overseas companies operating in the same sectors.

The US reporting season is also viewed holistically, and a raft of statistics has been developed around this data flow. For example, market information companies and analysts will track the percentage of companies beating forecast profit or forecast revenue, and by how much. This is a key indicator of the state of corporate America, and analysts like to see strong revenue growth as well as strong profit growth. Analysis will also be undertaken at sector level. The output from these running averages has a considerable impact on market sentiment.

An additional requirement on US companies is to produce a 10 – K Report within 90 days of the end of their fiscal year. This provides more detailed financial information than the annual report.

There is an increasingly stated view that the quarterly reporting cycle places too much emphasis on short-term performance. Companies such as Amazon and Netflix are cited as companies adopting healthy long-term strategies. The ongoing failure of large numbers of hedge funds is used to illustrate the limitations of the short-term approach.

UK

The larger UK companies report quarterly while the rest report at the half year and at the full year. For many companies – but by no means all – their reporting year ends

March 31, and full year reports can take a couple of months to appear. Some companies issue preliminary results.

Though not a legal requirement, a company will often produce an interim management statement (IMS) perhaps three quarters of the way through a year to keep investors informed of the company's performance. These will be condensed versions of the year-end report and are unaudited.

UK companies also produce trading statements, which are an expanded version of a company's income statement, with emphasis on revenue and revenue trends, cost of sales and gross margin. They may be issued two or three times a year, or perhaps quarterly by larger companies. A trading statement is often issued just before a company's close period (see below). They may sometimes be used to issue a profit warning – an indication that the company's earnings will fall short of market expectations. A mid or large cap company will usually publish the issue dates for its trading statements on its financial calendar.

Guidance

In their reports and statements, sometimes in press releases and sometimes through their house stockbrokers, companies give guidance to the markets on expectations for key metrics such as revenue, earnings, and profit margins. They will usually project to the end of the current financial year or sometimes address the next financial year. This guidance, usually presented as a range, is important to analysts and investors in their assessments of company valuations.

Preannouncements

Given the litigious nature of the US, companies are sensitive to the need to provide bad news to the markets as soon as it is available – or risk a lawsuit from investors for withholding share price sensitive information.

It has become commonplace for US companies to update their earnings guidance in preannouncements, using, e.g., a press release or a webcast. The purpose is to manage expectations – seeking to maximize the impact of good news and to minimize the impact of bad news, thereby avoiding a drop in share price. They are most commonly used to lower investor expectations and make it easier to beat market expectations when they officially report. Preannouncements are typically made a few weeks before the official reporting date, in a period that has become known as the confessional season. There are now usually a few hundred such preannouncements every quarter in the US.

This is not a common practice in the UK, but preannouncements from major US companies can have a significant impact on the London market.

Close period

There is a close period between the completion of a company's financials and their release to the public, when insiders, e.g., directors, are not allowed to trade in the company's shares. The length of the close period is likely to be a month for a quarterly or half-year report and two months for a final report.

Conference calls

Conference calls for analysts and investors are now a quite usual follow up to the issue of a company's earnings report, typically held in the morning on the same day. These calls allow analysts to ask penetrating questions, and the way the CEO and CFO present the results and answer questions can be a significant influence on share price movements. Analysts will have full access to these calls and there are now service providers that enable retail investors to listen in.

You can access many conference call transcripts through Seeking Alpha Earnings Center for both US and UK companies.

Consensus forecasts

Analyst consensus is the average forecast for key company metrics. The metrics will typically be revenue, profit before tax, earnings – EPS – and dividend. Range as well as average will be presented. Forecasts usually don't give a timeframe. Analysts will take account of company guidance in making their forecasts. These data are the basis of market expectations, which are an important determinant of share prices. Companies will sometimes use the consensus to guide the market – saying that they expect to meet, beat, or miss market expectations. Some companies present analyst coverage of their company on their corporate websites.

In engaging with analysts over forecasts, companies endeavor to provide information that is only available to the markets at large, albeit with some digging. For example, they will not share budget information with analysts.

Some useful websites for consensus forecasts, covering both US and UK companies, are:

- CNN Money: provides up to five-year earnings forecasts and a range of forecasts for 12 months ahead.
- Nasdaq: provides detailed forecast data. Enter ticker and go to Analyst Research.
- DigitalLook: produces a summary of consensus forecasts for two to three years ahead for many listed companies.

- ▪ Financial Times Markets: website gives a 12 month consensus forecast as a range.

There are now some specialist companies, such as Vuma Consensus in the UK, that pull together forecast data to create market expectations for corporate clients.

When a company publishes its earnings report, at first look, the markets can see where the company is in relation to expectations, and with a deeper look they can judge the health of the company at a fundamental level – looking at cash flow, margins, debt, various ratios, etc. More complex companies will be assessed at subsidiary or divisional level. Particular attention will be paid to the outlook statement by the chairman or chief executive officer – is it upbeat or overly cautious, e.g., referring to continuing challenging conditions? If an investor is in the company for its dividend, then he will turn quickly to the pages that deal with the dividend.

Roadshows

A commonly used corporate communications tool is a financial road show where senior staff make a series of presentations to existing and potential investors and analysts on performance, strategy, and outlook. Roadshows are often used for promoting IPOs. Companies post details of their roadshows on their websites, including formal presentations. Some companies will make several roadshows in a year. A good roadshow can lift a company's share price.

Annual general meetings

A company will hold an annual general meeting (AGM) to formally present its financial results, to elect its directors, and to deal with other matters that need the approval of shareholders. They tend to be set pieces with major shareholders having already cast the majority votes on the resolutions of the day, but they do allow the retail investor to ask questions of the company directors – and to give them a piece of his mind. The proceedings of an AGM will not usually have much impact on share prices, but the possibility is always there.

These meetings are good opportunities for market participants to gain further insights into a company's health, by both listening and questioning. However, attending AGMs will not usually be time well spent for the retail investor unless he has committed a large proportion of his portfolio in the company, and is anxious to delve very deeply into its affairs. A possible exception might be if you are invested in some quite speculative shares, such as oil and gas or mining exploration companies – attendance can give valuable insights into the prospects of the company.

From time to time a company may need to call an extraordinary general meeting (EGM), when the board needs shareholder consent for a particular action, e.g., the removal of a director. The business of an EGM could well be of interest to investors, with implications for share price.

You will need a mandate to attend an AGM or EGM, which your trading platform/stockbroker should be able to obtain for you.

Investor events and product launches

Retailers and fashion houses run events to introduce new ranges, and will invite investors and company analysts. A well-received show can give a share price a lift.

Product launches by technology firms are eagerly awaited by the markets, who quickly assess if the new product, such as a smartphone, is a milestone improvement or just a bit of tweaking. Consumer reaction and early sales are carefully scrutinized by the markets.

Corporate news flow

A useful rule of thumb is that the larger the company – market cap is a good measure – the greater the news flow will be. And news moves share prices.

As well as their formal reporting, companies will issue press releases to announce events such as major contract awards, acquisitions, alliances, new products, etc. Most press releases will contain positive stories.

In addition to the news flow from the corporation itself, there will more than likely be considerable news picked up on a company's fortunes by a small army of financial journalists, company watchers, and eager investors who follow the company's fortunes closely and post their views on bulletin boards.

Dividend policy

In 2013, Microsoft, awash with cash, finally bowed to shareholder pressure to pay a dividend and to establish a dividend payment program. Up to that point it had adopted a policy of investing surplus cash into R&D, but it was becoming increasingly clear that it could afford a dividend as well. A glance at the Microsoft chart suggests that this stabilized a falling share price after a spectacular rise. Microsoft's dividend yield is about 3%.

During 2012 and 2013, shareholders were applying considerable pressure on the big mining companies not to spend money on new mines because of global overcapacity – and instead return money to shareholders through their dividend policies.

If you search multpl.com S&P 500 dividend yield, you will find that the average dividend yield has trended down from 6% to 9% in the 1870s to a little over 2% now. If you click on S&P 500 Dividend Yield on the chart, you will find a chart showing that the value of the dividend has increased from 6 cents to around 42 cents per share over this period of time.

Dividend streams, as already mentioned, are crucial to pension funds and other large institutional investors. When they invest in a company, they will have attributed a substantial weighting to its dividend policy. A company will convey its dividend policy to the market, but the proof of the pudding is in the eating, when the company declares its dividend payout in its annual report. The markets like to see a steady increase year on year, and if a company disappoints, its share price is likely to be punished.

A closely watched metric is dividend cover – the ratio of profits or earnings to dividends. Dividend cover is watched carefully by dividend investors, as if it falls too low, the company may have difficulty in keeping up the level of its dividend payments. Cover falling much below two would be a worry. So analysts will try to gain insights into a company's cash flow, and any threats to it. If they anticipate a cut in dividend, they will signal this to the markets and this will put the share price under pressure. According to a report in late 2013, the average dividend cover for FTSE 350 companies fell to 1.40 in early 2013, a reduction of 40% in under three years – fallout from the global financial crisis. The drop was most marked with financial and mining shares.

From time to time a company will pay a special dividend. This will be because it has generated cash surplus to its needs. There can be several different backgrounds to this. It might be that the company has run out of ideas for growth, or it may be that it is accruing surplus cash through profitable activities.

Some companies can be so keen to keep their record of increasing dividend yield year on year intact, that they will raise money with a bond issue to support the dividend, rather than having to 're-base' it, a 'technical' expression for a dividend cut. The company would have to be confident that it is just experiencing a temporary downturn before engaging in this type of activity.

The markets will digest all available information around a company's dividend policy and take a view that may have an impact its share price.

Exceptional and extraordinary items

In November 2013, Starbucks was ordered by the courts to pay US$2.7bn compensation to Kraft for breach of a supply agreement. An analyst at a leading US brokerage firm wrote 'the ruling would not hurt Starbucks in the stock market because this is a one-time charge so it doesn't change the earnings power of the company.' This was perhaps a little optimistic as this *represented roughly a year of pre-tax profits for a company trading on a P/E ratio in the upper twenties. The share price drifted down from about US$82 to about US$75 over the next three months before running up to US$100 in 2015. The analyst was not far off the mark. (Note, Starbucks did a 2-for-1 stock split in March 2015).*

Exceptional and extraordinary items have been mentioned in the context of a company's income statement in *Chapter 4.* It can be very convenient for a company's management to classify a significant cost item as exceptional or extraordinary and place emphasis on 'underlying profit.' If the markets buy this, then the share price will hold up and management bonuses may be unscathed. As ever, the markets will look closely at the background to the adjustment and take a view.

Material events

Under US securities rules, a 5% movement in a company's average pre-tax earnings for the last three years is defined as a material event.

In US parlance, a material event is one that could be reasonably expected to influence a company's share price. For example, a fall in sales, an offer to acquire another company, an important contract win, an improvement in earnings, or a change in accountants. Material events must be notified to the public and to the Securities and Exchange Commission in an 80 – K form.

Profit warnings

In January 2015, 27 FTSE 100 companies had to alert investors that they were likely to miss earnings targets. Total profit warnings from them was 38 – more than the 26 seen in 2008 at the height of the financial crisis!

An important responsibility of a listed company is to keep the markets informed, and this process creates a market expectation. The company continually strives to meet or exceed market expectation and not to disappoint. If a company is struggling with its earnings, it will have to report this to the market at some point. The ideal approach for a company is to use skilful communications to give the market advance notice, while reassuring it that management is on top of the situation and recovery plans are already in place. This ideal is very often not met, with a company issuing a profit warning out of the blue and precipitating a sharp fall in share price. It is then not uncommon for a company in difficulty to give a series of profit warnings culminating in management changes driven by dissatisfied major shareholders. A well-managed and one-off profit warning may result in a fall in share price of around 10%. A third or fourth warning can devastate a share price. Profit warnings are normally announced through stock exchange news feeds – see below.

Analysts and market information firms monitor the number of profit warnings emanating from a particular stock market or index, perhaps quarterly, as a useful measure of economic strength or weakness.

A sharp fall in revenue growth can be as bad as a profit warning, or anything that might compromise future earnings.

Stock exchange news feeds

Listed companies have to comply with a mass of regulations, and are required to report on a wide range of their activities including, in the US, through Securities & Exchange Commission (SEC) filings. The New York and Nasdaq stock exchanges run an RSS Feed – where RSS stands for both Rich Site Summary and Really Simple Syndication. This is a constant stream of market information. You can set up to receive these feeds using an RSS Feed Reader. In the US, SEC filings are part of the RSS feed. Also, you can access SEC filings directly through the SEC website.

A source used by US professional investors is Edgar Online, which specializes in uncovering market intelligence from financial disclosures.

In the UK, the London Stock Exchange runs a Regulatory News Service (RNS) feed. The ADVFN website is a handy way to access the RNS feeds along with other company news – look at Recent News under the Quote tab.

Many companies publish SEC filings or RNS filings on their websites. As well as providing compliance information, companies use the feeds for conveying other key financial information to investors.

Examples of news flow through the news feeds are:

- Changes in directors
- Plans to raise money e.g., a rights issue
- Information relating to mergers and acquisitions
- Significant movements in share holdings

These news feeds can have an important bearing on company fortunes, and are watched closely through the day, though posts can – and frequently do – appear out of market open hours.

Taxation

You will have seen from *Chapter 4* that tax rate for a company has a significant impact on EPS. Where a company has operations overseas, its tax rate will reflect all taxes paid. Overseas tax disputes are quite commonplace, and represent a significant risk for companies with international operations.

Company taxation is a vexatious issue, and it goes without saying that companies seek to minimize their corporation taxes wherever they operate. On a fairly regular basis, companies review the possibility of transferring their headquarters overseas to enjoy a lower tax rate. Sometimes they move! They may achieve an improvement in EPS and share price, but on the other hand they may suffer from loss of reputation in their home country, resulting eventually in an adverse impact on earnings.

Companies based in the US and UK will be reluctant to move away from these key centers of financial activity. Remoteness from the markets and analysts could lead to a gradual erosion of their 'analyst rating.'

Companies that have been particularly creative in minimizing their global tax bill could be vulnerable to concerted government action to extract more taxes from them.

Free float

Share prices of companies with small free floats may be subject to increased volatility and wider bid-offer spreads as a result of their low liquidity. Institutional investors may be disinclined to invest in such shares.

Rights issues

A rights issue is a way for a company to raise more money – usually because it is running out, but sometimes because it has a strong business case for further investment and can't readily raise the funds by issuing bonds or raising a bank loan. And apart from fees (which will be heavy!), the company does not pay for new equity. The investors are accepting risk for a possibly greater return than they would get by taking up a bond issue. The company issues new shares, and existing shareholders have the 'right' to take them up before they are offered more widely. Existing shareholders will be offered the new shares at a discount to the current market value. With more shares in issue, the EPS goes down and this mostly – but not always – takes the share price down. Rights issues tend not to be well received by shareholders, and a company's shares can sell off if there is anticipation of a rights issue. It is not uncommon for an analyst to review a company's accounts and then publicly speculate that the company may have to make a rights issue.

Stock overhang

The expression 'stock overhang' is used to describe various situations.

It sometimes becomes known that a market participant is seeking to offload a large block of shares, and he may not be able to achieve this without depressing the share price. This is known as a stock overhang and the market will tend to mark the share price down until the overhang is cleared. Clearance of an overhang can result in a significant share price rise.

A significant stock overhang will occur if a company is relegated from an index. Tracker funds and ETFs based on that index will then have to sell the share. A significant overhang would be the equivalent of several days of trading volume.

Many companies award options to directors and key employees to buy some company shares at some future date at a specified price. The idea is that the share price rises nicely and then the option holder exercises his option, thereby buying at a price lower than the current price. The company sets aside shares to sell to option holders, and these represent a stock overhang – they have the potential to dilute EPS if and when options are exercised. A company grants options as a performance incentive, and this should boost EPS, offsetting the effect of dilution. So all is fine as long as the company gets the balance right. The granting and exercising of options will be reported in the company's regulatory news feed.

Share buybacks

Companies regularly buy back their own shares. Along with dividend payments, it's a way to deliver cash to shareholders.

Leading up to 2007, buybacks were fashionable and many companies paid a very high price for their own shares, given what happened in 2008. Then it started all over again. In March 2015, it was reported that during 2014, S&P 500 companies spent around US$550bn on share buybacks, double the level of five years previously, and paid out only US$350bn in dividends. Evidently these companies bought back around 20% of market capitalization, valued at around US$3.8tn, since the collapse of Lehman Brothers in 2008. Activity took place across all sectors, and greatly exceeded the aggregate investment in shares by US mutual funds and ETFs.

Sometimes companies will hold buyback shares in their treasury as an asset with a view to resale, but more commonly they will cancel them. If they cancel them, this will increase the EPS, which should be good for the share price, though many other factors can come into play, e.g., a reduction in interest receipts if a company has paid cash directly from its bank account. Buybacks decrease the net asset value (NAV) per share for a company, due to a reduction in cash on the balance sheet, but if the markets are focused on earnings and earnings growth in valuing the company's shares, this won't matter too much.

As share prices rise, buybacks become more expensive, and the record shows that S&P 500 companies do not have a good record in buying low.

It is argued by many that buybacks were a major factor in artificially sustaining the post–financial crisis bull run. The increase in share buyback volumes has been accompanied, unsurprisingly, by a decline in corporate investment in key areas such as research and development and capital equipment. In this period, there is little doubt that share buybacks were sustaining share prices, injecting vast quantities of money into the major markets, while there was a net outflow of mutual fund and ETF monies. There is a view that this phenomenon is boosting a short-term approach by chief executives and their teams, as increasingly their remuneration is linked to share price performance. In some US companies, the proportion of remuneration linked to share price is approaching 90%.

The US Federal Reserve strategy of maintaining low interest rates during the current decade was in part to encourage investment in higher risk assets, such as company shares. Somewhat perversely, this contributed to the unintended consequence of companies borrowing money, often through bond issues, to finance buybacks rather than using cash already on their balance sheets to invest in their core businesses. Many US companies that operate globally have billions of dollars in overseas bank accounts that they are reluctant to bring home because of US tax liability, and this has reinforced the borrowing trend.

Activist investors like share buybacks because it is their business to do so. They apply considerable pressure to CEOs to deliver cash to shareholders, though in many instances they will be pushing on an open door. On the other hand, Larry Fink, CEO of BlackRock, has accused US business leaders of eating their own seed corn. Undoubtedly, buybacks are occurring at the expense of investing in the future, but in 2015, economic conditions were not favorable for substantial investment programs. Possibly a 'chicken and egg' situation.

Somewhat depressingly, studies of S&P 500 companies have shown that the share prices of companies with large buyback programs have significantly outperformed those with substantial capital investment programs. You can check out the S&P 500 Buyback Index.

Some brokers encourage buybacks as a line of business and will seek to build a book of institutional investors interested in selling their shares back to a company. In the US stock market, the number of shares available for investment is probably shrinking.

Acquisitions – predator or prey?

It is estimated that the major mining companies have written off 90% of the acquisitions they have done since 2007, with impairments totalling US$85bn. In the US, merger and acquisition activity reached a record level of US$243bn in 2014. It accelerated in 2015 with the number of US$10bn plus deals reaching an all-time high.

> *Pfizer spent some US$240bn on three big acquisitions since 2000 – but its market cap is just US$205bn today (October 2015).*

If there is a rumor that a company is a takeover target, its share price can move up substantially, as the purchaser will usually have to pay a premium to complete the deal. If you are lucky, you can get a big boost in one of your holdings from this effect – this can be 30% or more. Though it doesn't have to be entirely by luck – someone who knows a sector well may have a shrewd idea about which companies might be a target. Of course if the rumor goes away, or the suitor calls things off, the share price is likely to go down as rapidly as it went up.

This can work the other way around, and if a company announces that it is in takeover discussions with a target company and the market doesn't like the deal, its share price can suffer – sometimes quite a lot. However, as we have seen in *Chapter 4*, during 2013 and 2014, a significant change in sentiment occurred, with investors tiring of share buybacks pumping up EPS. If a company was struggling to grow organically, then why not make some shrewd acquisitions? Predator companies found their share prices rising rather than falling when they announced an interest in another company.

Towards the end of 2015, Pfizer was at it again with a US$160bn offer for Allergan, a Dublin-based pharmaceutical company. This was the largest 'tax inversion' ever attempted, which would have dramatically reduced Pfizer's tax liability. Allergan is basically a US company headquartered in Dublin to take advantage of Ireland's low rate of corporation tax. However, at time of writing, President Obama had put an end to the deal through changes to Treasury Department rules. The global value of mergers and acquisitions activity in 2015 was heading for a record value north of US$4tn.

A significant factor in the dynamics of mergers and acquisitions is the golden parachute syndrome for CEOs. The theory is that shareholders want CEOs to put shareholder interests before their own, and not resist a good offer for the company in order to protect their own positions. In both the US and the UK, this has led to unreasonably large incentives for CEOs to cut and run. For large companies, CEOs have received packages in the tens of millions of dollars for selling the companies they are charged with running. This inevitably clouds the valuation process for target companies, and the valuation of the entity created by the acquisition.

There is no shortage of studies showing that a great many acquisitions fail to meet expectations. Combine this with a somewhat capricious market view of M&A activity, and you have the ingredients for 'irrational markets.'

Award of contracts

The business model of many companies is based on winning and executing contracts, e.g., companies involved in construction, oil field services, facilities management, transport operations, etc. They will value long-term contracts and repeat business over random wins, and the markets will pay close attention to both their portfolios of framework, or service contracts, and the health of their order books. A major contract win or the failure to renew an important contract can have a strong influence on a company's share price.

Management changes and quality of management

Many a company chairman and CEO has experienced the embarrassment of his company's share price moving sharply up when he has announced his resignation. Conversely, a very well-respected senior executive moving on can have the opposite effect. Chairman, chief financial officer, and chief operating officer are also sufficiently weighty positions to move the share price up or down with one of these executives leaving or joining a company.

Strong leadership and a strong management team are important to the success of any significant company. Analysts will take a keen interest in both the individuals in a senior management team and the dynamics within the team.

Executive pay

In 2015, top pay at media and communications companies was overhauling executive pay in the financial sector.

High executive pay in large cap companies has never been more controversial.

In his recent book *The Road to Recovery*, Andrew Smithers argues that the linkage that has developed between share prices and executive pay and bonuses, created by the structure of incentive schemes, is resulting in excessive focus on short-term company performance. Outcomes from this focus include reductions in investment, perhaps in plant and equipment, and increases in share buybacks, which boost earnings per share and, notionally, share price. The problem with all this is that top-line growth is impaired and the long-term trend for the share price may well be down. Also, this focus does not lead to much job creation, which is a drag on the overall economy. This is likely to impact company performance in the long term – but the executives with their large bonuses are long gone, though replaced by a new generation who, hopefully, might do a better job.

However, the investor might as well take advantage of the boost in share prices – which for some companies will be sustained, and for others not.

Insider/director transactions in their company shares

On February 8, 2013, a CEO disposes of shares of value over £4mn; on 1 May, he disposes of a further tranche, value nearly £4.8mn, reducing his holding to shares of value about £0.56mn. A rising market takes this in its stride but then the finance director disposes of most of her shares of value about £5mn and a generally nervous market sells the company heavily, with its share price losing about 13% in three days.

Insider/director transactions in their company shares are tracked very carefully by the markets, with analysts and traders looking for clues about the prospects of a company. Many websites and newspapers report insider and director transactions on a regular basis. A heavy sale of shares by a CEO or main board director will attract keen interest and may well cause a sharp drop in share price. It may simply be that the person requires the money to buy a house or for a divorce settlement, or that the transactions relate to tax management, but the share price can be affected nonetheless. On the other hand, directors buying heavily can be propitious for the company.

Competitor behavior

A major US consumer staples company declares that it is going to aggressively expand its European operations; this may squeeze the margins of its European competitors, whose share prices come under pressure.

Companies don't like competition. Ways of achieving competitive advantage or even market domination include:

- Developing world class products; Apple being the most obvious modern example.
- Developing a disruptive product such as streaming movies.
- Acquiring the competition!
- Creating an innovative or lean business model, such as the German food retailers, Aldi and Lidl, taking the UK supermarket sector by storm.
- Building a world-class brand – and managing it well, e.g., Nike.
- Effective R&D backed by patents.

Share prices are continually rising and falling within this competitive dynamic, which is closely followed by company analysts.

Disruptive products

A market can be disrupted by a new product. One of the most striking examples of this in recent times was the digital camera, which largely consigned traditional camera film to the dustbin of history. Digital cameras were then attacked in turn by smartphones with high-quality digital cameras built into them. Companies such as Tomtom and Garmin were disrupted when Google provided free mapping and smartphones included guidance apps. A step change improvement in battery technology for electric cars would be one of the most powerful disruptors the world has seen!

Movie streaming companies, such as Netflix, contributed to the demise of Blockbuster Video. Ironically, Blockbuster gave up the chance to acquire the early-stage Netflix.

To develop a successful, disruptive product is the holy grail for any high tech or creative company with profound implications for the company's valuation.

Activist investors

August 13, 2013 – Carl Icahn tweets that he has taken a large position in Apple and believes the company to be extremely undervalued. Apple's share price rises nearly 5% increasing market cap by over US$12bn. Icahn also tweets that he has met with Apple CEO Tim Cook, to press for a larger share buyback, and they will meet again soon. Three months later, Apple announced that it would return US$100bn to shareholders over the next three years through a combination of share buybacks and dividend payments.

It is increasingly common for activist investors in large, underperforming companies to apply sufficient pressure on management that the company eventually manages to turn around its performance, and its share price recovers. However, this can be a very long, unhappy, and uncertain process. Large institutional investors will take a view and may decide to run with it for the long term, but the retail investor can be much more nimble – if a share price is going nowhere, and recovery prospects don't look too great, there are always ways for him to put his money to better use.

The role of activist investors is discussed in *Chapter 6 The market participants, facilitators, and influencers.*

Shareholder register

The names on a company's shareholder register are significant. CNN Money (under Shareholders) and Morningstar (under Directors & Shareholders) provide information on ownership.

The presence of some major funds and institutional investors such as Vanguard, BlackRock, or Fidelity with substantial holdings is comforting for the retail investor, but they don't always get it right.

Ownership of some companies will be dominated by a founder or a dominant individual. Several former Soviet Union mining companies listed in London are controlled by Russian oligarchs. Idiosyncratic behavior may arise from these major shareholders, which makes it difficult to forecast the fortunes of the companies.

Committed institutional shareholders can give a company some stability, with strong and productive shareholder engagement, and will stand by the company's directors – for example, in the event of a hostile takeover attempt. Investors just there for the short term are likely to cut and run, taking a quick profit.

Some companies are quite closely held, perhaps by a founder and his family and company employees, with a relatively small number of shares actively traded. This will not necessarily create stability in the share price, but could signal commitment to success over the longer term.

The markets take a keen interest in company ownership, and look out for signs of important shareholders building or unwinding positions.

Market factors – general

Sentiment – bull or bear?

> *Sir John Templeton once said: 'Bull markets are born on pessimism, grow on scepticism, mature on optimism and die on euphoria.'*

The concept is fairly straightforward – a rising market is a bull market and a falling market is a bear market. A bull thrusts its horns upwards; a bear swipes its paw down. Some commentators worry about how often bear markets occur, and how long they last. A 20% fall in share price indices is generally regarded as defining a bear market. Some commentators worry about how often bear markets occur, and how long they last, but the simplest thing to do is to take a look at the long-term chart of the S&P 500 and form your own view. You can use Google Finance or YAHOO! FINANCE, which have a facility for a log (logarithmic) vertical scale, which gives a very informative view. You will see that the market has spent a lot more time rising than falling – and that the major falls can be rapid.

Sentiment is crucial. Investor confidence will be influenced by macroeconomic factors, outlook for corporate earnings, and severity of risks hanging over the markets. During any phase of market activity, there will be a tussle between the bulls and the bears. Quite often, the forces will be finely balanced, but from time to time, one or the other will decisively gain the upper hand – and the market will move dramatically up or down. You will see from the S&P 500 chart that the crests around 2000 and 2007 lasted for around a year. The Google chart going back to 1975 shows this well. The markets had overshot to the upside, and it took some time for the bears to prevail – but when they did, the falls were dramatic. After 2000, the index fell for about 2 years; after 2007, it fell for about a year. So it didn't take all that long for the bulls to regain the initiative.

To invest successfully, you must keep in touch with sentiment. It is far better to swim with the current than against it. It is much easier to make money in a rising market than in a falling market, as correlation studies have shown. Through a great deal of 2013, there was high correlation, with most US and UK share prices moving up. Moving into 2014, markets were fairly tranquil, but company reporting days were then the moments of truth – the share prices of companies reporting well, for the most part, held or rose; those that didn't were punished, often quite harshly, by the market.

Psychology

During the bull run in China in 2015, apple farmers were only farming when the stock markets were closed. Technology had enabled farmers in the remotest parts of China to actively invest and trade. In the summer of 2015, it all ended in tears for many of these retail players.

The psychology of the markets is a vast subject, and is only touched on lightly here.

It is very often stated that greed and fear are major drivers of stock markets. If you follow the markets in any detail, you will find it difficult to disagree. These emotions express the psychology of the market at the most basic human level. Psychology manifests itself in many different ways, but perhaps always with greed and fear playing a role.

At a macro-level, some very senior bankers postulated that 'groupthink' was a key factor in the financial crisis unfolding during 2007 and 2008, i.e., no one was able to depart from the consensus view. Money was being made and everyone else was playing along and if you didn't, you may underperform your peers and risk incurring the wrath of your management or shareholders. This implies that men and women of formidable individual intellect combined to produce a rather unimpressive group intellect.

At the next level down, fund managers are caught up in the same mindset as the senior bankers. They are ranked and assessed against their peers and benchmark indices and will invest and trade with the flow. Not much mileage in a contrarian approach – too risky! The fear of failure is a significant factor in fund manager behavior, and can lead to many poor investment decisions. This syndrome is no doubt influencing the steady shift to low-cost tracker funds. Fund managers are capitulating – accepting that they probably can't beat the market. So psychology is a factor in the seemingly inexorable shift to passive fund management. A great section of the fund management industry is exhibiting herd behavior.

Tail risks make markets nervous and volatile. Black swans can hit markets hard, with trading algorithms all working in sync, causing panic selling across the broader market. Markets very often overreact to news, both good and bad.

A significant factor in stock market bubbles is fear of missing out leavened by greed – across all market participants, not just the inexperienced retail investor. Stock market bubbles are always driven by high leverage – borrowing to invest – and panic can set in rapidly on a market scare as highly leveraged investors rush to close their positions.

Investors have a fear of idle money, which resulted in a frantic search for yield in the low-interest era borne out of the financial crisis. The search was very often futile, with small dividend gains being wiped out by capital losses or perhaps unfavorable currency swings.

Massive amounts of mutual fund and ETF money chase 'hot funds' as they peak, driven by poorly informed greed!

And so on.

For an academic standpoint, we have seen in *Chapter 4*, that Professor Fama propounds the efficient market theory which posits that share prices absorb all relevant information in close to real time – making it very difficult to beat the market. The shift to passive fund management would tend to bear this out. On the other hand, Professor Shiller posits that investor behavior cannot be fully rational, and that psychology must play a role in the stock markets. In 1996, when stock markets were in bubble territory, he inspired Alan Greenspan, when he was chair of the US Federal Reserve, to coin the expression 'irrational exuberance.' Shiller subsequently published a book with this title.

Unsurprisingly, the truth must lie somewhere in between. It is beyond doubt that many market participants systematically beat the index and that psychology plays a significant role in the markets. Professor Fama's theory would fit a fund management industry with substantial amounts of money invested in large cap shares and without the ability to time the market or go into cash to any significant degree.

Interaction between global stock markets

We looked at the concept of stock market correlations in *Chapter 3* and again at the beginning of this chapter. The US markets dominate – in particular the S&P 500 – and the UK markets often show strong correlation with them, especially on a short-term basis.

On a day-to-day basis, the US markets exert a strong influence on global markets through index futures, regular market open hours, and extended hours trading. However, significant events from around the world can impact very strongly on sentiment in the US – so it is best to think in terms of interactions between global markets while recognizing the weight of the US markets.

Analyst reports – upgrades and downgrades

The role of analysts has been introduced in *Chapter 4*. Analysts play a fundamental role in the valuation of company shares. The findings of the sell-side analysts are collated by the markets for each company, to produce a consensus forecast. Sell-side analysts' research reports work to some extent interactively with company's earnings reports. An analyst's report can move share prices significantly between earnings reports – notwithstanding that they may be knocked back or boosted by macroeconomic data. When earnings reports appear, they will often trump the analysts' reports because they contain the information that the analyst is endeavoring to predict. However, there is plenty of scope for disagreement between analysts and company executives on earnings prospects, which will play out as analysts revisit their recommendations after an earnings report.

The role of market analysts is described in some detail in *Chapter 6 – The market participants, facilitators and influencers.*

The sales desk

Investment banks operate sales desks with sales forces tasked with selling shares to institutions and other major investors to earn commissions. They are free to promote whatever shares they like, and may promote the shares of important customers of the bank. Companies make presentations to investment bank sales desks and this can move their share price to the good if they can stimulate some sales through an upbeat presentation.

Ex-dividend action

There will always be share price action, even gaming, around a company's ex-dividend date – the larger the dividend, the larger the action. On the ex-dividend date, the share price will open lower than it closed the evening before – it will gap down. The theory is that as soon as the company becomes liable to pay a dividend, the value of its balance sheet falls by the quantum of the dividend payment, e.g., if the dividend payout is 3.5%, the share will most likely open 3.5% down. The ex-dividend fall in share price will take place in the market opening activities, and with market maker involvement, especially for the smaller cap shares. Then usual trading activities will get underway.

Apart from the predictable gapping down on the day, ex-dividend action around any particular share is hard to read. It will depend on the characteristics of the company, the state of the market, and the buy and sell decisions of a large number of investors and traders. Some will buy the shares well in advance of the ex-dividend date in anticipation of a share price rise. If there is a strong rise, they might well take their profit before the share goes ex-dividend. If a company's dividend is high because the company is struggling and its share price is already depressed in a gloomy market, the share may be sold heavily on ex-dividend day. Those who have perhaps naively bought the share for its high-dividend yield may experience a significant loss, and a long wait before the share price recovers.

The short-term share price movements around ex-dividend dates are exploited by savvy traders. Longer term investors will be content to lock the dividend in and hold through the volatility, if they are confident in the quality of the company.

When several large cap companies in an index go ex-dividend on the same day, the effect can be strong enough to move the index down by several points.

Dividend cut

When a large UK insurance company announced an unexpected dividend cut, its share price fell 14.2% in a single day. As the company had been paying out 77% of its profits as dividends, perhaps the cut should not have been unexpected. The markets thought that the company's response could be price cuts, putting pressure on the profitability of the sector, and other insurance companies suffered significant falls in share price.

The importance of dividends to pension funds has been mentioned. In addition, there will be a great many fund managers and other investors who are relying on the compounding effect of dividend reinvestment to meet their investment objectives. A cut in dividend is therefore a very serious matter for them, in particular if it comes out of the blue. The markets don't like surprises! A significant dividend cut will be regarded in the same way as a profit warning and the share price is likely to be seriously punished.

Large investors run detailed analyses of a company's dividend streams, and closely monitor factors that could put pressure on dividend payments, e.g., a fall in a commodity price, which would affect the earnings of a resource company. These investors may begin to reduce their holding in a company as soon as they become concerned about the dividend program. Or some investors may decide to become more active in the affairs of the company, and engage with management with a view to improving earnings performance. Shareholder activism sometimes works, and if the market has confidence in the quality of the company, then its share price may prove resilient.

To make life more difficult for the retail investor, sometimes when a company cuts deep into its dividend stream, the markets takes the view that management is 'getting a grip' and the share price may actually rise!

Sector sentiment

On January 6, 2014, LSE-listed Ashtead falls 8% after the US market closes on January 5 due to United Rentals in US suffering a broker downgrade. Analysts at Evercore went from buy to sell. Ashtead is listed in London, but has substantial plant rental operations in the US.

Companies in an index are assigned to a sector, in which there may well be sub-sectors, and the sentiment of the sector or sub-sector will bear on the share prices of the constituent companies. There will often be concerted share price movement within a sector, e.g., if a major construction company disappoints with its results, other construction companies – especially those with a similar client base and business model – can be sold off. When a sector suffers, its supply chain companies are also likely to feel the pain.

There is also a proxy effect between stock markets. For example, if Halliburton or Baker Hughes, major US oil field services companies, report well or poorly, then the share prices of similar companies in the UK, such as Petrofac and Amec, are likely to be affected.

Sector rotation

'Wide diversification is only required when investors do not understand what they are doing.'
Warren Buffett

Many traders and investors like to have exposure to a range of asset classes, mainly shares, bonds, commodities, and property – both in their home country and around the globe. The growth of exchange traded funds (ETFs) has greatly facilitated access to these diverse markets. However, the attractiveness of these markets varies continuously, resulting in restless flows of capital in and out of asset classes around the globe. Within stock markets, there is constant rotation between sectors, and many professional investors work with sector rotation strategies. If competently executed, these strategies can be effective. As the world's economies run relentlessly through their cycles, various geographies and sectors will strengthen and weaken, and market participants will try to build their positions in strengthening sectors and reduce their positions in weakening sectors. A proactive retail investor should be aware of this phenomenon, as he adjusts his portfolio over time. But he should not try to follow it slavishly – jumping in and out of markets is rarely productive.

For company shares, factors that inform an effective sector rotation strategy include:

- The economic cycle
- Political policies

- Interest rates
- Geography
- Seasonality

The larger market participants will try to lead the markets, seeking to execute sophisticated sector rotation strategies, but poor performance from a great many fund managers and hedge funds suggests that this is easier said than done.

If you search <u>Fidelity Learning Center</u>, you will find useful material on sector rotation under <u>Markets & Sectors</u>.

The economic cycle

Share prices anticipate, so stock markets tend to rise as economies recover from recession and top out as economies slow down. Though the US is a strong influence on all significant economies around the world, they do not always move in sync. During 2013 and 2014, the US and the UK – and to a lesser extent Europe – were on the rise, while China was steadily slowing down. At the same time, there was a strong flight of investment money from 'emerging markets,' indicating a possible slow-down in these economies.

During times of uncertainty, a great deal of money will move into shares regarded as defensive; for example, utilities and consumer staples – companies providing products that people need through good times and bad. These companies are not always very exciting, but often pay good dividends, which are very attractive to investors searching for yield in difficult times. This can result in the share prices of these defensive companies running up to unrealistic levels, and then falling sharply as economic conditions improve and defensive shares get dumped. The unwary investor runs the risk of picking up some good dividends but then suffering a capital loss as the markets move on.

As economies begin to grow again and confidence picks up, market participants will rotate into cyclical companies, i.e., companies likely to benefit from an economic upturn. These will include consumer discretionary, such as luxury goods, expensive clothing and hotels and restaurants. Technology, industrials and automobiles will also pick up and possibly house building. In mid-cycle there can be a sell-off in these shares with energy and industrials coming into favor.

You will find many articles on the Internet describing how various sectors behave during the economic cycle. You will find different views, and in the real world many factors will come into play. In the first half of 2014, some of the so-called momentum stocks had become very expensive, especially in the technology area, leading to sharp falls in share prices. The prevailing wisdom at the time was that the markets were cutting and running from expensive momentum shares and rotating into 'value shares.' Some of the value shares may simply have been laggards in the market.

While some of the momentum shares had become overvalued, some had not. Not really very much of a strategy.

Political policies

Money will move between economies depending on the effectiveness of governments to stimulate growth and different sectors will benefit from the spending plans of particular governments – which will depend on the nature of their politics. Moving into 2014, the US economy was enjoying a strong stimulus from reducing energy costs with fracking playing a crucial role. In Europe, there is considerable opposition to fracking and green taxes are driving energy costs upwards. There is a fear in Europe that many energy-dependent companies will shift operations to the US to take advantage of much lower energy costs. There will be implications for company fortunes and share prices.

The main pledges in the 2015 Conservative UK election manifesto were:

- Eliminate the deficit and run an overall surplus by the end of the parliament.
- Aim for full employment for all those willing to work.
- Use money saved in reducing the benefits cap to fund 3 million apprenticeships.
- Triple the number of start-up loans to businesses to 75,000.

In addition, the UK government reduced the rate of corporation tax from 28% in 2010 to 20% in 2015, with an undertaking to reduce it to 18% in 2020. The UK now has the lowest rate in the G20 economies. These pro-business measures have made the UK one of the fastest growing economies in the developed world.

On the other hand, many regard Barack Obama as an anti-business president. US corporation tax stands at 40%, and you may recall his words during the 2012 election campaign:

'If you were successful, somebody along the line gave you some help. There was a great teacher somewhere in your life. Somebody helped to create this unbelievable American system that allowed you to thrive. Somebody invested in roads and bridges. If you've got a business, you didn't build that. Somebody else made that happen.'

Obama was emphasizing the importance of government in managing the economy. It is perhaps harsh to maintain that Obama is anti-business, but his sometimes lukewarm approach to business has possibly played a role in encouraging US companies to under-invest, buying back their company shares and hoarding cash overseas.

Interest rates

The movement of money between shares and bonds is a significant factor in share valuations. Simplistically, when bond yields are low, shares become more attractive and vice versa. During the long recovery from the financial crisis, US Federal Reserve and other central bank policies created a low interest rate environment, which pushed many investors reluctantly into shares, thought by many to be overvalued. There was a sense that the bull run, which was running out of steam from early in 2014, was 'unloved.'

In the associated search for yield, shares regarded as reliable dividend payers became popular. These included utilities and REITS – Real Estate Investment Trusts. For those that rotated into these shares early enough to capture some value, the issue became when to exit, so it was a time for them to keep close to central bank policy. In the final quarter of 2015, the S&P 500 utility sector and REITS were underperforming the index.

Utility shares are sometimes referred to as 'proxy bonds.' It has even been suggested that some hedge funds are proxy bonds – a strange concept, presumably a desperate marketing pitch by underperforming hedge fund managers.

The influence of interest rates in the market is discussed in more detail below.

Geography

Geography, touched on in the context of leading stock markets in *Chapter 2,* is much too large a topic to cover here, except for a few very broad-brush comments, and a suggestion to look at the history of a number of market indices over the years. Go to YAHOO! FINANCE and go through Investing/Indices/World/Europe and take a look at some European stock market performances.

Then go into, for example, Asia/Pacific and take a look at the Nikkei 225, Japan; the SSE, Shanghai Composite; the Hang Seng Index, Hong Kong; the KOSPI Composite, Korea, and so on. Click on 'max' for each chart and a picture of very mixed fortunes will emerge.

Alternatively, you can use Reuters Markets.

Investing overseas is discussed briefly in *Chapter 18 – Managing your portfolio.*

Seasonality

Many companies' earnings depend on a strength in a particular season, perhaps in the summer months – travel and leisure; or leading up to Christmas – retailers. If the markets sense that, for example, a wet summer is going to adversely affect the fortunes of a particular sector, this could stimulate some rotation into other sectors. A cold winter will boost the earnings of energy companies.

In the first quarter of 2014 severe bad weather, allied with a slowdown in job creation, caused US economic growth to fall to an annualized growth rate of just 0.1%. Fortunately, President Obama's reforms led to a sharp increase in healthcare spending in this quarter. Subsequently, the fears of economic slowdown were allayed, but the uncertainty spooked the markets and no doubt led to some sector rotation – short-term, tradable perturbations.

Seasonal effects tend to be short-term and are probably more the domain of traders than retail investors.

Company enters or exits an index

From time to time, depending on the practice of an index, companies will be promoted or relegated. See *Chapter 3*.

There are many tracker funds that by definition invest in all companies in an index, so changes in the composition of the index will result in an increase in trading as shares are bought and sold to bring the tracker fund back in line with the index. Professionals will seek to anticipate companies entering and exiting indices, and to exploit accompanied share price movements.

In the UK, companies are regularly promoted to and relegated from the stock market indices based on market cap, so it is particularly easy for professional traders to foresee and exploit the associated share price movements.

Company strategy

Companies describe and evaluate their strategies in their annual reports. They will also signal significant changes of strategy in these reports as well as through the various communication channels described above. The reaction of the market to adjustments in strategy can be highly significant for a company's share price.

Common strategy changes include withdrawing from unprofitable areas of business or starting operations in another territory. Or perhaps increased spending in R&D.

One of the most important strategic considerations for a company is mergers and acquisitions. A company announcing that it has made an offer for another company will wait with bated breath for the market's reaction.

Insider dealing

In 2014, New York State's attorney-general, Eric Schneiderman, described 'insider trading as trader's efforts to create and exploit small information gaps with the rest of the market.' As part of a continuing crackdown, he said that he planned to investigate brokerage firms that might have provided early market-moving information to preferred clients – 'looking at folks who obtain information, and at the analysts who provide the information.'

For large cap shares in the main US and UK markets, it is unlikely that insider dealing has a major influence on share prices. Usually, it will just allow a trader to make a quick return on release of news, or an investor to sell before bad news. Some of the more dubious market participants claim that insider trading is a victimless crime and it has even been proposed by some that it should be legal.

For small cap shares, insider dealing can be a more important consideration. A tip to one of the larger investors in a company could allow him to sell ahead of the market at large, causing a sharp fall in price but still obtaining better prices than other market participants. In other words, the playing field is rendered significantly unfair.

Fortunately, regulators in the US and UK have been cracking down on insider dealing, and the incidence of this is thought to have fallen.

Media coverage – journalists, broadcasters, bloggers

Check out Carl Icahn's Twitter feed!

Media, in all its forms – broadcast, print, and Internet – providing a constant stream of financial information, is an important influence on the markets. Discussion and analysis are virtually 24/7, covering topics that range from the macroeconomic climate and current tail risks, to individual companies. Shares and funds are plugged on a continuous basis by a range of people, including company CEOs, fund managers, and analysts. Sometimes investigations into a company's activities are reported. More recently, influencers and opinion formers have taken to Twitter, and services have sprung up that search Twitter feeds for price-moving information and opinions.

The question 'where are the markets headed?' is ever-present.

The financial television channels – Bloomberg and CNBC – are important sources of commentary. These are discussed in *Chapter 18 – Managing your portfolio.*

Newspaper financial pages and financial magazines such as Forbes Magazine, Barron's, MoneyWeek, and Investors Chronicle provide a constant stream of share analysis and tips that can move share prices. As do countless websites. Many newspapers give a set of tips at year end for the year ahead. These are very varied in quality. Tips from a well-respected source with a good track record can move a share price, at least in the short term.

The Internet is full of bloggers pumping out advice and trading techniques. Check out:

SWING-TRADE-STOCKS or

Dailyreckoning - the 50 best investing blogs

In the UK, you can check out the Penny Share newsletter, which specializes in small companies.

Without the media, investors would be reliant on company communications and analyst reports to inform their investment decisions. This would be a dull world.

There is further discussion of the media's influence in *Chapter 15 – A day in the markets.*

News flow

In March 2014, claims emerged that drug maker BTG had sourced venom from a Texas rattle snake hunt that wildlife officials wanted to ban, because petrol was being used to gas snakes out of the rocks! BTG denied buying wild rattlesnake venom and said a ban would not affect its supply chain. BTG's share price fell 3.2%.

News flow has been discussed in the previous chapter and its importance cannot be overemphasized. Though a great deal of news will be inconsequential, the markets will take a view quickly on what is significant and this will feed rapidly into the market as a whole or into an individual share price. Significant news, such as a profit warning or sharp fall in a commodity price, is always likely to trump the Technicals. There is a great deal of news flow for large cap companies.

There is no shortage of information sources to inform the retail trader and investor in their activities. However, provision of financial information including key economic data is big business, and bespoke and expensive services have evolved to support professional trading activity. A very big player in this market is Bloomberg, the provider of the ubiquitous Bloomberg Professional Service data terminal which:

'Brings together real time data on every market, unparalleled news and research, powerful analytics, communications tools and world-class execution capabilities – in one fully integrated solution.'

This provides a trading platform and flows of real time market data, as well as a range of analytical tools for 325,000 terminal users. The index companies and other service providers will sell their services through the Bloomberg Terminals. Many major market players use Bloomberg Terminals, paying a fee of around US$20,000 per annum per user. A single subscription costs around US$24,000, putting them beyond the reach of most retail investors and traders. Bloomberg is also famous for its financial television channel that competes with CNBC. Both operate informative websites.

A similar service is provided by Reuters, with over 400,000 users of its data terminals. Thomas Reuters is a global media and financial information group and is prominent in this space.

'Thomson Reuters Eikon provides easy access to trusted news, data, and analytics, all filtered by relevance to your exact needs, and displayed in a highly visual way that's easy to grasp and act on.'

More recent market entrants include FactSet, with over 50,000 data terminals, Capital IQ, and Markit. 51% of Markit, which has enjoyed near exponential growth, is owned by a consortium of investment banks which are all significant customers. They will also enjoy good business when Markit is the subject of an initial public offering (IPO). Markit describes itself as:

'A leading global diversified provider of financial information services. We provide products that enhance transparency, reduce risk and improve operational efficiency. Our customers include banks, hedge funds, asset managers, central banks, regulators, auditors, fund administrators and insurance companies. Founded in 2003, we employ over 3,500 people in 10 countries.'

These systems provide information on a global basis and across asset classes – to those that can afford it.

Chat rooms and bulletin boards

In 2013 it was reported that Bloomberg electronic chat rooms, where some 15mn instant messages are exchanged daily, have been used for rigging interest rates. It also emerged that Bloomberg journalists had been monitoring chat rooms for stories.

Integral to the Bloomberg and Eikon systems are chat rooms and messaging services that handle vast traffic. An early use of chat rooms was in investment banks, to enable quick communication between bank workers, their colleagues on other desks, and their clients. More recently they have attracted the attention of regulators investigating manipulation of interest rates and foreign exchange benchmarks. Evidence emerged that traders were using chat rooms to share sensitive client information. The investments banks are subjecting them to increasing levels of scrutiny and control in the context of the integrity of their operations. As well as market abuse, internal investigations are turning up quite a lot of profane, racist, and sexist language.

Internet chat rooms are now playing an integral role across the markets in all asset classes. They facilitate information sharing and concerted action between groups of market participants, which sometimes will sail close to the wind.

Chat rooms are not just for the professionals using bespoke systems. There are many chat rooms and information-sharing forums accessible to the retail investor. See, for example, StockRants.

Bulletin boards are prolific on investment and market information websites and tend to be the domain of countless small investors in their never-ending search for the 'tenbagger,' i.e., the share that increases in value by a factor of 10. For small cap shares with low news flow, bulletin boards can be a valuable source of information for the retail investor and trader. The participants, always with a bulletin board *nom de plume* or pseudonym, can display apparently deep knowledge of specialist companies and their business models and products – and their value. They often become enraged with each other and with the duplicitous market makers and 'stupid' fund managers who don't recognize the value in a share. Occasionally, well-informed views might move share prices.

Market factors – technical

Technical factors operate at both a strategic and tactical level. This section deals with some strategic technical factors, while technical factors that influence daily trading activities are covered in *Chapter 10 – Trading.*

The S&P 500

The S&P 500 is a key barometer for assessing market sentiment. Just about everything going on in the world that can affect the global economy is absorbed into the S&P 500 cash index through two processes. First, it draws in fine grain information on the 500 constituent companies and second, it incorporates, in a highly dynamic process, the well-informed views of index futures traders working around the clock in trades of breathtaking size. As we have discussed, other major indices often follow the direction taken by the S&P 500, though the movements can be quite different in magnitude. Every serious investor and trader in the US and UK will keep a close eye on the S&P 500. In March 2015, the Office of Financial Research of the US Treasury reported that the S&P 500 was in bubble territory at close to two standard deviations – 'two sigma' – from its historic norm. The index had been in similar territory leading up to the crashes of 1929, 2001, and 2008.

Stock market cycles

Economists like to think that markets move in cycles. In a sense they do, and you can find their various theories on the Internet. Evidently, since the end of the second world war, there have been around a dozen periods of economic expansion. However, in modern times, we have not observed a series of orderly economic cycles, with phases of economic growth followed by periods during which economies consolidate and draw breath before commencing another period of growth. Go to YAHOO! FINANCE and bring up the S&P 500 index. Choose the Max time frame and you will see the index going back to 1950. Choose the linear vertical scale. From 1950 to 1995 – 45 years – the market does not look very cyclical, though keep in mind that due to the scale, some quite significant volatility in shorter periods of time will not be very apparent. If you choose the log vertical scale, perturbations will be more evident and you will see very clearly the 'bull' and 'bear' market phases.

In 1995, the market commenced a sharp ascent, moving into three great 'cycles' which are discussed in *Chapter 7 – Recent history – and what we can learn.* It is more accurate to describe the first two ascents as bubbles, in which share prices moved well above value and then collapsed dramatically, with severe recession setting in. Taken as a whole, the economist community did not predict these very accurately using their theories of cycles. A more realistic interpretation of events is that the overvaluation of share prices and ensuing crashes have to a large extent created the economic cycles that we have experienced. In other words, over-exuberant market activity has created booms and busts, rather than the markets reflecting the ebbs and flows of economic activity. The sector rotation discussed above takes place within this context.

At the outset of 2016, the jury is out – the third 'cycle' has not run its course. The hope is that as a result of continual improvement in the 'globalization project,' regulation and governance, allied with perhaps a new ethical agenda and more maturity from the market participants, future crashes will not be nearly as severe as those that occurred in 2001 and 2008 and we might get back to business as usual in terms of classic market cycles. However, the proactive retail investor should never drop his guard.

Interest rates

Central banks set interest rates at which they lend to banks, and they borrow money on the primary bond markets. Bonds are then traded on a vast scale on the secondary bond markets. The size of the global bond market, assessed in terms of total debt, is over US$82tn. There is competition for investment funds between asset classes, not least between equities – shares – and bonds, and the historical record shows strong correlation between share prices and bond prices. They tend to rise and fall together. Bond prices are inversely related to bond yields, so as bond prices rise, yields fall. And as share prices rise, dividend yields also fall.

In 2015, the average dividend yield of S&P 500 companies was around 2% and the US 10 year Treasury yield was ranging between 1.7% and 2.5%. So the main benefit of being in an S&P 500 tracker fund or ETF was the possibility of capital gain. The S&P 500 performance in 2015 was flat.

After the financial crisis, the US Federal Reserve and other central banks executed substantial quantitative easing (QE) programs in order to inject liquidity into the markets. QE involves buying long dated bonds from financial institutions. This puts upward pressure on bond prices, and lowers interest rates. The idea is that the institutions increase their lending and buy assets, including shares. All this is meant to stimulate the economy. The problem is that QE eventually has to be tapered down, resulting in less money flowing into the stock markets.

As central banks raise interest rates after the financial crisis, investors will sell bond holdings and buy new issues with higher yields. The bonds with the longer times to maturity will most likely be hit the hardest. There will be strong downwards pressure on bond prices. Concurrently, investors may sell shares to seek safer, higher yields in new bond issues. The result will be some turmoil in both share and bond markets. Eventually, the markets will stabilize with strong fund flows into the bond markets and perhaps with the stock market indices reset at a lower level.

Rising interest rates are bad news for leveraged companies, as the cost of servicing their debt will rise. The market analysts will pay very close attention to the impact of this on a company's earnings. Also, higher interest rates will take money out of the pockets of consumers, and this will have an impact on the earnings of many companies.

Another effect of low interest rates is that they reduce the rate at which future earnings must be discounted, which is positive for share valuations. Rising interest rates will have the reverse effect. See 'Discounted cash flow methods' in *Chapter 4*.

Many US companies have taken advantage of cheap borrowing costs to fund buybacks and dividend payouts to shareholders.

Liquidity

In the summer, many people are on holiday, perhaps especially senior managers, and liquidity is low due to reduced trading activity – this makes markets vulnerable to shocks.

Broker-dealers, described in the next chapter, have an obligation to provide liquidity to the markets, e.g., through market making activities and facilitating trading activities. If their liquidity comes under pressure, this can have significant impact on share prices. Lack of liquidity was a significant factor in the demise of Lehman Brothers in 2008.

There has also been some loss of liquidity in the markets resulting from the Volcker reforms, which have forced the US investment banks to phase out trading using customer capital.

Historical P/E ratio

In March 2014, with the bull run in the US markets entering its sixth year helped along its way by QE, Richard Fisher, president of the Federal Reserve Bank of Dallas, went on record to say 'stock market metrics such as price to forward earnings, price-to-sales ratio and market capitalization as a percentage of GDP are at eye-popping levels not seen since the dotcom boom of the late 1990s.'

P/E ratio is most commonly calculated in terms of a company's previous one year of earnings – referred to as trailing P/E. It is updated each time a company reports its earnings. It is useful to look at the average historical trailing P/E ratio of companies making up an index in assessing if markets are over- or undervalued. The most important index is the S&P 500, and a chart of one-year trailing S&P 500 P/E ratio since 1929 by Seeking Alpha and Bespoke Investment Group, can be found by searching Seeking Alpha S and P 500 historical p-e ratio.

For historic data on FTSE 250 P/E ratio, search: UK Value Investor FTSE 250 Valuation and Forecast for Q3 2015 July 21.

CAPE – Robert Shiller's Cyclically Adjusted P/E ratio

Many believe that the Shiller P/E ratio is a more reliable measure of the expense of the market, and therefore more useful in prediction of stock market movements. In this ratio, P/E ratio is based on average inflation-adjusted earnings from the previous 10 years. The ratio is also known as the Cyclically Adjusted PE Ratio (CAPE Ratio). A chart of CAPE P/E provided by GuruFocus can be found by searching Gurufocus shiller – PE.

A version of the chart is also provided by MarketWatch. Search Marketwatch what shiller pe ratio says about market's top. For a chart going back to 1880, search multpl shiller – pe.

Forward P/E ratio

The markets also take a view on forward P/E ratio based on analysts' forecasts, which takes account of one year's future earnings. Regardless of the vagaries of analyst forecasts, they are in a better position than anyone else to forecast the earnings of a large number of companies; even though they may have some upside bias, their collective view is worth some attention.

FactSet provides a chart of S&P 500 Forward 12 Month P/E Ratio from the year 2000. Search FACTSET S&P 500 forward P/E.

Reuters provides data from 1986. Search Reuters S&P 500 12 m forward P/E.

Tobin's Q ratio

James Tobin, a Nobel Prize-winning economist at Yale University, postulated that the combined market value of stock market companies should be equal to the replacement cost of their physical assets.

Q ratio = Total value of stock market/Total asset replacement value.

US market and replacement values are available from the 'Federal Reserve's quarterly flow of funds accounts data,' under the section titled 'Balance Sheet and Reconciliation Tables for Nonfinancial Corporate Business.'   Line 35 is market value; line 32 is replacement cost. This can be difficult to find so don't try unless you are really interested.

Q can also be calculated for individual companies.

A Q ratio of 1 for a market implies that the market is at fair value. Historically, it has ranged between 0.3 and 1.7, reaching the higher level leading up to the dot-com bubble. The Q chart overlays the chart of the Cyclically Adjusted P/E Ratio quite closely.

Relative Strength Index (RSI) for the major indices

Relative strength index (RSI) is described in *Chapter 10 – Trading.*   It can be used to assess if indices are overbought or oversold. As for individual shares, RSI ranges between 0 and 100, with 70 suggesting overbought and 30 suggesting oversold.

Many websites allow you to display RSI below charts of indices and share prices. It cannot be taken as a definitive sign that a market is 'topping' or 'bottoming' out, but is a serious metric to be weighed in the balance.

Moving averages for the major indices

Moving averages are discussed in *Chapter 10 – Trading.*   The moving averages of the major indices are important technical indicators, closely watched by the markets.

Go to YAHOO! FINANCE and bring up the S&P 500 chart again. This time, select the five-year period and then go to Technical Indicators and select Simple Moving Average (SMA). Type '200' for the period and this will overlay the 200-day SMA on the chart.

Many traders get nervous when the S&P 500 gets up to around 6% to 8% above its 200-day moving average – you will see from the chart that there is some justification for this nervousness. Self-fulfilling prophecy comes into play and the market indices can settle into trading ranges strongly influenced by technical metrics – before a breakout to the upside or downside.

No one knows exactly where the 200-day moving average is heading, but its journey provides a steady stream of trading and investing opportunities.

Borrowing to invest

A great many investors borrow to invest in the stock market. This can be using a straightforward loan, or investing or trading on margin as described in *Chapter 9 – Futures and options, Chapter 10 – Trading,* and *Chapter 11 – Trading with Contracts for Difference (CFDs).*

When the markets are hit with some uncertainty, heavily leveraged investors will rush for the exits, contributing to panic and sharp falls in share prices.

A defining aspect of stock market bubbles is that they are inflated by borrowing!

6 The market participants, facilitators, and influencers

Introduction

There are vast numbers of organizations and people that participate directly in the stock markets through investment and trading activities. There are many more who facilitate activities and earn fees and commissions from the direct participants. Some also provide advisory services.

In addition, there are large numbers of analysts, commentators, journalists, and websites that influence the markets. Knowledge of these actors and how they behave and interact is important background to successful investing. This chapter attempts to describe them in an organized way, and includes many key words which should aid deeper research by the interested reader.

Economics and accountancy are probably the main disciplines of the markets, though people from virtually every background and education are drawn by the opportunities and excitement to be found there.

Dealers, brokers, and broker-dealers

In the context of shares (also known as equities), a dealer is a person, or more likely a firm, that deals in shares for its own account, sometimes through a broker.

Brokers trade on behalf of their clients for a commission. For trading on public stock exchanges, their main role will be to find the best price on offer for the client's trade size, to execute the trade, and then to oversee the post-trade clearance and settlement. Where a broker acts as agent for a client, he will carry the counterparty responsibility, i.e., to deliver the shares or cash.

A broker-dealer is usually a firm that acts as a broker as well as a dealer. Broker-dealers play a central role in equity markets, either as an independent firm or as an operation of a larger organization, such as an institutional investor or an investment bank. They deal using their own funds or on behalf of clients, and must keep a clear separation between their funds and those of their clients. In addition to trading or dealing for clients, they may provide them with investment advice and undertake research for them.

Other broker-dealer activities may include making a market in a number of shares and acting as house broker for listed companies and supporting them in raising capital. Also, they are important sellers and distributors of mutual fund shares.

Broker-dealers have to comply with stringent liquidity requirements. Liquidity issues were central to the demise of Lehman Brothers at the outset of the financial crisis.

The institutional investors

Between the 1970s and 2010s, the proportion of US shares held by institutional investors rose from 10% to more than 60%. Between 1985 and 2015, assets held by global mutual funds rose from US$1tn to US$35tn. Institutions now own most of the shares listed on the New York Stock Exchange.

The big institutional investors exert very considerable influence on the stock markets. Who are they? The definition of 'institutional investor' is fairly broad. It tends to mean organizations that invest large amounts of money on behalf of others, and are big enough to make a serious impact in the markets in which they operate. Institutional investors are deemed to be competent market participants, and more able to look after themselves than the smaller private investors. Therefore, they may receive less sympathy from a regulator if they believe that they have been unfairly treated. Other organizations will be keen to sell services to them, often at preferential rates and commissions. Institutional investors will be more able to gain access to a company's senior management than the retail investor.

The big institutional investors on the world stage include:

- Pension funds
- Insurance companies
- Asset managers
- Wealth managers
- Sovereign wealth funds

Pension funds manage the vast amounts of money set aside by individuals, governments, and corporations to provide retirement income. Insurance companies are big investors because they need to achieve returns on premiums collected in advance. As more people across the globe become seriously rich, the demand for wealth management steadily increases – investment banks and broker-dealers are mainstream providers of these services. Sovereign wealth funds have come into existence as some fortunate and prudent countries have created substantial surplus income, often from substantial oil and gas resources. It is estimated that the Norwegian sovereign wealth fund has assets of US$870bn and holdings in almost 10,000 companies. It owns on average about 1.3% of global stock market capitalization. It is in the list of 20 biggest shareholders in a great many companies.

In recent years, BlackRock and Fidelity vied for the accolade of the world's biggest asset manager, each controlling more than US$4.5tn of funds worldwide – roughly twice the UK's annual economic output of around US$2.3tn. BlackRock is the biggest shareholder in about one-in-three of America's top companies. Another player in this top league is Vanguard, which is specialized in low-cost tracker funds. In 2014 they broke the record for net inflow of funds for the third year running, with an intake of US$243bn, moving into second place for funds under management.

The monies under management will usually be organized into asset classes and funds, each with a manager. Dependent on structure, these large organizations may have an 'asset allocation manager' or a 'market strategist' with a global remit. They will continually assess how money under management should be deployed across the various asset classes – the main ones being shares, bonds, property, and commodities – and countries. This will lead to constant movement of monies between asset classes and countries, which impacts asset prices as the fund managers redeploy their money. One asset manager's panic to get out of a particular market will be another's perceived opportunity. The markets watch the activities of the asset allocators closely as they adjust their weightings.

Institutional investors are the most important influence in the medium- and long-term performance of the stock markets. They subcontract some of their fund management to fund management firms, whose fortunes are dependent on their ability to perform well and maintain and build market share for these services. In addition, there are investment consultants who advise pensions on fund manager selection. They also give transition advice, assisting pension funds to make changes in their investment portfolios; this will sometimes involve the hiring and firing of fund managers. Investment consulting is big business, but there is little evidence that it is effective in improving pension fund returns. In fact, recent studies have indicated the opposite (University of Oxford 2013 study of US investment consultants). Smaller pension funds in particular may lack the acumen to manage these services effectively.

Traditionally, institutional investors will have a five-to-ten-year horizon - or longer - for their equity investments and take long positions only. The larger fund managers have huge amounts of money to invest, and of necessity take substantial positions in the larger listed companies. Dividend flows from such companies make up a considerable proportion of the long-term returns, and are particularly attractive to pension funds which have to pay out a monthly income to their clients. Therefore, they are attracted to companies that pay a decent dividend and increase the dividend, even if by only a modest amount, each year. In the US, dividends are usually paid quarterly. In the UK, twice yearly is the norm, though sometimes quarterly payments are made to accommodate US investors. From time to time a special dividend may be paid. Of course the fund managers will not want to suffer an erosion of capital arising from a falling share price, but rightly or wrongly, they have traditionally taken a longer-term view of this.

These major market participants employ 'buy-side analysts' (see below) who will have determined a target price for a share, though they will keep this constantly under review, which will inform their advice regarding the eventual unwinding of the position. If a good dividend-paying company is performing well, the institution may decide to hold the position for many years – while taking an activist position to keep the company management on its toes.

It is a considerable undertaking to liquidate a large position in an S&P 500 or FTSE 100 company. A major shareholder may typically hold 5% of a company's shares, and based on average daily trading volumes the shareholder would have to sell the entire daily volume for several weeks to liquidate his position. The fund manager will then have a large amount to reinvest, which creates a big headache for him. In addition, he will most likely have trashed the share price, creating an even bigger headache. The alternative is to work with the company's management with a view to improving performance.

For further information search Investopedia, Introduction to Institutional Investing.

The banks

Investment banks

The London Whale is the name given to the trading activity of JP Morgan Chase's Chief Investment Office (CIO), when in 2012 it built a huge position in a derivative trade which it then struggled to close – ultimately losing US$6.2bn. The role of the CIO was ostensibly to manage the bank's investment risks, but it emerged that in reality it was trading aggressively with depositors' money – US$350bn, most of it federally insured deposits – to generate bank profits. It seems that as losses mounted, the traders conspired to conceal the situation from management.

The investment banks are the titans of the financial industry. A long list of names includes Goldman Sachs, JP Morgan Chase, Bank of America, Citigroup, Morgan Stanley, Credit Suisse, Deutsche Bank, Barclays, and Wells Fargo. An investment bank may be standalone or part of an integrated or universal bank with global operations. The integrated banks have both retail and investment banking operations under the same roof.

In the US, commercial banking and investment banking were separated by the Glass-Steagall Act, until it was repealed in 1999. This led to a rash of mergers and acquisitions and the emergence of large, integrated banks offering a wide range of services. Barclays were prolific with their acquisitions, which included Wedd Durlacher, de Zoete & Bevan, and, as a result of the financial crisis, much of Lehman Brothers. However, by 2015 Barclays were winding down a great many of their investment banking activities. JP Morgan amalgamated with Chase Manhattan Bank, and went on to acquire Bear Stearns, Bank One, Washington Mutual, and Cazenove in London. In the UK, Royal Bank of Scotland bought National Westminster and then went on to acquire ABN Amro, one of the worst deals ever made in the banking industry. Ostensibly, these banks were 'integrated,' but in reality quite different businesses were thrown together in short order. This created governance challenges for bank management, though it is tempting to believe that sometimes management didn't look too closely at what was going on, as long as it was making money. There is a view that the integrated banks in particular became vehicles for enriching senior employees at the expense of shareholders.

After many years of excess, the investment banks were beset by an endless stream of wrongdoings, and were hit very hard by a range of regulators, having to pay out record sums in fines. Barclays and Royal Bank of Scotland suffered more than most, and early in 2015, RBS announced that it was planning to cut 14,000 of the 18,000 jobs in its investment bank.

The investment banks are serious players in the stock market, where Goldman Sachs is reputedly the biggest winner. This is not too surprising when you consider their size, global presence, and range of operations. In addition to benefitting from world-class research and technology, the opportunities for legitimate information sharing and integration of expertise are extensive. As well as trading or dealing for their own account, they may also provide services to specialist trading houses to support their trading activities. The UK investment banks have struggled to compete with their US counterparts.

Investment banks have often enjoyed spectacular returns from the activities of star traders operating across a range of asset classes and running high levels of risk in the hope of generating substantial profits. The term 'casino banks' has been coined to describe these activities. The problem with this was that the bank's casino arm gambled with shareholder funds and the deposits of the bank's retail clients. If things went well, the star traders took the upside rewards through spectacular bonus payments. Their only downside was that they might lose their bonus or job. An unfortunate characteristic of some professional traders is that they want to make a lot of money, while taking as little risk as possible. This is evident from the rigging of Libor and Forex markets that has emerged, which suggests that the success of some star traders has been based on cheating. It is interesting to note that a number of star traders, who have moved on from investment banks to set up or work for hedge funds, have not managed to repeat their success. Undoubtedly the investment banks provide a strongly differentiated setting that is supportive of successful trading.

Following the financial crisis of 2008, a raft of legislation and regulation has been passed to constrain activities of the investment banks; these include, importantly, in the US, the Volcker Rule's restrictions on certain types of proprietary trading, i.e., trading for their own accounts. This did not prevent the specter of the London Whale appearing in the London office of JP Morgan Chase and pressure remains on both sides of the Atlantic to break up the largest of the integrated banks.

Activities undertaken by investment banks are wide-ranging and include:

- Broker-dealer operations. Central to these are sales desks, which act as a hub for the bank's relationships with major investors, such as fund managers and hedge funds.
- Investing and trading across a wide range of asset classes for clients.
- Trading FICC – **F**ixed **I**ncome instruments such as bonds, **C**urrencies (foreign exchange), and **C**ommodities.
- Corporate stockbroking, described below.
- Research for government and private entities.
- Running commodity merchant businesses.
- Commodity price hedging, e.g., fuel for airlines.
- Sometimes, even physical vaulting of precious metals.
- Market making.
- Futures and options trading.
- Back office support for specialist trading houses.
- High-frequency trading (HFT).
- HFT platforms and execution facilities and risk management for HFT houses.
- Risk management.
- Investment consulting and transition management.
- Portfolio consultancy.
- Wealth management, including tax efficiency advice.
- Corporate tax planning.

By 2015, FICC profits were under pressure in many investment banks as a result of regulation. Also, many banks had exited commodities trading and vaulting on the basis that it was no longer strategic, returns were shrinking, and there was pressure from regulators concerned with risk taking by 'too big to fail' banks.

From time to time, issues arise around the independence of the research undertaken by investment banks.

The banks are perhaps slowly improving their ethical behavior under pressure from governments, their regulators, and shareholders, but are unlikely ever to become perfect.

Retail banks

The retail-focused banks, e.g., regional banks in the US and some high street banks in the UK, increasingly offer services traditionally regarded as investment banking activities, such as wealth management and stockbroking, leading to a blurring of the distinction between these two types of bank.

Leading up the 2008 financial crisis, many of the retail sides of the large, integrated banks had built up sprawling overseas operations, thus creating vast networks through which money could be moved around, sometimes sailing close to the legal wind. These activities are receiving a great deal more regulatory scrutiny, and in these more straightened, post–financial crisis times, the banks are shrinking these networks.

Fund managers

As we have seen, the institutional investors employ fund managers to increase the value of their assets and those of their clients through investment programs.

A very significant change is underway in the fund management industry concerning the merits of active fund management, compared with passive fund management. Passive fund managers will simply track an index, such as the S&P 500 or FTSE 100, with portfolios replicating the constituent companies in the index. They maintain that any extra returns that an active fund manager might deliver are simply eaten up by additional costs. They and their proponents will also maintain that when active fund managers beat their index, they have just had a good run, but will find this difficult to maintain over the long term.

The main activity of an index tracker fund manager is buying and selling shares to keep his holding in each share in line with its weighting in the index, which will vary with time, and buying and selling shares to accommodate inflows and outflows of funds generated by investors. In addition, he will have to make significant adjustments when companies are promoted to or relegated from an index.

An active fund manager will be continually adjusting his portfolio as he takes profits and cuts losses, builds up positions in new companies, and accommodates the inflows and outflows of monies that occur on a daily basis due to investor activity. In a rising market, a successful fund will enjoy a net positive inflow of funds, creating new investment opportunities. There is a view that active fund managers will tend to do better when the markets are volatile, e.g., picking up bargains during sharp market pullbacks.

Despite the propaganda from significant parts of the fund management industry, it is a matter of record that the best actively managed funds consistently outperform passive funds. You can confirm this by spending a little time on websites such as Morningstar and Trustnet, which track fund performance. This proposition is explored in some detail in *Chapter 12 – About funds*.

When markets move into a sharp correction or fall, fund managers do not move into cash to any significant degree. In fact, funds are rarely more than a few percent in cash; 5% or 6% would be an unusually high cash component. If funds around the world rushed into cash, stock markets globally would collapse, so this is not a practical proposition. Fund managers in shares see their job as moving money around between companies and not between asset classes, e.g., from shares to bonds (though there are a small number of funds that invest in both shares and bonds). Some funds use derivatives, such as futures and options contracts, as a way of managing downside risk – preserving capital – though these incur trading costs. Futures and options contracts are described in *Chapter 9.*

Fund managers are continually benchmarked against their peers, and portfolio consultants working for the larger pension funds will analyze fund manager performance – recommending changes as they see fit. Pension funds have to meet obligations to pensioners over long periods of time, and they use actuaries to forecast these obligations. This will have an impact on their investment strategies, and they will instruct their fund managers accordingly. So the fund managers are not always given a free hand, and this may impact their performance. The jobs of the fund managers will ultimately depend on their performance, though it has to be said that a great many poor fund managers seem to survive indefinitely. There is a developing trend for fund managers, who are traditionally long only, to assign some of their funds under management to hedge funds, in an effort to boost performance. The hedge funds may well do some 'shorting,' particularly of indices, to protect portfolio values. Also, there is evidence that 'holding periods' are reducing with holding times for a company share often less than a year.

The trading desk

Professional market participants such as investment banks, broker-dealers, and fund managers, will have a trading desk for executing their trading strategies, building and reducing positions. The traders will endeavor to do this buying and selling in a way that doesn't move the share price significantly against them. If they find a share price moving up as they build a position, they will sell some shares in an effort to bring the situation back under control – and vice versa. The trader's mission is to acquire shares at an average target price. They will be guided by volume weighted average price (VWAP). For a company share:

VWAP = $\frac{\Sigma \text{ Number of shares bought x share price}}{\text{Number of shares bought}}$

Trading in line with the market in this way reduces the probability of the trader moving the price against himself.

An institution building a position in a company is often taken as a buy signal by other market participants – many of whom will be constantly looking for signs of institutional buying or selling in the market. When a manager sees that the share price of one of his holdings is reaching his target price, he may instruct his trading desk to reduce his position, and the process goes into reverse.

The development of 'dark pools' within private stock exchanges has provided a facility to make large trades with reduced transparency. Private stock exchanges are discussed below.

The fund management industry, on both sides of the Atlantic, is going through considerable change driven by competitive pressures. In the UK, there are continual regulatory demands for transparency and lower fee levels. These factors are driving many fund management companies increasingly into the provision of tracker funds. This will see some adjustment in the role of the trading desk towards index tracking.

Activist investors

In April 2015, it was reported that BlackRock, probably the world's largest asset manager, was pressing companies in its portfolio to give their shareholders the right to nominate directors, putting it in the forefront of the latest US corporate governance campaign – yet this is not a right the company is planning to grant to its own investors. In February 2016, Larry Fink, the BlackRock CEO wrote to FTSE 100 CEOs demanding transparency and openness with shareholders. This arose from his concern that they have been boosting profits at the expense of the long-term best interests of their companies.

In 2012, Neil Woodford, a fund manager with Invesco Perpetual, played a pivotal role in killing a proposed merger between EADS, the Airbus manufacturer, and BAE Systems. Woodford controlled 13.3% of BAE Systems. The coup de grâce was executed by Angela Merkel. The chairman of BAE Systems' employment contract encouraged him to make the deal.

Shareholder activism in various guises has increased on both sides of the Atlantic since the financial crisis, when a great deal of boardroom excess and incompetence came to light. The increasing tendency of major institutions to take underperforming management to task has already been mentioned. As a practical matter, these institutional investors and fund managers, because they have so much money to invest and can't be very nimble in the markets, have little alternative to taking a long-term view while applying pressure on management to improve performance. In addition, there are aggressive asset management companies and activist-focussed hedge funds that take positions in a company, and then seek changes, often pressing for board positions. Their motivation may be to enhance shareholder value or to make a killing for themselves – or both. Hedge funds are becoming increasingly involved as activist investors.

Activist investors, together with other major shareholders, will apply very substantial pressure on the target company, often engaging with management behind closed doors – with a view to getting the company back on track. They will seek to make changes in management and strategy, improvements in businesses processes, sales of non-core divisions, shutdown of unprofitable operations, etc. They may even try to break up the company into two or three new companies, to enhance shareholder value; or simply strip its assets – e.g., close down the business and sell its property portfolio. They might press the company to be acquired, in order to release value, or to find value-adding acquisitions.

Eventually, perhaps helped by improving economic conditions, the fortunes of the company may improve.

During 2015, more than 120 S&P 500 companies enabled 'proxy access' for large investors, which can now propose directors at company AGMs. Over the last three years, US activist investors have undertaken about 250 campaigns for board seats with a success rate of around 75%.

In addition, there is increasing regulatory pressure on company directors to improve their performance, and on institutional shareholders to improve their stewardship of the companies in which they have major holdings. Shareholder activism has increased dramatically in recent years, and many commentators believe that in some instances it has gone too far and has been detrimental to the fortunes of companies – in turning around or boosting company fortunes, activism has a mixed track record. The activities of activist investors, almost by definition, can lead to strong share price movements.

During bad times, an institutional investor will be looking for a reliable dividend flow to compensate for the fall in capital value of its holding. This can be a tough ask in a struggling company, and of course, companies don't always recover. Many major companies from 30 years ago are not around today or are greatly reduced. Sectors also can lose their shine. After the 2008 crash, most big institutions simply exited the big mining companies that had become seriously overvalued during the great resource boom created by Chinese demand. It can take years for a company to come around, and a proactive retail investor doesn't need to wait while the activist investors are at work with no guarantee of success. He can put his money elsewhere very easily – and should!

Hedge funds

In 2015, the US$38bn Harvard endowment fund reported that its US$6bn allocated to hedge fund management had returned only 0.1%.

Hedge funds have many of the characteristics of an institutional investor, covering the entire range of asset classes in their quest for exceptional profits. In the early days of hedge funds, the principal would invest his own money in the fund as an indicator of his confidence in his ability – putting his money where his mouth is. Many, but not all, hedge funds continue to adhere to this philosophy. In the stock market, they will use leverage and take both long and short positions, and account for a great deal of daily trading. The large hedge funds operate on a global basis, moving their monies in and out of positions sometimes quite rapidly, and making full use of futures and options contracts to hedge their risks. In the round they do not appear to undertake a great deal of high-frequency trading.

As well as traditional hedge funds, there is a relatively new breed of quant funds that rely on technology to produce their returns.

Traditional hedge funds

In 2015, hedge funds had some US$2.7tn under management – more than in 2007, just before the onset of the financial crisis. Their branding and image building has been extremely effective, and has convinced a great many people that hedge funds are where the 'smart money' goes. Pension funds are increasingly committing monies to hedge funds in an effort to boost performance. In some hedge funds, pension monies exceed 60% of total assets.

Hedge funds seek to differentiate themselves by achieving uncorrelated returns, i.e., returns that are not simply related to stock market movements. There are many hedge fund strategies. Some are based on trend following, some are event-driven, and some are specific company plays. Trend following makes use of sophisticated computer programs to exploit momentum across a wide range of asset classes, but it is not as easy as it sounds, and a fair measure of luck is involved in successful trading. Event-driven strategies involve identifying market-moving events, such as an acquisition or a large share buyback program, and speculating on their outcomes.

Hedge funds are also involved in shareholder activism, with research-led hedge funds building up significant minority stakes in companies and applying pressure on boards to change policy. According to Hedge Fund Research, total assets under management by activist hedge funds have doubled in the last four years. FactSet Research Systems tells us that in the past five years, activists have initiated campaigns at more than 20% of industrial companies in the S&P 500.

During 2007 and 2008, at the height of the financial crisis, many hedge funds experienced significant liquidity problems, with investors having to wait sometimes months before they could withdraw funds. Their money was tied up in complex investment strategies that took time to unwind.

We can take a look at hedge fund performance. According to Hedge Fund Research (HFR), in 2013 the average equity hedge fund return was 7%; in 2014, the average return was 3.6%, though there were a few outstanding performances of 30% to 35% return. In 2015, the industry as a whole incurred a loss, citing extremely difficult trading conditions.

You can study the performance of leading hedge funds by searching the <u>Preqin Global Hedge Fund Report</u>, and the <u>DATAROMA</u> website provides detailed information on hedge fund holdings – see <u>Superinvestor Portfolio Updates</u>.

Though there are some spectacularly successful hedge funds, in recent years a large proportion of the hedge fund industry has significantly underperformed the better fund managers and indeed a great many savvy retail investors.

A problem with the hedge fund space is that it has become very crowded and there are not enough great deals or trades out there to accommodate them all. Reasons for underperformance include a dilution of the quality of the people involved – inevitable as the industry has grown so fast; high fees – not justified by performance; the scale of funds under management and overtrading – the funds will simply move prices against them as they scramble for profits in intense competition with other hedge funds.

As already mentioned, there are many stories of star traders leaving investment banks to set up hedge funds and not making a fist of it, having failed to recognize the level of support that they had enjoyed within their banks.

Several hedge funds are now closing their funds to new entrants so that they can focus their efforts on achieving better returns, rather than increasing funds under management.

Quant funds

Technological advances have led to the development of specialized quant funds, which are fully automated trading systems.

The concept behind quant funds is that reliable, quantitative, rule-based, business models can be created for a company and provide the basis for an investment strategy – which is then largely driven by computer algorithms with minimal human intervention. Quant funds will use automatic data inputs seeking competitive advantage from the speed with which they can process input data and trade, and follow both momentum and non-momentum strategies.

Systematic trading strategies are now big business, with trading algorithms exploiting large numbers of small price movements. There is a body of opinion that these algorithms made a substantial contribution to the sharp market correction that occurred in August 2015.

Quant funds, unsurprisingly, have produced mixed results.

Stock exchanges

Public and private stock exchanges and dark pool trading venues have been described in *Chapter 3*. They facilitate trading, while competing among themselves for listings and trading business.

Stock exchanges are businesses, often listed, and are strongly profit-motivated. Competition between exchanges has never been fiercer, and they constantly seek to introduce innovative products. The stock exchanges capture vast amounts of data and, in their quest for profit, they will look to make best legal use of this data by packaging it and selling it. Commercial pressure can result in favorable treatment of preferred partners. Some exchanges format key economic data releases, so that they can be read by trading algorithms. A further revenue-generating activity is working with high-frequency trading firms, allowing them to co-locate their servers with those of the exchange to reduce latency, i.e., to increase speed of communication, taking milliseconds off trade times.

Market makers

Citadel Securities executes about 28% of US retail equities volume as well as making markets in more than 7,000 US-listed securities and in about 18,000 over the counter (OTC) securities worldwide.

Market makers are an integral part of stock exchange activities. They play a significant role in share price movements, especially in the short term. Their role and how this varies across the NYSE, the Nasdaq, and the LSE has been described in *Chapter 3 – Stock markets.* It is evident that the role of the market makers is particularly significant on the Nasdaq, where all trades go through a market maker. Because the Nasdaq is an electronic communications network (ECN), large numbers of market makers work remotely and compete fiercely. The Nasdaq market makers hold inventories of shares and trade aggressively on their own account as well as for their clients. Many of them are high-frequency traders. Market makers have a responsibility to maintain bid and offer quotes through the trading day, up to normal or exchange market size, while keeping an orderly market in the shares, using their inventories as needed.

Another area where competing market makers are particularly active is the smaller cap stocks on the LSE. As of February 2014, there were 23 registered market makers. The market makers are appointed by the stock exchange and take on an obligation to buy and sell shares up to normal market size, providing liquidity when the market is unable to do so. There is usually a minimum of two market makers per share, and the competition between market makers helps to keep spreads down. For more detail, search London Stock Exchange market makers. About eight market makers profile themselves on the LSE website, and these give interesting insights into their range of activities.

It is important to recognize that market makers are traders in their own right, and day traders in particular need to have some understanding of their behaviors – which are driven by their need to generate profits. Market makers make money in a number of ways, including:

- From trading their own inventory of shares. They will seek to capture momentum moves, long or short, especially where there is strong liquidity.
- They may employ high-frequency trading strategies to gain advantage.
- By earning commissions from institutional clients, buying and selling shares for them. They will often take large orders and guarantee an average buy or sell price. A common tactic is to drop price aggressively to panic shareholders into selling cheap, in order to enable the market maker to fill an order for a client.
- From the bid-offer spread – the difference between buying and selling a share is profit for the market maker.
- They will undertake arbitrage, buying in one market and selling the same or a similar security in another, looking to earn a riskless profit.
- They will loan shares from their inventory for shorting purposes for a fee.

When trading volumes become too low, the market maker will adjust his spread to stimulate activity. Market makers stay in close touch with market sentiment around shares that they make a market in. If a small cap firm with low liquidity reports well, the market maker will anticipate this and proactively manage price and spread accordingly – the share price is likely to gap up on market opening.

The overall impact of market makers is generally regarded as beneficial to the majority of market participants, as they contribute to the efficient operation of markets. However, if you search the Internet for <u>market maker tricks</u> (for example, Investopedia), you will find quite a lot of material.

Index companies

> *S&P Dow Jones Indices – Mission: 'As the world's largest resource for index-based innovation, data, and research, our mission is to bring independent, transparent, and cost effective solutions to the global investment community. S&P Dow Jones Indices is at the forefront of index change and innovation. Our goal is to continue to anticipate and respond to how our clients see global investment opportunities.'*

Stock exchange indices and the companies that run them have been mentioned in *Chapter 3 – Stock markets.*

The importance of indices has increased, in particular with the shift towards tracker funds and the emergence of ETFs, many of which are also based on indices. They are also the basis for index futures trading.

There are now hundreds of thousands of indices, many of them highly specialized, and even bespoke for clients with very specific needs. With the provision of new indices, index companies open up new investment markets.

A striking example of the importance of index companies was the decision in 2015 by MSCI to delay inclusion of Chinese mainland shares – the A-shares – in the MSCI Emerging Markets Index. The reasoning was that further progress was needed in opening up this market to global institutional investors. Inclusion of the A-shares in the index would have led to a rebalancing of funds and ETFs tracking the MSCI index. MSCI's proposal was to admit A-shares to the index at just 5% of their market value, and this would have induced fund managers to switch around US$20bn into these shares. Admitting them at 100% of market value would have resulted in a flow of US$400bn out of other assets into A-shares. The decision by MSCI not to admit A-shares in 2015 is thought to be one of the factors leading to the 2015 crash in the Chinese stock markets.

Green campaigners encourage the development of 'green companies.' The Nasdaq Stock Exchange runs the Nasdaq Clean Edge Green Energy Index (CELS). Established in 2006, by late 2015 the index – containing 46 companies – was down about 20%, compared with a rise in the S&P 500 of about 50%.

Investment advisers

US

The advisory terrain in the US is complex. Search FINRA Choosing an Investment Professional for a useful overview. An Investment Adviser (IA) owes a fiduciary duty to his clients, which is described by the SEC as follows:

'As an investment adviser, you are a 'fiduciary' to your advisory clients. This means that you have a fundamental obligation to act in the best interests of your clients and to provide investment advice in your clients' best interests. You owe your clients a duty of undivided loyalty and utmost good faith.'

You can find the full description by searching SEC Information for Newly Registered Investment Advisers.

IAs managing less than US$110mn are regulated at state level. An IA managing more than this must register with the SEC and is then a Registered Investment Adviser. An IA can be a firm or an individual, and the spelling of 'Adviser' is that used in US financial law. IAs advise on investing in securities, mainly shares, mutual funds, ETFs, and bonds and usually charge a fee negotiated in advance.

UK

In the UK, an Independent Financial Adviser (IFA) provides impartial advice to the retail investor. Since 2013, IFAs have been required to charge fees rather than receive commissions from investment product providers.

In 2015, the Financial Conduct Authority reported that about two-thirds of financial products are sold without reference to an IFA, indicating that the public at large is not too comfortable with paying supposedly transparent fees as opposed to hidden commissions. Many IFAs are not publishing fees on their websites, preferring to sell face-to-face. Unsurprisingly, some IFAs are charging fees at rip-off levels.

The website unbiased.co.uk will help you to find an IFA and gives guidance on reasonable levels of fees for various services.

Corporate or house stockbrokers

Many stockbrokers specialize in services to corporations, and are known as corporate, or house, stockbrokers.

Listed companies employ such stockbrokers to advise them on corporate affairs. A large cap company may well have more than one house broker. It is not uncommon for a company to be re-graded by another division under the same corporate umbrella as its house broker.

Corporate stockbroking services include:

- Helping to present and promote the company as a good investment
- Company analysis
- Monitoring and analyzing share price performance
- Assisting with liaison with the investment community and responding to concerns
- Corporate finance, including raising capital and underwriting initial public offering (IPO) if the company is pre-float
- Advice on capital structure and share register
- Rights issues – raising new investment
- Corporate strategy
- Mergers & Acquisitions (M&A) – company valuations and how company activity in this area is likely to be viewed by the markets, e.g., assessing overseas acquisitions, usually regarded as high risk
- Balance sheet restructuring

Retail stockbrokers

These days, a great deal of stockbroking is through execution-only online trading platforms with inexpensive trading fees. Platforms may provide some trading support.

Stockbrokers also provide advisory services and discretionary portfolio management where they are authorized by the client to trade on his behalf.

In the US, Registered Representatives (RR) provide an advisory service to retail clients on a fee or commission basis. They may be subcontractors sponsored by a brokerage. RRs are primarily securities salespeople, who may also describe themselves as stockbrokers/account executives – or as financial advisors, financial consultants, or investment consultants. They are legally bound to point out that they are not providing an Investment Adviser service, as described above, and they are not allowed to offer financial planning services, except in accounts regulated as investment advisory accounts.

In the UK, stockbroking firms usually provide advisory services by in-house stockbrokers, routinely on a commission basis. There is a large number of small and medium sized stockbrokers that will cater to the retail investor. The quality of service is variable and sometimes poor, despite regulatory attempts to raise standards.

The activities of US and UK stockbrokers are described in more detail in *Chapter 17 – Using a stockbroker.*

The analysts

In October 2013, Citigroup was fined US$30mn for passing unpublished research to clients, including SAC Capital, a hedge fund with a reputation for sailing close to the wind. This gave them an opportunity to trade on weaker sales of Apple's iPhone ahead of other investors. The analyst responsible was fired.

Company research analysts work for brokerages, investment banks, and research companies, and prepare reports on companies, industries, and markets for the investment community. Analysts are the most important source of information on companies and their prospects.

The sell-side and buy-side analysts

It was reported in May 2014, that based on cash flow, more than half of a major UK retailer's value lay beyond 2023 – possibly an analyst with an over-optimistic view of his ability to forecast company earnings.

The job of company analysts is to develop a quantitative understanding of businesses, their opportunities and prospects, and the risks that they face. The analyst is in a position to provide advice in a range of circumstances, but his most visible activity to the retail investor will be forecasting company performance and the determination of target prices for company shares. This activity is undertaken by the sell-side analysts, who seek to encourage investors to buy a particular share, and pay a commission or fee to the analyst's company.

Buy-side analysts are usually employed by major investors, such as fund managers, to provide in-house advice on investment opportunities – sifting through all the recommendations from the sell-side analysts, as well as a great deal of other market information, and advising the fund manager on the best investment opportunities. They will be more concerned about an objective assessment of a company than the sell-side analysts, who may err on the optimistic side. As they do not publish their research reports, the buy-side analysts are not of interest to regulators.

Both types of analyst will create equity valuation models for companies – often quite complex – and gather as much information as possible to feed into and update their models. But then they will use the outputs in different ways. An investment bank is likely to employ both sell-side and buy-side analysts who may well work with the same company financial models, but interpret them in different ways.

As well as looking at company earnings, analysts will also concern themselves with companies as acquisition targets and in terms of their breakup value. This requires deep understanding of a company down to divisional level.

It is the activities of the sell-side analysts that are of interest to the retail investor and which are addressed in some detail here.

Sell-side analysts

In 2014, it was reported that the shares in a major resource firm rose sharply after it had closed out a takeover, and the banks involved were now free to push the company's share to their clients.

Some typical firms undertaking research are Jefferies, UBS, Nomura, Morgan Stanley, Wells Fargo, Stifel, and Deutsche Bank. Companies have an incentive to engage with the analyst community in order to generate interest in their company shares.

A sell-side analyst follows the fortunes of companies closely, absorbing reports and news. A highly rated analyst working for a top brokerage is likely to be commissioned by a client, usually a fund manager, to research a particular company on a confidential, remunerated basis. Such reports may not be made available to the markets at large. A less highly rated analyst is likely to select his own research targets, and advertise his recommendations widely in the media. His motivation will be to identify companies that represent good value, and persuade institutions to invest in them – paying commissions to his firm. Sell-side analysts may send their reports directly to fund managers, who will then assess these reports, if they read them, together with assessments from their own buy-side analysts. A report may be made available to important clients without charge. Others, including the retail investor, will have to pay for them.

There is a great deal of competition between sell-side analysts, who are therefore constantly seeking out new information and perspectives, and endeavoring to get in front of potential buyers before the rest. Meetings with company management are highly valued by analysts. Many large cap companies hold regular analysts meetings while smaller companies will meet analysts on a selective basis. Only analysts with a favorable disposition to the company are likely to get meetings, and this can introduce a further element of upside bias. Analysts will also visit a company's facilities, e.g., a new production plant or a new flagship store.

Analyst recommendations and target price

> *When the Canadian pharmaceutical company Valeant's share price crashed from US$250 to under US$40 in late 2015/early 2016, only two important analysts switched to sell, reinforcing the suspicion that a great deal of sell-side analyst research is biased, possibly due to their propensity to cosy up to corporate management in a quest for new business.*

Sell-side analyst reports move individual share prices every trading day. Each report will include a forecast of earnings per share for a company, together with a target share price (TP). Timeframe for reaching TP is not given, but you should probably think in terms of months rather than years, in large part because even medium-term forecasts are notoriously unreliable. Based on his research, the analyst will make a simple recommendation such as:

- Strong buy, sometimes even conviction buy
- Buy
- Add
- Hold
- Reduce
- Sell
- Strong sell

As well as studying the detailed financial performance of a company, analysts also take account of macroeconomic factors, performance of sector peers, commodity price trends, relevant economic data, etc., as well as paying attention to guidance provided by companies. Analysts continually re-rate companies based on these factors. Particularly attractive to analysts is a company that has made a long series of earnings upgrades. Such companies are likely to be 'strong buys.' Conversely, it will only take one or two profit warnings to send a company sliding down the scale.

Active fund managers seek to beat a benchmark index, and analysts also advise whether a portfolio should be overweight or underweight a particular company share, in relation to its market cap weighting in the index. Another analyst practice is to keep a buy list and to add and remove companies as circumstances change. When analysts announce changes to their buy lists, this can move share prices.

A recent, perhaps a little unfair, characterization of analyst advice is as follows:

➢ Long-term buy – the share price has got ahead of itself

➢ Fairly valued – overvalued

➢ Add – it might come back

➢ Hold – sell

Analyst coverage

August 2014: a major European company moves its treasury staff to London. Its share price is at a discount to its sector and it wants to raise its profile with analysts with a view to raising investor interest and its share price.

There will be a number of analysts following large cap companies, perhaps 15 or more, leading to a constant flow of upgrades and downgrades, possibly 100 or more through the year. Many of the reports will be issued after a major event such as an earnings report, or an interim management statement. A significant unplanned event, such as a competitor going out of business, will cause the analysts to reassess.

Small cap firms may have only one or two analysts covering them, and some may have none. This can result in very substantial share price movements when such companies report. Smaller companies can be less good at managing market expectations – made more difficult when analysts only look at them from time to time. It's easier when coverage is more consistent.

Some companies list analysts' recommendations on the investor pages of their websites.

In the US, search Nasdaq Markets/Analyst Activity//Upgrades/Downgrades to find data from about 90 major brokerage firms. Nasdaq updates its table three times a day.

Another useful source is MarketWatch tools stock research updown.

In the UK, search <u>DigitalLook</u>, enter a company name or ticker and then click on <u>What The Brokers Say</u> for a chronological list of <u>Broker Views</u>. For a market wide list of brokers' views, search <u>DigitalLook UK shares broker views</u>.

These web pages give Target Prices (TP).

Analyst consensus

Brokerage and market information websites collate analysts' forecasts to create a consensus in the form of a mean and a range. This creates a market expectation. When a company reports, its results will be compared rapidly with the market expectation. For a large cap company, there will be many sell-side analysts. Sometimes there will be a strong consensus, e.g., most analysts on buy or strong buy. At the other end of the spectrum, there can be quite divergent views across the body of analysts.

You will find summaries of brokers' forecasts on a great many financial information websites. An example summary of analyst recommendations is shown in Table 6.1.

Recommendation	Number of analysts
Strong buy	8
Buy	2
Hold	1
Sell	2
Strong sell	3

Table 6.1 Typical analyst recommendations

Such summaries of recommendations are often presented by commentators and journalists at face value. If you look below the surface, you may find that the sell recommendations are quite out of date, and that since the company last reported, there has been a series of strong buy recommendations.

After a company reports, or in response to significant news or events, the analysts will reassess TP. The forecast TPs after a report should be the best informed.

It's useful to monitor how analyst recommendations are changing with time. This is referred to as momentum. Average broker recommendation (ABR) or consensus is calculated and monitored. The <u>Nasdaq</u> website provides a helpful summary of consensus recommendations, including momentum. Type a company ticker into the <u>Nasdaq</u> search box and go to <u>Stock Analysis/Analyst Research</u>.

The fortunes of companies can change rapidly. There is no guarantee that the share price will rise towards TP. Analysts are not always impartial! Some of the brokers that they work for may have a conflict of interest through making a market in the share, or as a result of being house stockbroker to the company and receiving a fee. Also keep in mind that there could be some influential reports that are only made available to the clients of particular sell-side analysts. While sell-side analysts will downgrade companies on a regular basis – e.g., from hold to sell – as a generalization, they make more upgrades than downgrades.

TP is a useful guide but cannot be taken as authoritative. The forecast time frames are not specific, but are quite short-term. The concept is that if the company has a following wind, or the headwinds are not too strong, then it will do well and the share price will rise to its target level. Think of TP as the level at which a share becomes fully valued and ripe for profit taking. When considering buying a share, look for some measure of headroom between the current share price and the consensus of forecasts, though sometimes there is little headroom. If there is a serious market crash, or sector crash, then quite possibly it will be that all bets are off.

A series of 'strong buys' after a company has reported doesn't mean that you should rush to buy the share. The chances are it has already risen as a result of the forecasts. As soon as an analyst's report has been published, personal networks go into overdrive, and by the time a hard-pressed retail investor catches up with the report, a significant price movement may have already occurred. Sometimes analysts' reports are leaked in advance of official publication.

If all you had to do was check TP before buying a share, then everyone would be a successful investor. The broker forecasts are often wrong, or overtaken by events, or indeed conflicted. Nevertheless, broker forecasts move share prices and a review of them should always be made before making an investment decision.

A series of 'strong buys' coupled with good momentum could cause you to put the company on your watchlist. See *Chapter 14 – Share selection methodology.*

Analyst influence

A share price can fall heavily on results that meet expectations, on an analyst recommendation to take profit.

Analyst forecasts are fundamental to company share valuations and the retail investor should follow them closely. However, there are a number of things to bear in mind.

As we have seen, there is a possibility of upside bias from the sell-side analysts and the assessments of the buy-side analysts are not available to the market at large.

Analysts carry different levels of weight in the marketplace. The Institutional Investor website provides rankings of analysts. Some analysts will have covered a company or a sector for years and their reports are likely to have the greatest authority in the market. Some analysts can get very prolific, pumping out numerous reports – seeking to drum up business and to build their reputations. Their research may be of dubious quality. The retail investor will find it hard going to develop an understanding of which analysts have the strongest reputation with any particular company, or to discern the quality of an analyst's work.

There will be friendly relationships between many fund managers and analysts. Professional traders are likely to have an extensive network of contacts with analysts, and will receive their reports in close to real time. The traders in the investment banks and hedge funds will receive phone calls from the analysts that they know best, as soon as the analyst is able (from a regulatory standpoint) to make the call, and chat rooms will be active. Retail traders and investors should take account of this in determining their strategies. Short-term traders will be at the greatest disadvantage.

Analyst reports

S&P Capital IQ is a main source of current and historical research reports from a global network of around 1,500 brokers and researchers. It is a subscription service used by professional investors. Most major brokerages sell their reports through this service. FactSet is another significant source of analyst reports.

In the UK, the Financial Times website makes available, for a fee, analyst reports from a range of sources. Search markets.ft.com/research/Markets Company Name.

Market information companies Morningstar and Zacks employ their own analysts and make their reports available on a subscription basis.

Hargreaves Lansdown provides research reports on a number of important FTSE companies.

For a useful article on accessing analyst reports, search Matt Krantz, Investing Online for Dummies, How to Access Analyst Reports Online.

Regulation of analysts

The activities of sell-side analysts in the US and UK are regulated.

In the US, regulation around the publication of research reports is strict and sell-side or Wall Street research analysts must register with the Financial Industry Regulatory Authority (FINRA). They are required to pass the General Securities Representative Exam as well as the Research Analyst Examination (series 86/series 87) in order to publish research for the purpose of selling or promoting publicly traded securities. In the UK, the regulatory regime appears to be less stringent.

Many firms in both the US and UK expect their analysts to achieve the Chartered Financial Analyst (CFA) designation through a series of exams.

Research reports move prices, and should not be made available to different parties at different times. Investment banks, which may have sell-side analysts, buy-side analysts, traders, house stockbrokers, and market makers under the same roof, go to some lengths to maintain confidentiality between these different activities but the record shows that they meet with varying degrees of success in managing these conflicts of interest. Noncompliance can result in heavy fines.

In the UK, rumours will often fly around and be reported in the mainstream press before a report is published, and just the rumour of a good or bad report pending can create a great deal of share price movement, e.g., 'a positive analyst report is expected to land on fund managers' desks the next day' or 'a particular share price was up today on expectation of an upbeat analyst circular.'

In the UK, the FCA is looking at the payment by fund managers and analysts for access to top corporate management. These meetings are facilitated by brokerage firms, and cost around £500mn per annum. Needless to say, the retail investor does not have access to the information that passes at such meetings.

The retail market

The percentage of US adults owning shares peaked at around 65% in 2007, and since then has been subject to a slow rate of decline. According to the Office of National Statistics, ownership of UK shares by individuals has fallen from 54% in 1963 to under 11% in 2012.

When stock markets have lost half their value twice in twenty years, it is not surprising that many people are turning their backs on investing in shares.

Retail investors

The community of active retail investors has a significant influence on stock markets, both directly and through its influence on sentiment. But who makes up this community? Well, just individuals who actively manage their investments – sometimes not very well – as opposed to those who simply put their money into funds or a number of shares, pay little attention to them, and simply hope for the best. They will vary from astute, high net worth individuals, often working with a trusted stockbroker, to someone who simply takes a punt on a well-known share.

There is a view, quite possibly with some truth in it, that many retail investors buy high and sell cheap. Perhaps piling in when the markets are hitting highs – afraid of missing out – and selling after sharp pullbacks have already occurred – cutting their losses. Some will be capable of making a good assessment of the state of the markets, and in identifying the right shares to buy. Many will simply follow share tips in magazines, newspapers, and websites. Many investments are made on a hunch – 'surely this share price can't fall any further' – or perhaps just following the herd.

The US has more active retail investors than anywhere else, and they make considerable use of mutual funds – pooled investments. The UK equivalents are OEICs and unit trusts. An increasing amount of retail investor money is invested through ETFs. Market strategists monitor flows of money in and out of these funds as they try to discern stock market trends – these fund flows have a significant impact on market sentiment.

The major players mentioned above will make the weather, but active retail investors will add to the momentum of individual share price movements, as they over- and undershoot.

In a strongly rising market when correlation is likely to be high, most share prices will rise and the retail investor needs to guard against overconfidence. Correlation will break down when the markets are high and macroeconomic factors have receded – and if there are no significant tail risks in the air. In these conditions, skilful share selection will be at a premium.

There are probably a lot more non-active retail investors than there are active ones. These are the darlings of the fund management industry, which earns its commissions on monies that stay invested year in year out, without having to do very much. If more retail investors were to switch out of poorly performing funds, the fund management industry would have to work harder.

The sources of data and information available to the retail investor – a great deal of it online - are vast, and many useful sources are referenced in this book.

Investment platforms

There are many web-based investment platforms that support investment in funds and individual shares. These provide both general market information as well as information to support investment decisions. Thereby they facilitate participation as well as exerting some influence on the markets. Some websites will provide information on their customers' investments in real time, for example, 'most looked at share today.' So they have the possibility to influence share price movements, while stopping short of providing investment advice.

A strong theme of this book is that the retail investor should invest through a combination of funds and shares. It makes sense to use an investment platform that supports both types of investment.

Investment platforms are discussed in some detail in *Chapter 10 – Trading* and *Chapter 12 – About funds.*

Financial websites

The proliferation of financial websites, many of them excellent, is greatly empowering, enabling the active retail investor to be better informed than ever before. Skilful use of data and information from these websites puts the retail investor who is prepared to make some effort in a position to outperform many professional investors – but probably not the best professional traders.

Undoubtedly these websites are a significant influence on the markets. Some influential financial websites are:

- Morningstar
- DigitalLook
- Zacks
- Nasdaq
- CNN Money
- Benzinga
- Kiplinger
- This is money (UK only)

Private equity

Many companies, perhaps family owned, are never listed. Also, companies are taken off the stock market from time to time by private equity companies, e.g., Alliance Boots was taken off the London stock market in 2007 by the American private equity firm Kohlberg, Kravis Roberts, and the Italian businessman Stefano Pessina. If the markets pick up that private equity is interested in a particular company, its share price is likely to rise sharply.

During 2014 and 2015, many private equity companies were looking to float or re-float, i.e., to make an initial public offering (IPO). The markets were high at the beginning of 2014, so many IPOs were rushed out to exploit this and some of them were priced too richly, with the share price falling away from its float level.

Some fairly recent high-profile IPOs include:

- Alibaba, whose share price surged to US$120 shortly after flotation, and then over the next six months declined to around US$60.
- Facebook floated in early 2012 at a price of around US$40, which promptly fell to under US$20. Since then is has confounded the analysts, and in 2015 the share price was testing US$100.
- The Royal Mail was floated at 450 pence in 2013 to accusations that it had been priced too low. The share price soared to over 600 pence before embarking on a roller coaster ride and settling down at around 450 pence.

There is an IPO lock-up period which prevents insiders from selling shares in a period before the flotation. Search Investopedia lock-up for details.

There are websites that provide information on IPOs, recent and upcoming. In the US, search MarketWatch IPO Calendar for a useful source.

In the UK, Hargreaves Lansdown provides information on 'expected' and 'rumored' IPOs. Search Hargreaves Lansdown ipos new issues.

Predator companies

As discussed in the previous chapter, a company seeking to take over another company is often referred to as a predator. It will sometimes start by building a shareholding in a target company discretely, to avoid the share price moving up against them. However, when its shareholding reaches a certain level set by regulation, it must make a declaration to the market. This is likely to cause a sharp increase in the share price of the target company – rightly or wrongly, the market believes that the predator company will be prepared to pay a premium on the price. Perhaps because of synergies from the acquisition that it expects to exploit; extra geographical coverage; or possibly it has identified some new market opportunities that it will be able to exploit. Rumors and speculation prior to any declaration can have the same effect.

Traders and investors, often working for hedge funds, will have a view on which companies are most likely to be takeover targets, and will often build speculative positions in them, causing the share price to rise. If it becomes clear that the acquisition is going to fall through, the target's share price can fall as far and as fast as it rose. So this is fertile ground for traders.

Corporate interests

As we have seen, companies transact in their own shares in a number of ways, including:

- Through rights issues – issuing additional shares, which reduces earnings per share.
- Through share buybacks – usually the shares are cancelled and this increases earnings per share.
- Issuing new shares for employee share option schemes. These schemes are used to incentivize and reward managers and key staff. For example, Long-term Incentive Plans – LTIPs – are commonly used in the UK.

Rights issues and buybacks in particular can lead to significant share price movements.

Company insiders

An insider is a director or senior officer of a company or any person/entity that owns more than 10% of a company's voting shares. In the UK, the shorthand 'Director Deals' is often used instead of 'Insider.'

Company insiders/directors must declare transactions in their own shares, in the interests of transparency and fairness. These are keenly observed by market participants as they can give insights into the prospects of a company. A director may judge that his company's share price has got ahead of itself (sell), or that the company is positioned for a strong recovery (buy). Or he may simply need the money!

Many websites provide information on deals, including Morningstar and Hargreaves Lansdown. Director Deals is a specialist website providing extensive data on insider/director transactions.

In the UK, the Weekend Financial Times provides a weekly summary.

Founders and owners

Founder shareholders can exert significant influence on a company's management, even though they no longer hold a majority of the shares – in fact, they may never have held a majority.

They can seek to influence executive appointments, investment programs, and dividend policy – quite often preferring to cut back on investment to increase dividend payouts.

Bill Gates of Microsoft is probably the most famous founder shareholder. He stepped down as chairman in 2014, having stepped aside from the company in 2008 to focus on his foundation.

Several of the large resource companies listed on the London Stock Exchange have powerful founders and major shareholders on the company boards who sometimes exert controversial influence.

Sir Stelios Haji-Ioannou, founder of Easyjet, became a turbulent shareholder after he handed over the management of the company, concerning himself with dividend policy and investment strategy.

Aggressive intervention by major shareholders can lead to volatility in a company's share price.

Short sellers

Short selling is an important dynamic in the stock market and is covered in *Chapter 8*. There are firms that specialize in short selling and hedge funds are prolific short sellers.

A great many trading and investment strategies are long only. However, market participants are increasingly using long/short strategies, which makes sense when markets are judged to be high. In addition, both traders and investors will take short positions on a tactical basis when they believe an index or a share price is ready for a significant fall.

Traders

Traders come in all shapes and sizes, ranging from high-frequency traders operating out of specialist trading houses to those who have a perspective perhaps up to several months. A common characteristic is that they are concerned with short-term price movements rather than with the long-term performance of the companies whose shares they are trading. They exert a strong influence on short-term share price movements, adding to volatility and to share price momentum in both directions. They will also seek to relieve inexperienced traders and investors of their money.

Trading is covered in some detail in *Chapter 10*.

Futures and options traders

Trading of indices on the futures markets has become a very significant factor in stock market trading. This is a form of derivative trading, as the value of the index is traded. The S&P 500 index is the most traded. Index futures trading volume is steadily increasing at the expense of the stock exchange cash markets.

The original purpose of index futures trading was to hedge against adverse movements in share prices, but now a main purpose is simply to generate profit. Futures contracts, i.e., to buy or sell the index at a future price, have to be met.

Options to buy or sell an index at a future date are also available for payment of a premium. Options by definition don't have to be exercised, but no one would want to exercise an option to buy at price that is above current market value, in which case the premium is lost. After purchase, options are commonly traded. Again, the purpose is hedging – or simply to make money. The options market is complex and mainly the preserve of professionals or highly skilled retail investors.

Futures and options trading is discussed in more detail in *Chapter 9*.

High-frequency traders

High-frequency trading has a significant influence on short-term share price movements. HF traders operate in both the cash markets and the futures derivative markets.

HF trading is a controversial activity. Specialist high-frequency trading houses systematically make money using virtually risk-free techniques. They claim legitimacy on the basis that they contribute significantly to liquidity in the markets.

A fuller discussion of HF trading is contained in *Chapter 10 – Trading.*

Financial information groups

Information drives markets and moves share prices. Unsurprisingly, provision of information is big business. People are prepared to pay for it – quite often a great deal – especially if they can get it fast and before their competitors.

A number of financial information groups, including Bloomberg and Reuters, have been mentioned in the previous chapter. A particularly significant service provided by these groups is chat rooms, which provide a means for information sharing, and even collaboration by market participants.

There are numerous financial websites offering investment and trading services, and all use provision of data and information to attract users.

Media

Media, in all its forms, both informs and influences all market participants, and has been discussed in the previous chapter.

Academics

Academics, especially those in the business schools, play an important role in the stock markets. Their greatest influence probably lies in the area of government and central bank policy.

Perhaps the most famous 'academic' in the world of finance is Ben Bernanke, who served two terms as chairman of the US Federal Reserve from 2006 to 2014, guiding the US economy through the financial crisis and the recovery – and overseeing the bold quantitative easing program, which pumped liquidity into the markets. Prior to serving at the Fed, Bernanke taught economics at a number of prestigious US business schools. In May 2015 it was announced that Bernanke had taken two new advisory roles – at Citadel, the Chicago-based securities firm, and Pimco, the California-based asset manager, specialized in bonds

As the financial crisis recedes into the past, there will be many academic studies on the impact of central bank policy, in particular in the US and Europe – and in Japan.

Other famous academics include <u>Robert Shiller of Yale University</u> who invented the influential, cyclically adjusted price-to-earnings ratio, commonly known as CAPE or Shiller P/E; and James Tobin who, together with William Brainard, introduced 'Tobin's Q' – the ratio between the market value and replacement value of a physical asset. See *Chapter 4 – About shares and shares are valued.*

The Sharpe ratio for risk-adjusted investment performance analysis, widely used by the fund management industry, was created by Professor Bill Sharpe of Stanford University School of Business.

Professor Eugene Fama has already been mentioned in *Chapter 4* in relation to efficient markets. Fama has undertaken important work on asset pricing with <u>Professor Kenneth French</u>.

As well as undertaking strategic studies of interest to governments and central banks, academics will undertake studies on such matters as high-frequency trading and its impact on the market and the influence of short selling on markets. Such studies are of considerable interest to policymakers and regulators.

At a technical level, academics work with commercial organizations e.g., developing sophisticated trading systems.

Regulators

US

At a federal level, the US Securities and Exchange Commission is the primary securities regulator and oversees the activities of the US stock exchanges. Futures trading is regulated by the Commodity Futures Trading Commission.

Broker-dealers are regulated by the Financial Industry Regulatory Authority (FINRA), which is a self-regulatory organization, formed from the merger of the enforcement divisions of the National Association of Securities Dealers and the New York Stock Exchange.

In addition, FINRA overseas the Securities Investor Protection Corporation (SIPC).

There is also legal oversight at state level, e.g., in recent times, Preet Bahara, US Attorney General for the Southern District of New York, vigorously prosecuted dozens of cases of insider trading accompanied by an increase in the severity of sentencing.

UK

In the UK, the Financial Conduct Authority supervises the financial services industry, deriving its remit from the Financial Services Act of 2012. Its remit falls into three main categories: consumer protection; protection and enhancement of the integrity of the UK financial system; and promotion of competition in the interests of consumers.

The FCA operates independently of the UK government, and is financed by fees charged to members of the financial services industry.

7 Recent history – and what we can learn

Introduction

Between October 1929 and July 1932, the Dow Jones Industrial Average fell from 381 to 41, a fall of 89%. Leading up to this, the market had been on a nine-year bull run that saw the Dow increase tenfold. This was the greatest stock market fall in history. The index did not reach 381 again until 1954.

If you are going to invest successfully, you need to be able to make an assessment of the current state of the market and likely future scenarios. For this, you will need to have some historical perspective – otherwise you will be flying blind. A great many people in the financial services industry constantly advise that it is impossible to time the market, so you shouldn't bother to try. This proposition is examined in this chapter.

As well as wanting to make money in the stock market, another crucial consideration is the preservation of your capital. So you need to understand the crashes as well as the bull runs.

In this section, the behavior of the markets is described mainly through the lenses of the S&P 500, which represents about 75% by capitalization of the entire US market in publicly traded shares, and the FTSE 100, which represents about 80% of the London Stock Exchange market capitalization. It is widely accepted that the S&P 500 is the most important stock market index, and it influences all other major world indices. There is a clear correlation between the S&P 500 and the FTSE 100 indices, though in percentage terms, the S&P 500 has strongly outperformed the FTSE 100, with a particularly strong surge ahead from 2013. The FTSE 100 global companies simply could not keep up with the US powerhouse of the S&P 500.

For the purposes of this chapter, recent history starts in 1987, the year of the Black Monday stock market crash. We take a look at the 1987 crash and then the crashes of 2001 and 2008 that got underway in 2000 and 2007, respectively. The 1987 fall, around 34%, was not as severe as the dramatic falls that took place in 2001 and 2008, which were around 50%. However, the 1987 crash was notable by the sheer speed of the fall, with the S&P 500 losing 20.6% in a single day, infamously remembered as Black Monday.

Charts

To get the most out of this chapter, you will need to go online and access some charts. The following are used.

For the main indices

YAHOO! FINANCE is a good source for main index charts. In the US, search <u>usa finance.yahoo.com</u>; in the UK, search <u>uk finance yahoo</u>.

Both show the Dow, S&P 500, and Nasdaq 100 indices on their home pages. The US site usefully shows the futures indices before the main cash markets open. The UK & Ireland site shows the US indices together with the FTSE 100, FTSE 250, and AIM (Alternative Investment Market) indices. The YAHOO! FINANCE charts have excellent functionality. They allow you to select a time frame up to 5 years, and then the next option is Max, which takes you back to 1950. If you click on <u>Basic Tech. Analysis</u>, you will be given a range of options. You can select <u>Linear</u> or <u>Log</u> for the vertical scale. Log is better for judging percentage movements. You can overlay a number of useful metrics, such as moving averages and relative strength index (RSI).

Another good source of charts is <u>Google Finance</u>. To bring up the S&P 500, click under <u>World Markets</u> on the right of the page, or if it's not there just insert S&P 500 into the search box. The Google chart has the ability to scroll back to 1975, allowing you to see episodes of activity in detail, e.g., a sharp pullback or a crash.

You can compare indices and individual share price indices with each other. It's useful to know the symbols for the major indices. The YAHOO! FINANCE and Google charts recognize different symbols. See Table 7.1.

Index	YAHOO! FINANCE	Google
S&P 500	^GSPC	.INX
Dow	^DJI	.DJI
Nasdaq 100	^NDX	NDX
FTSE 100	^FTSE	UKX
FTSE 250	^FTMC	MCX
DAX	^DAXI	DAX
CAC	^FCHI	PX1

Table 7.1 Index symbols

As an example, bring up the S&P 500 chart on Google Finance, and then add the Dow, Nasdaq 100, FTSE 100, and FTSE 250 by typing the symbol into the Compare box and clicking on Add. You can then compare the performance of these indices over various time frames.

Charts for the crashes

When we discuss the share price movements during the great crashes of 1987, 2001, and 2008, charts covering the episodes can be found at:

sniper.at S&P 500	1987	Search Sniper.at stock market crash of 1987
Jesse Colombo Dow	1987	Search Thebubblebubble.com/1987-crash
Istockanalyst S&P 500	2001	Search Istockanalyst.com/article/viewarticle/articleid/2688817
TheArmoTrader S&P 500	2008	Search jerrykhachoyan.com/how-the-retail-investor-was-lost-forever

Table 7.2 Charts for the crashes

Charts for P/E ratios

As we have seen, price/earnings ratio (P/E), is a simple and broadly used measure of share valuation where P is price per share and E is earnings per share – EPS. In this chapter, we work with average P/E for the companies in an index. Current valuations are conventionally based on the last, or trailing, 12 month's earnings – 'trailing twelve months' is often abbreviated to TTM. Forward P/E, based on a consensus of analyst forecasts for the next 12 months, is another broadly used metric.

Professor Robert Shiller has proposed a refined approach to market valuations, using a modified P/E ratio. P is current price, while earnings are the average, inflation-adjusted earnings from the previous 10 years. This is known as the cyclically adjusted PE ratio – CAPE ratio. This is also known as the Shiller PE ratio, or PE 10. The concept of CAPE is to take a long-term look at a company's earning power through the economic cycles. It is worth noting that the idea of 10-year averaging was conceived in 1988, after the Black Monday crash of 1987 but before the great crashes of 2001 and 2008 – which are not necessarily helpful to the concept of smoothing data.

It's worth staying in touch with these ratios, and Internet sources for them are provided below.

S&P 500 12-month trailing P/E

You will find a number of charts on the Internet for the S&P 500 12-month trailing P/E ratio. They do not provide consistent data. However, as we saw in *Chapter 5,* a plausible dataset from 1929 to 2014 is provided by Seeking Alpha and Bespoke Investment Group and can be found by searching <u>Seeking Alpha S and P 500 historical p-e ratio</u>.

The dot.com crash of 2001 stands out clearly, with trailing P/E reaching 30, but the financial crisis that was brewing in 2007 does not, with trailing P/E around 16 – which is not exceptionally high.

During 2014 and 2015, the S&P 500 trailing P/E was ranging up towards 20.

CAPE – Robert Shiller's Cyclically Adjusted P/E ratio

As we saw in *Chapter 5,* a chart of CAPE P/E ratio, for the S&P 500, from 1890 to 2010 can be found by searching <u>Gurufocus shiller – PE</u>.

A chart covering the same time can be found by <u>Marketwatch what shiller pe ratio says about markets top</u>.

For a chart going back to 1880, search <u>multpl shiller – pe.</u>

CAPE shows the great stock market crash of 1929 very clearly. Also, with the CAPE P/E, the 2000/01 crash stands out more sharply than in the basic P/E chart. Its value of around 27 in 2007 is more exceptional than the 12-month P/E at around 16.

At the outset of 2016, the Cape Ratio for the S&P 500 was approaching 25, more than one standard deviation above the long-term average of around 16.

It's easy enough to keep an eye on both the 12-month and CAPE charts, so that's what the proactive retail investor should do.

S&P 500 12-month forward P/E

FactSet provides a chart of S&P 500 forward 12-month P/E ratio from the year 2000. Search <u>FACTSET S&P 500 forward P/E.</u>

Reuters provides data from 1986. Search <u>Reuters S&P 500 12 m forward P/E.</u>

The data in these two charts compare reasonably well.

In 1999/2000, leading up to the dot.com crash, the forward 12 month P/E ratio was ranging between 24 and 26, and fell fairly rapidly to below 16. It then trended down, despite a rising market, and was ranging around 14 leading up to the crash of 2008. During 2014/15, the forward P/E was circa 15, ranging around the 15-year average, so somewhat below the S&P 500 trailing P/E, which was around 20.

VIX volatility index

VIX is the ticker symbol of the Chicago Board Options Exchange (CBOE) market volatility index, a much-watched indicator of the implied volatility of S&P 500 index options (described in *Chapter 9 – Futures and options)*. Often referred to as the 'fear index' or the 'fear gauge', it's a measure of the market's expectation of stock market volatility over the next 30-day period, assessed through the hedging activity on the futures market. Hedging is expensive, so the VIX index itself is volatile, shooting up rapidly when the market becomes spooked. The VIX index was created in 1986, succeeding the VXO.

Google Finance is a good source for the VIX index – type VIX into the search box. You can also find it on YAHOO! FINANCE, by typing ^VIX into the Look Up box.

When the VIX is significantly over 20, the US markets are widely regarded as stressed.

The crash of 1987

We will start with the crash of Black Monday – October 19, 1987, when stock markets around the world unexpectedly crashed, shedding huge value in a very short time. You can use the search words in Table 7.2, above, which shows the crash in the S&P 500 and Dow, or you could use the Google Finance chart of the S&P 500. Select 5 years and scroll back to 1987, and you will see the crash. Scroll back further and you will see that the market had been rising strongly since 1984, and in 1986 and 1987 the pace of rise was picking up. Interest rates were low and companies were raising money for acquisitions by issuing junk bonds, i.e., bonds paying high yields to compensate for risk. A great deal of financial engineering was going on to boost earnings, and many new and often overvalued companies were coming to the market as initial public offerings – IPOs. There was a sense that the stock market was a one-way, upwards bet.

During 1987, it became clear that the US economy was overheating. Inflation was rising, and the US Federal Reserve began to raise interest rates aggressively. The markets were becoming increasingly nervous, and many participants were taking short positions in the futures markets to hedge their portfolios. Concurrently, arbitragers were seeking to exploit differences between the cash and futures markets – aided and abetted by computer programs placing sell orders at high speed, creating volatility and instability. On Friday, October 16, 1987, the US futures markets were inundated with sell orders, became unstable, and collapsed. The negative sentiment arising from this led to the crash of the cash market in Hong Kong when it opened on October 19, 1987 - Black Monday. Europe followed suit and by the time the US markets opened and began their precipitous fall, other world markets had already declined significantly. Everybody was running for the door at the same time. Liquidity was totally inadequate – there were simply not enough buyers, and both the main markets and futures markets were overwhelmed. Greed turned rapidly to fear, and the rest is history.

The falls in major indices were as follows:

Index	Monday 19 October 1987 Fall	Tuesday 20 October 1987 fall
S&P 500	20.6%	
Dow	22.6%	
Nasdaq Composite	11.3%	
FTSE 100	10%	12%

Table 7.3 Crash of 1987 index falls

The FTSE 100 suffered an intraday loss of about 18% on 19 October 1987, with the index recovering sharply by market close but plunging again the next day. The situation on Black Monday was aggravated by the great storm that had closed the London stock market on the Friday, when the American market was already starting to slide.

Between an August peak and December low point, the S&P 500, Dow, and FTSE 100 all lost around 34% of their value.

1987 – the signs and lessons

Black Monday is particularly significant because it saw the largest one-day percentage decline in the US stock market. In practical terms, if you had invested in the US or London stock markets at the beginning of 1987, you would possibly have made a small gain by the end of the year. On the other hand, if you had invested in October 1987, just before the crash, and stayed invested, your shares, depending on which companies, would probably not have recovered until 1990 – more than two years on. A painful experience.

Was the crash predictable, considering that so many investors lost heavily? There are even stories of ruined investors turning up at the offices of their stockbrokers, armed and shooting. We can look at what was evident during the build-up to the crash. You will find it helpful to check out the charts referenced above.

- Take another look at the S&P 500 chart. The bulls were rampant in 1987, with the S&P 500 actually accelerating upwards during 1987 at an astonishing rate, and pulling other world stock market indices with it.
- The S&P 500 average 12-month trailing P/E ratio peaked at about 22, which was towards the top of its long-term range but not dramatically high – though a great many companies were seriously overvalued.
- The markets were euphoric and companies were expanding rapidly through acquisitions. Many company valuations were becoming unrealistically high, though to a considerable degree, this is hindsight. The markets were in unknown territory.

- There was a sense that the only way for the markets was up. This was the era of 'greed is good.'
- The Federal Reserve began raising interest rates aggressively.
- The VXO index, based on the S&P 100 and a precursor to the VIX, had been running at around 22 to 23 closing value, and began to rise above this level on October 8. By Friday, October 16, it had reached 36. On Black Monday it shot up to 150, indicating frantic hedging activity, but share prices were falling too rapidly for much of the hedging to be effective. This was an instance of the VXO/VIX not so much giving early warning as indicating that there was already a serious problem.

So there were tail risks swirling around in 1987, but the markets were gripped by fear and greed, and did not see these risks clearly. A minor black swan had turned up in the shape of a storm that shut down the London Market. It's impossible to calculate the impact of this, but it would have added to the developing panic.

Undoubtedly, the market professionals believed they would be able to manage their risk by a combination of swift selling and hedging – after all, with an average P/E ratio of 22, the S&P 500 was not seriously overvalued – certainly not compared with the dizzy heights reached a little over a decade later. The black swan that turned up was the inability of the stock markets to cope with the stampede for the exit. There was no question that the market was going down, but it seriously overshot!

So, was it foreseeable? To some degree it was, as many companies were seriously overvalued. However, the professionals, who though they could manage their risk, were caught out by the speed of the collapse as liquidity vanished from the market. For a great many retail investors, riding the market up, 1987 was a crapshoot – a game of chance!

If you want to study the 1987 crash in greater depth, you will find many useful articles on the Internet; for example, search:

Bubble Bubble the great stock market crash 1987

An informative paper on the 1987 crash is A Brief History of the 1987 Stock Market Crash with a Discussion of the Federal Reserve Response. You should find it with an Internet search.

The great bull run of the 1990s

It will be helpful again to bring up a long-term chart for the S&P 500. Then we can consider how the retail investor might have managed his portfolio during this phase of the market.

1990 marks the start of a great bull run, with the S&P 500 rising an average rate of about 9% per annum between the beginning of 1990 and 1995, and then from 1995 to 2000 at a staggering 28% per annum, though with a number of pullbacks. However, these were in the region of 13% to 16%, much less severe than the shock of October 1987. The sharpest drop of more than 200 points – around 16% – on the S&P 500, occurred in 1998 as a result of the Russian financial crisis. The Russian government devalued the rouble, defaulted on domestic debt and declared a moratorium on payments to foreign creditors. The markets mostly recovered in less than a year from these smaller crashes and then continued their upwards trend. You can check out the background to this series of smaller crashes on Wikipedia if you search List of Stock Market Crashes and Bear Markets.

The number of sharp pullbacks occurring from time to time during this bull run made it tricky – but by no means impossible – to exploit the full rise. You can infer from the chart that for pullbacks of up to 15% or 16%, a good strategy would have been to take some money off the table, perhaps half, and ride out the crash with the balance. Though with the benefit of hindsight, staying fully invested would have worked out quite well. Of course, the burning question is 'how do you know that the crash is going to be limited and not in the region of 30% or more?' Well, you don't, so you have to try to 'read the weather' and take a view. The more severe you believe a looming crash will be, the more of your investments you should take off the table, i.e., go into cash.

It's worth taking a look at the behavior of the VIX and the S&P 500 average P/E ratio through this great bull run. The VIX declined steadily during the first half of the nineties, but began to climb in 1995 as the S&P 500 began its steep ascent, with average P/E ratio climbing – but by no means in a straight line – from around 15 to 30. The volatility of the VIX from 1997 to 2004, i.e., through the boom and bust around the 2001 crash, is very evident from the chart. This was a long period of nervousness in the markets – but it was highly profitable for those that held their nerve and read the signs well.

One of the aspects of this bull run is that it eventually began to look as though it was defying gravity – many people would have taken profit well before 2001, rather than risk a sudden and very precipitous drop.

The crash of 2001

During the crash that commenced in 2000, and was in full flow during 2001, the Nasdaq 100 fell from 5,047 to 1,114 points, representing 78% of its value.

US technology stocks were at the centre of the storm in the US markets, so we will take a look at the Nasdaq indices, as well as the S&P 500. During the crash, the Nasdaq

100 and the Nasdaq Composite indices moved closely together, dominated by the tech giants of the day.

The Nasdaq 100, the main US technology index, climbed 39.6% in 1998 and in 1999 it soared by 85.6%. Then in 2000, things began to go seriously wrong. The famous 'tech' or 'dot.com' bubble was beginning to burst. Analysts did not know how to value Internet companies that were growing fast, but not 'monetizing' the activity that they were managing to generate on their websites – so they started counting 'clicks' and 'eyeballs', i.e., 'looks' on web pages. This approach ended in tears. At the same time, the Enron scandal was unfolding and Arthur Andersen, one of the big five accountancy firms, subsequently went under. It became evident that a great many firms had been overvalued – again – often due to dubious accounting practices, and to very poor or non-existent corporate governance.

By 2000, more and more overvalued companies were failing, and the collapse in confidence developed rapidly. It is useful to view the crash through the performance of the S&P 500, which is representative of the broad US market.

Bring up the istockanalyst chart for the S&P 500 chart cited in Table 7.2 above. The S&P 500 peaked early in 2000 at 1,527 points. It then moved sideways in a volatile trading range. Trading ranges occur quite commonly and have an approximate ceiling and an approximate floor. The index tried to recover its peak towards the end of the year, but didn't quite manage this and began a fairly steep, albeit volatile, decline. It hit a low of 966 points about six months later in April 2001, a fall of 37%. The index bounced hard off this level, and was quite possibly probing a new, but higher, low at about 1,180 points, when the September 11, 2001 attacks on the World Trade Center and the Pentagon took place, and the fall recommenced at a greatly accelerated pace. The index finally bottomed out at about 770 points towards the end of 2002, and then moved in a highly volatile trading range – 800 to 950 points, i.e., a roughly 20% range! – until a strong recovery got underway in April 2003. The loss from peak to trough was about 48%. This was a very severe fall, but much less than the 78% fall in the Nasdaq 100. The FTSE 100 fall was about 46%; the FTSE 250 got away with a fall of about 42%. That the indices fell by roughly the same amount on both sides of the Atlantic points up the connectivity between markets.

The London market in particular, through the 'global' companies of the FTSE 100, was a major accomplice in the collapse of the markets. There was a very particular exacerbating factor in the UK. The euphoria in the markets through the nineties resulted in corporations taking 'holidays' from contributing to employees' pension funds to the tune of around £20bn, though employees had to keep making payments. The contributions that companies could make were conveniently limited by regulation. The pension fund management industry was piling money into companies good and bad, and it was serious overvaluations that facilitated the holiday. The FTSE 100 hit an all-time high of 6,930 points on the last trading day of 1999. Then things began to go very badly wrong. During the early noughties, the value of pension funds fell from

£812bn to £610bn, and companies were compelled by regulation to divert large portions of their funds away from shares to safer bonds. Equity/share allocations fell on average from 61% to 45%, all adding to the gloom in the stock market. As a result of this, the pension funds derived only limited benefit from the stock market rally that took place from 2003 to 2007. The stock market then collapsed again, perhaps vindicating the increase in bond weighting, but none of this has done the UK's pension funds a great deal of good. So, as usual, the UK financial industry, centered in London, had made its own special contribution to a global stock market meltdown. It took about five years for the markets to recover from the 2002 lows. The S&P 500 achieved 1,562 points in 2007, slightly above its 2000 peak. Factor in some inflation and the markets didn't fully recover before they crashed again.

2000 – the signs and lessons

Following the dot.com crash, twelve investment banks paid out US$1.4bn to settle allegations of biased research by their sell-side analysts.

Before moving on to the great crash that was developing in 2007, we should stay with 2000, try to set aside the benefit of hindsight, and assess what an alert investor could have done to preserve his capital through the impending crash. Bear in mind that by 2000, a great many people would have been sitting on substantial capital gains, without having locked in their profits by selling their shares. As we have seen, there were two legs to the 2001 crash.

The dot.com leg

Go to <u>Google Finance</u>, and bring up the ten year charts for the Nasdaq Composite and the S&P 500. Then scroll back to 2000. You will see that during 2000, the S&P 500 index was moving sideways in a trading range – in the language of the markets, it was range-bound. In the period we are looking at here, there was considerable volatility, 7% or 8% between the floor and ceiling of the range. Now look at the Nasdaq Composite. You will see that in 1999, it broke away from the S&P 500, and in the first part of 2000 it rose in a gravity-defying way to 5,000, a level that it wouldn't see again until 2015. It then suffered a 36% correction during the first half of 2000. Amazingly, it rallied strongly before beginning the long decline that ran through 2001 and most of 2002, back in sync with the S&P 500.

What would market participants have been aware of during 2000? As always, there would have been any number of commentators presenting their views on the direction of the markets, but any serious investor would have been aware that:

- From 1995 to 2000 the index, smoothing through the dips, is rising at an astonishing rate. This was a period of 'irrational exuberance', a term coined by Alan Greenspan, chairman of the US Federal Reserve in December 1996.

- Throughout 2000, the S&P 500 has been nervously rising and falling but essentially moving sideways. The Nasdaq Composite has gone ballistic.
- There is a great deal of euphoria over the new technology stocks, many of them trading at astonishingly high valuations – but there are problems in valuing companies that are not close to making a profit.
- In 2000, the trailing 12-month P/E ratio of the Nasdaq 100 reportedly rose to well over 100 (at the outset of 2016 it was 22 and thought to be high!).
- Shares are more expensive than they have ever been. The trailing 12-month P/E ratio for the S&P 500 is reaching around 30, compared with a long-term average of about 15.
- The S&P 500 forward 12-month PE is ranging between 24 and 26, indicating continued, but perhaps a little restrained, optimism from the analysts.
- During 2007, for a great deal of the time the S&P 500 is more than 400 points above its 200-day moving average (you can check this out on Google Finance).
- The average FTSE 100 trailing 12-month P/E ratio is around 27, compared with a long-term average of around 18.
- The Enron scandal is unfolding.
- From 1997 to 2004, the VIX volatility index ranged between 20 and 35 – quite an elevated level, indicating a long period of nervousness or stress in the US markets.

Interestingly, the Shiller CAPE ratio reached around 44 just before the crash, but as this was because of low earnings five years earlier, its portending of the crash could be regarded as largely a matter of luck. Indeed, proponents of CAPE maintain that its purpose is to provide realistic assessments of share valuations, rather than to predict stock market crashes.

The extraordinarily high valuations, especially in technology shares, represented a very substantial tail risk hanging over the markets. The inability of the analyst community to place sensible valuations on technology stocks amplified this tail risk.

So without having to say 'with the benefit of hindsight', an informed and alert investor in 2000 should have been distinctly nervous. He should have been asking 'what is the upside potential of this market – and what are the downside possibilities?' If he judged that the upside potential was only around 5% but that something of a crash was quite plausible, he should have been taking money off the table. What would have been propping up the market? Certainly there would have been many coming to the market believing, wishfully, that it was not too late to get in – the people that traditionally buy high and sell cheap. And of course the greedy, looking for an extra few percent on their money, either disregarding or not recognizing the downside risk – or perhaps prepared to run it. And as always, there would be the traders, looking to exploit any remaining upwards bias with short-term trades while developing their shorting strategies.

With clear signals of an impending crash, the astute investor would know how to trim his portfolio, starting with taking some profits and selling some investments that are not really going anywhere. If market conditions continued to deteriorate, he might decide to reduce his market exposure quite rapidly – going entirely into cash or holding at around, say, 25% invested, in case of a sharp upturn.

The September 11, 2001 leg

Then, in the middle of 2001, it looked as though the crash had hit the bottom – hindsight is 20/20, but at the time it probably looked as though the markets were trying to rise off a higher low than the previous low, with the S&P 500 down about 23% from the high of 1,527 points. At this point, an intrepid retail investor might have begun to ease some money back into the market, thinking that he has played a pretty good game. And then a black swan arrives in the form of the September 2001 terrorist attacks on America. The markets finished up losing around half their value over a period of about two and a half years.

It is quite difficult to draw lessons from a black swan event. Hopefully, our investor did not pile into the rally before the second stage of the crash, but was just dipping his toes in. You can see from the chart that when the market did finally bottom out, it rose fairly sharply. During periods like this, you must keep very close to the news and various commentators, and make the best calls that you can. And as you go back into the market, select your funds or companies very carefully for the prevailing conditions.

It has to be said that a 'two-leg' crash with two quite different triggers was unprecedented and did not occur rapidly, so there was plenty of time to assess the unfolding situation and be prepared to accept a significant loss, say 5% to 10%, to get some or all of your money out of the market. The problem is that once the market is down around 5%, wishful thinking can take over, with investors staying heavily invested, hoping for a quick bounce – which doesn't come and losses continue to grow. There is no simple rule of thumb to help with this. You must have your finger on the pulse and make a realistic assessment of the situation – and then act decisively and be prepared to live with your decisions.

It is salutary to note that it took the market five years to recover from this crash and that this was not unrelated to the depth of the fall. If you take account of inflation, the market didn't fully recover before it crashed again. So, if our investor had stayed fully invested and rode out the crash, he would have done very badly. Interest rates during these five years were respectable and he could have got quite a decent 'guaranteed' return on cash. Also, he may have been in some companies that didn't recover all that well.

The purveyors of 'buy and hold' strategy would point to the effect of compounding dividends without reference to the quality of invested companies or to fund management charges that detract considerably from investor returns. Another important consideration is that after a crash, most likely a new set of companies will rise the most strongly. A crash is an opportunity to refresh your portfolio rather than ride a severe crash with some companies that are going nowhere.

2008 – the global financial crisis

After peaking at around 7,000 pence in 2008, shares in Rio Tinto plc, a London-listed global mining company, plunged to 1,000 pence later in the same year – an astonishing fall of about 85%.

It's beginning to look as though there might be some mileage in seeking to time the markets, despite the strong messaging from the financial industry that it's too difficult and you shouldn't bother to try!

Regarding the immediate backdrop, you can see from the charts that the run-up to 2007 looks very much like an exuberant bull market. China was rising, with GDP growing at over 9% per annum, peaking at 11.4% growth in 2007, and drawing in something like half the resources that were being mined from the ground around the globe – the great resource supercycle. The emerging markets were booming, with demand from China playing a strong role. Social programs in the US were providing housing for all and mountains of dubious debt were building. It was as though little had been learned from the crash that had occurred less than a decade before.

As with the crash that commenced in 2000, there was a chain of events leading up to the great crash of 2008. Bring up TheArmotrader chart for the S&P 500 referenced above. There were many 'key events' and the following ones tell the story quite well:

- The major market indices peaked in October 2007 with the S&P 500 reaching 1,562 points.
- In January 2008, US GDP growth came in at just 0.6% and the US economy lost 17,000 jobs – actually not a very high number, but high enough to rattle already nervous markets.
- In mid-January, the S&P 500 hit a low of 1,275 points, almost 20% off its peak. The market recovered, traded sideways, and then was testing new lows when the US Federal Reserve bailed out Bear Stearns on March 17, 2008.
- The market rallied, but by now the subprime mortgage crisis was underway and by July 2008 had spread to Fannie Mae and Freddie Mac, the US Federal Government mortgage associations. The markets hit a new low at around 1,200 points – the S&P 500 was now 24% off its peak.
- Again the markets rallied, but by now Lehman Brothers was in deep trouble and declared bankruptcy on September 15, 2008. This sent the market into panic and after a short period of extreme volatility the crash was underway, finally bottoming out with the S&P 500 touching a low of 673 points in March 2009, a drop of 56% from its peak.

2007 – the signs and lessons

In 2011, Carmen Reinhart and Kenneth Rogoff published This Time is Different: Eight Centuries of Financial Folly. *They demonstrate that short memories make it all too easy for crises to reoccur.*

There were several strong signals to the alert and prudent investor to begin taking cash off the table well before the Lehman bankruptcy.

- The S&P 500 trailing 12-month P/E ratio was ranging between 16 and 18, compared with a long-term average of about 15; however, the S&P 500 forward 12-month P/E has fallen steadily from around 25 in 2000 to a modest 15, indicating a fair measure of pessimism among the analysts.
- During 2007, for a great deal of the time the S&P 500 was more than 200 points above its 100-day moving average. You can check this out on Google Finance.
- The VIX volatility index had been climbing since the beginning of 2007, moving into a range around 25, indicating that the market had become stressed.
- The need for a bailout of Bear Stearns by the US Federal Reserve in March 2008 was very worrying.
- By mid-2008, the subprime mortgage crisis had come to the fore, and the Lehman Brothers collapse in September 2008 sent the markets into a steep decline.
- The VIX surged to an all-time high of nearly 70, though the VXO had hit 150 on Black Monday.

Even after the Lehman Brothers declared bankruptcy, there was still time to get out of the market and to take a 25% fall from the peak on the chin. Of course, a great many did, which led to the precipitous fall that only bottomed out when the S&P 500 was 56% down.

The alert and experienced investor would have been taking cash off the table steadily from October 2007, while carefully tracking valuations through average P/E and keeping an eye on the VIX. The fatal trap was to stay with a high level of investment, believing that there had to be a bounce soon.

2009 through 2012

Emerging markets, led by China, were responsible for three-quarters of the increase in global nominal gross domestic product between 2009 and 2014.

The markets bottomed out early in 2009 and then recovered about 20% in the next 12 or so months. This was a time to be investing briskly. The markets continued to trend upwards until April 2010.

By April 2010, a new tail risk had emerged. Standard & Poor downgraded Greece's sovereign credit rating to junk four days after the activation of a Euro 45bn EU-IMF bailout. This was an intensification of the Eurozone debt crisis and it triggered a sharp decline of stock markets around the world as well as a fall in the value of the Euro. However, the crisis receded, and the S&P 500 and the FTSE 100 recovered their losses in under six months and then enjoyed a good run up until August 2011.

In August 2011, the European debt crisis erupted yet again with the major market indices in the US, UK, and Europe losing 16% to 18% of their value in just a few weeks and with the VIX soaring to over 40 during the decline. You will see from the chart that the next 18 months proved very difficult for investors. In the middle of 2012 there was a run of poor nonfarm payrolls data in the US coinciding with the Greek election crisis. A negative outcome for the Greek election was a substantial tail risk.

The period of April, May, and June 2012 highlights the importance of tail risk in managing your portfolio. Greece was going to the polls again in June 2012 and the Syriza party, led by Alexis Tsipras, was threatening that if they gained sufficient influence from the election, they would tear up the 'EU Austerity Deal' that Greece had previously agreed to. Greece would then more than likely have exited the Eurozone with the collapse of the single currency. Based on recent stock market history coupled with the severe consequences of the collapse of the Euro, the possibility of markets losing 50% of their value was yet again plausible. This was not a time to be heavily invested. Hindsight shows that to have stayed heavily invested in the markets would have worked well because these markets had recovered their losses in less than 6 months and then continued to run-up strongly. But hindsight is 20/20 and this doesn't mean that to stay heavily invested would have been a prudent strategy. Perhaps an appropriate level of investment during this period would have been about 30%.

In July 2012, Mario Draghi, EU Central Bank President, made his famous speech – he would do 'whatever it takes' to save the Euro. The positive effect that this had on the markets is very clear. Draghi was saying that the risk of a collapse of the Euro and a breakup of the Eurozone was negligible – he had removed the tail risk. Of course there could be other cataclysmic events – black swans – but while you need to be alert to these, you have to get on with life and investing!

Another serious complication in the second half of 2012 was the US fiscal cliff crisis – the threat of legislated, automatic tax increases which would have put a serious drag on the US economy. The interplay between President Obama and House Speaker John Boehner caused the S&P 500 to move vertically up or down on a number of occasions. This was a nerve-wracking episode for investors.

It is worth noting that many hedge funds performed poorly during this period. Despite their much-proclaimed ability to judge and manage risk, they evidently struggled to do this successfully. However, their fees are unlikely to have suffered much.

2013 – bad news is good news!

2013 was a very good year for bold investors. Major index gains are shown in Table 7.4.

Index	Gain %
Dow	26
S&P 500	29
FTSE 100	14
FTSE 250	28
Nikkei 225	52
SSE – Shanghai Stock Exchange	7
Hang Seng – Hong Kong	4
Dax – Germany	23
CAC – France	19

Table 7.4 2013 index gains

Only China disappointed with lackluster performances in Shanghai and Hong Kong. The backdrop to this was fear of a 'hard landing' for China's economy, i.e., sharply declining growth developing into recession.

In 2008, the Fed had embarked on a major quantitative easing program (QE). The purpose of the QE was to stimulate the US economy as it struggled to recover from the financial crisis. It involved the government buying back substantial volumes of government bonds before their maturity dates as well as mortgage-backed securities. This was combined with an increase in the monetary base – also known as 'money printing.' As a result of QE, banks and other bond-holding organizations find cash on their hands that they didn't expect. The government's demand for bonds pushes their price up and interest on these bonds moves down. A great deal of the unexpected cash finds its way into shares and at the same time a low-interest environment is created – which is good for share prices.

In December 2012, the Fed stepped up its QE operations to the tune of US$85bn/month. In December 2013, it began to reduce – taper – its asset purchases by US$10bn per month on the basis that certain key economic objectives had been met. Perversely, the markets took the view that good economic news would cause the Fed to taper more rapidly and that this would be bad for shares. So 2013 – and well into 2014 – was an era of 'bad news is good news' and vice versa. The markets would move up on bad news!

The great tail risk overhanging the markets was how the US Federal Reserve, personified by chairman Ben Bernanke, was going to manage the taper of QE. If you bring up the S&P 500 chart for 2013, you will see that there were a couple of 4% to 6% retreats along the way – the 'taper tantrums' – so Bernanke managed the tapering well.

During 2013, the possibility of the Euro collapsing had greatly reduced – but not disappeared. It continued to be a significant tail risk and the ability of the peripheral Eurozone countries to finance themselves continued to be closely monitored by the markets. Countries raise money through bond auctions. Seven percent was regarded as the critical level of interest for 'affordability' by a troubled economy and by and large the peripheral countries were able to borrow below these levels.

A few more significant aspects to 2013 are worth a mention. In the US markets, investors were anticipating much better times ahead for companies and a great deal of the share price rise was attributable to 'expansion of multiples', i.e., rising P/E ratios – in anticipation of rising revenues and associated growth in earnings. The possibility of these market expectations not being met was a significant tail risk hanging over the markets. The second aspect is that companies were accumulating a great deal of cash. Some of this was simply being hoarded, but many companies were buying back their shares from the market – which gives a boost to earnings per share. Another tail risk hanging over the market in 2013 was the imposition by the US Congress of a US budget ceiling to rein in Federal Government spending. This added to the volatility in the markets until the issue was resolved in October 2013.

At the outset of 2014, both governments and investors were agitating companies to pick up their rate of capital expenditure; either capex to stimulate organic growth or outlay to acquire other companies.

No serious black swans appeared in 2013 and there were no market corrections – defined as a fall of 10% or more – though there were significant tail risks throughout. The end of QE was a constant concern, though it ran on through most of 2014. Isil/Daesh came into existence in the Middle East in April 2013. New tail risks emerged towards the end of 2013 with the Ukraine crisis beginning in November 2013 and an outbreak of Ebola occurring in Guinea in December 2013.

2014 – nowhere to go!

In October 2014 the Fed announces the end of QE in the US – soon bad news is going to be bad news. Ben Bernanke, the outgoing Federal Reserve chairman, remarked that the problem with QE was that 'it works in practice...but it doesn't work in theory.'

2014 was a good year for the S&P 500, but more or less flat for the FTSE 100 and FTSE 250, which ran out of steam at the beginning of 2014. The FTSE 100 was at about the same level as it was in 2007 before the financial crisis.

During 2014, the S&P 500 was sustained by share buybacks and the falling oil price. In the year, the price of Brent crude oil fell from about US$110, where it had been steady for some time, to under US$55. The index reached a record high of 2,010 in September

2014 and then embarked upon a near 10% correction, with the market finally giving way to fears around conflicts in the Middle East and the Ukraine, the Ebola outbreak, the state of the European economy, and the impending end of QE. All these factors had been tail risks hanging over the market. With an average time of about 26 months between corrections, the S&P 500 was due for a correction. There had been a 17% correction in August 2011 and a 9% correction in May 2012. However, the US market proved resilient and recovered its losses within two weeks. The London market fell a little further and did not recover as strongly.

2015

> *'Of the dozen economic expansions since the end of the second world war, the*
> *current one has been the slowest.'*
> **Patrick Newport, US economist at IHS Global Insight, January 2016.**

Early in 2015, asset managers globally had cut their holdings in US shares to the lowest level since 2008. During 2015, the S&P 500 was range-bound between 1,860 and 2,125, suffering a circa 12% correction in August caused by fear of an interest rate rise. It recovered most of this lost ground and some composure by the beginning of November. Towards the end of 2015, optimism picked up in the US. The S&P 500 trailing 12-month P/E ratio was about 21 against a long-term average of 15, while the CAPE was about 26 against a long-term mean of 16.6. The S&P 500 12-month forward P/E was standing at just over 17 compared with the 15-year average of 16. According to FactSet, analysts were predicting record S&P 500 EPS for the second half of 2015. During the third quarter of 2015 earnings season, 68% of S&P 500 companies were beating expectations compared with a historic average of 66%. A US interest rate rise for December 2015 was in the air and came in at 0.25%.

The FTSE 100 started 2015 at about 6,500, rose sharply to just over 7,000 in April, and then fell back to about 6,250, dragged down mainly by bank and mining shares. In November 2015, the FTSE 100 average P/E was 15. The FTSE 250 fared better, starting the year at about 16,000, rising to 18,000 in April, and then retreating to about 17,000 with an average P/E ratio of around 20.

Outside the US, there was little optimism. Towards the end of 2015, global growth forecasts were being downgraded, and surveys were indicating that around two-thirds of fund managers and analysts around the world considered developed world equities to be overvalued. Institutional investors withdrew US$277bn from US equities during 2015, counterbalanced by share buybacks running at unprecedented levels. On the upside, the Eurozone tail risk had receded and its economies were showing some strength.

Around the world, banks were regaining some swagger in their ongoing battle with the regulators, though underlying this, 2015 saw a flat performance from the five major

US banks. In the corporate world, managers hardly missed a step in overpaying themselves. Whether corporate governance is improving is an open question.

At the end of 2015, the markets finally let go and fell sharply. The oil price had rallied to around US$70 at the outset of the 2015 but then fell relentlessly through the year. The markets, with the S&P 500 dominant, panicked that the oil price had fallen too low and it was unclear whether this was due to oversupply or lack of demand – which would signal a slowing global economy.

2016

January 2016: US GDP is slowing and the US is poised to report its third consecutive quarter of year-over-year earnings declines, the worst performance since the financial crisis.

There was a depressing start to 2016 with the markets spooked by dramatic falls in the Chinese stock markets and in the Chinese currency; tensions were flaring between Saudi Arabia and Iran; S&P 500 earnings were under pressure; the possibility of the UK leaving the European Union was coming to the fore; and Donald Trump was forging ahead in the race for the Republican Party presidential nomination.

And the price of oil continued to fall. In January 2016, the sense of panic in the markets was palpable. Having assumed since the middle of 2014, that the fall in price was due to oversupply and could only be good for the economy, the markets attention became riveted on the issue with the major indices strongly correlated with the oil price – virtually moving in lockstep. As well as concern that demand for oil was falling, there was concern about the impact of budget cuts by the oil industry on their supply chain companies – representing a significant portion of major economies.

There was also a concern that banks could be hit by bad loans to energy companies. Early in 2016, there was a serious compounding factor – it was reported that a number of oil revenue based sovereign wealth funds were liquidating significant share holdings to prop up their economies in the face of the dramatic fall in oil price.

The price of Brent crude fell briefly below US$30 in mid-January before rallying to US$40 by the end of March. The main stock market indices continued to be strongly correlated with the price of oil, though in percentage terms, the fall in oil price was much greater than that of the indices.

The retail investment community was seriously spooked at the outset of 2016 with market information companies reporting dramatic outflows of cash from both mutual funds and ETFs. However, by early March the flow reversed and retail investors were cautiously moving into US equities again.

Early in 2016, S&P 500 dividend payouts increases were running out of steam, with energy companies slashing their dividends. At the same time, a number of FTSE 100 companies in the banking, mining and retail sectors, as well as Rolls Royce, announced cuts in their dividends. Capita UK Dividend Monitor reported that UK dividends were set to fall by 0.9% to £83.6bn. In early February 2016, it was reported that hedge funds had opened over £3bn of short positions in ten FTSE 100 companies: Glencore, Anglo American, Tesco, J Sainsbury, Burberry, BG Group, Royal Dutch Shell, Rolls Royce, Aberdeen Asset Management and Ashtead Group. Inconveniently for the hedge funds with short positions, mining companies staged a spectacular rally in February/March, helped along the way by serious short squeezes – see *Chapter 8 Short selling*. Some mining shares, for example Anglo American, were close to doubling in value (after a pause for breath, Anglo American share price doubled again in April 2016!)

The outlook for 2016 will be dominated by central bank interest rate policy and time will tell if the powerhouse US economy can take rising interest rates and slowing global growth in its stride.

So what can we learn?

It's useful to look at some metrics. A useful table for key S&P 500 metrics from 1960 to the present is provided by LongRunData – use the dropdown menu under Macro.

Take a look at earnings and P/E trends against the long-term chart of the S&P 500, and a number of useful insights will emerge. For example, through the financial crisis, earnings only fell by only about 35%, while the index fell by 56%; between 2013 and 2014, average earnings grew by 6.9%, compared with 10.8% growth in the previous year. Earnings fell in 2015, though dividend payouts were at a record level.

Another useful dataset provided by the Wall Street Journal can be found by searching Online WSJ Market Data Center 3021-peyield. This provides current levels of average trailing and forward P/E ratios and dividend yields for the major US indices.

Bull runs

Since the crash of 1987, there have been three great bull runs which you can see on the long-term chart of the S&P 500 chart and of the other main US and UK indices. You will see that bull market conditions have pertained a great deal more than bear market conditions. Several important insights for the stock market investor can be drawn from the record, to the extent that the past can be a guide to the future.

Buy and hold strategies would have worked well during the bull runs. However, there were several sharp pullbacks along the way. Two of the most severe occurred in 1998 during the Russian financial crisis, when the S&P 500 pulled back around 16%, and during the Eurozone crisis of 2011, when the S&P 500 pulled back by around 17%.

These would have been nervous times for the proactive retail investor, though the markets recovered quite quickly. Investors with strong portfolios would have been rewarded for holding their nerve and quite possibly done better than more nervous types jumping in and out of the market. When markets turn up after a sharp fall, more often than not, they move quickly.

When the markets become unusually nervous, it is important to be abreast of valuations and any severe tail risks that are hanging over the market. We have looked at a number of ways of checking out valuations at an index level. You can only keep abreast of tail risks by tuning into the media for events and discussion. If a worrying situation is developing, then the retail investor should be looking into taking some money off the table. An approach to this is described in *Chapter 18 – Managing your portfolio.*

The greatest challenge during a bull run is to ride it strongly and to judge if a major crash is imminent. If it looks as though the market could crash by 30% or 40%, it is best to reduce your holdings quickly, even if this means taking a loss. Recovery from the crash that began in 2000 took five years – and if you factor in inflation, the market had not fully recovered by 2007. Similarly, recovery from the crash that commenced in 2007 took until 2013 and again the remark about inflation applies.

Investors who judged the bottom of the financial crisis crash, i.e., March 2009, and invested in good companies either individually or through funds, and adopted a buy and hold strategy until the present time, would have done well. But, they would have done better if they had managed to successfully reduce their positions during the significant pullbacks that occurred in each of 2010, 2011, and 2012 – up to 17% and then built back up again as the market recovered each time. On the other hand, the charts indicate that an investor riding out these falls would also have done reasonably well and not experienced the hassle of active investing in a turbulent market. However, this does not take account of the risk associated with riding out a significant crash. It's important to be alert to tail risks that could make a sharp fall much worse. In 2012 in particular, the Greek election issues were exacerbating the already serious Eurozone debt crisis and for the markets to lose half their value – yet again! – was not implausible. Taking some money off the table would not have been a bad idea.

In 2001 and 2008, the major indices roughly halved and took years to recover. It's also worth noting that the recoveries were abrupt – 'v' shaped, particularly in 2009 – and the indices rose very steeply off the bottom. So bold investors increasing their percent invested rapidly would have been well rewarded. More steady investing during the bull runs would also have been rewarding, but gains would not have been as strong.

During a bull run, and especially during a sharp rebound, it is not hard to pick winners – just about everything goes up. 'When the tide rises, all the boats are lifted' – there is high correlation. As always, an alternative to share picking is fund picking. Or you could have simply 'bought the index' through a tracker fund or ETF, but keep in mind that good active fund managers consistently beat the index – as we shall see in *Chapter 12 – About funds.*

The crashes

How are you meant to judge if the market is about to seriously crash?

1987

As discussed above, the crash of 1987 was to some degree foreseeable. However, the speed of the crash was not and could be regarded as a black swan. The retail investor can draw some comfort from the improvements in trading systems that have been made in recent years together with a more sophisticated regulatory approach. The possibility of another loss of more than 20% in a day, or in the case of London, in two days, should be very low. The S&P 500 and other indices recovered fairly quickly. It can be seen in the LongRunData table, just mentioned, that S&P 500 earnings rose by 50% between 1987 and 1988, which would have underpinned the relative rapid recovery in the markets.

2001

The 2001 crash that was getting underway in 2000 was different in that the markets were seriously overvalued on any objective basis. They were in bubble territory and the record shows that leverage is a significant factor in the creation of stock market bubbles, i.e., a great deal of borrowed money, much of it from margin, is piling into both the cash markets and the index futures markets. So when the tipping point is reached and the bears are taking control, panic sets in. Leveraged investors suffer leveraged losses when the market falls sharply.

A particularly difficult aspect of 2001 was that it occurred in two distinct legs arising from unrelated events, one of which was a very large black swan – 9/11. However, in contrast to 1987, it occurred in slow motion over about two years. To some degree in hindsight, a good strategy would have been to exit the market in perhaps three or four stages as things got progressively worse.

2008

2008 was more easy to deal with as there were many signs that a great meltdown was coming. The markets were not overvalued to the extent that they were in 2000, but the collapse of a number of major financial institutions sent a series of shockwaves through the markets. As we have seen above, company earnings did not collapse to the same extent as the market indices – but that is the way that markets behave! Market sentiment was so bad as the crash was getting underway that an alert and savvy retail investor should have got out of the market no later than the demise of Lehman Brothers.

Riding out the 2001 and 2008 crashes, i.e., staying fully invested, would have been an unproductive use of money – though some dividend income would have softened the blow. However, the recovery from several much smaller crashes since 1987 took less than a year, and staying invested would have worked reasonably well.

Conclusion

The dramatic crashes of 2001 and 2008 were to a considerable extent foreseeable and were foreseen by the author who went almost 100% into cash as the crashes unfolded.

An important consideration for the retail investor is the likelihood of another stock market fall in the region of 50%. After many corporate scandals, such as Enron in the US and Polly Peck in the UK, efforts have been made to improve market regulation and corporate governance around the world. However, it is evident that by 2007, not a great deal of progress had been made. As we enter 2016, the regulators on both sides of the Atlantic have worked hard to minimize this risk, and there is perhaps cause for cautious optimism. Time will tell.

There is no doubt that there will be significant falls in stock markets in the years to come, and though accurate timing of the markets is not a practical proposition, there is a strong case for varying your exposure to the market – your percent invested – with market conditions. An approach to this is described in *Chapter 18 – Managing your portfolio.*

Don't be taken in by people that tell you it's impossible to time the market, so you should just invest a set amount of your money into the market every month and always stay 100% invested.

8 Short selling

Introduction

In 2015, the US$38bn Harvard endowment fund was seeking asset managers with short selling expertise.

If you believe that a company's share price is going to fall, you have the possibility to profit from it by selling it short. You borrow the share (there will be a borrowing cost), sell it straightaway and then buy it back when it has fallen to a lower price – provided that it has! You then return it to the lender, having made a profit from the fall in share price. If the share price rises, in order to close your position you will have to buy the share back at a higher price and you will suffer a loss. On the face of it, short selling sounds like a useful proposition. It contains the attractive possibility to make money in a falling market as well as in a rising market.

You can short an index using a derivative product such as index futures, as well as an individual share. The volatility of an index is usually less than the volatility of an individual share, and the dynamic of shorting an index is different to that of shorting an individual share. An individual share price can fall dramatically when market indices are rising.

In the index futures market, discussed below and in the next chapter, for every long position there is an equivalent short position – so a great deal of shorting goes on in the index futures markets! This chapter is mainly concerned with the shorting of individual shares.

There is no theoretical limit to how high a share price can rise and the short trader or investor can lose more than his original stake or investment. In a long position, the worst that can happen is that the share price drops to nil. Risk is amplified if the party is trading on margin, i.e., using borrowed money.

A great many investment strategies are long only. However, there are always some shares that are rising and some that are falling, and market participants are increasingly using long/short strategies. This makes particular sense when markets are judged to be high. Shorting is done both tactically and strategically. Many traders will take a short position as readily as they will take a long position, guided strongly by Technicals. Traders will often adopt an aggressive approach, buying back the shares at a low to close their position then seeking to judge a high point before selling again – attempting to drive the share price relentlessly down. Participants with more of an investor mind set will pay close attention to Fundamentals and take medium- or long-term short positions, believing that a company's share price is on a downward journey or that a company is a good candidate for shorting in a bear market.

Historically, bull market conditions are in place a lot more than bear market conditions, and during a bull market there will be significant periods when most share prices are rising, especially the larger caps and even some of the not-so-great companies. So much of the time, shorting will be going against the grain of the market.

To what extent should shorting be in the toolkit of the retail investor? This chapter should help you take a view on how shorting might fit into your investment strategy.

Hedging

Shorting is often used to hedge risk. Take an investor with a large portfolio of, say, S&P 500 shares, who is concerned that the market is about to move sharply lower but it's a bad time for him to sell his shares from a tax standpoint. Also, he will have to pay commissions to re-enter the market (UK share purchases are subject to the additional cost of stamp duty). He can short the S&P 500 index as an alternative to selling all his shares. He can short the index to the value of his portfolio or, as a matter of discretion, a proportion of it.

The perfect hedge will have taken place if a fully hedged portfolio value falls by 10% and the index also falls by 10%, thereby giving the investor a gain of 10% on his short – so he finishes up neutral. If the market rises unexpectedly, the short position will lose money, but the investor's shares will probably also rise in value and, again, he may finish up more or less neutral.

Ways to short sell

Disruptive products appear on a regular basis and can seriously impact the fortunes of companies. For example, Garmin was affected when GPS became available on smartphones; Blockbuster was devastated by movie streaming technology; Blackberry was hit hard by the rapid rise of smartphones; camera film has been virtually eliminated by the digital camera, which has in turn been hit hard by the ubiquitous smartphone camera. The ultimate disruptor is the Internet, which has fundamentally changed the way just about all business is done.

There are various ways to take a short position. For the retail investor, an option is to find a stockbroker that will provide this service, though it is likely to be expensive to borrow relatively small numbers of shares. If a position moves strongly against the investor, the broker may require him to close the position in the interest of credit risk management. As a practical matter, there will be some shares that are difficult to borrow. The lenders of shares have to manage their risk – the proposition for them is that they lend shares with a value of, say, US$20 and have them returned when they are worth only US$15, though they can hedge against this risk. Shares of small cap companies, companies with a small free float, or that are lightly traded will not be an attractive proposition for lending, as the short selling may contribute to some serious damage to the share price from which it may not easily recover.

The retail investor also has the possibility to take a short position through the index futures market, which is discussed in *Chapter 9 – Futures and options.* Index futures are traded on margin, i.e., borrowed money. You can trade index futures on the Chicago Mercantile Exchange (CME) and on the Intercontinental Exchange (ICE). Margin is variable on both exchanges. Many UK investors trade on the US index futures markets. Also, you can trade more than 2,000 individual company shares through OneChicago, a specialist exchange for trading single stock futures (SSFs). The margin offered by OneChicago is 20%, providing x 5 leverage.

In the UK, the retail investor can use a Contract for Difference (CFD) platform for both short and long positions. There won't usually be a problem to short the larger cap shares but the platform may decline to allow short positions for some small cap companies. The margin available on CFD platforms is variable, but 10%, providing x 10 leverage, is commonplace. CFD trading is described in *Chapter 11.*

Who are the short sellers?

In May 2015 TalkTalk, an Internet service provider, reported strongly sending the share price to an all-time high and triggering a short squeeze on short sellers. 15% of TalkTalk shares were out on loan – up from 2% a year before. During this period the share price had risen 35%, to the discomfort of several hedge funds betting against the company. TalkTalk market cap was about £3.5bn at the time. However, the short sellers that held their nerve would have done very well, as TalkTalk's share price halved in the following 18 months.

Investment banks and hedge funds are probably the biggest short sellers. Also, investment banks sometimes provide back office support to short sellers. Hedge funds are increasingly used by fund managers looking to boost their performance, to manage both long and short portfolios for them. They believe that by being both a long and short investor, they gain an advantage over the long-only investor.

Some hedge fund managers with a reputation for successful short selling are Jim Chanos, who helped to detect the accounting fraud at Enron, David Einhorn of Greenlight Capital in the US, and Crispin Odey of Odey Asset Management in the UK.

Odey shorted Northern Rock, the UK mortgage company that collapsed in 2008, and did well out of the meltdown in the Chinese stock market in August 2015. If you are interested, you can research their activities on the Internet.

Also, there are some high-profile firms that specialize in short selling, such as Muddy Waters, described below.

The main field is made up of vast numbers of retail and professional traders and investors who believe that they will be more successful if they take both long and short positions. They may short shares systematically or opportunistically.

Data shows that the Anglo-Saxon world has a much greater appetite for short selling than continental Europe.

Where do short sellers borrow their shares from?

Towards the end of 2013, gun sales in the US surged following a series of mass shootings, and the share prices of many gunmakers were outperforming the S&P 500. A number of institutional investors were building positions in these companies – and as fast as they were doing this, potential short sellers were borrowing their shares.

The main lenders of shares for short selling are the institutional investors and stockbrokers who will lend them from their own inventories or perhaps those of another stockbroker – for a fee. Normally, there will be a security loan agreement and the borrower will have to put up cash as security. Any dividends missed because the shares have been sold to effect the short position will have to be paid to the lender by the borrower.

Market makers also lend from their inventories. Investment banks and hedge funds will have the scale to enter into the necessary arrangements on a routine and cost-effective basis.

Lending by institutional investors might raise the eyebrows of people with pensions under their management – the institution may be lending a portion of their pensions to someone who, in effect, wants to drive the value of the pension fund down. The institution will say that it doesn't make much difference in the longer term. They probably reason, somewhat questionably, that they may as well make money out of the often pointless zero-sum speculations of short-term traders in the market, and that no long-term harm to the shorted companies is done. The short sellers will argue that this will put pressure on the management of the business to improve its performance. Not all institutions will lend shares for short selling.

Information on short positions

Shares out on loan

The quantity of shares out on loan is a good indicator of short selling activity in the market as a whole, and the number of a company's shares out on loan is a useful indicator of sentiment towards that share. It is usually expressed as a percentage of the tradeable shares, i.e., the company's free float.

In October 2013, according to Markit, across the US markets just 2.4% of shares were out on loan – close to an all-time low. Only six companies had 3% of their shares sold short; in Europe, there were even fewer short positions. This was a useful gauge of market sentiment. 2013 was a very good year for stock markets.

The proportion of shares on loan, taken together with data on actual short positions, will provide a useful perspective for potential short sellers. At any particular point in time, not all borrowed shares will have been sold. The borrower will have a strategy to sell the shares at a rate which he believes will be most productive for him. Professional traders and investors may well act in concert, selling strategically with a view to creating the greatest downwards pressure on a target share price. When hedge funds sense that a company or even a sector is in trouble, shares on loan can reach surprisingly high levels. Around 25% of a company's free float would not be unusual.

Markit tracks volumes of company shares out on loan for both the US and UK and provides this data on a subscription basis. Euroclear provides data on shares out on loan for the FTSE 350 shares. You need to register to see monthly data for no charge. You can obtain daily data for a subscription.

This is a key indicator of short selling activity. Professional traders will routinely access this information. The retail investor will find it more difficult.

The quantity of shares out on loan for a particular company is sometimes usefully reported in the financial press.

Short interest

The proportion of tradable shares, or free float, which have been sold short is another valuable indicator of the way a company is perceived by the market professionals. This is defined as short interest, expressed as a percentage. Stock exchanges provide short interest data, as do a number of specialist market information companies. In the US, stock exchanges report short interest monthly or twice a month. For example, search Nasdaq short interest and insert company name or ticker. Nasdaq also provides days to cover, which is the number of days of average trading volume needed to close out short positions. Other specialist market information firms provide daily information on short interest; for example, see shortsqueeze.com and Barron's Short Interest Tables.

A useful source of information on disclosed short positions in the UK is provided by Castellain Capital's Short Interest Tracker, which you can find by searching on their website. The tracker provides data on fund managers' short positions by both company and fund manager.

This data is a strong indicator of market sentiment towards individual companies, and information sharing – perfectly legal – will take place among some market participants. The availability of data on short positions can feed the concept of self-fulfilling prophecy and create momentum to drive a share price down – with market participants going short on Rockbottom Inc., simply because many others are!

Keep in mind that markets are often fast-moving, and large volumes of short positions can develop rapidly in response to bad news.

A strategic approach to short selling should, ideally, be informed by data on both shares out on loan and disclosed short positions.

The case for short selling

In 2001, James Chanos, a well-known short seller, identified fraudulent accounting practices in the Enron Corporation, an energy-trading and utilities company. The company's activity became known as the Enron scandal when the company was found to have inflated its revenues. It filed for Chapter 11 bankruptcy at the end of 2001.

The proponents of short selling maintain that shorting assists price discovery, but there are hundreds of thousands of long buys and sells in the major stock markets each day – and you might think that this was sufficient for reliable price discovery.

Short selling will strike a great many people as not very nice – as short sellers will be hoping that a company is failing and wish to help it on its way. This will be to the detriment of managers, employees, and shareholders as well as, in some circumstances, a substantial supply chain.

What are the positive justifications for short selling?

- Short selling helps with liquidity in the market – on the basis that short sellers are sellers of a share, when there are mainly buyers around. Short sellers argue that by counteracting this bullishness they are providing useful liquidity.

- Short selling contributes to price discovery – in that it can represent a considerable body of opinion saying 'this share is overpriced.'
- There is a plausible proposition that some of the best research on companies is undertaken by short sellers. This would be supportive of price discovery.
- Overexuberance in a market, a sector, or a share can be suppressed by short sellers. In the year 2000, a stronger dose of short selling might have led to a less pronounced boom and bust in share prices, by causing a light to be shone on firms' accountancy practices. Short selling provides a contrary view in the marketplace where overenthusiastic promotion of companies is commonplace. Company management, investment bank analysts under pressure from the company management for favorable ratings, and house brokers are all capable of bias.
- There is an argument that where a company is in poor shape with obdurate management unable to turn things around, a strong and sustained bout of short selling can cause perhaps inactive major shareholders to take action to protect their investment.
- Two great crashes have occurred so far in this millennium, and a powerful hedging tool for investors to have available for use if another great crash looms cannot be a bad thing.

The case against short selling

Though the case for short selling undoubtedly has merit, no one should believe that short sellers are in business for altruistic reasons. Some of the negatives are:

- Aggressive and concerted short selling can drive share prices down to unrealistically low levels, damaging confidence in the markets and even causing companies to cut back on hiring and investment. Lower profitability can become a self-fulfilling prophecy. Many commentators believe that short sellers considerably exacerbated the stock market crash of 2008, causing overreaction to bad news and fomenting panic.
- There is considerable scope for malpractice around short selling. Unscrupulous traders will sometimes use a technique called 'short and distort' – taking a short position and then spreading negative rumors about the company to drive down its share price. Disinformation campaigns can be very well-planned and are often anonymous.
- Shorting activity is much smaller than long activity and therefore coordinated activity can be more viable. The scenario that there is cooperation between parties that take 'long-term' short positions and traders who relentlessly hammer down a share price on a daily basis using a range of techniques is plausible. Sometimes, perhaps, these activities will fall under the umbrella of a single organization. Consider the amount of illicit cooperation that occurred to manipulate Libor rates and forex trading post–financial crisis – no doubt aided and abetted by the degree of connectivity that is now possible between

market participants. 'Bear raids' and 'bear squeezes', as discussed below, are a reality of the marketplace and may sometimes involve collaboration across market participants.

- The growth of 'under-regulated' dark pools and increasing volumes of trading within them – not the original proposition – may be providing a cover for sharp practice. There may be more malpractice taking place around short selling than the authorities care to admit.

- Short selling is fundamental to trading and in particular to high-frequency trading, which many argue increases share price volatility – an essential factor in the profitability of trading. So it's hardly surprising that the investment banking and hedge fund community will be vocal in favor of short selling.

Naked short selling

It is widely believed that naked short selling led to the demise of Lehman Brothers and Bear Stearns – kicking off the global financial crisis.

Naked short selling is where market participants sell shares that they don´t actually possess. They then have three days up to settlement date to deliver the shares to the counterparty, i.e., the purchaser. If they don´t deliver, they are subject to heavy fines. If a share price is falling fast, naked short sellers will sell instantly and then look for the shares to borrow – time is money!

Shorting the subprime market

It is widely accepted that the collapse of the subprime mortgage market kicked off the great financial crisis. And supporters of short selling say that if it had been possible to short the subprime market, it may have not gotten so out of control. Actually, it is reported that Goldman Sachs shorted the market through a new and somewhat obscure index – the ABX, an index of tradable asset-backed securities and credit default swaps. By shorting this index through extremely turbulent times, Goldman Sachs managed to negotiate these troubled waters better than most. If you are interested to know more about this, search <u>Goldman Sachs shorting subprime mortgage crisis</u>. These were not shares, of course, but it is a good example of the power of shorting. For much of the time, Goldman Sachs was swimming against the stream, but they managed to hold their nerve.

Bear raids and short squeezes

On December 5, 2014, software group Sage's shares rose sharply for a second day, up 6.5% as a short squeeze followed its full-year earnings. Nearly 5% of Sage's free float was out on loan ahead of the results, the highest percentage outside a dividend payment period in more than five years.

A bear raid is a concerted effort by a number of market participants to drive down a share price in order to profit from short positions – and can cause a share price to plunge well below a realistic price level. Also, bear raids can lead to a company going out of business – in which case the short sellers do particularly well. If the shorted company suddenly comes out with some good news, e.g., in an earnings report, or its share price rises with a strong upward movement across the market, then the short sellers have to move quickly to buy back their shares – short covering – before they have risen too sharply. All of a sudden you have a strong reversal of fortune, with the share price achieving some strong upward momentum. This is known as 'bear squeeze.' This can be quite a panicky time for the short sellers. A share price can rise at frightening speed helped along as the price surges up through the many short trader stop-losses that are likely to be in place. Each layer of stop-losses will precipitate another surge in buying.

Dynamics and risks of short selling

'Never short a dull market – VIX below 14.'

The mining sector globally had a very bad financial crisis, recovered well up to 2010, and then went into a long-term decline. Reduced demand for resources by China – at a structural level, i.e., not a short-term blip – as well as the market for gold moving into a serious bear phase, put sustained pressure on the share prices of mining companies. The large miners, such as Rio Tinto (RIO.L), BHP Billiton (BLT.L), and Anglo American (AAL.L), faced many headwinds – such as commitments to large investment programs which commodity prices simply could not sustain – as well as a range of political difficulties and environmental concerns. Check out their share price charts.

It is widely accepted that short selling is a more risky activity than long investing. The cost of holding a short position adds to the risk, and the obligation to pay dividends to the lender is a further complication.

When a company is in difficulty, there will be many people trying to get it back on track, and also, failing companies tend to become takeover targets. A predator company could well be tempted by the opportunity to take out some competition, perhaps gaining some valuable patents, a good research program, a foothold in a particular geographic region, or perhaps the brand. A rumor of a takeover could cause a very painful price rise for unwary holders of short positions.

The best time to go systematically short is during bear markets, when just about everything is falling and short strategies will enjoy a following wind. Records show that, on average, share prices fall more rapidly than they rise. So if you get it right, you can make money more rapidly going short than going long – provided you can close your positions quickly when things turn. However, the charts of major stock market indices show that between 1940 and 2000, the trend has been mainly up – despite sharp downwards shocks from time to time, such as in 1987. Then the two great crashes of recent times were followed by fairly consistent upward trends. Studies have shown that during phases of strong correlation in a rising market, the majority of share price gains – 70% and more – occur as a consequence of an overall market movement, rather than company fundamentals. Correlation has been discussed in *Chapter 5*. So for most of the time, short sellers would have been working against an upwards bias in the markets – why take on a rising tide?

During the crashes of 2001 and 2008, shorting of major indices and most companies would have been profitable, though nerve-racking, trying to anticipate the bottom of the market. Keep in mind that it is very difficult to judge the bottom of a major crash and when the market finally turns it can rise very fast. It can take some time to close large positions, especially in shares with poor liquidity.

There is a range of professional short sellers, from specialist groups to expert individuals who will identify candidates for shorting, research them in considerable detail and then take long-term short positions. On the other hand, a great deal of short selling is done by day traders, swing traders, and high-frequency traders looking to profit from short-term price fluctuations. These types of trader are described in *Chapter 10 – Trading*.

Despite the risks of short selling, even in bull markets there will be sectors that struggle, and there are always companies that are in difficulty. If you browse through a number of, say, five-year charts, you will identify some companies that would have been great to short – and might still be. For example, in the US, the Energy sector lost close to 28% and the Materials sector over 18% in the twelve months leading up to January 2016; in the UK, the Oil & Gas sector lost around 30% and the Mining sector around 55% in the same twelve months. However, hindsight is 20/20 and there were several severe bear squeezes along the way. The further a share price has fallen, the closer it will be to its eventual bottom and an increasing amount of nerve is required by determined short sellers to re-establish a short position.

There are some participants who seek to drive a share price down rather than simply seek to profit from a fall. From time to time a short selling specialist, such as Muddy Waters (see below), will announce that it is heavily short on a particular company, in the hope that they will encourage some profitable downward momentum of the share price. Other short sellers can get on board, with perhaps concerted action developing, with the players sharing information – a bear raid. Information on shares out on loan and short interest enables short sellers to focus on companies that have been targeted for short selling by the major players.

A different dynamic can operate for mid and small cap stocks. A crash or panic sell-off isn't required for a successful short trade. In many cases, a simple lack of news will be enough to quell buying interest and cause a price decline sufficient to produce a nice short-selling profit. The risk with mid and small cap stocks is that due to lack of liquidity, when news does arrive, the share price can rise sharply! A much-used tactic is to open a short position just before a company reporting date, speculating that earnings will be poor.

Some short selling specialists

High-profile short selling specialists include Muddy Waters, Gotham City, Pershing Capital, and Citron Research. Some of their exploits, which often lead to law suits, are described below.

Muddy Waters

Muddy Waters Research is a firm specializing in identify overvalued firms and taking short positions in them. Search <u>About Muddy Waters Research</u> for an interesting description of the company's values and activities.

The founder of Muddy Waters is Carson Block, a famous American short selling specialist. It would be nice to think that he really is 'on the side of the angels,' and perhaps he is. Undoubtedly, Muddy Waters is a significant market participant.

Sino-Forest

Muddy Waters is probably most famous for its research reports on Chinese companies, most notably Sino-Forest Corporation, which was traded on the Toronto Stock Exchange. A Muddy Waters' report of June 2011 accused Sino-Forest of fraud and its share price plummeted by around 80%. Sino-Forest filed for bankruptcy protection in March 2012. Of course, Muddy Waters would have had a substantial short position in Sino-Forest. Subsequently Sino-Forest sued Muddy Waters for US$4bn alleging that, along with around a 100 hedge funds, they took short positions on Chinese companies listed on western stock exchanges. The lawsuit accused Muddy Waters of launching a bear attack on Sino-Forest with vague accusations that led to a 'cataclysmic' effect on the share price.

Standard Chartered

On Saturday May 11, 2013, Carson Block of Muddy Waters announced at a financial conference that he had gone short on Standard Chartered Bank. After a good run-up since a recent low, the share price had already begun a sharp fall, gapping down on May 8 and gapping down again when the market opened on Monday, May 13. The share price eventually stabilized on May 13, down over 10% – which can almost certainly be attributed to Block's intervention. He appeared on the financial channels on the Monday, 'talking his book.' His assertion was that Standard Chartered had recently made some large, poor quality loans in Asia that it might eventually have to write down.

Since Muddy Waters' warning, the Standard Chartered share price has declined from around 1,600 pence to about 600 pence in November 2015.

Blinkx

In May 2014, an American academic, paid by an anonymous client, wrote a blog on Blinkx, a UK online video company, questioning the way in which it reported its revenue. Blinkx shares lost a third of their value and Muddy Waters declared a short position. In 2015, Blinkx shares were languishing at around 25 pence, down from an all-time high of over 200 pence in 2013. An analyst commented that Muddy Waters research was of consistently high quality and had the effect of driving down a targeted share price by an average of 77%.

Gotham City

Quindell

In April 2014, a US company called Gotham City Research LLC put out a report on Quindell plc, a London Stock Exchange AIM-quoted company specialized in software and computer services, predominantly for the insurance sector. The report begins with:

'Quindell PLC: A Country Club Built on Quicksand

Gotham City Research initiates coverage on Quindell PLC, with a price target of 3 pence per share (92% downside).'

There followed an extremely damaging assessment of the business, including the statement that there was 'No free cash flow and negative operating cash flow.' It also stated that 'Quindell's shares would qualify for a de-listing if the shares were trading in the US markets.'

The market instantly panicked. Quindell's share price plunged from 39 pence to around 23 pence. Within a few days, Quindell published a strong rebuttal, which stabilized the share price at around 20 pence. The bear raid halved Quindell's market capitalization, which had been about £2bn. Subsequently, with all confidence gone, the share price fell to around 2 pence before recovering to around 7 pence (the share price was since adjusted by a factor of 15, so 105 pence on the current share price chart). The company had been planning a listing on the London Stock Exchange main market.

At around this time, the Morningstar website listed the main shareholders in Quindell as:

- Rob Terry (Founder and Executive Chairman)   11.12%
- Prudential plc   7.11%
- FMR LLC (Fidelity Management and Research)   5.77%
- Merrill Lynch International   3.17%

Prudential, FMR, and Merrill Lynch can hardly be regarded as inexperienced investors with little research capability! The stock market is a dangerous place.

US hedge fund Tiger Global was a major short seller of Quindell through a Cayman Islands company. Quindell shareholders who lost money on the collapse of the share price will be interested to know if there were any links between Gotham City and Tiger Global.

Pershing Square Capital

Herbalife

Bill Ackman's highly successful hedge fund, Pershing Square Capital, was so convinced that Herbalife, a nutritional drinks company, was an illegal pyramid selling scheme that it took out a US$1bn short on the company and announced it to the world. At the beginning of 2015, Herbalife's share price fell below US$30 and it looked as though Ackman's trade was going to pay off. Unfortunately for Ackman, the share price then staged a strong recovery and was trading in a range of US$50 to US$60 towards the end of 2015.

Citron Research

In October 2015, Citron Research, famous for its analysis of some Chinese companies, published a research note on Valeant Pharmaceuticals International, a Canadian company. The note drew attention to a recent disclosure by Valeant regarding its links with Philidor, a company that it used for drug distribution. Valeant revealed that it had purchased an option to acquire Philidor for nil value and had been consolidating Philidor's financial results into its own.   Valeant's share price fell dramatically, exhibiting extreme volatility. From mid-October to mid-November, its share price fell from US$180 to around US$90.   Major concerns were the possibility that it was overinflating its revenues; that steep price rises that Valeant was applying to some important drugs were not sustainable at a time when Hillary Clinton was railing against the same practice by a number of pharmaceutical companies; and that Philidor was using questionable sales techniques. Valeant asked the SEC to look into the possibility of malpractice by Citron. In November 2015, hedge fund specialists Bill Ackman and

John Paulson were nursing heavy losses from their investments in Valeant. A great many short sellers joined in Citron's short selling action.

There are many other players that undertake research, take short positions, and then do their best to undermine market confidence in a company. With the explosion of modern communications systems, it is easier than ever before to get your message out there.

Regulation

During the financial crisis, some governments banned short selling of financial companies – banks and insurers – for various durations to massive roars of disapproval from vested interests. Post-crisis studies of the effectiveness of the bans are inconclusive.

US

In January 2005, the SEC implemented Regulation SHO, which updated short-sale regulations that had been essentially unchanged since 1938. Regulation SHO specifically sought to curb 'naked' short selling where the seller does not borrow or arrange to borrow the shorted security, by imposing 'locate' and 'close-out' requirements for short sales. Naked short selling had been rampant in the 2000-02 bear market.

Between 1938 and 2007, the SEC enforced the 'uptick rule,' which required every short sale transaction to be entered into at a price that was higher than the previous traded price, i.e., on an uptick (a tick is any movement in a share price, up or down). This inhibited the tendency of short sellers to accelerate the downward movement of a declining share price. The uptick rule was repealed by the SEC in July 2007, and this may have been an important contributory factor in the market collapse that got underway in 2007. In 2010, the SEC adopted an alternative to the uptick rule that restricts short selling when a stock has dropped 10% in one day.

In the US, regulators are assessing the value of introducing disclosure rules on short positions.

Europe

In 2014, the UK government attempted to overturn the European Securities and Markets Authority, which was seeking the right to ban short selling in emergency situations. The attempt was unsuccessful.

> *'The introduction of the short selling regulation has had some positive effects in terms of enhancing market transparency and reducing risks of settlement fails in EU financial markets,' said Steven Maijoor, Chairman, European Securities and Markets Authority, 2013.*

In Europe, short selling is regulated, and you can find information on this on the Financial Conduct Authority website. An extract from this website follows:

'Regulation (EU) No 236/2012 of the European Parliament and of the Council (the Short Selling Regulation – SSR) requires holders of net short positions in shares or sovereign debt to make notifications once certain thresholds have been breached. It further outlines restrictions on investors entering into uncovered short positions in either type of instrument. It gives powers to competent authorities to suspend short selling or limit transactions when the price of various instruments (including shares, sovereign and corporate bonds, and ETFs) fall by set percentage amounts from the previous day's closing price.'

It was reported in June 2013 that short selling in the EU was dominated by 10 investment firms and asset managers holding 28% of all significant short-selling positions.

In the UK, short selling is governed by the new EU Short Selling Regulation which came into effect on November 1, 2012 with the purpose of reducing volatility and increasing transparency. The new rules are a response to potential for market abuse and ban some specific naked short selling practices. They require investors to report short positions of larger than 0.2% of free float to the regulator and positions of 0.5% and above to be publicly disclosed. These data are available on the Financial Conduct Authority (FCA) website – search <u>FCA Short positions disclosed to us</u>.

China

The 2015 stock market crash in China is worth a mention. After peaking on June 12, 2015, a third of the value of the Shanghai stock exchange A-shares was lost in a month. When things were going from bad to worse, the Chinese authorities severely limited short selling as one of a basket of measures to stem the fall.

Private investors hold around 80% of Chinese shares.

Critics of short selling bans maintain that it deprives the markets of much-needed liquidity and it would have been much better to have limited trading on margin as the market was rising.

Some guidelines for shorting

2015: Long-only funds have been beating long/short hedge funds.

The retail trader or investor looking to have a shorting component to his strategy should closely follow the shorting specialists. There is a view that specialists in shorting carry out very high-quality research. The checklist below may be helpful.

- To short strategically, you need to undertake some research and then try to get your timing right. Timing is arguably more critical for short positions. It may take markets some time to give up on a share – it may be just rising with the tide.
- Take a view on the health of the sector of your target company.
- Seek out data on shares out on loan.
- Check out level of short interest – you don't want to be the only person shorting a share.
- Look at the current valuation – run through your buy criteria – assess if the share is overvalued.
- Check out analysts' recommendations.
- Study the share price chart over at least 5 years, preferably 10. Take a view on volatility and trend.
- Consider how attractive the company is as a takeover target.
- Check out the Technicals around the share price, e.g., RSI, trading range, Bollinger Bands, Keltner Channels; the professionals will be following these carefully and will react to them.
- Consider liquidity – it is important to be able to close a short position quickly. Small cap companies are the most risky to short. Spreads can be wide and liquidity low, making it difficult to close positions.
- Manage your risk – consider use of stop-losses and guaranteed stop-losses, especially if you are using gearing.
- Watch your short positions closely.

9 Futures and options

Introduction

'Derivatives are financial weapons of mass destruction.'
Warren Buffett

This chapter is mainly concerned with the 'stock index futures' markets and their influence on stock market trading and investing.

A security is a financial instrument capable of having a negotiable value ascribed to it. Types of security include shares, bonds, and commodities. A derivative security derives its value from an underlying tangible security. An index futures price – just a number – is a derivative security and tradable. The futures markets trade a wide range of securities. In shares, they trade stock market indices, sector indices, and individual shares, all with high leverage. They are used by traders for speculation, hedging, and arbitrage. Index trading dominates the futures markets for shares.

Futures trading developed from forward contracts, which allow a producer of a commodity to agree a selling price at a convenient future time for his commodity. This would perhaps be a modest price that he would be content to have, and he is prepared to give up some upside potential to protect against an unattractive downside price. The speculator who enters into the forward contract takes the chance that he will ultimately obtain a better price than the forward contract price, i.e., he buys at the forward price and then sells for a higher price. Both parties then have the possibility to trade their futures contracts, which has led to the development of exchange trading.

There are now modern, regulated exchanges that enable futures trading between parties – on the one side, a party who believes that an index or share price will rise, and on the other side, a party who believes it will fall. The party who is wrong pays the party who is right – very different conceptually from a forward contract between a farmer wanting to lock in a price for his harvest and a speculator, both of whom can benefit from the arrangement. Or a mining company wanting some protection against a sharp fall in the price of the commodity that it is producing.

Traders on the futures market are mainly either 'hedgers' or 'speculators' and it is estimated that around 97% of futures trading is undertaken by speculators. A great deal of the speculation is very well-informed.

The market-leading exchanges for futures trading are the Chicago Mercantile Exchange Group (CME) and the Intercontinental Exchange (ICE). In 2013, ICE bought NYSE Euronext, with a major motivation being the acquisition of Liffe, the London derivatives exchange. ICE specializes in index futures based on MSCI indices, in particular emerging markets, leaving most of the US index futures trading to the CME.

Trading index futures contracts is now a fundamental and highly influential component of exchange trading – and the US index futures are the most important. Index futures are traded in specified contract sizes and the most traded type of contract is the E-mini (see below). You can find charts for the performance of the E-mini indices on the CME and ICE websites. Futures contracts are settled quarterly – they expire on the third Fridays of March, June, September, and December.

If you watch the CNBC financial TV channel, you will notice that it displays the Dow, S&P 500, and Nasdaq 100 index futures on its screen. The CNBC website under Pre-markets provides close to real time data for these US index futures, together with the Russell 2000. In the UK, the FTSE 100, DAX, and CAC index futures are also shown by CNBC.

The amount of money at play in the US index futures through leverage is huge and the number of participants is quite small compared with the number of people that trade individual shares.

This chapter concentrates on index futures trading of the main US indices and the S&P 500 in particular, which is heavily traded on the CME. An understanding of the role of index futures in the markets is essential to successful trading. The longer-term investor will also benefit from an understanding of futures trading in terms of judging sentiment and timing the market.

For detailed information search CME Group Understanding Stock Index Futures.

Fair value

The main stock market indices are referred to as the 'cash indices' when there is a need to distinguish them from the futures indices. Index futures are priced at 'fair value,' which is the value of the cash index adjusted for time value of money – based on current interest rate – and dividends.

Futures contracts have an expiration date. If you believe that the index is going to be higher than the current value on expiration date, you contract to buy the index on expiration date at the current value adjusted for interest and dividends. This is the fair value – the cash index is adjusted upwards to reflect the time value of money between contract and expiration, and downwards because dividends becoming due in this period are not included in the deal.

As the expiration date is approached, fair value and cash value converge. When interest rates are low, the dividend adjustment will cause fair value to be below cash value for most of the time.

During the regular stock market trading day, the index futures fair value and cash value will trade more or less in parallel, separated by the fair value increment. However, overnight, the futures value may diverge significantly from the cash value, presenting an arbitrage opportunity between, for example, the NYSE and the CME when the cash markets open. The futures fair value will also step up on market opening if any of the companies in the index go ex-dividend on the day.

You can find a CME Group fair value calculation by searching CME Group Calculating Fair Value.

As mentioned, CNBC provides the state of the main US future indices in near real time on its TV screen each day. CNBC provides the same data on its website. Search CNBC Markets/Pre-markets.

A snapshot of the CNBC display is shown in Table 9.1.

FUTURES

Index Close	Current Future	Change	From previous
2121.1	2120.75	^3.75	expiration date

FUTURES FAIR VALUE (0.5)

Fair Value Close	Current Future	Change	From previous
2117	2120.75	^3.25	day

Table 9.1 CNBC index futures display

It is not immediately obvious how the table works. The left-hand column shows the previous day's closing values. The figure in brackets is the change from the previous quarterly settlement date – the previous futures contract expiration value. The bottom right-hand figure is the change since the previous day's close. The top right-hand figure is the change from the previous expiration date, i.e., 3.25 + 0.5 = 3.75. So the 'Change' figures are the change from previous expiration date and previous day, respectively.

How futures trading works

In stock index futures trading a simple number is being traded which is a derivative of, i.e., derived from, an index of share prices.

To see how it works conceptually, let's look at it in terms of a futures contract on the S&P 500 index with an expiry or settlement date 60 days ahead. Let's say that at the time the contract is struck, the S&P 500 stands at 1,800 – the spot price. Trader A goes long, undertaking to buy the index in 60 days' time at 1,800, believing that the index will have gone higher. If it has gone to, say, 1,900, then he buys at 1,800 and can sell immediately at 1,900 – a profit of 100 points (in reality, there will be an adjustment for fair value). The counterparty, Trader B, is the loser as he took a short position, undertaking to sell the index at 1,800 in 60 days' time (again, there will be an adjustment for fair value). So he has to buy at 1,900 in order to deliver at 1,800. His loss is 100 points.

A trader can effectively close his position before settlement date by opening an opposite position as described below.

An intriguing aspect of futures trading is that notwithstanding the possibility to close a position, it is a 'zero-sum game,' i.e., there is a winner and loser on each side of every trade.

The futures exchanges and their role

Stock index futures trading is dominated by professional firms and, as with everything else to do with the stock markets, the US is dominant.

Index trading accounts for the bulk of futures trading in shares and as we have seen, the main exchanges are the CME and the ICE. OneChicago is a specialist exchange where single stock futures are traded. Many other countries have important futures exchanges, e.g., Japan. The exchange websites provide information on the futures markets and give an insight into the complexity of this area of activity.

As described above, index futures trading is based on a forward contract between two parties with a set expiration date and a final trading day. The futures exchange facilitates this by matching parties – sometimes referred to as the contractees – wishing to take long or short positions.

The futures exchange provides a regulated environment for the trading. Each party to a futures contract has a counterparty and the exchange minimizes counterparty risk – risk of default – by use of margin accounts. Before a party can enter into a futures contract, he is required to place funds in a margin account (effectively a deposit) controlled by the exchange. The amount of margin required will vary on the state of the market, e.g., if the markets are unusually volatile, larger margins will be required. If the margin falls below a specified amount, the party will receive a margin call from the exchange – he will be required to top up his margin. If a party fails to meet a margin call, the exchange is exposed to a possible loss. Once his margin account is established, the party can start to trade.

US stock index futures

The most traded indices are the Dow, S&P 500, Nasdaq 100, and Russell 2000 and each has a standard trade size and a mini trade size. E-minis are electronically traded and represent a percentage of their corresponding standard futures contract sizes.

For the S&P 500, the standard size package is US$250 x the value of the S&P 500 index, so if this index stands at 2,000, the standard trading package will be US$500,000. This size of package suits the larger investors, though trading in the standard package is light.

The most traded package is the E-mini S&P 500 (ES). For the S&P 500, the E-mini is one fifth of the size of the standard package. It is sized at US$50 x the value of the S&P 500. So if the S&P 500 stands at 2,000, a standard E-mini S&P contract will be valued at US$100,000. E-mini S&P 500 futures are traded in these units and are popular with smaller traders. The main US E-minis are:

CME - Globex platform

- E- mini Dow
- E-mini S&P 500
- E-mini S&P Mid Cap 400
- E-mini Nasdaq 100

Intercontinental Exchange

- E-mini Russell 2000

The CME has recently introduced an E-mini FTSE 100 index futures contract.

As we have seen, when you enter into an index futures contract, you are undertaking to buy or sell one or more standardized packages at current price – strike price – on a specified future expiration date and time. For the CME, the established quarterly expiration points are 9:30 am EST on the third Fridays of March, June, September, and December, when contracts are either settled or rolled over.

Trading

Only the largest participants, such as US mutual funds, pension funds, hedge funds, and insurance companies will normally trade the standard index futures packages. A wider range of market participants will trade the E-mini contracts.

The E-minis are traded on electronic platforms using an order book. Starting on a Sunday afternoon, the E-mini contracts trade 23 hours a day, five days a week on the following time table (CT):

> ➢ 4:00 pm – Pre-market Sunday

> ➢ Monday to Friday: 5:00 pm previous day, including Sunday, to 4:15 pm next day, with trading halt from 3:15 pm – 3:30 pm

Between 3:00 pm and 3:15 pm, and 3:30 pm and 4:15 pm, a 5% up and down limit on prices is imposed.

3:00 pm CT is the close of the cash markets in New York.

A trader can enter into a futures contract at a time of his choosing at the current, fair value price of the index – the strike price – taking either a short or long position. He can enter into a contract for the next settlement date or for one further into the future on the quarterly cycle. At the close of each trading day, money is transferred between margin accounts to account for the difference, if any, that has occurred during the day between the strike price and the closing price. This is called 'marking to market.' Both parties must fulfil the contract on the settlement date and the exchange facilitates this by means of this mechanism. The final cash transfer is made on the settlement date.

The pricing mechanism works by keeping a balance between long and short positions. If there is demand for long contracts, the strike price will rise and vice versa. As with regular share trading, the order book has 'depth' which varies with time. Traders will place their orders, for long and short contracts at distances from the current strike price, hoping to pick up contracts at favorable prices as the strike price fluctuates during the trading day. High volumes of trading will lead to greater liquidity and tighter spreads, as with regular share trading.

When a trader is in profit and wants to lock in his profit before the expiry date, he opens another contract in the opposite direction. If the trader is long, he will simply open a short position of the same value. So if his profit is falling away, he is compensated because his short position is making money. Or to prevent a losing short position from getting worse, he can open a long position.

Another option available to traders on the CME is to roll their positions from one settlement date to the next. They can do this at any time but the convention is to do this on the roll date, which occurs eight days before the contract expires, on a Thursday. After the roll date, the lead expiration month for the futures index flips to the next quarterly period. Liquidity tends to pick up towards the roll date and declines afterwards as interest shifts to the next quarterly period.

Trading costs and leverage

We have seen that the E-mini S&P 500 (ES) standard package is valued at US$50 times the value of the index, so that if the index moves up one point, the value of a position moves up by US$50. The index trades in increments of quarter points, or ticks, so it follows that each tick is worth 0.25 x US$50, i.e., US$12.50. The ES spread is typically one tick, so it will typically cost US$25 to open and close a position plus commissions, which may be around US$5 for a 'round trip' for a retail trader (less for an 'exchange trader'). If the index stands at 2,000, the value of the position based on one standard package will be US$100,000 and the cost of a round trip will be about US$30 or 0.3% of the position. Trading costs will be somewhat higher if made through a full-service broker but still should be reasonable. Index futures trading is not expensive.

Margin requirements will vary with time as the value of the index fluctuates. At time of writing, typical levels by a stockbroker for the ES are US$5,060 initial to be maintained above US$4,600. So leverage is not far off x20. For day traders, who open and close their positions each day, the margin will be at least 25% of the position, as this is regarded as a high-risk activity.

Trading volumes

The bulk of index futures trading in the US is through ES, with between 1mn and 2mn contracts traded daily. At an average contract value of US$100,000, daily monetary volume is between US$100bn and US$200bn – but it can go over US$300bn. Most of this money does not exist – only the margin is real money. This compares with a figure for trading the underlying shares of around US$360bn daily.

It is interesting to observe that S&P 500 cash trading volumes have declined considerably since reaching a peak in 2009 at about 11.3bn average daily share volume. It is now steady at about 4bn shares which, as mentioned, represents around US$360bn. Quite possibly index futures trading has taken some business from the cash markets.

Index futures trading is highly significant and influential!

The attractions of stock index futures trading

Trading stock index futures is increasingly popular, with a great many major market participants as well as with a growing number of retail traders, who can now trade through a stockbroker. ES is the most popular instrument. Individual share price movements are usually much larger than index movements and can deliver substantial profits – but also substantial losses. The movement of an index tends to be more predictable, and leverage rather than volatility provides the potential for substantial profits. Another factor is the plausible belief among market participants that technical trading is more effective for index futures than for individual shares, especially for E-minis with their strong liquidity – the more savvy traders of this instrument will tend to follow the same trading signals.

Other important aspects of index futures trading are:

- They trade virtually around-the-clock from Sunday afternoon to Friday afternoon, so the traders can absorb news as it's reported – so there are less shocks to absorb resulting from time lag. Traders who can't trade during their 'day job' working hours can readily trade the 'round-the-clock futures.'
- The S&P 500 standard packages in particular are somewhat exclusive to the larger market participants.
- The E-minis, due to their strong liquidity, are used to rapidly increase or reduce market exposure as well as to hedge against market falls.
- Due to regulatory changes in the US, actively managed mutual funds are increasingly trading index futures – and options – in an effort to boost a flat performance across the active management community.
- The index futures markets are fertile ground for the HF traders. E-mini order books have good depth, which is useful for HF trading strategies. Some trading algorithms will calculate the ex-dividends movements expected for an index on each market opening.
- There is a constant flow of opportunities for index futures traders, especially around main market opening and when the markets are hit by unexpected events.
- In an instrument such as an E-mini, there will usually be enough liquidity to keep spreads low. Both volume of trading and liquidity tend to increase as contracts roll over and expiry dates approach.

What is the significance of futures trading?

After the US main market close, futures continue to be traded, albeit at smaller volumes. The traders will pick up significant world and local events together with key data releases as the world turns, and this will inform their trading decisions. The index futures influence market sentiment and how the cash markets are likely to open. But a bright start reflecting sentiment can be quickly knocked by some bad news, or vice versa. Nevertheless, there is nearly always money to be made – or lost – in the volatility around market opening.

As the US opening is approached each day, a significant gap may have opened up between the index fair value and yesterday's closing prices in the cash markets. The arbitragers will go to work instantly to exploit the difference. If the futures index has risen above the anticipated opening price, they may sell – go short – the futures index and buy, say, the S&P 500 – through individual shares and ETFs. So the two indices will converge rapidly. When the main market is open, a much finer grain of price discovery feeds into share prices which will bear on the level of the index, and while the main market is trading there will be strong interaction between the futures index and the main index.

Notionally, futures trading is a zero-sum game with a winner and loser on either side of each trade, though this is tempered by the trader's ability to freeze his positions as described above. The major players, among whom the investment banks and hedge funds will be dominant, are playing for highly leveraged stakes. So they have a strong incentive to deploy their best traders supported by the best technology, researchers, economists, and business modelers and this adds to the authority of the index futures market. The big investment banks have futures traders, share and ETF traders, analysts, and arbitragers under the same roof and so will enjoy a significant advantage over the retail trader. The advantage they enjoy is to some extent evidenced by the number of so-called star traders who are not so good when they go it alone and try to establish their own funds.

Index futures traders can open short positions just as readily as long and this can be useful in tempering the overexuberance that often occurs in the cash markets, where the bulk of the trading and investing is in long positions.

There are countless stock index futures trading strategies, but it is not the purpose of this book to address this beyond some basics already covered. You will find information on trading strategies on the Internet.

Options

You can buy options to trade a wide range of securities, including share indices and individual shares. Options trading is complex and it is not within the scope of this book to deal with this subject in any detail. With a futures contract, the counterparties, a buyer and a seller, have an obligation to settle the contract on expiration. In options trading, you enter into contracts of fixed duration which give you an option, as opposed to an obligation, to buy (a call option) or sell (a put option), a security. Option contracts are entered into at a strike price, i.e., the current price of the underlying security. The holder of the option has the right to exercise it at any time during the life of the contract. With options you can make – or lose – money in both a rising and falling market.

Option traders pay a premium – the price – for an option to buy or sell a share, which will vary with the level of risk. Option prices take account of fair value, time to expiration, and volatility. If a trader buys a call option to buy a particular share, and the share price rises above the strike price, he can exercise his option to buy the share at the strike price and sell at the current price, thereby making a profit. If the option holder decides the share price is not going to rise above the strike price, he can seek to trade his option. Or, he can let it expire and lose his premium. There is no point for him to exercise his option if the strike price is above the current price.

If a trader buys a put option to sell a particular share and the share price falls below the strike price, he can opt to sell the share at the strike price. So buying a put option is a defensive play. If the share price rises above the strike price, the option to sell at a lower price is not advantageous, so the trader can seek to trade the option, or let it expire and lose his premium.

The premium can represent a sizeable loss, as a percentage of the share price in play.

Options are exchange-traded. In US practice, options can be exercised at any time during the duration of the contract. Options stop trading on the third Friday of each month and expire the next day – remember, futures contracts expire quarterly. In Europe the convention is to exercise only on expiration date.

As with futures trading, options trading has increased dramatically over the last 15 years. S&P 500 option contracts have increased from an average daily volume of about 0.1mn in the late 1990s to currently around 0.8mn, which compares with around 1mn to 2mn ES contracts traded daily. No doubt this is also at the expense of the cash markets. Options trading has become an important part of the price discovery process.

There is a great deal of material available on the Internet describing options trading strategies. A good start is to search buying and selling volatility.

The main significance of options trading to the retail investor is that it is extensively used to hedge risk and is the basis of the VIX volatility index and the put-to-call ratio, which are described in *Chapter 10 – Trading.* These are useful indicators of sentiment.

A useful website for futures and option trading data can be found by searching barchart/futures/marketoverview.

Triple witching

Four times a year, on the third Fridays of March, June, September, and December, the contracts for share index futures, share index options, and individual share options all expire on the same day. This is known as 'triple witching' or 'freaky Friday' and tends to result in frantic and volatile trading as traders close out or roll over their positions before market close. For investors, it's something of a non-event.

10 Trading

Introduction

The markets hate uncertainty – traders don't.

Trading is a vast subject, and the purpose of this chapter is to provide an introduction that might be useful to the retail investor who is already trading or considering having a go at it. Some trading will give you useful insights into how the stock market works, but many retail traders are likely to achieve better returns from a sound investment strategy.

In the context of the stock market, you can trade an individual share on the cash markets and an index futures price or single stock future (SSF) on the derivatives markets. Exchange Traded Funds (ETFs) are increasingly used for index trading. Index movements tend to be less volatile and more predictable than the share prices of the companies that comprise the indices. On some significant news, trading the individual shares most affected is likely to be more rewarding than trading the index. You can also trade stock options. Futures and options trading have been briefly described in the previous chapter.

In the UK, a great deal of trading in both individual shares and indices is carried out through Contracts for Difference (CFDs). See *Chapter 11.*

This chapter addresses trading in individual shares, though some of the material here will be relevant to index trading. Successful stock market trading requires experience, discipline, and both fundamental and technical knowledge. Many traders and trading gurus place too much emphasis on Technicals and not enough on Fundamentals. Traders need to understand how share prices behave and how they are influenced by news flow and by key market participants. For the possibly under-resourced retail trader, keeping up with news flow and rapidly moving Technicals is a real challenge. See *Chapter 5.*

There is little doubt that profitable trading is a professional or semi-professional activity and the retail investor should enter this domain cautiously – if at all. A serious issue for the retail trader is that he becomes so focused on rapid share price fluctuations in real time that he will fail to see the bigger picture around a share price movement, and miss out on substantial movements that often take place over several days, weeks, or months – why close a winning position? However, many retail traders will be using gearing – trading on margin – and this will make their trading fingers very twitchy, and they will be inclined to close their positions each day.

Many traders will set themselves up on professional trading platforms. Others will trade on a more basic brokerage platform and use a couple of screens. For example, one screen may display the movements of indices and share prices in real time, with the other used to follow emerging chart patterns overlaid with customized metrics, e.g., trading volume, relative strength index (RSI), and moving averages. The trader should also be alert for news which could impact his positions and have good information systems so that he can rapidly discover the background to dramatic movements in indices or share prices.

Analysis of the share price chart has been taken to extremes and a vast amount has been written on it, quite a lot of it getting into the realms of snake oil salesmanship. Many people claim to have developed fool-proof techniques for reading charts that have made them multimillionaires – and offering to make you a multimillionaire, for a fee!

It is a matter of record that many, perhaps even most, retail traders lose money and sooner or later quit. Some will have the well-known gambling syndrome, perhaps laced with a fondness for adrenalin, and just keep going regardless, encouraged by the big wins that they will probably have from time to time. But for many retail traders, over time their losses exceed their gains. The trading platform industry needs to have a constant feed of new players, and to this end runs very slick and seductive campaigns to sell their increasingly sophisticated platforms and trading systems. Most retail traders will never be able to exploit the full range of functionality available on these platforms.

Reading this chapter will not make you an expert and profitable trader, but you might find it to be a useful introduction that will help you to position yourself as a trader. Or it may persuade you that it's more trouble than it's worth.

The difference between trading and investing

There are so many different approaches to trading and investing that a distinction cannot be precise. However, most basically it can be said that traders seek to profit from short-term movements in share prices – where 'short-term' can encompass positions held for fractions of a second to several months or longer. Day traders will look to open and close their positions each day. Other traders will take a view and may leave positions open for much longer. The higher or lower a share price moves, the greater the probability of a significant reversal, and judging this is an important trading skill. It is worth realizing that a recovering or collapsing share price can move a long way in months rather than years – up or down by a factor in the region of 10 is not unheard of.

An investor will tend to think longer-term, but within the investment community there will be entirely different approaches to, for example, taking profit or closing positions that are not working. Data shows that fund managers hold positions for shorter periods than they used to. The overall behavior of the markets at any particular time, particularly with respect to volatility, will influence approaches. When an investor is turning over positions rapidly, perhaps in a volatile phase of the market, then his activities will be closer to trading than investing.

There are shares that are regarded in some quarters as 'investing shares,' and others as 'trading shares' – or even 'spiv' shares in the UK, where a spiv is a flashy or slick operator. A factor in this will be the quality of the shareholder register. The presence of some large institutional investors with significant positions in the company and with a long-term perspective may give some stability to the share price.

Algorithmic trading

This is the age of robot traders.

Algorithmic or computerized trading is now routinely used by a great many market participants, including investment banks, institutional investors, and hedge funds. It dominates the activities in major stock markets around the world, where it is estimated that well over half of trading is algorithmic. For large cap stocks, most trades are algorithmic. Trades executed by algorithms are designated AT for automatic trade. The development of algorithmic trading led to the evolution of high-frequency trading, which is particularly profitable when markets are volatile. A great deal of algorithmic trading can be classified as high-frequency. Algorithms are used in both the cash and futures markets.

There are countless trading algorithms in operation in the markets every day. They are proprietary systems with their developers seeking competitive advantage. There is a wide range of algorithmic trading strategies that are based on codified rules and at the most basic level, they will seek to identify and exploit trends.

Most commonly, an algorithm will be designed to undertake a large buy or sell instruction, seeking to achieve a specified average target price. Trading rules are often based on a share price in relation to its moving average combined with analysis of trading volumes. The algorithm will seek to trade close to the volume weighted average price (VWAP) of a share. It will divide a large block of shares into packages and seek to trade them in a way that will have the least possible effect on the share price. Iceberg orders are commonly used for this, where the main order is hidden from the market and partial orders are released, sometimes over several days. In other strategies, the algorithm will interrogate the stock exchange's electronic order book. The order book comprises a constantly changing universe of limit orders, i.e., orders to buy or sell tranches of shares at a specified maximum or minimum price. The stock exchange computer system organizes these to show 'best bid' and 'best offer' prices and the trading algorithm attempts to analyze and interpret the rapidly changing patterns therein to inform its trading.

Some of the algorithms have additional functionality, e.g., scanning key data releases and incorporating them into their analyses. Some stock exchanges are creating news feeds that can be automatically read and analyzed by trading algorithms. This gives a clear trading advantage to well-equipped professional traders, especially when 'highly actionable' news occurs. High-frequency trading is discussed in more detail later in this chapter.

Market makers also make use of trading algorithms. They operate in a particularly complex world, competing with other market makers, providing liquidity and managing sometimes extreme volatility while seeking to generate a profit.

The influence of trading algorithms is highly visible. On significant unexpected news, the stock market indices are likely to rise or fall virtually instantaneously. If you pay for share price data in real time, you will observe the same with very rapid rises and falls in share prices. For the retail trader, the main price movements will have taken place before he can open a position in just one share. However, as you might expect, with technology advancing relentlessly, the retail investor can now buy trading algorithms for his private use.

Trading on margin and leverage

'When you combine ignorance and leverage, you get some pretty interesting results.'
Warren Buffett

Most stockbrokers will allow you to gear or leverage your money by trading on margin. In the US the amount of credit that brokerage firms may extend to customers in their cash accounts is regulated by the Federal Reserve Board. According to Regulation T, a customer may borrow up to 50% of the purchase price of shares that can be purchased on margin – the initial margin. In the UK, the 50% rule also usually applies.

In effect the stockbroker is lending you money to invest, e.g., at 50% margin, you can place, say, US$10,000 with a stockbroker and open a position of US$20,000 in a share. If your position moves against you, the stockbroker may make a margin call to manage his risk of bad debt and you will have to add money to your trading account. Interest rates will be steep, typically in the range 5% to 10% per annum. This is a useful source of income to stockbrokers. Trading on margin will amplify your gains, but the other side of the coin is that it will also amplify your losses. It is a risky activity with a degree of complexity, and you should make sure that you fully understand your stockbroker's terms and conditions if you are planning to trade on margin. Also check out commissions and interest rates.

You can also leverage your positions through trading derivatives, taking long or short positions. With a derivative, you simply trade on the value of a share (or index) rather than the share itself.

In the US, most derivative trading in shares takes place on the index futures markets where high leverage is available. With futures contracts, margin and leverage are at the discretion of the exchange and your stockbroker.

In the UK, you can typically obtain up to 10% margin, i.e., borrow 90% of a position, on a CFD platform. So you can open a £10,000 position using only £1,000. This is an attractive proposition as a 5% increase in the position translates to £500 – a 50% gain for the trader, but of course it can go the other way. A significant benefit of CFD trading is that 0.5% stamp duty on share purchases, which would be a serious drag on short-term trading, is avoided. CFD trading is illegal in the US.

Professional traders will use leverage to make the most efficient use of money. Many retail traders will use leverage because they want to play for high stakes. Using leverage of course amplifies your risk, and if you do, then you would be well advised to use stop-losses. However, this makes you particularly vulnerable to the aggressive tactics of high-frequency traders and market makers. Stop-losses and their use are discussed below.

Trading platforms

If you are going to make short-term trades, then you should consider setting yourself up on a good, professional trading platform. There are many brokerages providing this service. This should provide real time bid and offer prices or quotes and a good order management system ensuring best price, with efficient execution and settlement. Many other features will be available, some of them for a subscription, such as:

- Access to stock exchange Level 1 and Level 2 – see below.
- You should be able to set up a watchlist with real time share prices, and for an additional subscription, you should be able to get selected stock market indices in real time. This is important because indices rapidly signal a change in market sentiment, which a trader concentrating on a small number of shares will not necessarily detect as quickly.
- A good platform will provide a powerful charting package and analysis tools, such as share screening, as well as good technical support – they want to keep you trading!

- Streaming of other key market data, such as currency exchange rates and commodity prices.
- An economic calendar showing timing of key data releases.
- A company reporting calendar.
- Contact with other traders and interactive chatting.

For information on US trading platforms, search <u>Online Stock Trading Review Top Ten Reviews</u>.

For 2016, their top six trading platforms are:

- OptionHouse
- TradeKing
- optionsXpress
- TradeStation
- Fidelity
- Scottrade

In the UK, there are a number of good brokerage platforms to choose from, including:

- Hargreaves Lansdown
- Charles Stanley
- Barclays
- Fidelity
- BESTINVEST
- Interactive Investor
- TD Direct Investing

Providers of CFD and spread betting platforms include:

- IG Index
- Saxo Capital Markets
- CMC Markets
- InterTrader
- City Index

An Internet search will bring up more. These platforms facilitate trading across a range of asset classes. Many of them promote themselves through flashy and seductive advertising. The image of a successful young trader enjoying the high life is a common theme.

You should shop around the brokerages for the lowest commissions and interest rates and also read the terms and conditions carefully.

The brokerages want you to trade, and will incentivize you to do so through discounts on commissions for frequent trading, and quite possibly with trading support and sometimes with trading advice.

Information and trading levels

Trading Levels 1, 2, and 3 have been described in *Chapter 3 – Stock markets.* Level 2 is important for the serious trader, providing a view of the ever-changing limit order book. The trader can see the quotes offered by various stock exchanges and market makers dealing in each share, as well as the depth of the limit order book.

Types of order

The most common types of order have been described in *Chapter 3.*

Types of order have proliferated in recent years and it is now becoming recognized by regulators that the major stock exchanges have been too responsive in creating a great many 'sophisticated' types of order that accommodate trading strategies rather than the proper needs or functions of the stock markets.

The NYSE and LSE websites each list about thirty order types covering opening and closing sessions and regular trading, with many involving a request for delayed publication of the trade. This points up the complexity of modern share trading.

At Level 1 and Level 2, you can follow trading volumes and types of trades, though not all trades are reported in real time, in particular those from unlit trading venues – the dark pools.

Technical analysis

Technical analysis (TA) of charts and trading volumes can give valuable indications of future share price movements, and technical traders place TA at the center of their trading strategies. The ultimate technical trader (though not necessarily successful) will take the view that he can trade successfully based largely on Technicals – on the basis that all significant news flow will be reflected very quickly into these. He may make use of automatic trades, such as limit orders and stop-losses, to respond to sudden rapid changes in share prices.

Notwithstanding, a theme of this book is that both traders and investors will have the best chance of succeeding if they work with a blend of Fundamentals and Technicals. There are dozens of technical indicators and parameters. Some of the most common are described below, in most cases briefly because more detailed information is readily available on the Internet.

Investopedia and Wikipedia are good starting points:

- Volume
- Beta
- Relative strength index (RSI)
- Chart patterns
- Moving averages
- Bollinger bands
- Keltner channels
- Candlestick charts – price action
- Support and resistance levels
- Accumulation and distribution
- Put-to-call ratio
- VIX – volatility index
- Slippage

A useful website focused on technical analysis is Investors Intelligence, which has both US and UK sections.

Volume

Trading volume has been discussed in some detail in *Chapter 3.* For a particular share, daily volume is the total number of shares traded in the day. Daily volume can also be expressed in terms of value. Among market participants, volume is one of the most studied metrics as traders and investors look for indications of share price direction. Also, volume is a key parameter in some technical indicators, such as the accumulation/distribution line, and is fundamental to algorithmic trading strategies. Participants will scrutinize volume data, looking for the hand of an institutional investor building up or winding down a position in a particular company share. Or perhaps for short-term trading in small cap shares, they will try to understand what the market makers are up to.

Market information websites and trading platforms will provide real time volume information that draws together volume from the relevant trading venues. Examples of websites providing this service are FREEREALTIME and InvestorsHub in the US and ADVFN in the UK.

FactSet provides a proprietary volume analytics service targeted at buy-side analysts, which sweeps up reported volumes in real time, but the cost of the service may stretch some retail investors.

Somewhat illogically, these information sources will not always indicate an equal volume of 'buys' and 'sells.' This is because of the ways the trades are defined. The most-used convention is that buying volume is the number of bargains that are associated with a market participant buying at the offer price; selling volume is the number of bargains that are associated with market participants selling at the bid price. Buying volume is associated with an upwards sentiment for the share price, and selling volume with a downwards sentiment. However, the action going on at the yellow touch bar is complex and fast-moving as we have seen, and aggressive orders can cross the bid-offer spread.

Bid and offer prices are continually fluctuating across all the venues that are trading the share, and the trading computer's protocols will throw up anomalies on a regular basis with, e.g., a share price rising against strong selling volume.

However, significant movements in share price will nearly always be accompanied by high trading volumes, and usually it will be most useful to focus simply on trading volumes and share price movements rather than trying to interpret buying and selling volumes.

Another complication in respect to volume in the UK is that around 30% of activity in share trading is through CFDs, i.e., in derivatives of share prices rather than in the shares themselves. The only reported volume in these shares is the buys and sells by the CFD service provider in hedging his unmatched 'longs' and 'shorts.'

Beta

Beta is a measure of a share price's volatility in relation to the market, expressed as an index. By definition, the market has a beta of one, and individual stocks are ranked according to how much they deviate from the market. A stock that moves more than the market over time has a beta above one. If a stock moves less than the market, the stock's beta is less than one.

According to market wisdom, high-beta stocks are supposed to be riskier, but provide a potential for higher returns; vice versa for low-beta stocks, but you need to keep in mind that that volatility and risk, while related, are not the same.

Relative Strength Index (RSI)

Relative Strength Index (RSI) ranges between 0 and 100 and is a numerical device that seeks to assess whether a share is overbought (with RSI approaching 70), or oversold (with RSI approaching 30) – and therefore about to top or bottom out. Over a selected recent timeframe, it compares 'up days' with 'down days.'

RSI is an important metric much-used by traders and investors. It is applied to both individual shares and indices. Many websites allow you to display RSI below charts of indices and share prices.

Chart patterns

Charts are invaluable in looking back to see how a share price has behaved over periods ranging from, say, 10 years to a few days or even an hour or so. Are you looking at a steady riser, a recovery play, a volatile journey, a share that is going nowhere, and so on?

The use of emerging chart patterns is probably the most researched and written about aspect of trading. If you check out Investopedia, you will find an excellent treatise covering:

- Head and shoulders
- Cup and handle
- Double top and double bottom
- Triangles
- Flags and pennants
- The wedge
- Gaps
- Triple tops and bottoms
- Round bottoms

No doubt studying these patterns is of some value in short-term trading, but an emerging pattern can very easily be blown away by a significant news release or an analyst re-rating.

A good chart, when viewed over a few days, will show share price movement in great detail and you will be able to see the degree of volatility. However, when you go back over a few weeks or more, the chart may be based only on closing price, and the intraday volatility will not be shown.

Moving averages

On a share price chart, a 'death cross' occurs when the 50-day moving average falls below the 200-day moving average, creating a cross – which often corresponds with a sharp fall in share price. This also applies to indices.

Moving averages are closely watched for both indices and individual share prices. When a share price moves well above or well below its moving average, a pullback towards it is expected. A good charting service will allow you to overlay moving averages based on varying time periods.

There are various types of moving average, such as Simple Moving Average, Weighted Moving Average, and Volume Weighted Moving Average, which you can readily research on the Internet. You have to take a view on whether the 15-day moving average is going to be more insightful than perhaps the 100-day or 200-day for your trading situation. The shorter period is perhaps more useful when looking at an individual share, and a longer period when looking at the performance of an index that will display less volatility than the constituent companies. Charting packages will have a default number of days for their moving averages, perhaps 15 days, but it will be easy to change this to suit a particular perspective.

Bollinger bands

A band plotted two standard deviations away from a simple moving average of a share price, above and below it. By definition, it is a representation of volatility that rises and falls with time. Technical traders study the movement of the actual real time price within the Bollinger bands, paying close attention to breakouts. This is similar to RSI in indicating overbought and oversold conditions.

Keltner channels

Keltner channels are a similar concept to Bollinger bands, but a 20-day exponential moving average is used, which gives more weight to recent data. Instead of using an envelope based on standard deviation, average true range (ATR) is used, a volatility indicator that you can check out on the Internet.

Candlestick charts – price action

Candlestick charts are a simple way of displaying a day's share price action. A vertical bar will show the day's high and low price, as well as indicating the opening and closing prices. The body of the candlestick will be color-coded to indicate an up day or a down day.

There are many refinements to the candlestick chart and there is extensive coverage on the Internet.

Support and resistance levels

The price level which a share has historically had difficulty falling below is regarded as a support level. It is thought of as the level at which a lot of buyers tend to enter the share. Conversely, traders seek to identify a level that a share price struggles to rise above. This is known as a resistance level. There will be some subjective judgement in determining these levels.

The markets take a view on support and resistance levels for indices as well as individual share prices, and these help to define trading ranges.

Accumulation and distribution

The accumulation/distribution line is a volume-weighted momentum indicator based on the concept that during 'accumulation,' buyers have the upper hand and the price will be bid up through the day, or will recover if sold down and most likely finish nearer to the day's high than the day's low, and vice versa during distribution.

The Accumulation/Distribution metric is calculated at the end of each trading period using the formula:

$$A/D = \frac{(Close - Low) - (High - Close)}{(High - Low)} \times Period's\ volume$$

Put-to-call ratio

The put-to-call ratio is the ratio of the trading volumes of put and call options on any given day. It can be calculated for an individual share or an index and based on numbers or values.

Call options are bought by those expecting a price rise, so a lower put-to-call ratio, say around 0.6, indicates a bullish sentiment. A ratio above one is bearish. Current data on put-to-call ratios are provided by the equity derivatives clearing organization OCC. Search: OCC put-to-call ratio.

VIX – Volatility Index

The VIX Volatility Index has been discussed in *Chapter 7*. It's a measure of activity in buying S&P 500 index futures options – to buy or sell 'the index' at a future date at a guaranteed price to mitigate against losses, a form of insurance. It's based on a weighted blend of option prices for S&P 500 companies.

The VIX is very closely watched by stock market participants. When the markets are calm, the VIX will range between 12 and 20. The VIX above 20 indicates that the market is stressed, and in periods of market volatility it will spike up to 30 or more. Specialists trade VIX futures and options indices.

The VIX reacts very quickly to market-moving news and probably the main value of the VIX to the retail trader is as an indicator of sentiment. The skillful trader will be able to exploit the anticipated period of volatility.

News flow

News moves share prices – and so does lack of news!

Factors that influence share prices are discussed in *Chapter 5*. These factors provide a flow of news in many forms. Successful trading depends on rapidly accessing and interpreting news flow. Professional traders will be well-supported by researchers and information systems and will enjoy a significant advantage over most retail traders. Large cap companies lie within strong flows of news, some of it generated by the companies themselves, so there is much for the well-equipped trader to work with. There will be less news available for small caps, and their share prices will sometimes drift lower simply because there is no news to keep the market interested.

At a macro level, a significant news event in the US or China can boost or knock just about every share price, and winning positions can turn bad in milliseconds with trading algorithms around the world swinging into action in concert. News can also exert influence across whole sectors, for example, a sharp rise or fall in the price of oil or copper.

Professional trading teams will be up to speed with the economic calendar and have taken a view on which reports are likely to influence each company's fortunes – for example, employment data, purchasing managers' indices, industrial production figures, house price indices, and many more. Even then, the high-frequency trading people will have traded first, winning an advantage. Technology companies are now developing algorithms that assess how sectors and individual shares are likely to react to data releases. This is work traditionally done by junior analysts. Economic calendars are readily available on the Internet and on any good trading platform.

Of great importance are the sell-side analyst reports. Some of these, responding to a company report which has appeared before market opening, will often go public very quickly, calling the opening price up or down by a certain percentage. Then, especially for a larger cap company, analyst reports will emerge throughout the day, and a consensus is gradually built.

The heavy volume of news flow means that serious trading is an intense, time-consuming activity and most retail traders – especially day traders – will struggle to keep abreast of the news. The tempo of swing trading may work better for many. Both day trading and swing trading are discussed below.

Significant news causes volatility in share prices, but it's not always easy to exploit this with successful trades. Some information will be absorbed rapidly by the markets with a pronounced and enduring effect on share price. For example, a strong earnings report, a profit warning, an acquisition, or an important contract win. Other information may be more ambiguous, with traders making a quick assessment, while the major players take a more measured approach. They will carefully evaluate the new information before embarking on a program of building or unwinding their position in a company. Share prices very often settle down at levels very different to those resulting from the initial frenzied trading activity – if indeed they settle down at all. Traders will follow the Technicals closely, to gain insights into where the share price is heading in the short term, as well as keeping a close eye on relevant major indices and sector indices. These indices are also amenable to technical analysis. A sharp move in an index on significant news can very quickly reverse individual share price movements.

Trading signals and tradable moments

Buy on the rumor; sell on the fact.

The concept of trading signal tends to apply to recognizable patterns that appear on share price charts, and notionally signal a significant movement in a share price. You will find extensive treatment of this in articles on the Internet. If many traders recognize a signal that for them has a good track record, and trade on it together, they can create a profitable momentum in a share price movement, up or down.

In addition to chart patterns, traders like anything that they are likely to interpret in the same way that enables them to trade in concert – or more accurately, their trading algorithms. They don't need to collude to know that a strong rise in industrial production is going to move share prices in that sector upwards; or if Chinese GDP seriously disappoints and there is a poor US durable goods orders report on the same day, the major indices will fall and the professional traders will know which company shares to sell the most aggressively. If you are signed up for index movements in real time, you are likely to see an instantaneous near-vertical fall in all the major US and European indices.

In the context of individual shares, the signal can be a dismal company report or a profit warning. Events of this nature are 'tradable moments' and the speed of response is largely due to the activities of trading algorithms as the response to the tradable moment unfolds. For a while, things will be going well for everybody and then some participants will decide that things have gone far enough and there will be a tussle for direction, with the market eventually settling down.

There is rarely certainty in trading and the signals don't always point in the 'right' direction. During 2013 and 2014, bad US nonfarm payrolls reports were sometimes interpreted by many as good news because they might cause the US Federal Reserve to delay its taper of quantitative easing. And the markets rose!

The architecture and details of trading algorithms are confidential, but those of the same genre will tend to follow a similar logic, resulting in the significant concerted movements that take place on major events. In *Chapter 4,* reference is made to a well-respected essay by Keynes on share valuation and introduces the concept of convention. Keynes wrote his essay before the era of trading algorithms, but the obvious similarity between them can nevertheless be regarded as convention, and a successful market participant will have some understanding of the controlling conventions in any particular set of circumstances.

A significant event for traders, particularly those in the US, is the triple witching hour, which was described in the previous chapter.

The trading environment

A day after Google invested US$1.9bn buying American technology firm Nest, shares in an unconnected automotive equipment firm soared 1,900% as investors confused the two. The high volume of trades points to more than a few investors making the same mistake.

A great deal of diverse activity, driven by a range of motivations, takes place every day in the markets.

The trading – and investing – environment is increasingly competitive, and two key competitive factors are speed of communication and speed of execution. There is a ceaseless quest for innovation and competitive advantage. Bloomberg chatrooms were in the news in 2013 over multi-firm chat rooms used in particular by forex traders. Traffic volume was phenomenal, with Bloomberg subscribers sending between 15mn and 20mn instant messages and 200mn emails each day. Bloomberg reporters added to the consternation by tuning in, looking for stories. The Bloomberg Compliance Center improved the compliance tools available to its clients, but a light was shone on the volume of communication that takes place among market participants.

The rise of Twitter and many other forms of instant communication is a significant enhancement on gossip in elevators and bars. A number of companies are developing algorithms that search for tweets and other forms of messaging that might have an impact on share prices and filter out actionable information. See *Chapter 18 – Managing your portfolio* for information on these service providers.

In speed of execution, the high-frequency traders lead the way. They will be hard at work in both the cash and futures markets, executing a variety of strategies, which will all be based on the generation of profit with minimal risk.

An important modern phenomenon is the increasing popularity of index tracking funds and index ETFs. ETFs in particular facilitate rapid movements of massive amounts of money into and out of the markets and between asset classes. There are many regulatory concerns around the proliferation of ETF products, in that they can have a destabilizing effect on markets and that there is potential for market abuse.

Trading and investing around the globe is strongly influenced by the US index futures trading, which is described in *Chapter 9.* The futures indices absorb market-moving information around the clock, and often set the tone as the world's stock markets open and close. In addition to main index futures trading, futures trading at a finer grain takes place at a sector level and in individual shares. Participants in the futures markets include the global heavyweights - investment banks, hedge funds, and high-frequency trading houses.

Many shares are cross-listed and traded on more than one stock exchange. There are opening and closing auctions and extended hours trading adding to the complexity of the environment. The news flows never stop. Large organizations with strong research departments and the capability to absorb and analyze vast amounts of information and data in close to real time, and in a coherent way across company divisions, will enjoy a substantial trading advantage.

Usually, the heaviest trading activity takes place early in the trading session. Where there has been significant overnight divergence between the futures prices and the previous closing prices on the cash markets, there will be considerable trading activity, including arbitrage, to bring them back in line. On most trading days, the second busiest time is towards the end of the trading day, when participants take money off the table and/or position themselves for the next market opening.

Fund managers are classified and ranked and seek to beat their specified benchmark index and to outperform their peers. A much-used measure of portfolio performance is 'alpha,' which is described in *Chapter 12.* Viewed simply, if a mutual fund beats its benchmark index, alpha is the percentage measure of this, adjusted for risk. The point being that a fund manager is not credited with alpha if his outperformance is based on a high-risk strategy. His success will be regarded as just luck.

Many fund managers now refresh their portfolios on a regular basis and an important facet of their portfolio management will be building their positions at attractive price levels – they rely on their trading desk to achieve a best average price in competition with other trading desks. The institutions' trading desks are very influential during the trading day, handling large trading volumes. They have to cover the spectrum of activity between trading and investing in order to fulfill their briefs. Part of this dynamic is the high-frequency traders seeking to front run the fund managers and their trading desks – anticipating their intentions, and seeking to pick up tranches of shares on offer in, for example, a rising price situation, beating the fund managers on speed, and then selling the shares on to them. They are 'capturing alpha' from the fund managers which, unsurprisingly, the fund managers don't like. Other market participants will take account of significant institutional activity, to the extent that they can identify it, in their buy and sell decisions.

In efforts to boost performance and capture alpha, there is increasing incidence of fund managers using long/short strategies and allocating monies to hedge funds for management. Hedge funds in particular will be executing their long and short strategies, and during the day there will be bear raids and short squeezes. And there will be unlit activities in the dark pool trading venues, sometimes with unwelcome interventions by the high-frequency traders.

Individuals in investment banks will be seeking to build or burnish their reputations and to earn spectacular bonuses. Investment banks have many activities under one roof, including stockbroking, trading, market making, and mergers and acquisitions, and interaction between activities can clearly be advantageous. After the scandals of the last decade, the investment banks work hard at managing their Chinese walls and conflicts of interest, but there will always be people who sail close to the wind.

Sell-side analysts and their networks of contacts are basic infrastructure within the trading environment. Analysts' reports, in particular sell-side, play a crucial role, and rapid access to these will give a trader an advantage. There are regulations around release of reports, but as soon as there is a general release of reports, peoples' networks will come into play aided by modern communications systems. Unsurprisingly, there will be some 'leakage' as well, which may test legal boundaries.

The stock exchange trading systems and market makers 'make the market' in every share and they strain to keep the markets stable while seeking to make their own profits. There have been 'flash crashes' and sometimes trading in a particular share has to be suspended.

Stock exchanges make commercial deals with market participants, for example co-locating the servers of high-frequency trading firms with their trading computers.

Rumors are always plentiful, for example, advance warning of a takeover or merger can be very profitable, and suspicious share price movements are an indicator that leakage is occurring from within a company or from its advisors. Suspicious share price movements are now receiving more regulatory attention, and incidence of these falls in jurisdictions where the regulators up their game.

Traders thrive on volatility – they want market indices to overshoot and undershoot and also individual company shares because they make the most money on large price movements. They will encourage volatility whenever they see an opportunity.

This is not a calm environment. Unsurprisingly, many retail traders will struggle to play in it and may not discover why a position has moved against them until they read about it the next day.

About trading – some important factors

Experienced traders will usually prefer to trade in company shares in which there is a fair amount of trading activity, somewhere between 10,000 and 100,000 trades per day.

Market makers

The role of market makers has been discussed in *Chapters 3* and *6*.

All trading activity on the Nasdaq Stock Exchange is through market makers, and each share on the NYSE is managed by a designated market maker. On the LSE, the role of the market makers is most prominent in trading of the smaller cap shares.

It is important for short-term traders in particular to be aware of the trading tactics and methods of market makers.

As a matter of risk management, market makers will hold as small an inventory of each share as possible. When the market opens, there may be great demand to sell a particular company share – perhaps it has reported badly – and the market makers will have to work hard to bring order and some semblance of stability to the share price. This can result in significant widening of bid-offer spreads and considerable volatility in early trading.

If a market maker's inventory of a particular share runs too low or he has a large buy order from a favored institutional client, he may decide to drop the price sharply to induce panic selling – known as 'shaking the tree,' to get some shares in. The spread is another tool at the disposal of the market maker. He can widen this to discourage trading if a share price becomes too volatile and he is concerned about losing control. However, there will be more than one market maker for each share and the competition means that they do not have unlimited latitude to manipulate prices and spreads.

Traders are often incensed by what they see as the 'hand of the market maker' in 'disagreeable' share price movements. Sometimes they are right to be cross. For more information, search 'market maker tricks.' This does not tend to be a serious issue for the investor taking a longer-term perspective.

The bid-offer spread

For the larger cap shares, liquidity is usually good with tight bid to offer spreads, typically 0.01% to 0.05%, and only those traders buying and selling very rapidly, such as the 'scalpers' – see below – or the high-frequency traders, will focus sharply on spreads. However, for the smaller cap shares, liquidity will be lower and there may be greater market maker activity in setting bid and offer prices. For these shares, the trader needs to watch the spread carefully. Spreads can be particularly high immediately after market opening, reaching 5% or more, which means you will incur a significant loss simply by opening a position. This makes trading small cap shares expensive and risky. A bright start on market opening can evaporate rapidly and if exchange or normal market size is low, you may not be able to close a position as quickly as you would like – see 'slippage,' below. Nevertheless, traders are tempted, as share prices movements circa 20% or 30% in one day are a regular occurrence.

When you are interested in a smaller cap share, it can be better to wait until the share price has settled down after market opening before you buy. If the share price runs up strongly while you are waiting, it may be best to let it go. Be dispassionate, there will be plenty more opportunities!

As with any market, share prices are determined by supply and demand, and it is imbalances in these that cause the fluctuations in share prices, which can be rapid and pronounced.

For large cap stocks, there is usually plenty of trading interest with a high volume of trading taking place every day, providing liquidity. Absent significant news, share prices may not display much volatility and spreads are likely to be narrow. Good or bad news will lead to a surge of buyers or sellers, and sharp share price movements, most likely accompanied by an increase in spread, until supply and demand are back in balance – most likely at a new price level or within a new trading range. For the larger cap shares, this will usually happen without too much market maker intervention. Small companies will not be so liquid and it may not always be possible to match up buyers and sellers in real time. This tends to amplify share price movements. It is then the role of market makers to keep the market in these shares orderly. They can influence price by adjusting the bid-offer spread as well as by trading from their own inventories to provide liquidity.

Slippage

Slippage usually refers to the difference between the price a trader is hoping to get and the price he actually gets, due to rapid share price movements.

Another problem that occurs with small cap shares is that the trader may have picked the perfect time to buy, but finds that his order doesn't get filled because it's larger than exchange or normal market size. By the time he has broken it down and opened his position, the share price may have moved several percent. The same can happen on exit of a position with not enough buyers around and the share price slipping away. This is a frustrating experience!

Opening and closing auctions

Public stock exchanges run auctions to set opening and closing prices, and the professional traders are active participants in these. There are bargains to be had, both buying and selling. When a company reports well above or well below market expectations, there can be a lot of action in the auction and the matching engine will have to work hard to do its job with a delay of several minutes before the stock exchange computer finishes the uncrossing process and the share price opens for the day's trading. When it finally opens, a 'gapping' compared with the closing price the day before of 10% or more is not unusual.

Some stock exchanges run auctions during the trading day, sometimes on a routine basis for all shares, or sometimes for an individual share if there is a need to stabilize it.

It is now possible for the retail trader to participate in auctions through direct market access (DMA) arranged through a stockbroker.

Stop-losses

An important issue for traders, especially those using high leverage, is use of stop-losses. When you open a position, you have the option to place a sell order – a stop-loss – at a level that you specify, triggered if the share price falls to or below this level. For a short position, it will be a buy order. In effect, you employ an agent, probably computerized, to sell the share for you at a loss. Alternatively, you may place a stop-loss on an open position to lock in a profit or limit a loss should the share price fall sharply. Stop-losses are problematic, not least because they can be gamed. The concept of a stop-loss that you place several percentage points below your buy price or current price sounds very attractive in principle, but the retail trader needs to be very thoughtful about their use and effectiveness in his trading strategy.

Stop-loss orders are not transparent to the market. Typically, no charge is made for placing a basic stop-loss. However, a serious problem with basic stop-losses is that share prices very often gap up or gap down on market opening, i.e., the share price opens at a different level from the previous day's closing price, a consequence of the pre-opening auction. If the share price gaps beyond your stop-loss, it won't work. Also, if the share is not very liquid, there simply might not be any buyers to match your sell order and your stop-loss will fail to execute or may execute at the first matching order below your stop-loss level. To overcome this problem, you can opt to pay for a guaranteed stop-loss. The cost of a guaranteed stop-loss is a variable depending on the share and service provider, but for a liquid share it might be 0.3% of the position. So US$3 for a US$1,000 position – not insignificant on top of your other trading costs.

A strong message from both traditional stockbrokers and the providers of trading platforms is that you should always use a stop-loss. It sounds responsible and comforting – and professional. However, it is very much in the interests of the brokerage for its clients to use stop-losses so that they don't incur losses that exceed the level at which they are securitized by the cash on their accounts. This keeps bad debt down for the brokerage, and a commission will be earned every time a position is stopped out. And then more commission will be earned when the trader opens a new position.

Professional traders are watching their screens all day and may well choose not to use stop-losses – they will make their own sell decisions in real time. Many retail investors will not be watching their screens all day, so want someone to sell for them. However, in using stop-losses, you are to a significant degree giving up control over your investments – you are denying yourself the opportunity of 'taking a view' on a sharp share price fall; you just get stopped out and that's it. There is little point in setting stop-losses at around 3% or 4% as you will probably get stopped out on most positions by normal market volatility, leading to a steady erosion of your funds. This logic leads to setting stop-losses perhaps closer to 8%. If you set your stop-loss at around 8% the chances of it getting 'taken out' are still uncomfortably high – to be stopped out at 8% and see the share price finish only 5% down on the day is frustrating. An £8,000 loss on a £100,000 leveraged position is severe.

As discussed previously, trading algorithms are good at triggering stop-losses. If you study a number of charts where a share price has made substantial gains, you will probably see that there have been many sharp pullbacks on the way which would have triggered stop-losses. If a share price comes under pressure, the professionals may well decide to increase the selling pressure and drive the share price down through the stop-losses that are in place and in a sense waiting to be 'taken out.' As the stop-losses become sales, the selling pressure is increased even further and the share price falls far and fast. Eventually the share price will reach a low and then bounce very sharply – only to be traded down again. Great for the high-frequency traders and anyone with a short position, but not so great for the hard-pressed retail trader.

When markets are calm, the greatest risk to the retail trader will lie in events such as a profit warning, an analyst downgrade, a takeover bid (which may have an impact on a short position), or perhaps an economic report that bears strongly on the activities of the company. If you have the time and are supported with high-quality research and real time news flows, you may be able to manage your risk effectively without using stop-losses. Otherwise, you can try to be very technical and look for support levels or areas of accumulation for your share and place your stop-loss below this level. In addition, you can take a look at the limit order book, if you are signed up for Level 2, to see if the support level is currently corroborated by buy orders in place (though orders can be cancelled!). So when your stop-loss agent seeks to sell, he is likely to find a buyer (not an issue if your stop-loss is guaranteed). But then you are planning to sell just at the level at which buyers are coming into the market. Again, this is not playing the market odds very well. The research to inform placing of stop-losses takes valuable time.

It can make sense to use a trailing stop-loss to protect an unrealized profit that you have made on a share. Use of trailing stop-losses makes good sense in a rising market to protect profits – but this may be more to do with emotion, because you are seeking to lock in a profit rather than to minimize a loss.

If you are trading on high leverage, the case for using stop-losses is compelling.

Technical trading

Technical traders are not very concerned with the fundamental value of a share. They believe that there are many recognizable chart patterns which, when studied together with a wide range of other metrics, can be used to forecast share price movements. An aspect of this approach is that the charts and metrics, if studied perceptively, can provide insights into what the major players are doing, and this enables the technical traders to trade off their strategies.

The successful technical trader will be strongly tuned into the overall state of the market and news flow, both at macro level and company level. He will also be aware that strong, positive or negative news will often trump the Technicals. This is very evident from the near-vertical movements in indices when trading algorithms act in concert in response to a significant signal. However, there is strong tendency in the world of trading to exaggerate the usefulness of Technicals and the effectiveness of technical trading, and the retail trader needs to be wary.

Trading platforms place great emphasis on technical trading, and provide a range of sophisticated tools for their traders to use – with such an amazing array of tools available, surely it should be possible to make money hand over fist! They encourage use of leverage, which enhances their commissions and leads to high exposure in individual share trading. Their cheerleaders will make profound statements such as:

- Strict trading discipline is required and tight stop-losses should be used to cut losses.
- Until a trader is supremely confident in his mental discipline, well-placed stop-losses provide the trading discipline necessary to exit losing positions before losses become catastrophic.
- Traders must learn to exit losing positions early. Mastering this skill requires discipline and a short memory.
- Losing trades are an inevitable part of stock market trading. Keeping them under control will allow you to get out and trade another day.
- The best investors aren't right all the time; they just lose the least amount of money when they're wrong.

To a considerable extent this is the language of gambling, but such an approach is of considerable benefit to the trading platform operator. As mentioned above, every time the platform has to make a margin call, it runs the risk of bad debt if the trader cannot meet the call. Also, constant churning of positions means extra commissions for the platform.

Nevertheless, considering the great many 'non-technical' factors that influence share prices, technical trading is perhaps more successful than you might logically expect. If large numbers of market participants are using the same techniques, for example, following accumulation and distribution, closely watching the 15-day moving average, or being guided by RSI, then the concept of self-fulfilling prophecy comes into play. If enough people believe that a share price is going to rise sharply, momentum is created and it probably will. But the technical traders have to be very alert for the 'disruptors' that can put a price rise into reverse in a heartbeat, for example, an analyst downgrade or the company directors selling their company shares heavily.

The technical trader will regularly cut his losses and take his profits guided by the Technicals. If he has mistimed his buy and has suffered a loss, he may see that this is an opportunity to increase his position rather than to cut losses – this is sometimes referred to as averaging or doubling-up. He will let profitable positions run and may protect his profits using trailing stop-losses.

Long or short?

There are significant differences between the dynamics of long and short strategies. Short selling has already been discussed in *Chapter 8* and is revisited here, albeit briefly, within a short-term trading context.

Shorting is an important tool in the toolkit of the day trader or short-term trader. Every day, week, or month there are falls in share prices to be exploited, so why not? However, it is important to realize that there is a specialist shorting 'community' at work. It will be tuned into shares out on loan and short interest data as well as the dynamics and occurrences of bear raids and short squeezes. There will be a great deal of collaboration in the market. Another complicating factor will be the activities of the high-frequency traders who are able, perhaps more than most, to influence short-term share price movements. The retail trader should assess if he can equip himself to play and win in this game. In the retail context, the swing trader will be playing with better odds than the day trader or scalper, all described below.

A great deal of emphasis is placed on charting in short selling strategies. There are significant generic differences between strong upwards and downwards share price movements which are worth studying. A good example is the precipitous falls that can take place when a share price is falling and triggering stop-losses on the way. As the professional short traders often interpret chart patterns in the same way, they assume considerable importance. If you search 'short trading/chart patterns,' you will find a great deal of material.

Psychology

In 2015, researchers at Imperial College, London dosed traders with testosterone, to increase aggression, and cortisol, to increase stress. Both these hormones caused traders to invest in more risky assets.

While the broad psychology of the markets has been touched on briefly in *Chapter 5,* the trading environment has its own particularities with a variety of mindsets associated with different psychological types.

Many professional traders have the mindset that they should be able to make considerable profit from trading while taking little or no risk. A stark manifestation of this is the performance of the high-frequency trading firm Virtu – it was reported in 2014 that it had had only one down day in 1,200 trading days! Not too many sleepless nights there then, unless of course you were Knight Capital, which went belly up in August 2012, after a programming glitch lost the company US$460mn. Virtu no doubt operates within the law, but this is surely an area for regulatory scrutiny. Also seeking to be in the low-risk space are some traders in the investment banks who sail close to the wind and sometimes cheat. As we have seen, they have access to information and collaborative tools that are beyond the dreams of the retail trader – they shouldn't need to cheat.

Another mindset, quite laudable, is that you can use your 'smarts' to beat the market using game theory. In some situations, it will be the trader against the market in general, in others, it will be the trader pitted against a small number of other traders, e.g., high-frequency traders battling each other for alpha. The concept is that there are many parallels between playing the markets and playing different types of games. Gaming skills include strategic thinking, assessing risks, memorizing, decision making, pattern recognition, and so on. Search 'trading and game theory' for an interesting read.

Then there are the purveyors of trading platforms who give a particular spin to the role of psychology in trading. They project the image of shrewd-looking young men (rarely women!) watching a trading screen, when they're not swimming in the ocean or climbing a mountain, and beating the markets to make serious money. The reality is that you are only likely to make money trading if you have a sound grasp of both Fundamentals and Technicals and are able to assess situations rapidly – and be right more often than you are wrong. Share price movements can be violent, and you will often need to hold your nerve if you believe you are right. Often you will get it wrong, and then you need to draw the lessons and 'get back on the horse.' So psychology does play a role and trading is not for the fainthearted. But you will not succeed just because you have the 'right psychology.' For retail traders, trading is a risky business and a great many of them lose money and quit.

There are many high-risk takers who trade on margin and make a significant contribution to the stock market bubbles that have burst so spectacularly, such as the Nasdaq bubble in 2000/01 and the China bubble that burst in the summer of 2015. Among these numbers will be retail traders seduced into taking more risk than is good for them, and traders in investment banks operating under the radar of their compliance teams.

At the retail trader level, greed and fear play a significant role. Less experienced traders will buy a share that has already risen too sharply (greed), and sell a share that has fallen sharply just before it bounces back (fear).

So there are many different psychologies at work within the trading community, and it is difficult to draw any general conclusions. But being aware of the various psychologies at work helps the retail investor to understand the market and develop his strategy.

What is for sure is that to succeed as a trader, you will need to work hard and be constantly in touch with the markets and your positions – in an obsessive way, and you need to enjoy it!

Some trading approaches

If you don't understand it, don't touch it!

Information is key

April 18, 2013: commodity prices have fallen sharply based on disappointing growth in China, causing mining share prices to fall precipitously on the LSE including ENRC and Khazakhmys, which owned 26% of ENRC. On the same day reports emerge that the Serious Fraud Office is weighing the launch of a criminal inquiry into ENRC. April 19, 2013: at 13:50 hours ENRC issues an RNS advising that an offer for ENRC might be in the air. ENRC's share price surges by 10% in under 4 minutes in heavy volume, goes into auction for about 5 minutes and then surges another 12%. Total rise in the day is 26.6%. Khazakhmys' share price follows a similar pattern and finishes the day up 24.4%. Only professional teams are likely to have had the information resources to enable them to benefit from share price movements of this nature. The possibility of a SFO criminal inquiry was not an inhibitor.

Many professional traders use a Bloomberg terminal, which provides a stream of market-moving information. A Bloomberg terminal will cost a loan retail trader

US$24,000 per year. Another widely used system is Thomson Reuters Eikon, and FactSet is building a position in this space. Some information on these services has been provided in *Chapter 5*. These systems will be beyond the means of most retail traders, but there are many sources of free information that can be used to create quite efficient information systems. Many are cited through this book.

Many retail investors have productive relationships with stockbrokers. See *Chapter 17 – Using a stockbroker*, which suggests how this might be achieved. You will be paying for the stockbroker's knowledge through commissions and it is important to be sure that he really is adding value to your trading activities. You probably will need to work through a stockbroker if you want direct market access and to be able to participate in auctions.

Another possibility is to make use of services such as the <u>Prompt Trader Chatroom</u> which you can find with an Internet search.

Day Trading

Day traders look to open and close positions, both long and short, mostly on the same day and will often make many trades each day, sometimes only holding a position for a few minutes. They may well use leverage as discussed above, and should be able to negotiate fee discounts if their daily trading volume is high. High-frequency traders also don't hold positions overnight.

In the US, the NYSE and FINRA have imposed rules to limit the small investor day trading on margin. Customers that these organizations classify as Pattern Day Traders are subject to special Day Trading Restrictions for U.S. securities. The rules limit day trading in accounts holding less than US$25,000 in cash, shares, and options. For more information on this, search <u>Interactive Brokers/margin accounts</u>.

If you look at a chart of a major index, such as the S&P 500 and bring up the volume data, you will see that most of the volume occurs at the beginning and end of the trading day – periods that are rich with trading opportunities. As we have seen, if overnight the futures index has moved significantly away from the cash index – the S&P 500, for example, is a cash index – a significant amount of trading in both the futures index and the cash index, as well as in the underlying shares, will bring about a re-convergence. This is classic arbitrage play. Towards the end of the trading day, many traders will be closing positions, with the day's work done, or perhaps opening positions to take advantage of sharp share price movements that they anticipate or speculate will occur on the next day's market opening.

The professional day trader will have gathered as much information as he can on his target shares, including any analyst reports available early, and may participate in the pre-market opening auction – placing buy and sell orders, hoping to obtain a more favorable price than he would achieve after the opening bell. After an initial burst of activity, many share prices settle down, possibly entering into a trading range for the day, and the number of good trading opportunities diminishes. It is useful to recognize that early share price movements will be based on rapid evaluations of the impact of overnight news and perhaps a company report. It's very tempting to jump in to catch the momentum, and just as easy to be caught out! The major players may take longer to take a view and early movements can be sharply reversed – or reinforced. Where a company has fallen sharply on market opening, sometimes it will recover nicely during the day – or it may lurch down several times during the day, with participants continually trying to judge the 'bottom.' This is a challenging environment for retail day traders.

In London, the US market opening at 2:30pm London time can have a significant impact on share prices, providing another period of lively price action.

Many day traders will focus on high beta shares, i.e., shares that move more than the index of which they are a part. Sectors can experience periods of strong volatility, e.g., since the 2008 crash, many mining company shares have exhibited particularly strong volatility. You will also find considerable volatility among mid to small cap shares, but poor liquidity and wide bid-offer spreads can be unhelpful to the day trader and the hand of the market makers can be an unpredictable wild card.

Whichever trading system is in use for a share, the early trading can be highly volatile, especially in the smaller cap stocks, as the system seeks to balance the buy and sell orders. Price movements in excess of 20% in a day are not unusual. Spreads can be 4% to 5% or higher until trading settles down, so it can be a good thing to watch and wait. A hasty purchase just after opening can leave you substantially down if the price turns against you and you have paid a 4% spread. On the other hand, you can finish up kicking yourself if you decide not to buy when the price is up 8%, and it finishes the day up 20%. Small cap stocks in particular are not easy to day trade.

Day traders will use a variety of strategies which can be based on, for example, analyst upgrades and downgrades, company reporting, publication of key financial data and other news flows, momentum, and on charting and surrounding technical data. Crucial for the UK day trader is what the US futures are doing and the direction that the US markets take when they open. It can be handy for a UK day trader to close all his positions before the US markets open, as an unexpected sharp fall in the US markets can knock back even some very strongly performing shares in the London market.

Many day trading strategies, in particular those of the high-frequency traders, are based on price action. There are service providers that will sweep share price charts at the end of each trading day to examine the price action and to identify, possibly using pattern recognition techniques, price action that looks prospective. Take a look at the Price Action Lab website.

A common phenomenon is investors and traders seeking to judge the bottom of a dramatic share price fall, where you will see the share traded up sharply in the morning and then bashed down sharply in the afternoon. The pattern is often repeated for several days. This can be profitable territory for the wily day trader.

A competent day trader will follow his positions closely and continuously, and will usually not be tempted to leave them open overnight to avoid the risk of losses should his positions gap down sharply on market opening. A day trader will often be working with quite small percentage increases that may not survive the overnight news. He may feel confident that he can manage his downside risk without using stop-losses or he may put them in as a backstop, but close unsatisfactory positions before they get stopped out.

Some day traders will 'scalp,' i.e., make hundreds of trades a day, holding positions for just a few seconds or minutes, exploiting daily volatility in share prices – employing high leverage with the hope of generating a significant profit on small movements in share price. It has become very difficult for scalpers to make money in the face of competition from the high-frequency traders. The share that a scalper is following may move so quickly that he will not be able to exploit the movement, or if he is able to react to it, he will only partially catch it.

So why do many retail day traders lose money? It surely can't be that difficult to pick up a 1% movement in a share price and make money out of it amplified by a leveraged position. Well, actually, it is. Take another look at *Chapter 5* to see the range of factors that can influence share prices.

At one end of the spectrum are highly experienced day traders who have set themselves up with the processes and information sources that they need to succeed. At the other end of the spectrum will be gamblers. In the UK, playing CFDs will be little different from playing the horses and quite possibly undertaken by addictive gamblers who find CFD trading exciting. From time to time, they will have spectacular successes from their gearing, which keep them in the game. In between the ends of the spectrum, there will a wide range of approaches.

Swing trading

Another category of trader is the swing trader. Share prices do not move in straight lines, and if you look at virtually any share price chart over, say, a month or three months, you will see many significant swings whether the share price is trending up or down or moving sideways. The swing trader will look to exploit these, quite often guided by Technicals, holding positions for a few days or a month or so. It is important with this approach to be aware – to the extent that you can be – of the overall trend in the market and be prepared to let good positions run even through quite significant pullbacks. Again, you can get some sense of this concept by studying a number of share price charts.

Swing trading is a good option for retail traders. They will never beat the professionals on speed of trade but they can beat them on timing.

A proponent of swing trading is Dr. Melvin Pasternak, who has posted valuable material on swing trading on the Internet. Search his name with 'Swing Trading's Eleven commandments.' Interestingly, Dr. Pasternak describes himself as a 'techno-fundamentalist,' blending technical and fundamental approaches, and tells us that philosophically he has moved over the years from 70%/30% technical/fundamental to 55%/45%. This is more or less where you would expect a logical mind to be:

The website MyRollingStocks aims to identify shares that exhibit a behavior that can be exploited by the swing trader.

Momentum trading

The trend is your friend.

A share price having a strong run up or down is a very common phenomenon. The run can last days or years. Traders will seek to ride this momentum. Momentum can carry good companies, popular with the markets, way above fair value, but all good things come to an end and the alert trader will understand the Fundamentals of the company, watch the Technicals closely, and be ready to take profit quickly.

You can just keep a weather eye out for momentum situations, or you can find a good charting service that allows you to run rapidly through the charts for companies in an index or a sector. There are market information services that specialize in this, scanning thousands of charts at the end of the trading day, searching for signs of momentum. Price Action Lab has just been mentioned.

As the profit in a good momentum play builds, the probability of a reversal increases and this is not a time to relax in following the news flow, in particular company and analyst reports. A trailing stop-loss would offer some protection against a sudden and very sharp fall in share price.

There are a number of websites offering to assist with momentum trading strategies, e.g., Warrior Trading in the US.

In the UK, the Momentum Investor Newsletter has already been mentioned.

Some examples of good momentum plays are given in *Chapter – 18 Managing your portfolio.*

Trading on company reports

Some of the best trading opportunities occur when earnings reports and company reports are released. In the UK, publication of interim management statements and trading statements can be just as significant. These are moments of truth for a company when Fundamentals take center stage, and setting aside 'the macro picture,' company reports tend to be the greatest influence on share prices.

Reporting calendars are available on the Internet, e.g., Fidelity, DigitalLook, Bloomberg, Morningstar, and Zacks. Companies will often post their reports before market opening, though in the US, it is quite common for companies to report during the trading day or after the markets have closed for the day. In addition, you can check a company's earnings calendar for upcoming earnings reports. If you like the look of a company that is reporting imminently, run it through your checks and put it on your watchlist. Watchlists are discussed in *Chapter 18 – Managing your portfolio.*

Take a look at the company report as soon as it is released and check EPS against consensus expectations. The Nasdaq website is a good source of forecasts. Enter the company ticker in the search box and when the company comes up, click on Analyst Research and then on EPS for historical and forecast EPS values. These are provided on a quarterly basis. DigitalLook is another good source for both US and UK companies, providing EPS forecasts for typically one to three years ahead. CNN Money also provides EPS growth forecasts but in less detail.

Also important is the chairman or chief executive statement, which will usually give some indication of outlook and possibly guidance. If earnings beat expectations, and there is a confident outlook statement, then the share price is likely to move up on market opening.

You could make a quick decision to buy or you could wait a few days to absorb market commentary. A good source of commentary is CNN Money. Type the company name or ticker into the search box and it will provide the latest news and press releases, often using Zacks material. Or go straight to Zacks. In the UK, citywire money is a good source of near real time news and the Hargreaves Lansdown website updates its Share Research on companies that it covers, often the same day. For the larger cap companies, there will be widespread coverage of earnings reports in newspapers and on the Internet.

Keep in mind that there will be a great many professionals rapidly absorbing the report who will have been studying the company for years – they will have much deeper insights into the company's performance than most retail traders. Nevertheless, company reporting day does go quite some way to levelling up the playing field for the retail trader with respect to availability of company information. There are a number of ways to exploit reporting day though none of them is fool-proof.

Traders may decide to take positions leading up to publication date – long if they believe the company will beat expectations, short if they expect a miss. They then stand to capture the gap up or gap down in the share price on market opening that will be lost to the trader that takes his position on market opening. There is a strong element of speculation in this, but the more a trader knows about the company, the lower his risk will be. If there is a strong beat or miss, the share price is likely to gap sharply up or down. 10% plus movements after market opening are not unusual. In these circumstances, there may be prolonged opening activity, with a several minute delay before the opening price becomes available to the market at large. If a company reports in line with market expectations, the share price may not do very much - unless the whole market is moving strongly up or down in a correlated way as a result of a significant news event.

The professionals and more sophisticated retail investors may participate in the pre-market or opening auction. Most retail traders will look to make their trading decisions as soon as the opening price is available. They will have absorbed the company report as best they can and then seek corroboration of their view from the early price movements, perhaps waiting to see how the share price settles down after the initial flurry of activity. Then, as we have seen, the larger players will come onto the scene. Their buy-side analysts will have taken a view and many sell-side analysts will have sent their reports to an army of fund managers, who will need to work though their compliance processes. Early share price movements can be reinforced or reversed quite dramatically as consensus builds and the market takes its view.

Some analysts will take the view that even though a company has reported well, its upside potential is limited and they will recommend taking profit. Other analysts may take an opposing view and upgrade the share. Sometimes opinions will be divided and not all trading desks will be working in the same direction – the best opportunities for the traders will be when they are, and this results in a strong trend in a share price movement. A company share is often traded down in anticipation of a poor report. If the report is not that bad, there may be a relief rally. The large cap companies will be followed by many analysts and the consensus view will emerge through the course of the day – and be reported on various websites and, on the next day, in the print media.

It can be worth looking out for some big last-minute trades the day before a company reports!

Trading on the financial calendar

A great deal of trading takes place around pre-planned announcements of key economic data. There are dozens of data releases each week. The professionals undertake their research and will know the likely effect of each important release on sectors and companies.

Trading platforms provide financial calendars, as do many financial information websites. Continuing the list from *Chapter 5, s*ome typical reports are listed below. All have the possibility to move share prices:

- US Durable Goods Orders – a proxy for business investment
- Import and Export Prices
- Business Inventories
- Productivity and Costs
- Consumer Price Index
- Bloomberg Consumer Comfort Index
- Index of Consumer Confidence
- Treasury Budget
- Business Inventories
- Institute for Supply Management – Services Sector Index
- China Manufacturing Purchasing Managers' Index
- EIA Natural Gas Report
- Baltic Dry Index – measures the cost of shipping raw materials

Using the analysts

It was widely reported in 2013 that if you wanted to work for Steven Cohen's controversial SAC Capital hedge fund, you had better be the first to get the heads up from an analyst that has just gone public with a company upgrade or downgrade.

Analysts have been discussed in some detail in *Chapter 6.*

Across the financial sector there are analysts with a track record for making good calls. For many a company, there will be perhaps one or two analysts that have been following it for many years and are regarded as expert on its fortunes. They will be adept at obtaining market-sensitive information. The Institutional Investor ranks analysts by asset class and sector, with this information available for a subscription. Top-ranked analysts will have the greatest influence on share price movements and will be known to the markets.

Professional traders, from those in hundreds of specialist trading houses to those in investment banks and hedge funds, will network with analysts and the strength of their networks will be an important factor in their success. Some analysts have access to sources of insider information.

The retail trader will find it difficult to develop a network of analysts that will provide him with information as soon as the regulations allow, though those that have worked in the financial industry will be better placed. There are Internet sources of analyst reports in close to real time. Nasdaq under Markets/Analyst Activity//Upgrades/Downgrades provides data from about 90 major brokerage firms and updates its table three times a day. In the UK, DigitalLook provides a continuous feed of analyst recommendations – upgrades and downgrades – under UK Shares/Broker Views. Benzinga's website provides useful and timely information on analyst upgrades and downgrades and a variety of other useful trading ideas.

For short-term trading, the retail trader will struggle to compete with the professionals, who will have rapid access to analyst reports as they are published. The high-frequency traders will be capturing most of the alpha! Swing trading on analyst reporting is likely to be more productive, as an analyst upgrade or downgrade can result in a sustained movement in a share price. It's likely to be more productive to focus on the large and mid cap companies, as these will have strong news flows that can inform profitable trading.

Keep in mind that analyst reports can become quickly out of date and you should pay most attention to those that follow an earnings report or some other significant data release that has a bearing on a particular company's outlook.

Ex-dividend plays

Share price movements around ex-dividend dates have been discussed in *Chapter 5*.

Traders will usually not be much interested in collecting dividends, but are keen on trading the often very significant share price movements that occur leading up to and following ex-dividend dates, when the dividends are significant. The share price will fall on the ex-dividend date as the liability for the company to pay the dividend crystallizes. Sometimes the share price will recover quickly from the fall, but quite often it will fall a lot further.

The share price movements around an ex-dividend date can be much higher than the dividend percentage. So while a patient investor waits six months to pick up a final dividend worth perhaps 3%, a trader can pick up quite possibly twice that by savvy trading in the few days either side of the ex-dividend date.

Some traders will short a share before the ex-dividend date, anticipating that it will fall by more than the dividend amount – keep in mind that the gain on the short will be partially offset because of the obligation to pay the dividend to the lender of the share.

Specialize

Sector specialization can be productive, getting to know the characteristics of a sector and the companies in that sector, then trading around reporting and data releases that impact the prospects of these companies. Sector rotation has been discussed in *Chapter 5*.

Another possibility is to trade around movements in commodity prices, which impact the performance of resource companies.

Specializing in mining companies and shorting them would have been productive from 2014 and into 2016. Another productive area of specialization would have been to be long in biotech shares from 2012 up to the summer of 2015.

Devising your approach

Opposing opinions make a market.

There are a great many approaches to trading and to succeed systematically it is important for the retail trader to develop a manageable approach that works for him. It will need to be based on a sound rationale, supported by real time data – and shown to work on a sustainable basis. If you trade or plan to trade, some key issues are:

- To develop a personal strategy that takes account of how much time you are prepared to spend on research and monitoring positions. News flow frequently trumps Technicals.
- Take a view on how long you will hold positions for. A day trader will not be overly interested in the big picture. He will be content to lock in his profits each day and start again the next. This is his philosophy. However, day trading is probably the most demanding approach to trading and swing trading will be a good option for many retail traders. Share prices often make very strong runs though usually with significant volatility, which is a challenge. If you are using leverage, i.e., trading on margin, it is important to understand the daily cost of keeping a position open.
- Be very careful using leverage, even though this is one of the main attractions of trading to many retail traders. If you are new to the game, start with modest positions and only increase them once you are confident that you are trading profitably on a sustainable basis. Big wins will come from time to time, keeping people with a gambling mentality trading, though the reality may be that in the round they are losing money.
- Be very thoughtful about the use of stop-losses. They are not an easy answer to risk management and managing them can be time consuming. Keep in mind that the more leverage you use, the more is the need for stop-losses, and this is not a good direction of travel for most retail traders. An alternative to comprehensive use of stop-losses is to limit position size, as discussed in *Chapter 18 – Managing your portfolio.*
- Check out the liquidity of the shares that you are going to trade; you could usefully check out normal or exchange market size through your stockbroker.
- Don't trade small cap stocks unless you have some deep insights into particular companies. You will be competing against professional traders and market makers.

- If you are trading shares that pay a dividend, make sure that you have noted the ex-dividend dates.

High-frequency trading (HFT)

Warren Buffett on high-speed trading, CNBC 'Squawk Box', 6 May 2013:

Rebecca Quick: On Friday, I sat down with Charlie Munger. And he talked a little bit about the high-frequency traders. Listen to what he said in terms of who he was comparing these traders to. Oh, we don't have the sound bite. But at the time, Charlie said this is basically legalized front-running. What do you guys think about that?

Buffett: I agree. I agree. I mean, that's why these fellas exist and why they spend enormous sums on trying to get the speed of transmission, you know, that's a millionth of a second or a thousandth of a second faster than the other guy. I mean, you know, and it is not contributing anything to capitalism.

High-frequency trading was given considerable prominence by Michael Lewis' *Flashboys – Cracking the Money Code*, published by Allen Lane, 2014.

Trading, as opposed to investing, on the secondary stock markets is dominated by high-frequency trading (HFT) houses. Trading algorithms and some algorithmic trading strategies have been described above. HF traders have not the slightest interest in the efficient allocation of capital.

Many market makers use HFT to support their activities.

About high-frequency trading

'The best minds of my generation are thinking about how to make people click ads. That sucks,' said well known data scientist Jeffrey Hammerbacher, when he was working at Facebook. He now works for Cloudera, a company he founded. The same could be said of a generation of young mathematicians and computer scientists that have been hired to develop HFT systems.

A good insight into HFT can be found in the <u>London Stock Exchange Group Response to CESR Call for Evidence on Micro-Structural Issues of the European Equity Markets (CESR/10-142), 30 April 2010</u>. CESR is The Committee of European Securities Regulators. An Internet search will readily find this document, which provides a useful definition of HFT as well as useful background.

In essence, HF trades are executed in milliseconds on electronic limit order books and holding times can be less than a second. HF traders use their own capital, i.e., they do not trade on behalf of clients.

HFT is used for trading shares in both the cash and futures markets. It relies on very fast – low latency – connections to stock exchange trading systems to enable rapid trading. It is also used in foreign exchange trading. Because all trading on the Nasdaq is through market makers, many HF traders have set themselves up as market makers on that exchange.

HFT houses are increasingly co-locating their servers with stock exchange servers to reduce latency. They are constantly seeking opportunities in stock exchanges around the world, as regulation in the major exchanges bears on their activities. Some jurisdictions, for example Hong Kong, apply a financial transaction tax which inhibits HFT, and the International Monetary Fund has lobbied for widespread application of such taxes.

While HFT algorithms can execute any trading strategy, they have developed a range of strategies that particularly exploit speed. HFT operators will seek to close out their positions each day, and it is claimed therefore that they compete among themselves and not against long-term investors. However, this is challenged by other market participants, who maintain that the HF traders have an unfair advantage in capturing alpha. The first to trade on the publication of some key economic data will capture the most alpha.

A great deal of HFT activity is based on moving in and out of a position in a fraction of a second, generating profit through a large number of small price movements. The HFT operators will use a combination of Fundamentals and Technicals to identify opportunities. For example, they will interrogate electronic order books and monitor order flows seeking to forecast price movements 3 to 4 seconds ahead that they can exploit. As well as responding to short-term price action, they will also seek to create it. For example, some trading algorithms will place and cancel orders to wrong-foot the competition and to move share prices to their advantage. Legally, this is sailing close to the wind. High-frequency trading algorithms are also used to execute arbitrage strategies, seeking to buy a share on one exchange and sell it instantaneously on another, where price differences are detected, i.e., exploiting 'short-term pricing inefficiencies.'

Some HFT strategies will seek to anticipate large institutional trades and 'front run' them, e.g., buy ahead of an institution that is building a position in a share, and then sell to it at a profit. In 2014, several dark pool trading venues run by investment banks were severely criticized for allowing access to HF traders without informing their institutional clients. The large cap shares are very popular with the HF traders. Every day, they seek to extract some money from your pension.

Because high-frequency trading depends on substantial trading volume, the E-minis, particularly S&P 500 E-mini, make ideal trading instruments. HFT firms regularly trade the E-minis because of their technical behavior patterns.

On major stock exchanges, this computer-driven activity dominates the trading – especially for the larger cap stocks. There are over 200,000 quote updates per second on the New York Stock Exchange! There won't be as many on the London Stock Exchange but still, the hapless retail trader studying Level 2 to inform his trading activities will be challenged to keep up.

The high-frequency traders and their markets

In April 2013, a commentator on one of the financial TV channels described the purpose of high-frequency trading programs as to 'separate fools from their money.'

Studies of HFT have suggested that in 2009, HFT accounted for 60% to 70% percent of share trading volumes in New York and London, falling to about 50% to 60% in 2012 as a result of increasing regulation and competition putting profits under pressure. The other side of this coin is that less than half of stock market turnover is executed orders from investors seeking to take a meaningful position in a share. An additional factor in the UK is that a very considerable proportion of stock market turnover is executed through contracts for difference (CFDs), which are derivatives of share prices, and this robs the market of liquidity. CFDs are exempt from the 0.5% stamp duty, so trading through CFDs is an attractive proposition. This avoids billions of pounds of stamp duty every year.

Recent estimates are that the bulk of HFT is undertaken by specialist HFT houses and investment banks with a relatively small volume by hedge funds. Investment banks also provide HFT platforms to other market participants.

A list of well-known HFT houses would include Citadel, Optiver, Infinium, Algorates, and KCG Holdings. It's interesting to check them out on the Internet. You will find some colorful stories. Search company name high-frequency trading. Unsurprisingly, most of these companies were incubated in the major exchanges in New York and Chicago. They are capable of generating high profits in both bull and bear market conditions.

KCG Holdings came into existence as a result of the takeover of Knight Capital Group by Getco. This followed a disastrous loss of US$460mn by Knight Capital Group due to a trading error in a new system in August 2012. Knight Capital, a global financial services firm, was the largest trader in US shares.

The flash crash

In 2010, HFT was accounting for around 70% of equity trading in the United States and was blamed by regulators for the May 6, 2010 flash crash during which the Dow Jones Industrial Average suddenly plummeted about 1,000 points, or 9%, and the S&P E-mini index dropped about 3% between 2:41 pm and 2:44 pm. A large order in the S&P 500 index futures market is thought to have triggered a wave of selling by HFT practitioners resulting in a dramatic loss in liquidity. The 9% fall in the Dow was the second largest intraday points swing ever, though the index recovered rapidly.

The flash crash prompted a strong regulatory response, and in September 2013, the US Commodity Futures Trading Commission issued a concept release on risk controls and system safeguards for automated trading environments. The release offers a view of the automated trading environment, and presents a system that would involve:

- Pre-trade risk controls
- Post-trade reports and other measures
- System safeguards related to the design, testing, and supervision of automated trading systems
- Additional protections designated to promote safe and orderly markets

The case for HFT

In February 2016, IEX, a dark pool trading venue, applied to become a registered stock exchange. IEX employs a 'speed bump' system to deny the HF traders their speed advantage. This involves the application of a 350 microsecond delay to all trades and was described as un-American by one of the established exchanges.

It is maintained by many experts that HFT improves market liquidity, with HF traders acting in a market making role and making a smaller profit from the spread than the traditional market makers; and that a claimed narrowing of bid-offer spreads benefits both the retail investor and the large institutional investor. Proponents of HFT maintain that it contributes to price discovery by arbitraging and eliminating discrepancies between trading venues and that it dampens volatility. However, as studies of HFT become more rigorous and are undertaken by impartial bodies, serious doubts are emerging regarding these claims. The proposition that HFT improves price discovery is being increasingly questioned.

Concerning volatility, proponents of HFT have long argued that HFT's liquidity provision into the market has the impact of dampening volatility. However, studies in 2011 found that 'intraday volatility has risen most in those markets open to HFT' (Andrew Haldane, Head of Financial Stability at the Bank of England at the time). This is corroborated by other contemporaneous studies.

The case against HFT

In October 2014, the SEC charged Athena Capital Research, an HFT firm, with fraudulent trading to manipulate closing prices of Nasdaq-listed shares. Over a six-month period, Athena had made a large number of trades in the final two seconds of nearly every trading day, moving prices in its favor. The trading algorithm was code-named Gravy. Athena paid a US$1mn penalty to the SEC without admitting or denying its findings. You can find more details on this case by searching SEC Athena Capital Research gravy.

No doubt issues around liquidity, volatility, and bid-offer spread will continue to be controversial. There is increasing evidence that HFT increases correlation, quite possibly because HFT econometric models are increasingly disconnected from fundamental share valuations.

However, what is inarguable is that HFT is a highly profitable activity that is intent on taking money out of the market without running normal market risk.

By their very nature, HFT practitioners will always sail close to the wind with respect to ethical behavior and there are many areas of dubious practice. For example, there are suspicions that there is some illicit flow of information within dark pool trading venues where HF traders have been tipped off with respect to the trading intentions of institutional investors.

A concern around speed advantage relates to the so-called 'stealing of alpha' where alpha is the investment manager's return in excess of the compensation for the risk borne in an investment. In simpler language, the HF traders simply get their trades in first e.g., on release of US nonfarm payrolls data, where a strong miss on expectations causes sharp share price movements with fairly reliable predictability. A perhaps more serious example of unfair practice occurs when a HF trader detects that an investor is seeking to buy a large volume of a particular share and seeks to disrupt the market to its advantage, perhaps by exploiting a temporary shortage of supply in the share and trading the price up aggressively.

Investment banks are criticized for providing enabling services to HFT houses, enabling them to gain a crucial speed advantage over the investment banks' long-only clients, such as pension funds. Many market participants, especially buy-side analysts working for fund managers, maintain that this constitutes a conflict of interest.

HFT practitioners know that index tracker funds have to regularly adjust their holdings, e.g., as market capitalizations of companies change with their share prices; companies being relegated from or promoted to an index have a particularly significant impact. HFT strategies anticipate and trade ahead of fund manager block orders and capture some of the associated share price movements. Studies have shown that HFT relieves funds, including many pension funds, of substantial monies through this practice.

There is evidence that HFT trading practices are unfair to small traders and investors. Apart from enjoying an unfair speed advantage, in both receipt of information and execution, HF traders will sometimes focus on day traders and trade against them, e.g., by creating large falls in a share price to take out stop-losses and then making profit on the recovery. Another tactic is placing and cancelling limit orders with the intention of misleading other participants. This is known as spoofing, an illegal practice because you shouldn't place orders you don't intend to execute. Sometimes, HFT firms will deliberately 'stuff' the market with bids to slow down the traditional traders and increase their competitive advantage. The exchanges are not always as on top of these abuses as they might be. Another tactic to move prices to their advantage is 'washing' – where the HF trader buys and sells to itself.

Stock exchanges are perhaps working too closely with HFT houses through co-location of servers. They are driven by profit, and in information sharing with HFT houses may sail close to the wind.

The response to this range of HFT trading practices has included the relatively recent intrusion into the investing and trading environment of the dark pools – private 'off-exchange' venues. But as we have seen, the HFT traders have managed to insinuate themselves into these trading venues.

There are concerns that HFT creates a two-tiered market between firms with higher and lower technological resources. In the UK, algorithmic trading through CFDs undoubtedly creates a two-tier system as this activity is free of stamp duty.

Recent surveys have shown that a majority of institutional investors regard HFT as a negative factor in the functioning of stock markets.

You can find a very informative blog on HFT by searching <u>Financial Markets Analytics, Sam Cheekong, How High-frequency Traders Are Ripping Off Investors.</u>

11 Trading with Contracts for Difference (CFDs)

Introduction

Trading Contracts for Difference (CFDs) is a form of derivative trading widely used in the UK but illegal in the US and many other countries. The value of the derivative is exactly the same as the value of the share price that it is derived from at any point in time. It allows trading on specialist platforms with high leverage – typically x 10. This is known as trading on margin, effectively trading borrowed money.

It is estimated that around 30% of trading on the London Stock Exchange SETS is through CFDs. Particularly significant is that in the UK, CFD trading is exempt from the 0.5% stamp duty applied on share purchases, and this is a substantial advantage for any short-term trading strategy. The viability of high-frequency or rapid trading would be significantly impaired if it was subject to stamp duty on buy orders. This effectively means that there is a 'two-tier' system operating in the London markets, with traders working through CFDs and exempt from stamp duty, enjoying an unfair advantage over everyone else.

You can take both long and short positions on a CFD platform and also trade indices, such as the FTSE 100. UK-based traders can take positions in overseas indices, such as the S&P 500, and in overseas shares.

There is no stamp duty or equivalent tax on buying shares in the US, and you can trade on margin, typically with x 2 leverage, through a stockbroker. Higher leverage can be obtained in the US by trading derivatives on the futures markets.

Financial spread betting is a close cousin of CFD trading and also illegal in the US. Spread betting is perhaps associated with more of a gambling mentality and is only briefly described here for the sake of completeness.

There is much confusion over the concept of a European financial transaction tax, with even prime minister David Cameron saying that the UK already has one in the form of stamp duty. However, as a great deal of trading in the London market is through CFDs, a large amount of stamp duty – many billions of pounds worth – is avoided on this activity. A tax on CFD trading would be a massive drag on trading in the London market – one of the reasons why it is so fiercely resisted. A tax on the profit of each transaction has been mooted, but the practicality of this must be questionable.

The mechanics of CFDs

With a CFD, the trader enters into a contract with the CFD service provider based on the value of a share price or an index of share prices. He doesn't actually buy the share. The trader can open both long and short positions and close the position at any time during market open hours. If the trader takes a long position and the share price goes up, the CFD provider pays the trader the value of the rise; if the share price goes down, the trader pays the CFD provider the value of the fall. Vice versa for a short position. The platform will refer to long positions as 'buys' and short positions as 'sells.'

There is no expiration date on a CFD contract. CFD service providers are discussed below.

One of the main attractions to most CFD traders is the ability to trade on margin. Leverage of up to x 10 is readily available. A trader can put a £10,000 deposit into his trading account and open a £100,000 position – in effect borrowing £90,000. If the share price then moves up 10%, he will make £10,000 profit, i.e., he will double his £10,000 deposit (less charges). On the other hand, if the share moves down 10%, he will lose his entire £10,000. The CFD trader has the possibility to take a very high level of risk! Many CFD traders use stop-losses to limit losses. However, use of stop-losses carries its own type of risk, as discussed below.

Another significant benefit of CFDs is that they allow the trader to take short positions as readily as long. Short positions are generally regarded as more risky than long because, theoretically, there is no limit to how high a share price can rise. It is plausible that you open a short position in a company in difficulty, and that all of a sudden it becomes a takeover target with its share price doubling or tripling.

For long positions, the worst that can happen is that the company goes bust and the share price drops to zero – it cannot go below zero.

The charges for CFD trading are competitive. The trader will pay commission of perhaps 0.1% to open a position and another 0.1% to close it – applied to the size of the position, not the deposit. Discounts based on high volumes of trading may be available. The platform is likely to have a minimum position size, perhaps £10,000. There will be an interest charge to keep a position open overnight, for example 2.5% above interbank rate, so there is some incentive not to leave positions open indefinitely. A guaranteed stop-loss will cost something in the region of 0.3% of the position. However, if a position moves against him, at some level, the trader will be asked to top up his deposit – he will receive a margin call.

When you trade CFDs, your trading platform will show the value of your positions in real time. It will probably provide other share prices with a 15-minute delay without charge. For a monthly fee, it will provide you with share prices in real time for a specified number of shares. Trading CFDs without real time share prices is arguably a complete waste of time, as you need to know both your entry and exit prices in real time.

CFD profits for the retail investor are liable for capital gains tax. You can't trade CFDs in an ISA and you will be liable for tax on profits above any tax-free allowance that you enjoy. For traders leveraging up to high positions, seeking profits in the tens of thousand pounds, this is a serious risk factor. How much risk can you justify if you are going to pay a high rate of tax on your profits? Curiously, some SIPP (Self Invested Pension Plan) platforms allow CFD trading on invested cash, and profits are not taxed. On the face of it, it does not seem like a good idea to trade your pension, but it's for the individual to assess his portfolio risk and the tax-free aspect is attractive. However, when cash is withdrawn from a SIPP, it will be assessed for tax.

Trading CFDs

Trading CFDs with leverage without using stop-losses is risky; trading CFDs with leverage using stop-losses is also risky.

Some approaches to trading have been described in *Chapter 10* and will be applicable to trading with CFDs. However, there are some particular aspects of CFD trading that are worth mentioning.

In the UK most day traders work through CFDs – to avoid stamp duty and to obtain gearing. Their focus is to anticipate movements of indices or share prices, either up or down, and to exploit them. They are more likely to contribute to share price movements than to drive them decisively as a professional trading firm or major institution might.

If you trade CFDs, you will be competing with professional traders. The shorter the time frame of your trading, the greater will be your disadvantage against the professionals and the closer you will be to playing a zero-sum game, i.e., your loss is someone else's gain.

So what is the best way to manage your risk when CFD trading? The best way is to eliminate risk at source and not trade CFDs! Research shows that only about 20% of CFD traders make profit. In July 2013, the CEO of a major CFD service provider admitted under pressure from Geoff Cutmore on CNBC Europe that most of his clients for CFDs and spread betting lose money.

Notwithstanding this advice, you can manage your risk by using stop-losses to close out positions – both to protect profits and to cut losses; you can monitor your positions closely supported by good information sources; or you can use an alerts service. Use of stop-losses to limit your downside is covered in some detail in *Chapter 10* and *Chapter 18 – Managing your portfolio*.

If you don't really 'use' leverage, for example, you use £1,000 to open a £10,000 position and you can afford to lose, say £3,000, then staying in very close touch with your position, perhaps using alerts, may be an acceptable – and efficient – way to manage your risk. If you use this approach, you should research and plan your information system carefully. If a position suddenly turns bad, you need to be able to discover why as soon as possible. After a very precipitous and long fall, there is often a sharp bounce – and the need for an informed decision – whether to cut your losses, hang in for the bounce, or even increase your position. Keep in mind that the larger cap stocks will have the strongest news flows – but this can be a double-edged sword, depending on your ability to pick up share price moving information in close to real time.

On the other hand, if you use £10,000 to open a £100,000 position and a 20% or 30% loss would put you into serious financial difficulties, then use of a guaranteed stop-loss is strongly advisable. If you keep a large position open overnight or over the weekend, you should seriously consider using a guaranteed stop-loss.

Many traders follow a strict rule to always use a guaranteed stop-loss for short positions and many will never leave positions open overnight.

One of the causes for lack of success by CFD traders is that many of them do not understand the markets and the companies whose shares they are trading all that well – they place far too much store by rumor and overly rely on Technicals rather than a sensible balance between Technicals and Fundamentals. The best traders have quite deep knowledge of the companies they are trading.

CFD traders have very little interest in picking up dividends. In long positions, they will be more interested in exploiting the share price movements that take place leading up to and after ex-dividend dates. If the share goes ex-dividend while a short position is open, the trader pays the value of the dividend to the CFD provider. The CFD provider has to borrow the share, then sell it to hedge his position, and so the lender misses out on any dividend that may become due while the trade is in place. The lender of the share will want his dividend! A CFD trader will try hard not to be short on an ex-dividend date unless he has reason to believe that the share price will fall by more than the dividend percentage.

Some professional traders – for example in hedge funds and high-frequency trading houses – 'play against' retail CFD traders. Many retail traders will not be able to continuously monitor their positions and will use stop-losses to manage their risk. However, they may place their stop- losses at predictable levels. This provides the professionals with an opportunity to undertake some heavy selling around these levels and the share price will then plunge down through the stop-losses – which are sell orders. Many other traders will be panicked into selling just before the share price bounces back. You can see this happen on any day in the market. Pattern recognition is common capability of trading algorithms, and some will be good at predicting where rafts and layers of stop-losses may lie, e.g., in areas of accumulation and distribution. Some traders will avoid use of predictable numbers, such as round numbers, in determining stop-loss levels.

A fairly common ploy by professional traders, aided and abetted by sophisticated trading algorithms, is to place and then cancel orders on an order book. This is sailing close to the legal wind! Cancellation of buy orders could greatly weaken a support level, which would be good for short positions held by these traders.

The CFD platforms provide information on the open positions of their client base. Whether this is helpful information for the professional traders is a matter of conjecture.

Serious CFD traders will make use of London Stock Exchange Level 2 information. If you search on the Internet for 'ADVFN Level 2 explained,' you should find a guide to Level 2 and how it can be useful. The London Stock Exchange also provides a guide to Level 2 market data, also available on the Internet. ADVFN and most CFD trading platforms provide access to Level 2.

Analyst upgrades and downgrades move share prices by significant amounts every trading day, and traders with rapid access to these will enjoy a significant advantage. The markets are full of informal networks, supported by chat rooms, where information is continually exchanged, and it is very common to read in the financial press that rumors of an upbeat broker's bulletin have moved a particular share price.

Another significant advantage that the professional traders enjoy is use of Bloomberg terminals, or similar products, which provide a continuous flow of market-moving information. At an annual cost of around US$24,000 for a single data terminal, these are beyond the reach of most retail traders.

Day traders use many complex trading strategies that you can research on the Internet, for example, search pairs trading and butterfly spreads.

CFD trading platforms – the service providers

Development of CFD and spread betting platforms has made trading possible for the retail investor. A number of companies provide CFD trading and spread betting platforms, for example:

- IG Index
- Spreadex

- InterTrader
- City Index
- CMC Markets

Their trading platforms offer a great deal of supporting data to their clients, such as financial calendars (dates and times of publication of key economic data), charting services, news flow, etc., and also data on numbers of clients long or short on a particular share, the ratio between long and short positions, and timeline trends.

CMC Markets describes its platform as follows:

- Customizable Reuters news feed
- Live Economic Calendar with event countdown
- Customisable price alerts
- See how our clients are trading with Client Sentiment
- Connect with our clients via the Chart Forum
- Intraday insights from our global team of analysts

How do CFD service providers operate? For any share or index, they will offset long and short positions against each other and take care of as much of their risk as they can in this way. For an excess (unmatched) of long positions, they will buy shares in the market. These transactions, because they are a CFD service provider's hedge, are curiously exempt from stamp duty. The legislators have been surprisingly accommodating.

Where there is an excess of short positions, the service provider will have to borrow and sell shares and will possibly have arrangements in place with a number of organizations that lend shares. When buying back the shares to close his hedge, again the transaction is exempt from stamp duty.

Where a CFD service provider is offsetting long and short positions, he will still collect dividends from traders in short positions for trades that go ex-dividend, and keep them, because he has not had to borrow the share.

In terms of price discovery, there can be a great deal of trader activity through which a view on share price is taken, but only CFD platform hedging volume goes through the stock exchange, so volumes reported by the stock exchange will not necessarily be reflective of all trading activity. It follows that high-frequency trading through CFDs will not promote stock market liquidity in the London market as much as is sometimes claimed.

Some CFD platforms provide direct market access.

Spread betting

Financial spread betting is quite similar to CFD trading. It is a derivative product in which the bettor is seeking to gain from a price movement, either up or down. You can spread bet on the price of many things, including shares, indices, commodities, and currencies. Leverage is a key component and any profits made are tax-free.

The 'spread' is simply the difference in the 'buy' and 'sell' price. Take a spread of £10.65/£10.55. If you take a long position and buy at, say, £10.65 and sell immediately at £10.55, you will lose 10 pence. So the price has to move more than the spread before you are in profit; for example, if you are able to sell at £10.75, you will be in profit. Therefore, the narrowest possible spread is attractive to the better, and spread betting platforms compete on the narrowness – tightness – of the spreads that they offer.

As with CFDs, spread betting is a leveraged product. A deposit is required, which allows you to open leveraged positions. The margin required for each position will typically be between 1% and 10% of the value of the position. As with CFD trading, if a position moves against you, and the margin requirement exceeds your deposit, you will need to commit more cash.

The spread bettors are significant market participants and contribute to share price movements. This is because the spread betting service provider will have to buy and sell some shares to cover his risk. The service providers give spread bettors 'opening calls' on the FTSE 100 and other derivatives before the markets open at 0800 hrs. These have sometimes been reported by the financial TV channels. These will be the opening position for spread bettors wishing to 'trade the index' as well as an early indicator of sentiment prior to the market opening.

The CFD platforms mentioned above also provide spread betting services – and a great deal of information on spread betting. The Internet is also a rich source of information on spread betting and trading strategies.

12 About funds

Introduction

Most books on investing in the stock market are concerned with buying and selling individual shares, and indeed much of this book deals with this subject. However, for many people, investing in funds is likely to be significantly more rewarding than investing in individual shares.

This chapter describes the most common types of fund, the advantages and disadvantages of investing through funds as opposed to individual shares, and provides some insights into the fund management industry and its performance.

In the context of the stock market, funds are pooled investments in companies with a fund manager. The most popular types of fund are mutual funds in the US and open-ended investment companies (OEICs) in the UK, which have a similar structure. OEICs evolved from unit trusts. The fund manager buys shares in a number of companies to create a fund and invites investors to buy units – or shares – of the fund.

Mutual funds and OEICs are bought and sold on a forward-pricing basis, i.e., they are not bought and sold in the market in real time.

Types of funds that are traded on the stock market in real time are investment companies, or trusts, where the fund manager sets up a company which invests in a range of companies, and exchange traded funds (ETFs), which are growing in popularity globally.

ETFs facilitate investment in many asset classes, including commodities and stock market index products.

A significant shift is underway from actively managed funds to passive funds, which simply track a stock market index. This is a serious consideration for the retail investor.

Many investment commentators are perhaps a little too negative on mutual funds and OEICs, citing in particular high management costs. However, if you can identify good funds that consistently 'beat the index,' the management costs are worth paying.

The fund management industry

In 2014 the global asset management industry reached a record level with US$74tn under management, generating a profit of US$102bn. About US$25tn of this is in equity – share – funds.

US

There are about 7,700 open-ended mutual funds in the US, with a total asset value of around US$15tn.

In the US, the Investment Company Institute (ICI) is a national association for investment companies. Its main focus is mutual funds, though it covers the full range of investment companies. As well as promoting the interests of these companies, it also champions ethical behavior and public understanding of investing through these special-purpose vehicles. Its website is worth a look.

Another useful website is run by 'statista' – The Statistics Portal. It provides a great deal of interesting information on the US fund management industry.

UK

The Investment Association (IA), formerly known as the Investment Management Association, represents UK investment managers. According to their website, it has over 200 members who manage more than £5tn for clients around the world. If you are a UK investor, it's worth a visit to their website, which gives useful insights into the industry. The IA database includes some 3,000 OEICs and unit trusts available to investors in the UK, investing in a wide range of sectors.

The IA passes data to companies such as Morning Star, Thompson Reuters Lipper, FE Analytics and Citywire, which operate market information websites and provide fund data to both professional and retail investors.

There is also the Association of Investment Companies (AIC) that represents the UK investment trust industry.

The dynamics of the fund management industry

There has been huge growth in the fund management industry. The remuneration of fund managers is not transparent and questions are being increasingly asked. Without more accountability, they will not be well-placed to hold the management of companies in which they have big shareholdings

> *to account, e.g., they won't challenge big bonuses and high pay culture.*
> *BlackRock is seeking more influence, but does not want to be influenced.*

Fund management companies are asset managers and typically they manage a wide range of assets, not just company shares – and they work for both institutional investors, such as pension funds and insurance companies, and retail investors. The fund management industry is large and invests in shares through a bewildering range of funds, each with its own fund manager. There are often different versions of the same fund for different types of owner and jurisdictions – many funds are created specifically for pension funds. The investment platform that you use (see below) will guide you towards the funds that are appropriate for you – these will usually be US or UK retail funds.

Because the fund management industry has so much money to invest, it has little choice but to invest in a great many large – and sometimes not very good – companies. They manage to characterize the funds holding such companies as moderate – as opposed to high – risk and encourage people to commit their money to these funds. Fund risk is discussed below. Despite the enabling power of the Internet, there are still many people who have their money languishing in underperforming, actively managed funds and lacking the confidence to make changes; many in the US may feel trapped by exit fees that they were led into by unscrupulous advisers. These are the favorite clients of the fund management industry.

The industry receives considerable bad publicity. Most people's pensions are invested through funds, and it is constantly reported that excessive management fees and charges drain substantial value from them. Published data and commentary indicates that there is quite some truth in this. A problem with the industry is that fund managers tend to be paid in proportion to the value of funds under their management, and not based on performance, though this is slowly changing. Some funds are introducing performance fees. Dealing with a rip-off pension fund will range from impossible to challenging and this is touched on briefly below. However, in non-pension fund situations, the retail investor can put himself very much in charge.

It is important to be aware that the fund management industry is driven by annual fees, so they want you to stay invested – even through a crash that halves the value of your holdings. Proponents of 'staying invested' have undertaken calculations based on stock market indices to demonstrate that even if you had invested just before the great crashes of 2001 and 2008, you would be ahead now. It is the reinvestment of dividends that has achieved this, but they are promoting a near-mindless approach to investing, which pays no attention to timing. Marketing by the fund management industry is aggressive and it promotes investment across a large range of funds regardless of their merit.

When you invest in funds, there are two main layers of fees or costs – external advisory fees around which funds to select, and internal costs for managing the investments in the fund. In recent years, fund costs have received considerable attention. The Internet is proving to be a highly disruptive agent and, in concert with investor activism and regulatory pressure, has created a more competitive environment for the fund management industry. There are now many low-cost investment platforms offering a great deal of market information to the retail investor, but not formal investment advice. In addition, there are many websites specialized in the provision of information on funds.

Many retail investors are now cutting advisory fees and making their own fund selections. They are not always well-equipped to do this. In addition, many fund managers are cutting their levels of investment management expertise and their company research budgets, and shifting their business focus to running low (or lower!) cost index tracker funds. These are funds that simply track an index by investing in all the companies in that index in proportion to their market cap. This is known as passive management – all the fund manager has to do is adjust his holdings as market caps fluctuate and some companies enter or exit the index. The performance of the tracker fund over time should be close, but slightly below, that of the index, due to fund costs. As market caps of the constituent companies rise and fall in daily trading, the fund manager will buy and sell shares accordingly.

Tracker funds are heavily marketed, and this is promoting migration of investor money from actively managed funds to tracker funds. This has created a dilemma for the retail investor – whether to go with the flow, or seek to identify active fund managers who consistently beat the index. In addition, he needs to assess value for money in fees paid to both advisers and fund managers. Good advisers can add considerable value to an investment portfolio, but they need to do more for their money than steer you into a low-cost fund tracking the S&P 500 or the FTSE 100.

In the UK, a 2014 study by Deloitte indicated that about 150 'gatekeepers' are responsible for steering investor money into a small number of large funds, with around 90% of investor 'new money' finishing up in just ten funds. These gatekeepers work for investment platforms, financial advisory groups, and discretionary and wealth managers. This is not helpful to the active management cause.

If you decide to invest in a tracker fund following a particular index, then you should simply seek out the fund with the lowest costs and check the small print for any hidden charges.

Branding is very important within the fund management industry, and the fund management companies work very hard at building brand recognition. Usually the focus is on the company rather than individual funds, as the companies want you to pile your money in across their range of funds and not be too discerning with respect to individual fund performance. And they may place too much emphasis on diversity. When the fund marketers are telling you how good the performance of a particular fund has been, they won't tell you that several funds in the same category have performed a great deal better. Bear in mind that this is a hugely resourceful and well-paid industry, and it will always find ways to thrive. New funds are launched on a regular basis and investors will invest through them based on a marketing story only, as a new fund has no track record. However, when a fund manager with a strong track record starts a new fund, it will be worth a look.

A very significant aspect of funds is that they do not shift significantly into cash even in the most threatening of economic circumstances. An average of 5% cash held by funds would be quite high, but can occur in periods of significant uncertainty in the markets. If funds were to go heavily into cash all at the same time, there would be a total collapse in stock market prices around the world. Hence the relentless 'stay invested' message. Fund managers see their job as moving money around between companies, and not in and out of the market. No matter how good your fund manager is, you could say that this is a staggering shortfall in level of service, i.e., to simply watch while the value of the fund loses half its value, as happened in 2001 and 2008, but that is simply the nature of the fund management industry. However, the retail investor can go into cash very rapidly and though jumping in and out of the markets is not recommended, it is an important backstop to have.

Poorly performing funds are subject to scrutiny and many are closed or merged with other funds, which is healthy but probably a minor influence on the overall performance of the industry.

There is now a new generation of funds under the banner 'Liquid Alternative Strategies.' These are concerned with development of new portfolio management theories and adopt, e.g., unconstrained and long/short strategies, claiming 'hedgefundification.' In other words, they adopt a hedge fund approach. Given the poor performance of much of the hedge fund industry, it's probably best to be cynical about Liquid Alternative Strategies.

Though the fund management industry is less than perfect, a strong theme of this book is that the retail investor should have more of his money invested through funds than in individual shares. There are some brilliant fund managers and funds and they are not all that difficult to identify.

Some fund management firms

US

Some of the best-known names in the US fund management industry are:

- Fidelity
- BlackRock
- Vanguard – heavily specialized in tracker funds

- State Street Global Advisors
- JP Morgan Asset Management

UK

For the UK, the list includes:

- Schroders
- Henderson
- Investec
- Aberdeen Asset Management
- Brewin Dolphin
- F&C
- Fidelity
- BlackRock

A number of the big fund managers are listed companies themselves, and the markets carefully monitor data on their inflows and outflows of investor money. This data can significantly impact their share prices. This is an added incentive for these companies to keep the flow of money net positive into their funds, though they don't always achieve this.

Pension funds

Where fund managers work for pension funds, there can be strong personal relationships that take the edge off competition, and therefore they will often command higher fees for a modest performance. Also, smaller company pension funds in particular are not well-placed for driving hard bargains with the fund/asset managers. A combination of high fees and underperformance is devastating for pension funds, and the man in the street – the retail investor – should scrutinize the performance of his pension funds carefully, and be prepared to take his business elsewhere if he is not constrained by imposed costs. Very many retail investors will be too nervous or lacking in confidence to have a go at making their money work harder for them. This mindset plays into the hands of the fund management industry. Hopefully this book will help at least a few people to be more proactive and successful in managing their hard-earned money. For further discussion on pension funds, see *Chapter 18 – Managing your portfolio.*

Paradigms of the fund management industry

Paradigm: a set of assumptions, concepts, values, and practices that constitutes a way of viewing reality for the community that shares them, especially in an intellectual discipline.

Consistent messages from the fund management industry take little account of the nature and quality of the companies that a fund contains or the state of the markets. They reflect the optimal business model for fund managers, though not for the retail investor. A number of paradigms of the fund management industry are described below.

Think long-term

A constant message from the industry is that you should think long-term, meaning five to ten years or more, and that you need to be patient. As a generalization, this is simply bad advice because it takes no account of fund performance or the possibility of a severe stock market crash. You need to be invested in strong funds and paying sufficient attention to the market to move fully or partially into cash if the circumstances for a serious stock market crash are developing. See *Chapter 7*. There is evidence that funds are increasing their turnover in companies, i.e., holding them for shorter periods. This reflects the realities of the markets these days – the fund management industry, or at least some of it, is recognizing that the long-term hold works less well than it used to. You need to give a fund that you are invested in a reasonable period of time to show what it can do, but you should be prepared to wind down your position in a fund that is clearly underperforming.

Don't attempt to time the market – it's just too difficult

It is difficult to time the market, but this does not mean that you shouldn't try. If you learn how the markets work, you are likely to get your timing more right than wrong and your investments will benefit from this. It is a reality that the markets always pull back and sectors always pull back. Even the best companies pull back. Some companies stumble or crash, sometimes due to internal problems and sometimes as a result of external factors. Such companies can make good recovery plays. There are some recovery funds. The pullbacks may not be very large during a strong bull market, but they should be enough for the alert investor to exploit.

Stay invested

The fund management industry wants you to stay invested through thick and thin. Their fees depend on it. A much-run argument is that there are only a small number of days each year when the market moves up sharply and if you are not in the market, you will miss these days – when there is a big upwards move in the market it is usually quick and you are likely to miss it if you are not in the market. Of course the reverse is also true – if you are in the markets, you can also suffer from the very sharp falls that occur from time to time.

A serious problem with this logic is that it is based on the proposition that you are either fully in or fully out of the market. You don't need to be either!

If you are invested in good companies – either directly or through good funds – it can be a good strategy to ride out the smaller pullbacks in the market. However, if you believe that conditions are developing that could lead to the market losing around half its value, then you should reduce your exposure to losses – percent invested – rapidly. Percent invested or PCI is discussed in *Chapter 18 – Managing your portfolio*. An important question is: what constitutes a smaller pullback? In the US and UK, recent history has seen markets recover quite quickly from pullbacks of around 15% or less.

It is worth noting that some funds show more resilience than others through market turbulence, and you can see this, at least in retrospect, by looking at a fund's chart and comparing it with benchmark indices.

You can get back into the market quickly – a very efficient way is through good funds.

Reinvest your dividends if you don't need the income

The compounding effect of reinvesting dividends is powerful over a number of years. However, this advice should be tempered with the proviso that it works best if you are invested in good companies. There is not much point to reinvesting the dividends of a company that is attempting to prop up a falling share price through a dividend policy that ultimately turns out to be unsustainable. Where you do decide to reinvest a company's dividend, you need to be careful about the level of commission paid on reinvesting the dividend – it can be a significant proportion of a small dividend. Some platforms will accrue the dividends before reinvesting them to reduce the impact of the commissions. However, there is much to be said for investing in funds that specialize in growth companies that invest their profits in the business rather than paying a significant dividend.

Stick with the funds you're in

> *'Individual investors in fact perform so poorly that one could use their mutual fund reallocations to predict future stock returns.'*
>
> *Don't be such an investor.*

In 2005, Andrea Frazzini and Owen Lamont, academics working in the field of finance, published a book called <u>Dumb Money: Mutual Fund Flows and the Cross-Section of Stock Returns</u>. (National Bureau of Economic Research Working Paper No. 11526). You can find it on the Internet together with discussion.

It postulates a lemming-like herd of retail investors rushing from one hot fund to the next – and concludes that they invariably rush into hot funds just as they are running out of steam.

No doubt it is not the intention of Frazzini and Lamont to suggest that adroit reallocation of money to various funds is not possible, but their findings suit a fund management industry that wants you to invest your money in their funds and just leave it there. It will take its annual fees and doesn't have to bear the costs associated with redemptions.

It is worth noting that Frazzini and Lamonts' research was undertaken before the 2008 financial crisis and the great bull run that followed it during which 'the herd' might have enjoyed better luck. And also, they are looking at trends involving large numbers of retail investors. It is quite possible for the savvy retail investor to separate himself from the herd. An examination of a number of fund chart performances will illustrate that exchanging or switching funds can be very productive. This is covered later in this chapter.

Older people should shift into fixed-income instruments

The conventional wisdom is that younger people can afford to have a greater proportion of their savings invested in the stock market because they can afford to take more risk. Older people should shift strongly into fixed-income instruments to decrease the level of risk in their portfolio. There are 'lifestyle funds' that are designed to achieve this for you.

In other words, there is more time for younger people to recover their losses – they don't understand the markets! And older people are not capable of following the markets and making good judgements for their investments. There is no doubt some truth in this, but the older retail investor who is prepared to do some work should be able to follow a more sophisticated investment strategy and reap the benefits of this.

And the younger investor can learn how to manage his risk.

If you invest in the best actively managed funds, whether within a pension fund or not, with a good approach to risk management and timing, you will most likely achieve good returns.

Types of fund

The fund management industry offers a range of fund types and it is important for the retail investor to understand the differences, and to work with those that are the best fit for his investment philosophy and style. A working knowledge of the costs associated with funds is also important, as this will enable the retail investor to obtain value for these in his investment activities.

Mutual funds

Mutual funds are long established in the US and play an important role in retirement planning. Covering a range of asset classes, they must be registered with the US Securities and Exchange Commission (SEC), which regulates them in accordance with the Investment Company Act of 1940. Investors purchase units or shares in the mutual fund from the fund itself, or through a broker for the fund. Unlike individual shares, there is no bid-offer spread when buying or selling units of a mutual fund. Mutual funds invested in shares are 'open-ended,' which means that the fund manager will create new units to accommodate new money flowing into his fund, and will cancel units to accommodate outflows. Therefore, mutual funds always reflect the value of the shares in the fund. Mutual funds are valued daily, based on the net asset value (NAV) of their holdings with a deduction for costs. It is a regulatory requirement that investors should be able to buy or redeem their holdings directly from the fund manager at each business day's valuation.

It is important to understand how dividends and capital gains within mutual funds are treated from a tax standpoint. Dividends will be earned regularly and capital gains will be realized when the fund manager sells shares within the fund (provided they have made a profit). In either case, all dividends and capital gains are 'distributed' to the fund holders at the end of the year, usually December. A fund holder must then declare these on his tax return, even if he has elected to reinvest the monies. There are different tax rates for short- and long-term capital gains. The gains are short-term when the investment has been held for less than a year.

The NAV of the fund will fall by the value of the distribution. If you are a recent investor in it, you could end up with a tax bill even though you haven't benefited from the gain. Many funds make distributions in December and some make projections of anticipated distributions, so if you stay in touch you may be able to anticipate a large distribution and exit the fund before it takes place. Tax rules would prevent you from buying the fund back within 30 days.

Mutual funds can be held in tax-sheltered accounts such as Individual Retirement Accounts and 401(k) and 403(b) accounts.

Always check out your individual tax situation carefully and if in doubt, seek professional advice.

Mutual funds costs

Lowest costs do not necessarily give best value.
Nor do highest costs.

The cost of investing in mutual funds can be high, so it's important for the proactive retail investor to understand the mutual fund cost regime.

For a useful summary of mutual fund costs, search US Securities and Exchange Commission, Mutual Fund Fees and Expenses or Fidelity Mutual Fund Fees and Expenses.

As mentioned, there is no bid-offer spread on mutual fund units. The NAV of a fund unit is the same whether you are buying or selling units. However, there are many other costs that fall into two categories that can be regarded as external and internal.

The external costs are levied by advisers and brokers and can be minimized by the retail investor who is prepared to shop around. The internal costs are levied by the fund manager and cannot be avoided, though they will vary from fund to fund.

External and internal mutual fund costs of are described below.

External costs

Many people use an Investment Adviser, registered with the SEC to manage their mutual fund portfolios for them for an annual fee that will typically lie in the range 0.25% to 2.5% of the value of the portfolio. The fees should be disclosed to the investor on regular statements.

Some funds use an intermediary, such as a broker-dealer or bank, to sell their mutual fund shares. If you purchase a fund through an intermediary, you will be charged a sales load, some or all of which is used to compensate the intermediary. This creates a possible conflict of interest because the intermediary may be directing you to funds which pay them the highest compensation. Loads cover brokerage costs and the cost of investment advice from the intermediary.

Loads are applied in different ways. Front-end loads are paid on purchase and back-end loads are paid when the investment is redeemed. They may also charge a sliding scale redemption fee where the fund is held for less than a specified period of time, typically five years. Some funds charge a sales load even if there is no intermediary involved. The Financial Industry Regulation Authority (FINRA) limits sales loads to 8.5% of the investment.

Funds can also levy front-end charges described as purchase fees, redemption fees, or account fees, rather than a sales load.

There is no evidence to show that there is a systematic difference in the performance of load and no-load funds.

Internal costs

The internal costs, or expenses, are applied to the value of the fund as an expense ratio. An expense ratio is typically 0.6% to 0.9% of the value of the holding, with tracker funds at the lower end of the range. This will normally be quoted upfront by the mutual fund and covers management fees, operating expenses, the costs of managing distributions, and possibly the cost of managing a 12b-1 marketing plan known as a level-load. This is an internal fund manager operating expense, and it is worth noting that a fund can describe itself as a no-load fund provided that it limits its level-load to 0.25% of the value of investments in the fund.

There are also transaction costs, which cover the costs of buying and selling shares within a fund. Many mutual funds provide their annual transaction costs.

A study by Edelen, Evans and Kadlec found that U.S. share mutual funds average transaction costs are 1.44% per year. Some fund experts will look at the makeup of transaction costs in fine detail, but this will be of limited value to the busy retail investor.

In addition, a mutual fund may charge for investment advisory fees provided to investors by the fund. And there will be fees for custodianship of monies and accountancy. These items can add an additional 0.6% or so to expenses.

Actively managed funds are likely to pay for research through 'premium' brokerage fees to a broker undertaking research for the fund manager and purchasing shares for him. These charges are not always very transparent and will fall under transaction costs. If the fund outperforms its benchmark index, then the research costs will be justified, at least in principle.

An additional cost may arise from tax overpayment. A newcomer to a fund may find himself paying tax through the distribution process when he has not benefited from long-term capital gains in the fund just crystallized by the fund manager. Tax overpayment will not be an issue for funds held in tax-sheltered accounts.

A significant cost advantage of a tracker fund will be in transaction costs, as they will only have to trade to adjust for market caps changing and companies entering and exiting an index; and to adjust holdings as monies flow into and out of the fund – and they will not have any research costs to cover.

So we may have, for internal costs for a tax-sheltered fund, something like the percentages shown in Table 12.1.

Type of charge	Active cheap	Active dear	Tracker
Expense ratio costs	0.6%	0.9%	0.6%
Transaction costs	1.2%	1.8%	0.3%
Advisory, custody, and accountancy	0.5%	0.7%	0.5%
Miscellaneous	0.2%	0.6%	0.3%
Total	2.5%	4.0%	1.7%

Table 12.1 Mutual fund costs

Financial websites report that annual mutual fund costs typically aggregate to a little over 3% for sheltered funds and a little over 4% for unsheltered funds. This is consistent with the figures in Table 12.1.

Whereas you don't want to overpay on internal fund costs, the performance of the fund is usually a more important consideration.

OEICs

Like mutual funds, OEICs are open-ended and always reflect the value of the shares in the fund – the net asset value (NAV) – with a deduction for costs. OEICs are valued daily.

Unlike mutual funds, gains from holdings within OEICs are not subject to tax, and UK residents can invest in an ISA 'wrapper.' ISA stands for Individual Savings Account. Capital gains and dividend income inside a stocks and shares ISA are free of tax. Outside an ISA, there is a tax-free capital gains tax allowance of £11,100 and a tax-free dividend allowance of £5,000 (tax year 2016/17). Currently, a UK investor can place up to £15,240 in an ISA each year.

Some fund managers have a 'fund of funds' offering – the proposition being that you can obtain considerable diversity while only having to manage one fund. You will be paying for an additional layer of management and you should assess the fund alongside other funds that you are considering – and seek to judge if the fund of funds concept is really likely to add value in the market circumstances pertaining at the time.

OEIC costs

As with mutual funds, OEIC investment costs can be high.

There is no bid to offer spread on OEIC units. The NAV of a fund unit is the same whether you are buying or selling units. However, there are many other costs that fall into two categories that can be regarded as external and internal. The external costs are levied by advisers and brokers and can be minimized by the retail investor who is prepared to shop around. The internal costs are levied by the fund manager and cannot be avoided, though they will vary from fund to fund.

You have the option to use an Independent Financial Advisor (IFA) operating on a fee basis. He may charge a fixed fee for an initial meeting, and then if you want him to manage your portfolio for you, an annual percentage of your assets. This is likely to be between 1.5% and 5% per annum, with the percentage decreasing for larger portfolios. Many investors are balking at such fees and increasingly making their own fund selections.

There is also an annual management charge (AMC) from the brokerage/fund platform, which typically varies between 0.4% and 1.75%, depending on the fund platform.

Fund management costs are expressed as total expense ratio (TER), an annual charge typically between 0.7% and 1.7% of the value of the investment. TER is also known as an ongoing charge figure (OCF) – for most funds the makeup of these metrics is practically identical. Transaction costs are not included within the TER, and are not usually identified within fund documentation.

Excluding IFA fees, OEIC costs are likely to lie in the ranges shown in Table 12.2.

Type of charge	Cheap	Dear
TER/OCR	0.7%	1.75%
AMC	0.4%	0.75%
Total	1.1%	2.5%

Table 12.2 OEIC costs

It is well worth checking out these charges when you select your fund platform.

Fund platforms are no longer allowed to include in their costs a hidden charge to the fund management firm (other than a nominal amount). This had given the impression to investors that the fund platform services were without cost.

In 2017, European Union regulation will require fund managers and brokers to 'unbundle' their fees, i.e., separate trading commissions from research costs. This will allow investors to be more discerning and will probably further reduce monies flowing to brokers for research. It is also likely to further encourage a shift towards tracker funds.

Pressure from the Financial Conduct Authority (FCA) has forced fund management costs down, placing pressure on fund management payments for research, though the fund managers can pay for these through brokerage fees, which are included in transaction costs. In these circumstances, the broker's research may not be impartial. In 2014, it was estimated that investment banks and brokerages could find their fees for equity research falling by as much as 50%.

There has been a tradition of fund managers paying brokerage companies for access to the top management of companies. In 2013, the FCA found that the industry was spending some £500mn on this activity. It is not possible for the investor to assess value added by research and access costs concealed within transaction costs. The effectiveness across the industry will undoubtedly be variable.

The regulatory pressure will encourage many fund managers to opt for an easier life and move towards more provision of tracker funds.

Unit trusts

Unit trusts were the forerunners of OEICs. There are a number of technical differences between an OEIC and a unit trust, which can be readily researched on the Internet. Most significantly, there is a spread on unit trust prices, often small, but it can be as high as 5% or more for some specialized funds. Given the vast range of OEICs and unit trusts on offer, such a spread would be difficult to justify, though not necessarily impossible.

The spread is in effect an initial fee which you will incur if you buy the fund directly from the fund manager. However, initial fees are often heavily discounted on a good fund platform. These are commonly referred to as fund supermarkets, which are discussed below.

Valuation time

To calculate its NAV, the fund determines the closing or last sale price of all shares in its portfolio and the worth of any other investments. Then it deducts any fees or expenses, and it divides the balance by the number of units, or shares, in the fund.

In the US, the SEC requires each mutual fund to calculate its NAV and report it to the National Association of Securities Dealers by 5pm Eastern time each trading day. This is the price that the retail investor will obtain if he has placed a buy or sell order in that trading day before the cutoff time.

Most UK funds are valued at noon while the London market is open. A few are valued first thing each morning based on the closing prices of the trading day before. Most overseas funds will be priced in the UK after the relevant markets are closed. When you decide to invest in a fund, you should find out the daily time at which the price is struck and what the deadline is for you to make your investment in order to get the next struck price. It's also useful to know this when you are exiting a fund.

When you buy or sell a fund, you are trading at a forward price and you won't know what it is until the price is struck, though stock market movements will give you an idea. This can be frustrating if the market is moving fast up or down – you can't get in or out of the market in real time.

Exchanging or switching

It is important to be able to exchange, or switch, between funds at little or no cost, and you should ensure that this is possible with your fund platform – see below. You don't need necessarily to exchange or switch directly from one fund to another. You can sell a holding, wait, and then reinvest in another fund as you see fit. You need to take account of possible tax implications.

Use of derivatives

Most open-ended funds are long-only, though some use shorting and this may be a growing trend. Also some funds use derivatives with a view to enhancing performance, for example, buying options to mitigate downside risk – however, this is a form of insurance which comes at a cost. The fund prospectus should advise you if the manager uses such approaches.

Investment companies and investment trusts

Another way of investing in a portfolio of companies is through an investment company (US) or investment trust (UK). This is a company that invests in the shares of other companies. When you invest in a mutual fund or OEIC, you are in effect investing directly in the companies in which the fund has holdings, whereas if you invest in an investment company or investment trust, you are investing in the company that owns the shares in the constituent companies.

These are known as closed-end investment vehicles. They are traded on a stock exchange with a fixed number of shares – they do not create or cancel shares or units on a continual basis. They can borrow money to invest – this is known as gearing, or leveraging, and this has the potential to boost or depress the performance of the company or trust, depending on the skill of the manager and the vagaries of the market.

The price per share is determined by the market and may well be different from the aggregate net asset value (NAV) per share of the investments held by the vehicle. The price is said to be at a discount or premium to the NAV when it is below or above the NAV, respectively.

(Note: in the context of an investment company or trust, NAV means the market value of the shares held by the vehicle; in the context of an individual company, NAV is the value of a company's assets less the value of its liabilities.)

A premium might arise because of the market's confidence in the investment manager's ability or the underlying securities to produce above-market returns. A discount might reflect the charges to be deducted from the vehicle in future by the managers, uncertainty due to high amounts of leverage, concerns related to liquidity, or lack of investor confidence in the underlying shares.

In the US, investment companies make distributions of dividends and capital gains in the same way as mutual funds.

In the UK, investment trusts are exempt from capital gains tax on their investments. The investor will be liable for tax as described above for OEICs.

With these vehicles, you can get in or out of the market in real time, though usually there will be a bid-offer spread on the price, i.e., you buy your shares at a slightly higher price than you can sell them at that particular point in time. Spreads will typically be around 0.75%. When it looks as though a major market crash is developing, or the market is rising very fast, the ability to trade investment companies or trusts at any time during market opening hours can be a significant advantage over mutual funds and OEICs. At other times, this benefit is not very significant.

A specialist type of investment trust is the Real Estate Investment Trust (REIT), available in both the US and UK. These vehicles invest in real estate directly through property or mortgages. They are a liquid way to invest in property and usually pay a good dividend. However, they tend to be heavily leveraged, i.e., they borrow money to invest in property and so their profits are sensitive to interest rate rises. So balancing capital preservation against dividend yield can be a challenge.

In the US, examples of REITs are:

- Cohen & Steers Total Return Realty Fund
- Alpine Global Premier Properties Fund
- Nuveen Real Estate Income Fund
- RMR Real Estate Income Fund

In the UK, major property companies with REIT status include:

- British Land Company
- Hammerson
- Land Securities
- Derwent London
- Great Portland Estates

Both open-ended and closed-end funds as investment vehicles have their fans, but the most practical consideration is that a good open-ended fund will outperform most closed-end funds and a good closed-end fund will outperform most open-ended funds.

ETFs – Exchange Traded Funds

In July 2013, fears were reported over ETF structural issues. Falling equity markets resulted in the highest level of failed trades in the US$2tn Exchange Traded Fund (ETF) market for nearly two years – reviving the debate about the structure and liquidity of these popular investment vehicles in times of volatility.

In January 2016, it is reported that global inflows into ETFs in 2015 were US$372bn, 10% up on 2014. Regulators on both sides of the Atlantic were becoming increasingly concerned that high ETF trading volumes were creating instability in markets, citing the wild price moves in the US markets on August 24, 2015.

An Exchange Traded Fund (ETF) is an investment fund that, as its name implies, trades on a stock exchange. An ETF will hold assets such as stocks – shares and bonds – and commodities, and trades close to its net asset value over the course of the trading day. Most stock ETFs track an index, such as a share index, a bond index, or a commodity price. ETF costs are normally lower than for mutual funds or OEICs and an ETF may be a cheaper way to track an index than a tracker fund. In the US, the tax treatment is different from mutual funds in that the sale of an ETF is a taxable event. For mutual funds, the distributions are taxable events. Depending on personal circumstances, ETFs may be more tax efficient investments for US investors. For UK investors, tax treatment is similar between ETFs and OEICs. There is a spread on ETF prices, which is usually small.

US ETFs have combined assets of about US$2.1tn. You will find an interesting article on ETF trading by searching The Amount of ETFs Being Traded Has Eclipsed US GDP.

Where an ETF is invested in dividend paying company shares, the ETF will either pay a dividend or capitalize dividends by buying more shares.

ETFs are used by a wide range of market participants, most notably hedge funds, to take quick positions to exploit shifts in global economic sentiment. There is a view that the possibility to trade ETFs in real time in the market, as opposed to mutual funds which have a single price point each day, leads to overtrading with inexperienced retail investors incurring significant trading losses.

The largest ETF is the SPDR S&P 500 (SPY). In early 2016, trading in this ETF was turning over at a rate of around 200%!

Some ETF providers covering both the US and UK are:

- Vanguard
- BlackRock
- iShares by BlackRock
- Wisdom Tree
- ETF Securities

In the UK, Hargreaves Lansdown offers a range of ETF investments.

The ETF marketplace has become very competitive, with many new funds launching. Funds are seeking to innovate, e.g., introducing smart beta products as described below.

You will find many ETF screening tools on the Internet. Trustnet provides screening capability for ETFs, including both US and UK products.

Smart beta

In the US in 2008, the SEC authorized actively managed ETFs in which the manager has discretion to depart from the specified benchmark index. These are known as smart beta ETF funds which depart from the concept of market cap based tracker funds. They are seen by many investors as a way of obtaining 'active fund management' at a reduced cost.

ETFs traditionally provide the investor with beta, i.e., gains or losses relative to the movement of an index or a commodity price. 'Smart beta' is a relatively new concept, where a more discerning choice of asset is made. A smart beta fund may be made up of companies complying with certain criteria relating to, for example, EPS, dividends, volatility, debt or even momentum.

Critics of smart beta maintain that a smart beta fund will only beat the index for a short period, because others will copy the approach and it won't be smart for long. A further issue is that some smart beta ETF criteria may lead to considerable turnover in the fund and therefore increased transaction costs.

Overseas

US and UK fund management firms run a wide range of overseas funds. If you go to Fidelity.com 'Search Fund Picks.' you will find your way into a range of funds which will give you a flavor for what is available. In the UK, Hargreaves Lansdown under Fund prices and research offers a Search by sector, which will take you into a range of available overseas funds.

ETFdb provides a tool for country screening – search <u>ETFdb ETF Country Exposure Tool</u>. For emerging markets, search <u>ETFdb Complete List of Emerging Markets Equities ETFs</u>.

For US investors, the tax treatment of overseas mutual funds is complex. That for ETF gains is more straightforward.

Investing overseas is covered in more detail in *Chapter 18 – Managing your portfolio.*

Fund categories

Most funds fit into a system of categories, and if a fund is actively managed, its performance will be benchmarked against a stock market index appropriate for its category. The active fund manager will seek to beat the benchmark index.

Morningstar has a comprehensive system of fund categories. In the US, search <u>Morningstar Category Classifications</u>. You can also search for <u>Fidelity</u> categories by going in its website to <u>Research</u> then <u>Mutual Funds</u>. At the top level, both have the categories shown in Table 12.3.

Small Cap Value
Small Cap Blend
Small Cap Growth
Mid Cap Value
Mid Cap Blend
Mid Cap Growth
Large Cap Value
Large Cap Blend
Large Cap Growth
Communications
Consumer Cyclical
Consumer Defensive
Equity Energy
Financial
Health
Industrials
Natural Resources
Real Estate
Technology
Utilities
Miscellaneous Sector

Table 12.3 Fund categories

They then drop down into Sectors, or Sub-categories, which you can explore on their websites. For all US equities, Morningstar uses the S&P 500 Total Return as its 'Group benchmark index' and then each category has a specific benchmark, e.g., for Small Cap it uses the Russell 2000 Value Total Return. Each fund fact sheet will identify its benchmark index.

Other companies promoting mutual funds have their own category systems, for example, the Kiplinger categories are shown in Table 12.4. Kiplinger is a US financial planning website.

Kiplinger Categories
Alternative
Diversified emerging markets
Global stock
Hybrid
International diversified large company
Large-company stock
Mid-size company stock
Regional and single country
Sectors
Small- and mid-size company international
Small-company stock
Target date

Table 12.4 Kiplinger fund categories

For the UK, some typical category systems are shown in Table 12.5.

FE Trustnet	Morningstar	Hargreaves Lansdown
UK All companies	UK Equity income	UK All companies
UK Equity & bond income	UK Flex-cap equity	UK Equity & bond income
UK Equity income	UK Large-cap blend equity	UK Equity income
UK Smaller companies	UK Large-cap growth equity	UK Smaller companies
	UK Large-cap value equity	
	UK Mid-cap equity	
	UK Small-cap equity	

Table 12.5 UK Fund categories

Again, each fund fact sheet will identify its benchmark index.

Income or growth?

Income and growth shares have been described in *Chapter 4* and many funds will specialize in either 'income companies' or 'growth companies.' Investors in income funds can opt to receive dividend income or to reinvest it. Income funds are usually categorized as 'value' funds.

Pension funds need dividend payments, so income companies are well-supported in the market. Many retail investors also opt for income. As we have seen, the power of compounding dividends, if reinvested each year, is important, especially if you are invested in good companies.

There is a school of thought that if you don't need regular dividend income, it's better to go with a company that reinvests its profits in a growing market than to reinvest dividends in a company that is not growing strongly. In other words, you should prefer growth funds to income funds.

The situations in the US and UK are a little different.

US

The average dividend yield in the S&P 500 is about 2%, so there aren't many good mutual funds that pay income over this level. There are some funds that specialize in dividend-paying companies, but it's hard to identify many that pay very much more than around 2%. There will be one or two distributions of dividends in the year and the investor can opt to receive the dividends in cash or reinvest them.

Fund fact sheets concentrate on total return, and may not separately identify dividend yield. Morningstar provides trailing twelve-month (TTM) dividend yield for US mutual funds.

UK

In the UK, the average dividend yield in the FTSE 100 is around 4.5% and in the FTSE 250, around 2.5%. So more attention is perhaps paid to dividend yield in the UK than the US. Many funds offer a choice between income and growth – for a particular fund you can opt for either the Income (Inc) or Accumulation (Acc) units. The Inc units will pay the investor a dividend or income once or twice a year. With Acc units, the dividends will be automatically reinvested.

The UK Investment Association requires specialist income funds to yield 10% more than the wider market, so dividend cuts in a sector can result in fund managers rotating out of that sector.

For funds which specialize in growth companies, there will be little dividend yield in any event, and the fund may offer Acc units only.

Active or passive fund management?

A new expression has entered the financial lexicon – the 'closet indexer.' A large proportion of 'actively managed' funds it seems do little more than track their benchmark indices. Some investors are mounting legal actions to claim back fees and losses from underperformance. The closet tracker funds will not have enhanced the credentials of the bona fide active management community.

In February 2016, it is reported that the European Securities and Markets Authority has found that nearly a sixth of actively managed retail equity funds could be closet indexers – raising the concern that many funds are charging high fees for active fund management while simply tracking an index.

During 2014, public sector pension funds on both sides of the Atlantic were migrating a great deal of their assets to tracker funds. They did not consider that they were getting value for money for management fees paid.

As we have seen, a key consideration for the retail investor is whether to opt for passive management, i.e., invest in tracker funds, or seek to identify active fund managers who can consistently beat the index. This has always been a matter of fierce debate within the fund management industry and its client base. The debate has raged particularly strongly post–financial crisis, and those against active fund management are in a broad sense winning the marketing battle – to some extent backed by data. But as with all data, it should be scrutinized.

Regrettably for the investing public, a great many funds have not performed well and resentment over fund managers' costs, some of which have included a component for a kickback to financial advisers, has grown over the years. On average, no broad relationship has been found between higher costs and outperformance. Regulatory pressures have helped with respect to transparency of costs – for example the 2013 Retail Distribution Review in the UK. A great many retail investors have opted not to pay excessive costs for funds that are languishing behind benchmark performance. All this, coupled with increasing competition, has resulted in a dramatic shift by the fund management industry away from actively managed funds towards passive, tracker funds. Ironically, there are many tracker funds that are not cheap – they rely on investors paying little attention to the levels of fees that they are paying.

However, there are still many strongly performing, actively managed funds out there that consistently beat their comparative indices, and their costs are modest in the light of the performances that they achieve. If an actively managed fund puts on 15% or so in most years, 2% in internal charges is good value. However, there are many funds that perform consistently poorly and for these 0.5% would be too much!

The factors at work in the market have caused many investors to dispense with the services of financial advisors, making use of the Internet to manage their own affairs. However, there are some very good financial advisors and undoubtedly some valuable expertise has been lost to the body of retail investors.

Some financial journalists have a tendency to obsess over fee levels when they could better spend their time writing on absolute fund performance. When they do, their writing is sometimes lazy. It makes little sense to spend a great deal of time and energy identifying the funds with the lowest costs while paying very little attention to fund performance. Also, journalists will frequently pick up on a marketing story pointing out that a fund has put on 10% in the year, while overlooking the fact that other funds in the same category have put on 15%!

A recent development in the market is the emergence of 'robo-advice' to serve the bottom end of the retail investment market. This entails people entering personal information into an algorithm that then recommends suitable investments for them. Considerable growth in this market for low cost advice is anticipated.

Active fund management

An actively managed fund will come with significant management charges, and the retail investor should stay aware of these to ensure that he is getting value for money. If you are paying a fund manager to beat the index, then you should check that he does. We can take a look at the track record of active fund management.

US

"Some estimates suggest that in 2014, as little as 10% of active fund managers beat the S&P 500.' This is simply not true, e.g., search 'Index funds beat active 90% of the time.' Really?" Rob Isbitts.

Data from S&P Dow Jones Indices shows that in the five years to 2014, 56% of large cap funds consistently failed to beat their benchmark index and that 68% of mid to small cap funds similarly failed. These figures are based on total return, i.e., with dividends reinvested. Search: businessinsider sp-indices-versus-active-funds-spiva.

Another study by nerdwallet found that only 24% of 7,630 active funds 'beat the index' over a ten-year period. Search nerdwallet study: Only 24% of Active Mutual Fund Managers Outperform the Market Index.

What can we say about this?

There are around 9,000 equity mutual funds in the US, with about 40% of these invested in US companies. There are less than a 1,000 listed companies, with a market cap over US$3bn in the US, and the quantity of shares available for purchase is shrinking as a result of share buybacks. The Russell 1,000 large cap index accounts for more than 90% of the US stock markets. So fund managers with large sums of money to invest will be invested in a selection from around 1,000 companies – they are all swimming more or less in the same pool. In such circumstances, statistically you would expect half the managers of large cap funds to beat the index, and half to fail. When you adjust for fund management charges, you would expect less than 50% of funds to beat the index. So the data is unsurprising – in fact, it is what you would expect.

The range of performance between the best and worst companies, with respect to share price, is dramatic. In a good year for the markets, the best performers will put on 40% or more while the poorest will suffer a price fall, so there should be plenty of scope for active fund managers to beat the index.

There is a far greater number of mid and small cap companies to choose from, and it is an easy deduction that a great deal of poor share picking is going on for the 68% of mid to small cap fund managers who fail to beat the index. The benchmark index may be the Russell 1000, comprising 1,000 companies, whereas our fund managers have many thousands of companies to screw-up with. Clearly many of these companies are simply failing to perform in terms of earnings or in catching the interest and confidence of the investing community. There is also the matter of fund charges, which eat away at returns for investors. A fund manager who is overtrading, i.e., turning over too many companies within his portfolio without picking enough winners, will pay excessive transaction costs and this will knock his returns.

Why do fund managers find it so difficult to beat the index? One theory is that a reduction in 'dispersion' – a measure of the variability of share price performance – in recent years has played a role. Quantitative easing (QE) is cited as a contributor to this phenomenon. The massive program of share buybacks in recent years has been supportive of share prices, but has brought an air of unreality and unpredictability to many of the larger cap share prices. The growth of tracker funds will also contribute to a reduction in dispersion, as the funds will simply pour money into good and bad companies based only on their market cap. Yet another factor tending to reduce dispersion is the large volume of HFT, which sets its own agenda in relation to share valuations.

UK

Research by Tilney Bestinvest has identified 100 fund managers that have consistently beaten the index sometimes over decades. The average outperformance of this group is about 4.6% per year. Search Tilney Bestinvest, The Top 100 Fund Managers.

In the summer of 2015, it was reported that active fund management was enjoying something of a renaissance, with around two-thirds of actively managed funds beating the FTSE All Share index, though this was not a difficult index to beat.

Outperformance in the UK is strongly associated with funds invested in small and mid cap growth companies, often predominantly FTSE 250 companies. The FTSE 100 companies have a combined market cap of about £1.2tn, whereas the market cap of FTSE 250 companies is just £161bn. The performance of the FTSE 100 has been lackluster since 2000, when it reached around 7,000 points. In 2015, it struggled to attain this level again, largely due to serious underperformance of banking and mining company shares. So there should have been plenty of scope for active fund managers to avoid these shares, and beat the index.

Passive fund management

Even Warren Buffett backs passive investing. In 2015 it was reported that Warren Buffett, one of the world's most successful investors, who has made a fortune from identifying undervalued companies and then investing in them, has instructed the trustees of his estate to invest his fortune in passive funds, such as S&P 500 index funds. However, with a net worth in 2015 of around US$67bn, his money would swamp the top-performing actively managed funds.

By 2015, passive funds accounted for around 35% of all mutual fund assets in the US, compared with around 2% in 1995.

In the UK 2015, £74bn was invested in tracker funds, accounting for about 10% of the UK fund management industry.

So, it's not worth paying for active fund management – or is it?

- Actively managed funds rarely beat the index.
- Whenever an actively managed fund does beat the index, it's likely to be largely down to luck and rarely lasts.
- Costs in actively managed funds eat away most of the returns.
- Tracker fund charges are very low, so just stick all your hard earned money into these. You just have to pick which indices to track.
- In certain developed equity markets, such as the US, it is difficult to identify a manager that consistently adds value through share selection, so investors should consider using passive funds.

These are consistent messages from large sections of the fund management industry that do very well from the rather simple task of tracking an index. You don't need a high-powered fund manager to run a tracker fund, and you don't have to bother with research. Also, the funds do 'what it says on the tin,' i.e., they track an index, so you can't get criticized for underperformance and you rake in the fees. The fund management industry has been more than happy to encourage this trend. Marketing has become the key skill rather than expertise in fund management. The marketing is proving highly successful, and this is resulting in a relentless trend of retail investors opting for tracker funds – and the emergence of giant asset management companies dominating the market.

An increasingly recognized problem with tracker funds is that they automatically pump money into the most overinflated shares. This is the opposite of buying cheap and selling high – the more a company share price rises, the more of it the tracker funds have to buy!

Keep in mind that as a result of its costs, a tracker fund will always perform below the performance of the index that it is tracking. It should only be by a small amount, but there are some tracker funds that overcharge.

When a retail investor is content to invest through tracker funds, he should pay very close attention to investment costs.

Active management potential

Should the retail investor simply settle for tracker funds? It's worth taking a look at the compounding effect of beating a tracker fund by a small amount each year over time. Table 12.6 shows the gain on a US$10,000 investment over ten years with tracker management fees of 1.7% per annum and active management fees of 2.5% per annum respectively. It is assumed that the index rises by 3% per annum, and the extra returns for 4%, 5%, and 6% active management returns are shown.

US$10,000 starting sum:

Index gain	Type of management	Active gain	Management fees	10 year value	Extra return
3%	Passive		1.7%	11,517	
3%	Active	3%	2.5%	10,700	-7.1%
3%	Active	4%	2.5%	11,786	+2.3 %
3%	Active	5%	2.5%	12,970	+12.6%
3%	Active	6%	2.5%	14,259	+23.8%

Table 12.6 Effect of active fund management

The potential benefit of being in an actively managed fund that beats the index by just 3% is 23.8% over ten years, a substantial improvement.

There are some outstanding active fund managers who beat the index year after year by considerably more than 3%.

Advantages of actively managed funds

There are some outstanding actively managed funds, not all that difficult to identify, so it's quite possible to get some of the best fund managers in the world working for you, and carrying much of the strain. Good fund managers are undoubtedly worth their fees. Most retail investors managing a portfolio of individual shares will struggle to match their performance.

Some of the advantages of investing through funds are listed below.

- The cost of market entry is reasonably low.
- There is the possibility to exchange or switch funds for little or no cost.
- A portfolio of funds is much easier to manage than a portfolio of individual shares. Ten or fifteen funds would be a good sized portfolio.
- It facilitates diversification – in companies, sectors, and company size. You get exposure to a wide range of companies, many more than you could manage effectively as an individual. If you are invested in, say, half a dozen funds, you will have a stake in several hundred companies.
- As a general rule, funds are much less volatile than most individual shares and can be less volatile than their benchmark stock market indices. There are always exceptions, for example, a fund of biotech or gold mining companies can be very volatile. Volatility of a fund is a useful metric and can be assessed directly from its chart.
- You can take a longer-term view of fund investments, because a fund manager will be taking profits and cutting losses for you.
- You can let the fund manager worry about the big price movements in individual shares. These can be time-consuming and stressful to manage well.
- A good fund manager will have more successes than failures in terms of large share price movements. He will be skilled at identifying undervalued shares and avoiding overvalued shares. He will have some insights into which companies are potential takeover targets – though there is a school of thought that you shouldn't invest in a company simply because it looks like a takeover target (though hedge funds do this a great deal). When you see a share price move up 20% or 30% in a day, you may think, 'Well, I missed that as an individual play, but there's quite a good chance that it's in one of my funds!'
- It's a good way and quite possibly the best way to get a lot of money into the market fast, which is sometimes necessary – when markets turn they can move up very fast. You don't usually want to invest a large amount in just one company. Investment in a fund gets you immediately into a range of companies – avoiding excessive exposure to any particular company.
- You can readily gain exposure to overseas companies – and currency movements.

Disadvantages of funds

The disadvantages of investing through funds will be largely a matter of the perspective of the individual investor. The main disadvantages perhaps are:

- Management charges. The Internet and competition has resulted in the availability of very low brokerage fees for individual share investment compared with fund investment costs – so you can invest more cheaply if you are prepared to take on the task of managing individual shares.
- You can't deal mutual funds or OEICs in real time – you can only get a forward price. However, you can deal investment companies/trusts in real time.
- You can't take a short position (though some funds now take short positions).
- Funds don't go into cash to any significant extent if the stock markets begin to crash - 5% cash would be high. However, the retail investor can go into cash.

The skilled and proactive investor in individual shares should be able to achieve some spectacular gains in quite short periods of time. A 20% or 30% gain in a share price in a few weeks or months is not unusual. The investor in funds will rarely, if ever, enjoy such gains, but neither will he be on the wrong end of such movements.

Trading funds

Mutual funds and OEICs are not really suitable for short-term trading. You could short-term trade ETFs, but there would be little point, as they do not display the volatility of individual share prices that is needed for successful short-term trading. A trading period measured in months rather than days or weeks could yield attractive results, especially in volatile markets driven by macro events – this would be akin to swing trading. The possibility to open and close positions with minimal cost is attractive to a swing trading approach, though some fund managers in the US will charge extra fees to an investor that they perceive to be overtrading a fund.

Fund risk

There are risks involved in investing in the stock market and particular risks associated with investing through funds.

Management and mitigation of risk

The fund management industry and its regulators have developed an approach to investment risk with the intention of serving the investment community and to allow the performance of fund managers to be compared. It is useful to understand this approach and its limitations. A good start is to look at risk in a fundamental way. The scientific definition of risk is that it is the product (multiplication) of the probability of an unwelcome event occurring and the consequences if it does occur. Faced with a risk, as the investor is, the party at risk has a number of options.

Take the example of the designer of a school addressing the risk of small children falling down the stairs. He has choices with respect to managing this risk. He can eliminate risk at source by designing a single story school, i.e., no stairs. If the designer is constrained by space and has to use stairs, he can minimize risk of a fall by careful design of the steps and landings, using non-slip surfaces, and provision of helpful handrails. He can further reduce risk by designing warning signs and by advising the school authorities on the importance of training the pupils in the safe use of the stairs, e.g., no running. These are all risk management and mitigation measures. A careless designer may just go for cheap, standard stairs, to maximize the profit in his fee or because he is incompetent, and simply accept the risk of some bad falls on the stairs and being sued for negligent design.

There we have it. Risk – eliminate at source, manage and mitigate, or accept.

The underlying premise of the fund management industry's approach to risk management is that the investor should invest some money in funds with a long-term perspective and simply accept the risk associated with this approach. This makes no sense for the retail investor, who will also not be interested in eliminating risk at source, as this would mean not investing. The retail investor who is determined to succeed will develop his skills in the management and mitigation of risk. A striking illustration of good risk management is to avoid committing an entire lump sum, perhaps from an inheritance or a pension scheme, into the stock market when indices are testing all-time highs. Another risk that a great many people do not properly address is that their investments underperform for many years, and they approach retirement in straightened circumstances, unable to pay off their mortgage. This risk can be managed and mitigated by informed, proactive investment.

The fund management industry approach to risk

Larry Fink, founder and CEO of BlackRock, believes that the biggest financial risk facing the younger generation is that they will keep too much money in cash, which will be eroded by inflation. This will have a serious impact on their provision for retirement.

With respect to the level of service that it provides to its customers, the fund management industry has a number of serious, inbuilt problems to which there are no generic solutions. These include:

- Its inability to go into cash to any significant degree, no matter how bad the market outlook.

- It has an aversion to any serious attempt to time the market – the closest it gets is advising customers to invest a regular amount each month.
- By definition, more than half of all funds put in below-average performance.
- There are not nearly enough good fund managers in the industry.
- Many fund managers are overpaid.
- Many funds are too large and are stuck with substantial holdings in underperforming companies.
- There is a shortage of good company shares to invest in.

Most people are dependent on the performance of the fund management industry for their retirement provision, and people are living longer into their retirement. A substantial risk facing most customers is that they will not generate sufficient investment returns to assure a comfortable retirement. The fund management industry has no credible response to this risk.

Nevertheless, the industry has made an attempt to develop an approach to risk management. The approach is backward looking - it makes no attempt at serious forecasting and it conflates risk and volatility, which are interrelated but different. The industry makes use of portfolio management theory which is typically based on models such as the capital asset pricing model (CAPM). In simple terms, it compares the performance of a fund – a portfolio of shares – with its benchmark index. The amount by which a fund beats its index in a particular period is known as its 'alpha.'

Unfortunately, attempts to apply such theories are not a substitute for competent, active fund management, but we will run through the principles.

Alpha and beta

The efficacy of active fund management has been discussed above – can an active fund manager add value to an investment portfolio? Alpha and beta, which are key parameters in CAPM, are commonly used to assess this.

A stock market index, by definition, has a beta of 1. A share price that moves with the index has a beta of 1. You can 'buy beta' cheaply by investing in a tracker fund. If you want to beat the index, you have to pay for an active fund manager. The amount by which he beats the index is alpha – if indeed he does!

Alpha is adjusted down for the risk taken by the fund manager assessed through beta. If the fund displays on average 30% more volatility than its benchmark index, then its beta is 1.3, and this is used as a measure of the systematic risk of the investment. If a fund's beta is high, it is construed that the fund manager is running excessive risk to achieve his return – simply because he has invested in volatile funds. In other words, the fund manager is not given credit for returns achieved through perceived, excessive risk taking and his alpha is adjusted down as a function of the fund's beta. So volatility and risk are conflated because no one has come up with a better approach.

Sharpe Ratio

The Sharpe Ratio is similar to alpha in that it is designed to assess 'risk adjusted returns,' but the benchmark used is the risk-free rate of return such as that from treasury bills or gilts. The risk that a fund manager is taking is assessed by calculating the standard deviation of his returns, which is expressed as the volatility of the fund.

Sharpe Ratio = (Return – Risk free return)/Volatility

Consider the two funds shown in Table 12.7.

Fund	Return	Volatility	Risk free return	Sharpe Ratio	
A	18%	9%	3%	1.7	(18-3)/9
B	14%	5%	3%	2.2	(14-3)/5

Table 12.7 Sharpe ratio illustration

A high Sharpe Ratio is good and Fund B is considered to be a better investment on the basis that you should seek the highest level of return for the lowest level of risk.

Unlike alpha, Sharpe Ratio is not calculated in relation to a benchmark index, so it can be used to compare the performances of funds in different categories.

Morningstar rankings

Fund rating companies, such as Morningstar, provide comprehensive fund management rankings, commentaries, risk-adjusted performances, and comments on the suitability of various funds in their reports and on their websites. It is well-worth exploring and getting to know your way around Morningstar and one or two similar websites. Morningstar is an influential website. It has both US and UK websites and covers ETFs as well as mutual funds and OEICS.

The top level Morningstar rating is its star system, which assigns a one-star rating to 10% of the funds it evaluates, a two-star rating to 22.5% of funds, a three-star rating to 35% of funds, a four-star rating to 22.5% of funds, and a five-star rating to 10% of funds. Morningstar also provides category ratings and peer-group ratings to help investors further compare funds. The ratings are based on the fund's past performance, the fund manager's skill, risk- and cost-adjusted returns, and performance consistency. The website also provides useful explanations, readily accessed by entering Morningstar and the metric of interest into your search engine.

These ratings are intended to be a starting point for further research and are not buy or sell recommendations.

EU Risk & Reward profile

In Europe, and therefore the UK, the fund management industry uses a Risk & Reward profile, which you will find in each fund's Key Information Document. This gives a risk/reward ranking on a scale of 1 to 7, though the main measure of risk in this approach is volatility – which is not the same as risk. The ranking has some use, but you should not select funds on this basis alone. The logic is that if you are in a volatile fund, it may dip just when you need the money and you will have to sell it cheap. The proposition, therefore, is that you are incapable of judging why a fund has been volatile in the past and assessing how it is likely to behave going forward.

The EU documentation is not easy to find, but if you are interested in the source, search for CESR's guidelines on the methodology for the calculation of synthetic risk and reward indicator in the Key Investor Information Document. The risk number is described as synthetic, because it is based on volatility and not real risk due to the difficulties in assessing this. The indicator is presented as shown below together with, as an example, the explanatory bullet points from the Fidelity Special Situations Fund.

Lower risk   Higher risk

Typically lower reward   Typically higher reward

1	2	3	4	5	6	7

- The risk category was calculated using historical volatility data, based on the methods set by European Union rules. Volatility is influenced by changes in the stock market prices, currencies, and interest rates which can be affected unpredictably by diverse factors including political and economic events.
- The risk category may not be a reliable indication of the future risk profile of the fund.
- The risk category shown is not guaranteed and may shift over time.
- The lowest category does not mean 'risk-free.'
- The use of derivatives may result in performance rising or falling more than it would have done otherwise.

The wording beneath the Profile will vary from fund to fund. Some funds includes the statement:

Recommendation: The fund may not be appropriate for investors who plan to withdraw their money within five years.

This is consistent with the characterization above of the drivers of the fund management industry.

The main factor behind a high number is the fund's volatility over the last three years. If it has displayed high volatility, this will push the risk number up. In a nutshell, the EU approach to risk is mainly based on the proposition that you should avoid high volatility funds in case you need to sell at a market low. Their proposition is that you simply select a fund or funds to invest in, taking account of risk ranking – and perhaps with the assistance or your financial adviser. And that's it. You then wait five years or more to see how your funds get on. This is a poor approach to investment, but it suits the fund management industry very well because their fees continue to accrue to them. All it has to do is persuade as many retail investors as it can to make their monthly contributions to their large, underperforming EU Risk & Reward Profile Category 3 and 4 funds. 'Retirement risk' has been mentioned above. From this perspective, the 'low-risk' funds could well be the highest risk!

You will get a much better feel for the funds strategy and risk profile by looking through the fund's Report & Accounts and other fund documentation.

Fund performance

Benchmarking

'Does Your Fund Manager Consistently Beat the Stock Market?
Probably not – but you shouldn't much care.'

This bizarre message was posted on a website by a mutual fund guru. Actually, you should care a lot! There are many active fund managers that consistently beat the index. We first need to look more closely at benchmarking against a stock market index. Most indices are based on share prices and take no account of dividends and the effect of reinvesting dividends. The exception to prove the rule is the German Dax, which does. Nonetheless, you need to benchmark against the total return of an index, i.e., the return based on dividends reinvested. The complication with this is that total return is dependent on timeline starting point, and this is not always clear for indices which have evolved over many years. Nevertheless, there are useful sources for total return indices, referenced below.

Small caps

There are studies on both sides of the Atlantic suggesting that, on average, small cap companies deliver better returns than large caps. Small cap companies can achieve higher rates of growth, but are subject to severe share price falls if there is an indication that the growth is running out of steam. In the US, there aren't many funds specializing in small cap shares, but there are many in the UK.

Mutual funds – performance

Mutual funds usually present their total returns over the last ten years compared with a total return benchmark index. You can find this comparison in the fund's fact sheet or a website such as Morningstar. Make a note of the ticker symbol of a fund that you are interested in and either search the Morningstar website (you may need to register) or try searching directly using the fund ticker, e.g., Morningstar POAGX. Note that a commonly used device is to show the chart of the fund performance in terms of the current value of US$10,000 invested ten years ago.

Table 12.8, below, contains a number of mutual funds that have consistently beaten their benchmark indices. You can check them out quickly using the ticker symbols shown. These are all no-load funds with a five-star Morningstar ranking. The 10-year performance is based on US$10,000 invested 10 years ago – the 'current values' are from March 2016.

Category Fund	Ticker Symbol	Total Assets US$bn	Number of holdings	Turnover of holdings	Expense ratio	10 year performance US$
Technology Fidelity Select IT Services Portfolio	FBSOX	1.5	201	56%	0.81%	32,775
Mid Cap Growth PRIMECAP Odyssey Aggressive Growth Fund	POAGX	6.9	148	15%	0.62%	29,930
Large Cap Growth Parnassus Endeavor Fund	PARWX	1.3	33	39%	0.84%	29,127
Large Cap Growth Fidelity OTC Portfolio	FOCPX	13.5	201	106%	0.76%	26,577
Mid Cap Growth Buffalo Discovery	BUFTX	0.84	112	43%	1.01%	24,444
Mid Cap Growth Hennessy Focus Fund Investor Class	HFCSX	2.2	21	4%	1.46%	24,590
Large Cap Growth Glenmede Large Cap Growth	GTLLX	2.1	82	95%	0.87%	23,393
Mid Cap Growth Goldman Sachs Small/Mid Cap Growth	GSMAX	2.9	75	52%	1.33%	22,610
Technology USAA Science and Technology Fund	USSCX	0.97	172	91%	1.24%	23,320
Large Cap Growth PRIMECAP Odyssey Growth Fund	POGRX	6.2	130	10%	0.63%	22,097
Large Cap Growth Vanguard PRIMECAP Core Fund	VPCCX	7.5	143	13%	0.5%	22,401
Large Cap Value Boston Partners All-Cap Value Inv	BPAVX	1.1	134	26%	0.95%	21,472
S&P 500 Total return						19,483
S&P Mid Cap 400 Total return						21,227
Nasdaq 100 Total return						28,000

Table 12.8 Mutual fund performance

Over the last ten years, all of these funds have beaten the S&P 500 total return index and the more strongly performing S&P Mid Cap 400 total return index. Some have beaten the Nasdaq 100 total return index. Unsurprisingly, the technology funds have done well. Technology has had a great run, but this may not continue. Arguably, it would have been risky to allocate too much of your money to this category, especially given previous problems with technology sector overvaluations.

Leaving technology shares aside, it is clear that some funds beat the S&P 500 significantly and systematically. It's worth taking a closer look at PRIMECAP Odyssey Aggressive Growth Fund (POAGX) to see what it is doing well. Go to their website and bring up the fact sheet for this fund. You will see that PRIMECAP:

'uses a multi-counselor investment model whereby each portfolio manager is responsible for a distinct portion of the overall fund. Each individual manager is able to invest across all 10 sectors of the S&P 500 index.'

This fund operates with five portfolio managers with a combined experience of 118 years. Their declared intention is to pick shares that will outperform the S&P 500 over a three-to-five-year time frame. In March 2015, their sector weighting showed Health Care at 33.1% and Information Technology at 27.2%, so we can infer that they judiciously exploited the strong tailwinds in these sectors at the time. At 31 March 2015, this fund had total assets of US$6.8bn and portfolio turnover ratio of only 15%.

If PRIMECAP can consistently smash the S&P 500 performance, then why does the fund management industry as a whole have such difficulty? Tracker funds are a totally different business model, as we have seen. Their challenge is in improving their operating platforms, creating new products, and sales and marketing. Presumably, this is a lot more straightforward than outperforming the S&P 500.

At time of writing, some of the best performing funds are closed to new investment. However, about 100 funds from Fidelity's US Equity mutual fund data base beat the S&P 500 total return index over the last ten years.

An investor's return on an investment in a mutual fund will effectively be lowered if he pays external charges.

OEICs – performance

Total return for OEICs can be checked and compared with a benchmark index, as for mutual funds through the fund fact sheet or Morningstar. A five-year time frame is typically shown for OEICs, and fund turnover is not usually available. An OEIC will often have an Accumulation (Acc) version and an Income (Inc) version. If a fund pays little or no dividend, it will have an Acc version only. The Acc version is with dividends reinvested and so its performance represents the total return. The Hargreaves Lansdown website allows you to select either Price or Total return charts going back up to five years. If you select Price, you will see the fund price without dividends. If you select Total Return, you will see the price with dividends reinvested. Even if you are seeking income, you should check out the total return, as this will give an insight into the quality of the fund. The website also has the facility to overlay the important stock market indices for comparison. Note that the website overlays total return indices for both Acc and Inc fund charts. Some individual OEIC fund performances as of March 2016 are shown in Table 12.9.

Category Fund	Fund Size £bn	Number of holdings	Ongoing charge OCF/TER %	Five year performance %	EU Risk & Reward Indicator
Offshore Polar Capital Healthcare Opportunities Inc	0.77 (US$1.1)	45	1.21	160 220*	6 current
Specialist Pictet Biotech Inc	1.26 (US$1.8)	37	1.22	110 200*	6 current
Global Fundsmith Equity	3.7	29	0.97	138	5 current
UK Smaller Companies Fidelity UK Smaller Companies Acc	0.26	107	0.96	120	6 now 5
UK All Companies Neptune UK Mid Cap Acc	0.67	38	0.82	130	6 current
UK Smaller Companies Henderson UK Smaller Companies Acc	0.13	113	0.84	95	6 current
Global Schroder Global Health Care Acc	0.225	59	0.88	120	5 current
UK All Companies Old Mutual UK Mid Cap Acc	1.69	48	0.78	100	6 current
UK Smaller Companies Baillie Gifford British Smaller Cos. Acc	0.21	67	0.68	75	5 current
UK All Companies Franklin UK Mid Cap Equity Acc	1.05	39	0.82	80	6 current
UK Smaller Companies Unicorn UK Smaller Companies Inc	0.059	34	0.84	75	5 current
UK All Companies Henderson UK Equity Inc and Growth Acc	0.58	138	0.84	70	5 current
UK All Companies Invesco Perpetual High Income Acc	12.4	87	0.92	70	6 now 5
UK Equity Income Standard Life Inv UK Equity Uncnstrnd Acc	0.94	60	1.15	80	7 now 5
UK All Companies Fidelity Special Situations Acc	2.9	126	0.94	50	6 now 5
IA UK Smaller Companies Total Return				60	
FTSE 250 Total Return				65	
FTSE 250 Cash Index Return				45	

*July 2015, prior to a significant correction

Table 12.9 OEIC performance

Returns are compared with the IA UK Smaller Companies Total Return, and the FTSE 250, both total return and cash return.

The health care and biotechnology funds have had a spectacular run, though Polar Capital Healthcare Opportunities and Pictet Biotech came back to earth by the end of 2015 after warnings to the biotech sector by presidential candidate Hillary Clinton about pricing of their products. Also, the table shows a number funds containing small and mid cap companies that have done very well. These are mainly funds with a size below £1bn.

You can see from the table that the EU Risk & Reward Indicator is not particularly helpful. For several funds in the table, the indicator has come down over the last two years. This does not make much sense, as the US and UK markets were trading around all-time highs through 2015 and almost certainly riskier than two years ago.

Why have these funds performed so well?

We can make a distinction between the specialist funds – Biotechnology and Pharma/Health Care – and the Smaller Company funds. The specialist funds have done well to a significant extent because their sector has done well. There has been great excitement around the development of new drugs, and a near-frenzy in merger and acquisition activity. The other funds are general and their small size enables them to be agile – winding down positions in companies that are running out of headroom and building positions in up-and-coming or recovering companies. And possibly taking positions in companies that are good candidates for takeover.

The performance of Fundsmith Equity has been outstanding. This is an unconstrained fund with about 50% of its holdings in US companies – so it has benefitted from US$ strength.

Fund size has been a particularly important factor – though its importance may vary over time. Towards the end of 2013, UK smaller companies funds had had an outstanding run, as we have seen. Towards the end of 2013, there was considerable discussion around this stellar performance and whether it was likely to be sustained. These funds lost momentum during 2014 and then put on a useful surge in 2015.

It is worth noting that the Neptune UK Mid Cap fund has just 38 holdings. Some retail investors may well have this number of holdings but would be hard pressed to beat the professional fund manager's performance – 130% over five years. It is much easier to select some top-performing funds than it is to manage a portfolio of individual shares.

As a footnote to this discussion, recent data (late 2015) has shown that a fifth of OEICs specializing in North American companies have failed to meet or beat their benchmark indices – actually not a bad performance, though helped by dollar strength.

Investment companies and investment trusts – performance

US

Investment companies or closed end funds (CEFs) in the US are specialized investment vehicles. There are only about 560 of them and the number is declining. Many are bond funds as opposed to equity funds.

The author has been unable to find any comparative data for investment companies and mutual funds.

UK

Many investment trusts range across a number of sectors, which complicates sector comparisons. At the beginning of 2014, the industry group – the Association of Investment Companies – reorganized its sectors to facilitate comparison with OEICs. This data indicates that over 1 year, 5 years, and 10 years, in terms of average performance, investment trusts have outperformed OEICs. Search Investment Companies v OEICs/Unit Trusts. However, in terms of the best performing funds of each type, performance is comparable, with the best outperforming the FTSE 250.

Possible explanations for the average outperformance is that the investment trust sector is much smaller and the quality of fund management quite possibly less diluted than it is in the OEIC sector; and that investment companies have greater flexibility to range across categories of companies and geographies, whereas most OEICs are constrained and seek to beat their benchmark indices. Some commentators regard this constraint as a serious drawback for OEICs.

An additional factor is that research has shown that the chairmen and directors of some investment trusts have significant shareholdings in their companies – a strong performance incentive.

Investment trusts can pay dividends out of reserves, so have the ability to smooth their dividend payouts through good times and bad.

As we have seen, investment trust shares have a distinct advantage in turbulent market conditions in that they can be traded in real time.

There is much to be said for assigning a portion of an investment portfolio to investment trusts, particularly in the UK, where they are commonplace.

The fund supermarkets

US

Some US platforms for mutual fund investment are:

- Broadridge Matrix
- Stifel
- Pershing
- deVere Group
- Fidelity
- charlesSCHWAB
- Scottrade
- BlackRock

UK

Several of the largest UK fund supermarkets are:

- Hargreaves Lansdown
- Charles Stanley
- Barclays
- Fidelity
- BESTINVEST
- Interactive Investor
- TD Direct Investing

They discount by 100% the upfront charge for most of the funds they handle, so the fund management companies make their income from their annual charge. This covers the cost of their fund manager as well as research, transaction costs, and stamp duty.

You may be able to buy some funds directly from the fund manager, but the fund manager may refer you to a list of fund supermarkets. In most cases, buying through a fund supermarket will be the best option.

13 Fund selection methodology

Introduction

For a great many retail investors, the key to successful investing in the stock market is to be invested in good funds.

In *Chapter 12,* we have seen that there are many funds that consistently beat the index, sometimes by quite a lot and over long periods of time – a decade and more. It is not difficult to identify these funds and then to make a useful assessment of them. By investing in such funds, you get an experienced professional team working for you. However, we don't want to be like lemmings jumping into hot funds just as they are cooling off. We need to identify funds with good upside potential and have a strategy for building and monitoring a portfolio. You shouldn't just pick some funds that have performed well and invest in them in isolation from what is going on in the markets.

Strategy

The previous chapters have sought to set the framework for a successful investment strategy. When you have read *Chapter 18 – Managing your portfolio, y*ou should have a view on how much money you are prepared to invest in the stock market and how it should be split between individual shares and funds.

You should also have a view on the state of the market and what percent invested (PCI) you are comfortable with. If you already have a portfolio, you could take a view on your PCI. If the markets are testing highs and there are some tail risks in the air, it might be a good time to take some profit or get out of some poorly performing investments. If the markets have just been through a serious pullback and you expect a strong recovery, then you might want to get some money into the market quickly, and funds are a good way of achieving this.

So, which funds? You need to take a view on the balance that you want between income and growth shares. If you want the comfort of regular income from dividends, then focus on income funds, but make sure you check the total returns that they have been achieving. Alternatively, you may take the view that growth funds are a better bet and you may be content to sell some units from time to time if you need some income. Or, you may want a portfolio containing a blend of income and growth funds. The fund fact sheet or market information websites such as Morningstar will indicate what level of income can be expected and frequency and timing of payments. Keep in mind that the dividend payout is not guaranteed and could be reduced.

Then you need to take a view on sectors. Economic cycles and sector rotation have been discussed in *Chapter 5*. If you follow the markets, you should be able to get some sense of which sectors are running out of steam, and which may be on the road to recovery after a period of poor performance. Biotech shares began a strong run in 2012, with the sector rising by a factor of over three until it ran out of steam in July 2015, losing around 20%.

As well as looking at mutual funds and OEICs, you might also look into investment companies/trusts, particularly in the UK, where surveys have indicated that on average, investment trusts perform better than OEICs. The approach to selection is similar.

If you interested in having some overseas exposure, you should tune in to a range of relevant information sources – you will hear views, quite possibly supported by good data, that the markets in particular regions are undervalued or overvalued. You also need to tune into the strength or weakness of the US dollar and sterling. The gains from a rising stock market in, for example, Europe, could be substantially offset by a falling Euro. You can enjoy excellent returns from overseas funds if you get your timing right, e.g., some of the BRICS – Brazil, Russia, India, China, South Africa – have had good runs, but you need to follow currencies carefully. Another way to get overseas exposure, if you like a particular country, is to invest in an ETF linked to the main market indices there, e.g., the Italian stock market FTSE MIB (the Rome bourse is run by the London Stock Exchange) – see <u>Blackrock iShares II IMIB</u>.

If you find that you are having a good run with some overseas funds, then you could gradually build up a position in them, but you should monitor their performance closely.

Fund documentation

Each fund has a fund fact sheet that provides information on objectives, main sectors, top ten companies, performance, and some key fund characteristics such as asset value and number of holdings. The fact sheet is likely to be updated quarterly or monthly. Some funds will provide additional information in a prospectus or key information document. Much of the information provision is to comply with regulations. In addition, each fund provides an annual report.

Market information and brokerage websites provide a great deal of information on funds under typical headings such as performance & risk, composition, fees, distribution, and ratings. Morningstar is a good starting point.

Fund categories

Fund categories have been mentioned in *Chapter 12.* The various market information and fund platforms use different category systems for funds. However, most common are Small Cap, Mid Cap and Large Cap and some have a sub-category of Value, Growth and Blend, e.g., Large Cap Value.

The concept of value has been discussed in *Chapter 4.* Value investors seek to identify undervalued companies. Other investors may prefer to focus on companies that are growing strongly and likely to continue to do so. You can hedge your bets by choosing Blend.

The fund fact sheet will tell you its category, though this may be obvious from the name of the fund.

In the US, you may find the best funds in the mid cap range, whereas in the UK, you are likely to find the best funds in the small to mid cap range. In Table 12.8, the best total return performance for US funds has come from growth funds, so it may be best to focus on these, perhaps with some blend. For UK OEICs, the best performances – apart from the specialist funds – have come from smaller companies funds. The possibility that this category is running out of steam cannot be ruled out and some exposure to mid caps is probably a good idea.

Unconstrained, or flexible funds, that have performed well will always be worth a look. The Energy sector has suffered from the collapse in oil price and may become a recovery play at some point. Financials and mining shares in the UK have had a dismal run and may eventually recover. The miners enjoyed a good start to 2016. However, strong recoveries may be years away and there may be many better, more immediate opportunities.

Fund information websites and rankings

Investment platforms have been discussed in *Chapter 12.* They cover a range of services, including provision of market information, brokerage, and sometimes investment advisory services. Some highlight or promote particular funds. It's worth exploring several of these sites to get a feel for what's on offer and how funds are marketed. You may have to register to access some sites.

There are a great many funds out there and some sites present quite a confusing picture for the retail investor. The best way through the confusion is to focus on rankings by performance over specific periods of time, such as one-year performance and three-year performance.

The following sites are worth reviewing.

US

Morningstar US

This is one of the biggest market information websites. It is not a brokerage and has separate websites for the US and UK markets. To access detailed information you have to register.

Morningstar US has a well-known star system for assessing funds and provides comprehensive fund rankings by category, together with very large fund datasets. The system shows fund performance over up to ten years. Morningstar offers a virtual portfolio manager.

Kiplinger

This is a personal finance website which provides fund rankings by category. To get to these easily, search Kiplinger Top-performing mutual funds by category. Then explore rankings by category.

U.S. News MONEY

Also a personal finance website. For useful rankings search US News MONEY, best mutual funds.

Fidelity US

Fidelity is one of the largest fund managers and provides rankings by fund category as well as a brokerage service for funds and shares.

Go to Research/Mutual funds. Under Asset Class select US Equity and then select the Category that you are interested in. Then select Fund Picks from Fidelity and click on Results and you will bring up a large selection of funds to run your eye over.

The Fidelity Learning Center is worth a visit.

UK

FE Trustnet

Trustnet is a very useful market information site that enables fund ranking by category.

Morningstar UK

As mentioned above, Morningstar UK is one of the biggest market information websites. To access detailed information you have to register. Morningstar has a well-known star system for assessing funds and provides comprehensive fund rankings by category. The system shows fund performance over up to five years. Morningstar offers a virtual portfolio manager.

Fidelity UK

A brokerage site for funds and shares which provides a great deal of information on funds, but not a simple ranking system. Fidelity has a Select List of over 100 funds which it believes stand out from their peers and it may be worth assessing some of these in detail.

Hargreaves Lansdown

A brokerage site for both funds and shares which provides a great deal of information on funds, but not simple rankings. Fund documentation is made available, and the site has charting tools that allow you to overlay fund performance charts and a variety of stock market indices.

Hargreaves Lansdown keeps a list of their assessment of best funds for their clients to select from, called the Wealth 150, which is worth a look. Again, it may be worth assessing some of these in detail. Funds that are attracting the most attention at any particular point in time are highlighted. The site has a virtual portfolio facility for both funds and shares.

BESTINVEST

BESTINVEST is a brokerage site which provides a useful listing of top-performing funds by category. Search Best Invest Top Performing funds.

Citywire Money

This is a market information website that shows a selection of top-performing funds over a three-year period with focus on fund manager performance. It has a virtual portfolio facility for both funds and shares. Search citywire uk funds.

Drawing up a shortlist

There are many criteria that you can use to assess a fund, but the most important is track record. This is important in just about any assessment. In this context, you can prefer a fund that has consistently beaten the index for many years, or you can prefer a fund that has not performed particularly well but maintains that in the future it will improve its performance. You will enjoy better odds with the former. A new fund being launched with a great deal of marketing hype may catch your attention, but be careful investing in a fund without a track record.

Will funds that have performed well continue to do so? Not necessarily, but it's a good place to start. The performance of a fund will be a function of its terms of reference, its size, the state of the marketplace, the quality of the manager and the quality of his research, and that of the fund management company that he works for. If the fund is in good shape with respect to these parameters, it should continue to perform well.

Use the websites described, and in particular use the fund rankings to select perhaps a dozen funds across a range of categories. Take the one-year performance as the most important while applying some weighting to longer time frames, though you will get a better idea of performance over time from the fund's chart.

Benchmarking performance

The proposition here is to look for outstanding total return against a benchmark index, but we don't just want to beat an index that has not performed strongly.

US

The Morningstar website benchmarks funds over periods of up to ten years against their category benchmark indices. If you refer to Table 12.8 of mutual funds, you can search the fund tickers shown there and then bring up the 10y charts. Most of the funds in the table are benchmarked against the S&P 500 Total Return Index. Some are benchmarked against the S&P Mid Cap 400 Total Return. FBSOX is benchmarked against Technology, which will be reflective of the Nasdaq 100, which is a more demanding index.

Morningstar also uses category indices, such as Large Value and Mid Cap Growth, and also some MSCI indices, e.g., the ACWI (All Country World Index), but you will do well enough just to focus on the S&P Mid Cap 400 Total Return and the S&P 500 Total Return as your key benchmarks, while paying some attention to Morningstar Technology for technology funds. The Mid Cap 400 has outperformed the S&P 500, while the technology indices have outperformed both. Time will tell if they continue to do so.

Fidelity also provides a useful fund charting service, again up to ten years, and enables benchmarking against a range of total return indices.

UK

Go to the <u>Hargreaves Lansdown</u> website and search for a fund through <u>Fund prices & research</u>, e.g., <u>Fidelity UK Smaller Companies</u>. Then go to <u>CHARTS & PERFORMANCE</u> and then go to <u>Add to chart</u> and you will be able to readily bring up the main UK indices cited in Table 13.1. These are total return versions of these indices.

FTSE 100
FTSE 250
FTSE 350
FTSE All Share
FTSE TechMark 100
FTSE Small Cap
AIM

Table 13.1 Main UK indices

Check out the FTSE 100 and FTSE 250. Select 10Y and you will see that the FTSE250 has seriously outperformed the FTSE 100 and that the FTSE Small Cap is also significantly ahead. You can add in the S&P 500 easily enough. This will be shown in sterling terms.

Take a look at the volatility of the indices and you will see that the FTSE 100 has exhibited a little more volatility than the FTSE 250.

You can also check out comparison with benchmark in the fund fact sheet. Benchmark indices from the Investment Association are sometimes used and may be less demanding than the FTSE 250, but the IA UK Smaller Companies has outperformed the FTSE 250. These are the indices to beat.

Fund selection

At this point you should have half a dozen or a dozen funds that you like.

For the US, all of them should have beaten either the S&P 500 total return index or preferably the S&P Mid Cap 400 total return. For the UK, your selected funds should all have beaten the FTSE 250 total return index. This is up about 65% over five years.

Then compare the relative performances of your selected funds. In the US, you can do this using Morningstar and comparing performance over various timeframes. In the UK, you can use <u>Hargreaves Lansdown</u> under <u>Fund prices & research</u>. Select any fund on your shortlist and then under <u>CHARTS & PERFORMANCE</u> go to <u>Add to chart</u> and overlay other funds and indices. Take a view on whether the displayed volatility is consistent with the fund risk rating. Again, use various time frames.

For both US and UK funds, take a view on volatility and resilience. The charts enable you to see how resilient these funds have been, i.e., how much did they fall by when the indices dipped, especially during major market pullbacks?

Fund attributes

There are a number of factors that have some bearing on fund performance that you can use to refine your selection of funds for investment. These are discussed below.

Fund manager

Many investors will follow a fund manager that they have faith in.

It is stating the obvious that the fund manager is crucial to the success of a fund. Also important is the research support available to him plus back-office support; the culture of the firm; and the size and category of the fund. The manager of a UK smaller companies fund will be playing with a better hand than the manager of a resource companies' fund struggling with the end of the China resource supercycle.

Despite the messaging from the tracker fund proponents, there are many actively managed funds that have performed well over decades. If a good fund manager moves on, then it is likely that the fund management company will replace him with someone of similar caliber. There should not be a shortage of quality candidates for a top-performing fund. If there is a deterioration of performance after a change in fund manager, you have the option to move your money to other funds.

There are some 'star fund managers.' They are likely to have had good runs, but their performance can fall off as the size of their fund grows – though sometimes the outperformance of 'star funds' is difficult to recognize!

Two US star fund managers are Warren Buffett of Berkshire Hathaway and Michael Aronstein of Marketfield Asset Management. In the UK, Anthony Bolton of the Fidelity UK Special Situations fund had a tremendous run. Neil Woodford is heralded as a star fund manager in the UK, and Terry Smith has achieved a high profile.

It's constantly reported that Berkshire Hathaway (check out BRK.B shares priced for retail investors) has struggled to beat the index in recent years. In fact, on a total return basis, it has more or less tracked the S&P 500 over at least the last five years, as can be seen on Morningstar. Not a bad performance, but many funds have done better.

Michael Aronstein's MainStay Marketfield (ticker MFLDX) fund took in record money in 2013 and suffered heavy losses in 2014. The fund is a liquid alternative fund mandated to take significant risk in the market. Such funds are managed to some extent like hedge funds and have been marketed as where the smart money is now going. The fund invested heavily in natural resource companies, anticipating a recovery in the sector that failed to materialize.

Anthony Bolton moved on from fund management in 2007, then returned to work in China in 2010, setting up China Fidelity Special Situations (an investment trust, ticker FCSS). The fund lost heavily in its first two years, falling with the market, and then enjoyed a strong recovery run. This is a good illustration of the importance of timing, even for one of the world's best fund managers.

Neil Woodford ran the UK Invesco Perpetual High Income fund for many years and developed a great following, though if you check its total return performance over, say 10 years, it has more or less tracked the FTSE 250.

In 2014, Woodford quit Invesco to start a new fund, the CF Woodford Equity Income Fund, which quickly grew to over £6bn in value as the faithful followed. The fund got off to a spectacular start, running ahead of most competitors. He was starting with a clean sheet of paper and without the drag of some large, underperforming holdings.

The Invesco Perpetual High Income fund experienced a strong outflow of funds as the faithful followed Woodford. This would have not been all bad for the fund as it would have given it the opportunity to get rid of some underperforming shares - over the last couple of years, it has outperformed the FTSE 250.

Another interesting UK story is Terry Smith, who resigned in 2014 from Tullet Prebon, where he was CEO, to concentrate on his 'unconstrained' Fundsmith Equity fund, valued at around £3.5bn. With 60% invested in the US market, the fund surged ahead of the best UK funds – the US markets were rising strongly through 2014 and into the early part of 2015, when the UK markets were running out of steam. Smith was not constrained by having to stick to a category theme. Interestingly, he has only about 28 companies in the fund – an example of a successful, idiosyncratic approach.

If you have time, check out the performance of these funds.

A metric used to measure fund manager performance is the Information Ratio. You can research it on the Internet. FE Trustnet provides Information Ratios for UK fund managers.

Academics undertake studies of active fund managers using concepts such as behavioral finance to identify the attributes of a successful fund manager. The purpose is to predict which fund managers are most likely to be successful, but the retail investor will have to rely on track record. Fortunately, this is a useful indicator of likely future performance.

Income

You may want a fund that pays regular income. In evaluating income funds, you should check total return, which is the best measure of the quality of the fund. Then review the income from your shortlisted funds to find one that meets your needs. Try not to select a fund only on the income that it pays.

Sometimes, in order to meet its stated income payments, a fund will pay out more in income than it is receiving in dividends by eating into the capital in the fund. It may struggle to restore its capital. This is more likely to happen with funds that position themselves to pay out high levels of income.

Sectors

The funds weightings across sectors is particularly important because of the way sectors strengthen and weaken as the markets rotate from sector to sector. If you are investing in funds, you don't need to have detailed knowledge of individual companies, but an understanding of the state of the market with respect to key sectors should add value to your fund selection. A fund fact sheet will indicate its main sector holdings. For example, the top sectors in the PRIMECAP Odyssey Aggressive Growth Fund at July 2015 and January 2016 were as shown in Table 13.2.

	July 2015	January 2016
Healthcare	33.5%	32.4%
Technology	27.0%	29.9%
Industrials	19.9%	17.6%
Consumer cyclicals	11.0%	12.0%
Financial services	2.7%	2.3%

Table 13.2 PRIMECAP Odyssey Aggressive Growth fund – sectors

Top sectors for the CF Woodford Equity Income fund at July 2015 and January 2016 were as shown in Table 13.3.

	July 2015	January 2016
Pharmaceuticals & biotechnology	26.64%	31.1%
Tobacco	15.8%	16.5%
Financial services	11.7%	10.3%
Support services	7.8%	8.3%
Aerospace & defence	4.8%	2.9%
General retailers	4.3%	2.2%

Table 13.3 CF Woodford Equity Income fund – sectors

Both funds had a heavy weighting in healthcare, pharmaceuticals, and biotechnology at the right time! They have made small adjustments to their sector holdings over six months.

You can check the state of a fund's main sectors by viewing the sector performance charts – see *Chapter 4 – About shares and how shares are valued* under 'Let's look at some charts.'

Fund size

There are some US mutual funds valued at over US$100bn total assets. However, we have seen some very good, sustained performances in mutual funds under US$10bn in value. There is anecdotal evidence that as funds get too large, they run out of steam, and US10bn may be a good threshold to stay below. If a fund is too small, its costs will become disproportionately high due to poor economies of scale. To avoid funds under US$75mn may be a good rule of thumb. A fund will sometimes show the weighted average market cap of the companies in its portfolio, a useful indicator of the typical size of companies that it invests in.

There are very few US small cap company funds, i.e., comprising companies below US$2bn, and there is no obvious evidence that US small cap funds outperform their larger cousins. In the UK, smaller companies funds have outperformed for many years. A typical smaller companies fund may have a fund value between £25mn and £200mn, containing companies with market caps ranging between about £500mn and £3bn.

Number of holdings

> *'Diversification is a protection against ignorance. It makes very little sense for those who know what they're doing.'*
> *Warren Buffett*

There has been a great deal of research into the ideal number of holdings in a fund manager's portfolio and the answer seems to be at least 25, but probably more than 50, to give sufficient diversity as a component of risk management.

Data drawn from Tables 12.8 and 12.9 is used to check out average size and number of holdings for the funds studied. The outcome is shown in Table 13.4.

	Average fund size	Number of holdings	
		Range	Average
US	US$4.3bn	33 to 201	135
UK	£1.6bn	34 to 138	70

Table 13.4 Average fund size and number of holdings

In the table, the average US fund is more than twice the size of the average UK fund and has about twice the number of holdings. However, an examination of the data in Tables 12.8 and 12.9 does not suggest that number of holdings is useful as a fund selection device. Remember, the funds in the tables have been selected based on sustained performance.

The number of holdings in a fund is probably most strongly related to fund size, sector factors, and the investment style of the fund manager, though a smaller number of holdings in a fund possibly keeps research costs down.

Turnover of holdings

You can see from Table 12.8 that for US mutual funds, the range of turnovers is 13% to 106% with an average value of 46%. You can also see that the second-best performing fund, PRIMECAP Odyssey Aggressive Growth Fund, has the lowest turnover of the funds in the table at 15%, while the fourth-best performer, Fidelity OTC Portfolio, has the highest at 106%. This suggests that turnover of holdings is unlikely to be a useful metric for fund selection, though funds with higher turnovers will incur higher transaction costs.

The annual turnover of holdings in a fund's portfolio gives an interesting insight into the dynamics of the fund. A fund that focuses on identifying value should have a lower turnover than a fund that seeks to ride momentum and takes a good profit as soon as it emerges rather than waiting patiently for a greater profit. Fund managers using momentum rather than fundamentals will most likely incur higher transaction costs.

UK OEICs do not appear to publish holdings turnover data, but industry surveys indicate a trend towards higher annual turnover.

Risk rating

The fund management industry's approach to risk has been discussed in *Chapter 12.*

In the US, <u>Fidelity</u> provides a useful discussion of sector risk for each mutual fund and also provides a brief explanation for the following volatility ratios.

- Beta
- R^2
- Sharpe Ratio
- Standard Deviation

The discussion in the fund documentation on sector risk is probably more useful than the values of the ratios. For the funds in the Table 12.8, the three-year Sharpe Ratio is between about 1.8 and 2.3.

In the UK, the EU Risk & Reward indicator features prominently on the fund fact sheet. As we have seen in the previous chapter, it conflates risk and volatility which, though related, are not the same thing. The usefulness of this indicator can be assessed with reference to Table 12.9. Use the Hargreaves Lansdown charting tool to compare these funds over five years. Regardless of the value of the EU indicator, you will not observe any significant difference in volatility between funds that have increased by 120% or more over five years and funds that have increased by around 70%. The three-year Sharpe Ratios for funds in the table range between 0.9 and 1.6.

On the Risk & Reward rating, look for around 6 – this will indicate a high-performing fund with some volatility. It should perform well if you get your timing right (or not too wrong!)

Top ten companies

In the US and UK, the fund fact sheet shows the top ten holdings and these are also carried by the market information websites. In the US, mutual funds have to publish online a list of all holdings quarterly, and this will usually be displayed prominently on the fund's website. In the UK, funds are required to publish their full lists of holdings twice a year, but these may not always be easy to find.

Take a look at the top ten holdings and see if there are any companies in there that you know and like the look of.

If you have studied the markets for some time, you will recognize some of the companies, especially if they are S&P 500 or FTSE 100, and if you like what you see, this could tip you towards one fund rather than another. Or, you will be able to research them fairly quickly because there is quite a lot of information readily available as well as a strong news flow. Smaller companies will not be so well-researched and you will probably have to simply rely on the track record of the fund manager and his team. If you don't recognize any, don't worry, it's the fund manager's job.

Fund costs

If you are prepared to spend some time understanding the market and seeking out good funds, there is not a great deal to be gained by paying external advisory charges. Also, you will see from the tables of fund performance in *Chapter 12* that the internal charges are quite reasonable given the high performance of the funds.

In the US, go for no-load funds with an expense ratio of not much more than 1% or less. The performance of the fund is more important than a slightly high expense ratio.

In the UK, you should look for funds with OCF/TER + AMC of around 1.1% or 1.2%. Also, make sure there is no initial charge through a bid to offer or buy to sell price spread. You have to have a very good reason to pay an initial charge that could be in the region of 5% – never say never, but given the number of good funds available, there should be a very compelling reason for paying an initial charge.

Fund selection

We can summarize the key points in fund selection:

- Select funds that have consistently outperformed the total return indices; in the US, the S&P 500 or S&P Mid Cap 400; in the UK, the FTSE 250.
- If you are considering US technology funds, select those that have matched or beaten the Nasdaq 100 – or the Morningstar Technology index.
- Take a view on Category and fund size. In the UK, take a close look at some smaller company funds.
- Decide if you need income from the fund, but make sure that the fund has a good total return.
- Read what the fund documentation says about fund risk.
- Check the main sectors that each fund is invested in and how they stand compared with the market cycle – check the sector charts.
- Look at top ten holdings and see if there are any companies that you like.
- Make sure that fund costs are reasonable.

Pay some attention to the track record of the fund manager, number of holdings, and portfolio turnover (in the US), but on the basis that these are secondary factors.

If you have existing fund holdings, check them out against these criteria and assess if you might do better switching into some funds with better credentials. If you decide to exchange or switch funds, do it gradually.

Then all you have to decide on is timing! This is covered in *Chapter 18 – Managing your portfolio.*

Virtual portfolio and monitoring

Using a virtual portfolio is described in *Chapter 18.*

Set up a virtual portfolio for your selected funds and use this to guide your fund investments. You will almost certainly find some significant divergences in performance, and you should guide your portfolio into the better-performing funds.

You should reset your virtual portfolio if you need to, depending on how the market is behaving. Some of your funds may fall sharply, presenting good buy opportunities, and this may be a good time to reset. You should try to check your virtual portfolio at least once a week, more frequently if the market is volatile or if you are invested in overseas funds. Funds are usually a lot less volatile than individual shares, but daily movements can be quite significant.

If some of your funds are performing poorly within your portfolio and also against the market indices, you should try to find out why. If you judge that you need to switch funds, do this cautiously. One of the best ways to improve the performance of a fund is to sell it! However, you only need to look at the charts of a strongly performing fund and a weak one over several years to see that switching would have been a good strategy and sooner rather than later.

The advantage of monitoring through a virtual portfolio compared with an actual portfolio is that the website with your holdings will display an average price when you have added to a holding. You need to focus on the absolute performance.

Investment companies/trusts

The procedure is quite similar for investment companies or trusts, though you will access them on websites under 'companies' rather than 'funds.' Also, there will be a company report rather than a fund report and there may be some directors' dealings that can be viewed.

Pay close attention to whether the company is trading at a premium or a discount to NAV. Usually it will be at a discount and you should take a view on its magnitude and why the market is discounting by this amount.

For an investment company or trust, there is likely to be a small spread, less than one percent – not really an issue for a high-performing fund.

Overseas

You can follow a very similar process for selecting overseas funds. In the US, you can find a good selection of overseas funds through Fidelity. Go to Research/Mutual Funds/International Equity and then take a look at All Categories. In the UK, you can usefully use Trustnet for browsing and ranking overseas funds.

Some overseas funds hedge against currency fluctuations. The fund documentation should advise on this and you need to take a view on whether you want currency exposure.

Some guidance to investing overseas is given in *Chapter 18.*

14 Share selection methodology

Introduction

Warren Buffett on chasing yield: Chasing yield is crazy. Just because you'd like to earn 8% or you'd like to earn 10% or you'd like to earn 6%, the world is not going to adapt to that. You have to think about what is the most intelligent thing to do, and if that produces 5% or 6% that's the best you are going to do. But to get enticed into some investment that is risky or that you don't understand because someone promises you a higher yield – I can take you down to the waterfront or something like that and they'll promise you 15% or something.

CNBC's 'Squawk Box', May 6, 2013.

This chapter sets out an approach to selecting individual shares for investment. The basis of successful investing is the selection of good companies and buying their shares at prices that represent good value. It is perfectly possible to invest in a good company at the wrong price – timing is important!

The previous chapters have sought to demystify and explain the workings of the stock markets, and to position the reader to develop a successful investment strategy. Now we have to get ready for the execution. This chapter places considerable emphasis on building market knowledge as well as going into the finer grain of identifying which companies might be a fit with your strategy, and how to assess them. This leads into buying strategies, which are discussed in *Chapter 18 – Managing your portfolio.*

Investing when the stock market indices are testing all-time highs is challenging, but as we have seen, the markets are testing all-time highs a great deal of the time. Sectors as well an individual shares can be subjected to momentum buying, and can become significantly overvalued. However, within each index there are many sectors and many companies and they do not all reach all-time highs at the same time. Sector rotation, discussed in *Chapter 5,* is a reality of the stock markets and continually presents buy opportunities, not least for the alert retail investor.

Major institutional investors with large amounts of money to invest have little choice but to be heavily weighted in large cap companies. Pension funds in particular rely on the dividends streams from the large caps. As well as investing in some good, large cap companies, the retail investor has the possibility to invest more extensively in mid cap and small cap companies – where many companies offering an attractive balance between income and growth are to be found.

If you are going to invest in individual shares, it's useful to have some understanding of company financials. Some basics are covered in *Chapter 4*. The three key elements are Income Statement, Balance Sheet, and Cash Flow.

Essentials

To invest successfully in a sustained manner in individual shares, it is necessary to develop a fairly deep understanding of the markets and a good knowledge of a number of sectors and companies. This involves some complexity, and requires hard work and discipline. If you don't have the appetite or time for this, you should invest in funds, underrated by many commentators as an approach to successful investing. Some key ingredients for successful investing in individual shares are discussed below.

- It is important to read! For many people, traditional newspapers are a thing of the past, but they do have the advantage that an editorial team works hard to create a useful digest of information for the investment community each day. You may not want to go to the expense of the Wall Street Journal or Financial Times every day, though you can get discounts if you take out a subscription; or you could work with their online content, possibly for a subscription. These newspapers are influential and their stories can move markets! Alternatively, many cheaper daily papers have good financial sections and it's worth finding one that suits you, either in print or online.
- There is a massive amount of information available online, and it's perfectly possible to get along without buying a newspaper each day. But try a newspaper and see what you think.
- There are many weekly 'share tip' magazines that you can subscribe to, such as Forbes and Barron's in the US, and Investors Chronicle and MoneyWeek in the UK. These magazines also run websites where you will find many articles on the markets and companies.
- You should watch the financial channels if at all possible – Bloomberg and CNBC. They cover many of the big companies that have reported each day prior to market opening. Quite often they will interview the CEO or CFO and you can listen to what they say about their company and its prospects. A great many people will be on their way to work at this time, but with tablet computers and smartphones, it may be possible to tune in at least for some of the time. A particularly valuable time for UK investors to tune in is around 2:30pm when the US markets open. Traders are regularly interviewed for their views on the direction of the market and you can pick up useful insights from them.
- Get to know several sectors. These have been mentioned for the New York and London markets in *Chapter 3*. You can filter in several different ways –

there may be sectors you like and sectors you don't like. For example, you may decide to avoid pharmaceuticals because of the competition from generics, the share price shocks that can occur if a major drug trial fails, or some of their drug pricing policies; or anything to do with big oil and gas if the oil price is trending down and you don't expect a recovery any time soon. You may decide that you don't like defense companies if governments are cutting their budgets, or telecoms where there is fierce competition and a great deal of evolving regulation. There may be companies that you know something about and like. Maybe you work for a listed company. If the economy is slowing down, then the markets will shift towards 'defensive' shares, such as utilities and consumer staples. If the economy is recovering, then the markets will be switching into the more cyclical shares, such as consumer discretionary, house builders, or online retail.

- Get to know quite a few companies and learn their tickers – this makes it very easy to look them up on websites. How many companies? If you are serious you will get to know 30 or 40 companies well – and then increase this over time. Follow their fortunes. If you don't enjoy this, then concentrate on funds!
- Develop a feel for market cap as this will determine market interest, news flow, and liquidity. All the large cap companies generate strong news flow that moves share prices. In the US, the titans of the stock market have market caps up to around US$200bn. The minimum market cap for an S&P 500 company is US$5.3bn. In the UK, the FTSE 100 also has its titans with market caps of over £100bn but size falls off rapidly and the smaller FTSE 100 companies have market caps around £4bn. All these companies generate intense interest and news flow. Towards the lower end of the FTSE 350 (FTSE 100 plus FTSE 250), market caps are around £500mn, and at this level news flow falls away.
- Establish your information sources. Many sources are cited in this book.

Where to start

You may be a successful investor already and just doing some reading to see if you can pick up a few useful ideas; or you may have been investing for some time without as much success as you would like; or you may be completely new to investing. Whatever your situation, hopefully, you will find some value here.

If you already have a portfolio of individual shares, you may find it useful to run a ruler over them using the approaches suggested here. If you are new to picking individual companies, then where to start can be daunting. However, there is no shortage of advice!

Many people just invest in 'popular shares,' often household names, and in a strongly rising market this can work quite well. Some stockbroker websites aimed at retail investors may show the most-traded shares on any particular day, with the associated volume of buys and sells. Stock exchange websites show share price movements each day, usually with a 15-minute delay, and this is good indicator of which shares are most actively traded each day. These shares can be worth a look.

In the US, you can check <u>Dataroma 'Superinvestor Portfolio Updates'</u> to see the holdings of leading hedge fund managers and movements in their portfolios.

Another thing you can do is to check out the top ten holdings of some of the best-performing funds. Though keep in mind this is a rearview mirror perspective, and the fund manager may be running down his positions in some of these holdings.

Newspapers and magazines are full of share tips, and if you register with a number of financial websites you will not be short of tips coming in by email. Some weekly share tip magazines pull together buy and sell recommendations from a range of sources each week, and it is worth checking these out on a regular basis.

Websites such as <u>InvestorPlace</u> in the US and <u>This is Money</u> in the UK are prolific sources of share tips. The <u>Motley Fool</u> is another UK source, but it charges a fee. Towards the end of the year is a prolific time for journalist tipsters. They assess the performance of their recommendations from a year ago, and announce their recommendations for the new year. Their performance is very mixed!

There is no shortage of share tips, but you need to have a quick way of sorting the wheat from the chaff.

First look

Business model

The typical retail investors will find it challenging to undertake deep research into a range of companies as he seeks to build and manage his portfolio. Many companies, in particular some small and mid cap companies, have simple business models that are easy to understand and it will be a straightforward matter to study an annual report and some reviews of the company and have quite a competent understanding of its products, markets, and outlook. On the other hand, most large cap companies have rather complicated business models, e.g., banks and insurance companies, sprawling multinational conglomerates, integrated oil & gas companies, pharmaceutical giants struggling with their R&D pipeline, miners impacted by commodity prices and the challenge of long-term projects, and so on. These companies present a considerable challenge even for experienced analysts. Either you become expert in the business models of these complex companies, or you rely to a considerable extent on the expertise of others.

However, you don't need to follow the 'experts' blindly. As covered in *Chapter 4*, even the most complicated company is assessed through its capacity to generate earnings by growing its EPS and dividend streams. An important rider to this is that for companies that generate their profits largely from their assets, such as banks and property companies, price to book ratio will also receive close attention from the analysts. If you use these simple filters, you will straight away have valuable insights into the quality of a company and whether it is worth detailed evaluation. At this point, the critical issue is the reliability of the forecasts – and you need to listen to the experts on this.

Concentrating on mid and large cap companies, because news flow is strong and trading liquidity will be good, it can be useful to think in terms of:

- Strong, well established companies with good track records and steady growth
- Young companies that are growing strongly
- Recovery plays

In building your portfolio, keep in mind that young growth stories and recovery plays can be very profitable but can be tricky to get right.

Income versus growth

There is an important choice to be made in emphasis between income and growth shares. These have been discussed in *Chapter 4* and there is further treatment in *Chapter 18 – Managing your portfolio.*

Study some charts

We looked at a number of charts in *Chapter 4*. A picture is worth a thousand words. You can gain useful insight into the way the stock market behaves by looking at a number of 10-year company share price charts – and comparing them with a relevant index. This is very quick and easy to do.

It's also instructive to look at shorter time periods to see the share price movements in a finer grain. As you work through, give some thought to various entry and exit points with an eye to the index as a guide, i.e., buying when the index has pulled back, or selling when it's testing a high. This will give you insight into how difficult investing in individual shares can be.

You will see quite a range of share price performances. Some where you just wish you had invested a number of years ago. Others that would have been good recovery plays. And some that would have been a nightmare for a 'buy and hold' investor but a delight for a skillful swing trader exploiting the volatility.

You will probably view a number of charts with high volatility, but an overall trend either up or down. You might take a look at a few utilities or consumer staples – regarded as 'defensives' paying a good dividend – and form a view.

Look at the basics

The following websites provide key company metrics that will allow you to run a ruler rapidly over a company.

DigitalLook

Pick a company and go to the DigitalLook website. Type the company name or ticker into the search box. Note the market cap of the company, and then go to the table of Key Fundamentals. You will see data for about five preceding years and a Forecast for one to three years ahead. This table is rich with crucial information.

- First look at Revenue and Pre-tax profit. This will tell you a great deal about the company. Is the company showing significant, consistent growth in revenue and profit, or has it suffered some setbacks over the years? Is continued strong growth forecast? You can assess CAGR – Compound Annual Growth Rate – readily from the revenue numbers.
- Then look at P/E ratio, both trailing and forecast. This will tell you how the company is priced. Over 20 is getting expensive. Finally, look at EPS and PEG.
- Is EPS growing strongly and consistently? Many companies have a wobble in their record and it can be useful to find out what caused it. Scan the company reports around the time of the setback.
- How does the PEG look? PEG is particularly important when assessing growth companies. Less than 2 is good; less than 1 is very good, but the market may have serious doubts around growth forecasts.
- What does the dividend record and forecast look like? Anything between zero and 3% or 4% is good as long as the company is achieving good EPS growth. If the dividend is much more than this, the company could be struggling for growth.
- Is the dividend growing consistently?
- Price to book, important for capital-intensive companies, is shown under Financials/Key Financials.

Nasdaq

Go to the Nasdaq website and search the company of interest – both US and UK companies are covered. Then go to Quotes/Revenue EPS to see the revenue history of the firm. Next, go to Analyst Research and you can check out forecasts for Revenue Earnings Growth, P/E Ratio, and PEG Ratio. You want to see that the company is growing revenue and EPS and has a low PEG, say, less than 2 or 3. Also check out Momentum to see if analyst forecasts are moving in the right direction.

It's worth getting to know the Nasdaq website, which is rich with useful information.

CNN Money

CNN Money is another good source of key company information covering US companies. Again, type the company name or ticker into the search box. The site provides useful information on earnings growth, in particular the consensus analyst growth forecast for the next five years. It also provides a graphic showing the high, median, and low forecasts for the next 12 months. Look for strong consensus in forecasts.

Next step

If the company doesn't look promising through these early filters, it's probably not worth a second look. There are plenty more companies. You may be surprised at the number of companies that will not look good through these filters – surprising, because many of them will be hot tips. Companies that look promising after a basic look should then be subjected to a more rigorous look as described below.

Share selection methodology – checklist

It's useful to have a checklist to support your buy decisions, and the knowledge you will build will also support your sell decisions. However, a checklist should not be used in isolation from a good understanding of how the market works.

Set out below is a fairly detailed checklist for evaluating a company as an investment proposition. It will be quite time consuming to go through this rigorously with each company that you decide to check out in more detail. However, if you are not an experienced investor, it will be a good discipline for you to follow it through for a number of companies as a learning process – you are likely to take a view fairly quickly on which checks you like the best, and you should create your own customized approach.

1. Look at the basics
Take a look at the key company metrics as described above. These simple checks should rule out a great many companies and save you time in more detailed research.

2. Note market cap
The greater the marker cap, the greater the news flow and analyst coverage.
Source: Any financial information website.

3. Note the free float

If the free float is a lot less than shares outstanding, this indicates that there may be significant government or private shareholders, possibly exerting influence on management that may not be in the best interests of the shareholders at large.

Source: YAHOO! FINANCE, US or UK – bring up company data and go to Key Statistics and you will find Float under Share Statistics.

4. Note the sector

Do some research on the sector. Are there strong headwinds? Has the sector already had a good run? How is the company rated in its sector by P/E ratio, P/B, etc.

Source: For up to ten-year performance of S&P 500 sectors, search sectorsspdr. GuruFocus under Market gives P/E and Shiller P/E by S&P 500 sector. For three-year performance of LSE sectors, go to shareprices.com and click on Sectors.

5. Learn the ticker

Knowing tickers allows you to look up companies on websites quickly.

Source: Any financial information website.

6. Check out the company website

The website of a large cap company will contain a great deal of information for investors, e.g., 'the investment case,' analyst coverage and consensus, presentations of results, road show information, etc.

7. Target price

Check out analyst target price (TP). See *Chapter 6.* Look for some headroom between current share price and TP.

Source: In the US, go to YAHOO! FINANCE, enter company name or ticker into the Search box, then click on Analyst Opinion for an Upgrade and Downgrade History and Price Target. In the UK, go to DigitalLook, search company and see chronological listing of Broker Views under Recent Recommendations, together with Target Price.

8. Check beta

Beta is an indicator of volatility compared with the relevant index. There is a view that high beta shares are riskier, but have the potential for better returns than less volatile shares.

Source: Many financial information websites.

9. Study the share price chart

Spend a few minutes looking at the share price chart over various time frames up to ten years and with a relevant index overlaid – in the US, use the S&P 500, S&P Mid Cap 400, or Nasdaq 100; in the UK, use the FTSE 100 or FTSE 250. Over- or underperformance against the market indices, especially in recent years, will give considerable insight into the performance of the company. Is the share price trending up or down or ranging sideways? How does the current share price compare with historic highs and lows? Is the share price volatile? The chart will give you a better

insight than beta alone. Is there a steady upwards trend, albeit there may be pullbacks, in line with the market trend? Keep in mind that on most share price charts, you will not be looking at total returns, i.e., with dividends reinvested.   For a high-dividend-paying company, the comparison will underestimate the performance of the share.
Source: Google Finance; YAHOO! FINANCE; ADVFN; and many more websites.

10. Company reports
Look over latest company reports, earnings reports, trading statements, etc. Review statements on company outlook by chairman and CEO. Try to find the company's current guidance – this could be in a press release. Look for media coverage after reporting day, especially for smaller companies, as this may be the only coverage. Be alert for profit warnings.
Source: The company website; in the UK, ADVFN under Quote, and for Hargreaves Lansdown, search the company and click on the Financials tab.

11. Analyst reports
You will probably find it difficult to obtain analyst reports, but you need to check latest upgrades and downgrades. Keep in mind that you should attach most weight to reports that come after the company's latest earnings report, and look for some headroom between current price and target price.
Source: US Nasdaq under Markets/Analyst Activity//Upgrades/Downgrades provides data from about 90 major brokerage firms and updates its table three times a day. In the UK, DigitalLook provides a continuous feed of analyst recommendations – upgrades and downgrades – under UK Shares/Broker Views; Hargreaves Lansdown provides useful analysis of latest reports for some larger cap companies – go to Share prices & stock markets, enter company name or ticker, click on HL RESEARCH.

12. Balance sheet strength
See *Chapter 4:* Check Current ratio; Cash to debt ratio; Debt to equity ratio.
Source: YAHOO! FINANCE under Key Statistics/Balance Sheet (Note: at time of writing this website is showing Debt to equity ratio x 100).

13. Articles
Look out for Internet, newspaper, and financial magazine articles on the company. An informed review can be very valuable.
Source: Internet and stores.

14. Dividend policy and history
Yield of 3% to 4% is about right for an 'income' company – much more than this and it could be because the share price is depressed, and this could indicate lack of investor interest in the share. Institutional investors rely on dividend streams and view very seriously the possibility of a dividend cut or rights issue. Most companies will have had their payment record impaired by the financial crisis, but that is sufficiently long ago for a meaningful recent trend to have become established.

Source: In the US, search <u>Nasdaq dividend history</u>; in the UK, go to <u>ADVFN</u> and look under the <u>Financials</u> tab.

15. Dividend payout ratio or cover

The company needs to be generating enough cash-backed profit to be able to cover comfortably the dividend payment. In normal circumstances payout ratio should not be more than around 70% or cover less than around 1.5 to 2.

Source: In the US, search <u>CSIMarket</u>, insert the company name or ticker and you will find dividend payout ratio under MANAGEMENT EFFECTIVENESS; in the UK, you can use <u>ADVFN</u> under the <u>Financials</u> tab.

16. Profit margin

It is self-evident that this is a particularly important metric, but surprisingly, commentators don't reference percentage profit as often as they might. A healthy net profit – earnings – is necessary for good cash generation and enables a company to be conservative in its profit recognition. A net profit of 3% to 4% is rather thin; 10% is healthy. Above or well above 10% indicates a strong, competitive position.

Source: In the US, <u>CNN Money</u> provides net profit; in the UK, <u>Hargreaves Lansdown</u> provides net profit, described as <u>Profit after tax from continuing operations</u>, under <u>Financials</u>.

17. Discount rate

Discount rate has been explored in *Chapter 4,* and this can be quickly explored using Benjamin Graham's formula. Make an estimate of the EPS growth rate – the formula used 7 to 10 years – and calculate IV = EPS(8.5 + 2g). If you obtain a value significantly above current share price, then a high discount factor is implied. This would indicate that the market is concerned about the risks that the company faces or is uncertain about the EPS forecasts – or both. Or that there is simply little market interest in the share. If you judge that the market is overly concerned, then you could take the difference between Graham's IV and current share price as margin of safety.

18. Pricing power and competition

A companies pricing power will be influenced by the quality of its output and its cost base and efficiency. Strong pricing power should be reflected in its profit margin. A good profit margin will attract competition and a key issue here is the cost for another company to enter the space.

Source: In the US, <u>CSIMarket</u> – click on the <u>Competition</u> tab at the top of the page; <u>CNN Money</u> – search company, see <u>Competitors</u>.

19. Commodity prices

If you are looking at an oil & gas company or a mining company, their share price will be strongly influenced by the oil price and by the price of iron ore, gold, copper, etc. Look at both current price and trend.

Source: <u>YAHOO! FINANCE</u>.

20. Insider/Director transactions in shares

This is an important consideration, but directors and other insiders buy and sell shares in their companies for a great range of reasons that are not necessarily an indicator of sentiment. However, if, e.g., a founder-shareholder sells heavily, the markets may punish the share price. The professionals will be hardwired to the regulatory news feed, so this will happen very quickly.

Source: In the US, go to the Nasdaq website, search the company and click on Insiders. In the UK, go to Hargreaves Lansdown, search the company and click on Director Deals. US and UK, see YAHOO! FINANCE.

21. Debt

Level of debt is a key company metric and will become increasingly so as interest rates rise post–financial crisis.

Source: In the US, go to CSIMarket, insert the company ticker, and you will find Financial Strength; in the UK, go to ADVFN under the Financials tab.

22. Pension liability

Some companies have a very large deficit on their final salary pension scheme even though it will probably be closed to new entrants. Making up the deficit, which they are bound by law to do, can be a significant drag on performance. Such companies, where the pension deficit is comparable to market cap, are sometimes referred to as pension zombies.

Source: Company annual report.

23. Shares out on loan and short interest

Check shares out on loan and short interest.

Source: In the US, shares out on loan may be difficult to find; for short interest, search Nasdaq short interest, shortsqueeze.com, and Barrons.com; in the UK, search Euroclear for shares out on loan; also check Castellain Capital short interest tracker.

24. Acquisition target

Is the company a potential acquisition target? You need to read to be tuned in! Beware a company whose share price has already risen as a result of predator interest. If the predator loses interest, the share price is likely to fall sharply.

25. Ownership

Check the main ownership of the company. Are major institutions prominent in the ownership? Is it closely held? Is ownership diverse?

Source: US Morningstar – search company and click on Ownership. UK Morningstar – search company and click on Directors & Shareholders.

26. Chat rooms

There are many discussion websites on the Internet.

Source: In the US, search Top Ten Investment Forums; in the UK, go to Interactive Investor under Discussion tab as a start.

There are many other criteria for assessing company shares, but the above is hopefully a useful start.

Conclusions

The purpose of this chapter is to set out a rational basis for selecting companies for investment. It is important to restate that there can be no certainty in stock markets, but a disciplined, well-informed approach will greatly enhance the prospects of success. Shrewd selection of companies, combined with a well-informed approach to the timing of buy and sell decisions is crucial for successful stock market investing.

Chapter 18 – Managing your portfolio provides guidance on the proactive management of a portfolio.

15 A day in the markets

Introduction

Stock markets trade around the globe, starting each trading day in the East, which includes Australia, China, Southeast Asia, and Japan, followed by India, the Middle East, Europe, and finally, the Americas. All the major stock markets are interrelated, often strongly, and understanding the interrelationships is important for successful trading and investing. With a global stock market trading volume of over US$60tn every day, the amount of activity is vast. A journey through a typical day in the markets can usefully illustrate the integrated nature of the world's markets, and make some sense of their complexity.

The cash indices and the futures indices

The major US indices, including the Dow, the S&P 500, and the Nasdaq 100 are the most watched in the world. In the UK, the most-watched indices are the FTSE 100 and FTSE 250. They are referred to as the cash indices to distinguish them from the corresponding futures indices, which are based on derivatives. There is a futures market in many of the major world indices. The relationship between the US cash and futures indices has been described in *Chapter 9.*

The S&P 500 daily volume is in the region of US$3.5bn and upwards, and value of shares traded has reached above US$11bn. It's difficult to find the FTSE 100 volume in sterling terms, though number of shares traded can be found, e.g., on YAHOO! FINANCE under charts of indices. A typical daily volume is around 0.6bn shares traded. On exceptional days, FTSE 100 volume has reached around 1.5bn shares traded.

Stock market performance is ultimately measured through the performance of the cash indices, so every day there is an intense focus on their performance. Are they moving sideways in a trading range with the possibility of breaking out to the upside or to the downside? Over the last month or so have the market indices hit a series of new highs? Will they hit another, and what then? Are the markets grinding steadily upwards? Are they in 'bubble' territory, with share prices overinflated by leverage? Or have the markets crashed and the burning question is 'has the bottom been reached?' Are the major stock markets around the world moving in sync, i.e., exhibiting strong correlation due to major macroeconomic factors, or are fundamentals to the fore?

The importance of index futures trading, in particular of the US indices, cannot be overstated. Each week the US futures commence trading in Chicago on Sunday at 5:00 pm (pre-market starts at 4:00 pm), one hour before the Tokyo stock exchange opens, which is no coincidence. Even though the index futures trading volumes are low until the New York markets open, the futures traders will be taking account of stock market performances as well as news flow, including economic data releases, as the world turns. The state of these indices will usually set the tone for the start of trading in the London market. Significant news out of Europe will influence the US futures and the opening sentiment in the US. However, the US markets are usually dominant, with the S&P 500 alone accounting for more than half of global stock market capitalization, and tend to influence European markets more than vice versa. So when you see that the UK indices have risen or fallen off with the US futures, it will usually, but not always, be that the UK indices are tracking the US futures.

The sentiment from the performance of the US futures can be short-lived when the cash markets get underway. An early US data release, an unexpected report from a Dow 30 company during the earnings season, an international political situation flaring up, or disappointing economic data from China can change sentiment very quickly. Also the cash markets absorb on a daily basis a much finer grain of information than the futures markets, interpreting vast amounts of news flow and data in relation to individual sectors and companies. With the interplay between the cash markets and the futures markets, price discovery is a round-the-clock activity.

Because of a strong correlation between the New York and London markets, after the burst of activity following the opening bell, the London market indices will often track the US futures until the US opening bell at 9:30 am ET (2:30 pm London time), when the US cash markets usually become dominant.

The state of the market – sentiment

'Be fearful when others are greedy and greedy when others are fearful.'
Warren Buffett

Notwithstanding a little repetition, important factors that bear on sentiment include:

Moods and themes

It is important to gauge the sentiment of the markets. Markets can be optimistic, pessimistic, nervous, jittery, euphoric, gloomy, tentative, and so on. A particular sentiment may pertain for some time and then change rapidly on significant events. Or there will be times when sentiment is swinging wildly. There are a lot of minds at work seeking to identify trends. It is not difficult to tune into endless discussion in the media on sentiment. Opinion is often divided, with very plausible views on either side of the argument. This is, after all, what makes a market between buyers and sellers! Sometimes, though, there will be fairly strong consensus regarding the direction of the market, which presents opportunities for the retail trader and investor.

Another significant market behavior is that they move from theme to theme. For example, the markets may react sharply to an outbreak of hostilities in a strategic region, eventually factoring the implications for company earnings into share prices, and then recovering before moving on to the next theme, which may be around interest rates.

Some influencing factors are recurring, others hang over the markets sometimes for months or even years, and others are 'events' that take place, sometimes leaving a lasting scar on the markets, sometimes not.

Market psychology

Market psychology is an all-pervading factor but manifests itself in many different ways, some of which have been touched on briefly in *Chapter 5* and *Chapter 10.* It's worth trying to tune into market psychology but there are no simple rules of thumb to follow – you need to listen to the market babble and try to make sense of it.

Global economic growth

Most companies need strong and growing economic conditions if they are to prosper, and gross domestic product (GDP) could be regarded as the ultimate influencer of sentiment. GDP data from the major economies, particularly the US and China, that is out of line with expectations can move markets significantly. During the recovery from the global financial crisis, GDP growth around the world has been uncertain and faltering.

GDP figures are typically published quarterly and revised monthly.

Central bank policies

Since the global economic crisis, central banks around the world, most notably in the US, Europe, and Japan, have had a profound influence on stock markets, particularly in relation to quantitative easing programs and interest rate policy. Policies are sometimes announced and sometimes inferred from minutes of meetings when these are published. A policy announcement by a major central bank makes for a significant day in the markets. Perversely, share prices will sometimes rise on deteriorating economic conditions – on the basis that this will result in central bank stimulation.

The reporting or earnings season

The earnings season has been described in *Chapter 5.* As US companies report quarterly, the US earnings season is particularly important. The next US earnings season is never far away and when it comes, strength or weakness in corporate earnings has a substantial impact on market sentiment. In the US, some companies publish their reports in the morning before the market opens. Others report during the day or after market close. In the UK, most companies upload their reports onto their websites at 7:00 am, an hour before market opening.

Tail risks hanging over the markets

Tail risks hanging over the markets can cause jitters and high volatility. When there is a substantial tail risk hanging over the markets, they can develop a 'risk on/risk off' mentality with the markets responding rapidly to news and changing perceptions of the level of the tail risk.

Interest rates and bond yields

We have been in a period of very low interest rates since the global financial crisis and rising interest rates will increase the costs of companies with debt – reducing their earnings with a knock on effect for their share prices. A great many indebted companies regarded as not particularly good have quite possibly only survived because of low interest rates. These are sometimes referred to as zombie companies. Rising interest rates will also hit consumers in the pocket with a knock-on effect for many companies. There is endless debate around when post–financial crisis interest rates will rise, and at what rate.

Share prices tend to rise with bond prices. As bond prices rise, bond yields fall, and shares look more attractive especially for the institutional investors who need dividend yield – and are not averse to rising share prices.

Every day, influenced by interest rate trends and policies, monies are shifted between shares and bonds and other asset classes. When markets are volatile, the flows are large.

Currencies

Currency trends and fluctuations are important and influence trading and investment activities on a daily basis.

Fluctuations in exchange rates impact directly on company earnings and therefore have a bearing on share prices – in a variety of ways. If a company is located in the US and generates significant profits in overseas subsidiaries, then a rising dollar will result in lower overseas profits in dollar terms. Another impact can be through input costs. For example, if a company's feedstock is a commodity that is internationally traded in US dollars, then a surge in the dollar will be unwelcome.

In 2015, emerging markets suffered substantial stock market falls, exacerbated for the overseas investor by collapsing currencies.

Dollar/Euro, Dollar/Yen, Dollar/Sterling, and Sterling/Euro are among the most closely watched exchange rates.

Commodity prices

Commodity prices and trends are closely watched because they directly affect the revenues of a great many companies, most obviously those operating in the resource or mining industries. Also, a great many companies' costs are influenced by the prices of raw materials. For example, copper is the most used industrial metal and so its price figures in the analysis of many companies, large and small.

Oil and gas prices impact the fortunes of all the oil and gas companies, explorers and producers, as well their supply chain companies. For many companies, energy is a significant cost and their fortunes are strongly affected by oil and gas prices. As the oil price fell sharply in 2015/16, the sector cut back sharply on investment, affecting the fortunes of many industrial companies in its supply chain.

Gold is always closely watched. Even though it has no industrial use, it has always been regarded as a safe haven when there is high tail risk around, but perhaps less so in recent years. But that could change quickly!

Sector rotation

Sector rotation has been discussed in *Chapter 5.*

Sometimes geographic areas get significantly out of sync in terms of economic performance, for example, between the US, Europe, Eurozone peripherals, Japan, Russia, and other emerging markets. Investors look for markets that have become cheap rather than invest in markets that are judged to be already expensive. Average P/E ratio for a market or index is a closely monitored metric. These perceived imbalances in valuations lead to continuous capital flows between regions. From time to time, investor flight occurs from economies in difficulties.

Sentiment varies across asset markets, and investors seek to execute rotation strategies, led by the major market participants with others seeking to follow. The market strategists and asset allocation managers are always hard at work reshaping their portfolios, responding to events and trends. There are many types of rotation strategy – between countries and regions; from bonds into shares and vice versa; from defensive shares, such as staples, into cyclicals, such as consumer discretionary; or out of momentum shares, perhaps growth company shares that have become overvalued, into value shares.

The Asian and European markets

The important Asian stock markets interact with the US and European markets in different ways at different times. Sometimes they are strongly correlated and sometimes they are not. The Chinese stock markets in particular tend to go their own way. From 2011 through 2014, the Chinese markets underperformed significantly compared with Europe and the US, after many years of outperformance. Then in 2015, they rose sharply and crashed! Many emerging market economies are strongly dependent on selling into China, the world's second-largest economy, and since Chinese growth began to slow in 2010, these economies have struggled. There is flight from the emerging markets every few years.

The London and New York markets

Connectivity

The US and UK stock markets, the largest and third-largest in the world, have been described in *Chapter 3*, including trading hours. While there is a measure of connectivity between most major stock markets around the world, the connectivity between New York and London is particularly strong with a time difference of only five hours and the large market participants, including investment banks and hedge funds, operating in both markets. Many UK companies are cross-listed on the US stock markets and trade as American depositary receipts with trading volumes sometimes comparable to those in the UK. So the London opening prices will be influenced by both extended hours trading in New York and the index futures trading in Chicago, which will have absorbed trading activity in other markets and news through the night.

The strongest correlation between London and New York is at major index level, but correlations at sector level can also be strong. There is also a proxy effect as analysts will study the performance of sectors and companies in the US for read-over into the London market. For example, if a major oil field services company in the US, such as Baker Hughes, has reported well or badly, this is likely to feed through to similar companies listed in London, e.g., Petrofac, Wood Group, and Amec; or if a major user of microchips, such as Apple, disappoints, the London-listed chip manufacturers such as Arm, Imagination, or CSR may also be hit depending on analysts' perception of how their earnings will be affected.

An early start

There is a five-hour time difference between London and New York. The markets open in London at 8:00 am and in New York at 9:30 am ET, though the pre-market trading in the US opens at 4:00 am ET, which is 9:00 am London time. On most days in the year, New York main trading opens at 2:30 pm London time – usually a significant moment for London.

This is a driven industry and the professionals will have started their deliberations well before market opening, seeking to absorb and weigh everything that has happened overnight and taking a keen interest in US futures trading as well as London, Frankfurt, and Paris futures. There is a lot to absorb since the stock markets opened in the East. Conversations between colleagues, collaborators, and accomplices will take place around the globe as it turns. They will participate in the pre-markets and opening auctions and develop their plans for the main trading day. Though as with all plans, these may not 'survive first contact with the enemy.' Then comes the opening bell and all the serious market participants are in full swing.

The financial TV channels and financial press

For the retail investor, the financial television channels are a useful way of getting up to speed on what has happened overnight. Newspapers, in particular the Wall Street Journal and Financial Times, provide useful insight into what happened in the markets the day before, as well as many articles relating to global developments and sentiment. The amount of information available on market information websites and investment platforms is virtually limitless, and active investors find a constant stream of unsolicited emails arriving in their inboxes.

Bloomberg and CNBC start well before market opening and both have European editions. They provide market coverage throughout the day, winding down as the US markets close at 4:30 pm ET – 9:30 pm in London. These are high-quality services providing constant streams of data, insightful commentary, and interviews with a wide range of market participants as well as politicians, central bankers, and regulators. And importantly, with the chief executive officers and senior executive directors of companies usually, but not always, on their reporting day and quite often before market opening. They want to talk up their share price of course, especially if their numbers are disappointing. This is an important 'playing field leveller' for the retail investors, giving them the opportunity to hear what key executives have to say about their companies and trading outlook – through interview by well-informed and expert 'interrogators.' In addition there is a constant stream of market strategists and fund managers offering their views.

The TV channels run throughout the day. The coverage up to marketing opening and during early trading tends to be the best. An hour or so after the markets have opened, the coverage often becomes more magazine style, though it picks up again in the UK as the US opening bell approaches. High-quality guests can pop up at any time – even prime ministers. These channels are regarded as important platforms by many senior politicians and major political announcements are well covered. Politicians can, and often do, move markets sometimes with just a few words.

Many of the guests on these channels are there to 'talk their book,' i.e., to promote a particular share or fund or perhaps a sector that they have an interest in. But it can still be well worth listening to what they have to say – they might be right.

A very useful feature of the TV coverage of the US markets is daily interviews with traders in New York who, as you might expect, are very strongly tuned into market sentiment. They are not always right but they are always worth listening to.

The economic calendar

A glance at a good economic calendar illustrates the amount of key economic data released to the markets each day. These move share prices, sometimes a great deal. The big data releases, such as the monthly US nonfarm payrolls numbers (first Friday of each month) and purchasing managers' indices (PMIs) for major economies bear strongly on sentiment.

It is worth noting that key releases from China often occur over the weekend.

The professionals will be hardwired into these data releases and know which ones will have the greatest impact on particular stock markets, sectors, and companies. Some high-frequency trading systems will machine read the releases – kindly provided by some stock exchanges in readable format – and their algorithms will be trading on the data within milliseconds.

These 'events' start in the East, with key releases from China and Japan attracting close attention.

If a particularly important release is due, such as an important PMI, the markets may just move sideways until the data is released. A significant deviation from expectations will then move the markets significantly.

Particularly important are the US data releases, many of which take place between 8:30 am and 10:00 am ET, bringing the London market to life again.

Spread betting opening call

In the UK, the spread betting industry makes opening calls on share prices and on the major indices. These are a useful indication of market sentiment. Opening calls are to be found on the spread betting company websites and are sometime announced by the financial TV channels.

The VIX index and options

Options are also traded almost around the clock on the CME, with traders and investors looking to hedge – insure – their risk. An important measure of option trading activity is the VIX Volatility Index – the US market fear gauge – which has been discussed in *Chapters 7* and *10*. Go to YAHOO! FINANCE and enter ^VIX in the Search box.

People don't want to pay commissions to buy an option if they don't have to, and fear can come and recede quickly, causing the VIX index to rise and fall sharply. It is a much-watched index, particularly by traders.

Stock exchange news feeds

Stock exchange news feeds have been described in *Chapter 5.*

The regulatory news feeds can have an important bearing on company fortunes, and are watched closely through the day, though posts can and frequently do appear out of market open hours.

The professionals will have people monitoring the news feeds, which gives them a significant advantage over the retail day traders.

Pre-opening activity

The auction processes leading up to market opening for the NYSE, the Nasdaq, and LSE have been outlined in *Chapter 3.* These pre-market processes are quite specialized and have been the domain of the major market participants. However, increasing numbers of retail investors are participating through direct market access provided by their brokers.

For a small company there may be very little or no activity prior to the bell and the market maker will assess the news and post his opening prices accordingly.

The opening bell in London

As soon as opening prices have been determined, limit orders and market orders – including aggressive orders – will come through and the day's trading is underway. Overnight differences between the FTSE 100 futures and the opening cash prices will be rapidly eliminated through trading and arbitrage.

The opening bell in New York

The US market opens at 9:30 am ET, which is 2:30 pm London time, except for a few days in the year as a result of different timings of daylight savings, and the behavior of the US markets, more often than not, sets the tone in London for the rest of the day.

The US futures have traded through the night and fair value may now be above or below the previous index close. The gap will be largely closed on market opening with direction depending on how much conviction there is in the futures fair value. Any remaining gap will be quickly eliminated through arbitrage – traders looking to benefit from price discrepancies between different markets and exchanges.

The New York markets inevitably start with strong trading volume. Then, absent key economic data, the US markets will often drift sideways in low volume for much of the day, making their minds up later, quite possibly with a decisive move up or down accompanied by a surge in volume as investors and traders position themselves for the next day's market opening. They will take a view on sentiment and seek to position themselves – to avoid losses from 'gapping down' of prices or to gain from 'gapping up.'

The crucial context to all this is the global economy, in which the US economy, as a global engine of growth, is key. Traders and investors around the globe never take their eyes of the US economy, and both the cash and index futures markets.

Corporate activity

Company reports

Many companies post their reports before the market opens. This is the moment of truth for companies, and the analysts and all serious market participants will be assessing the reports within seconds of their availability.

Share prices are about buying into a company's cash flow – through EPS and/or dividend stream. So company reporting, quarterly or half-yearly, is crucial when companies announce their EPS and dividend payments. Dividend is paid out of EPS.

The CEO will describe the company's outlook and may provide forward guidance, which is studied rapidly, and the market will take a view on how confident it is that the company will continue to achieve its objectives. Share prices move on both EPS and dividend announcements.

In the US, preannouncements, possibly in the form of a press release, and in the UK, interim management or trading statements will appear regularly and move share prices. These may contain profit warnings, often made a couple of weeks ahead of the formal reporting date in an effort to soften the blow. Unexpected guidance from a Dow 30 company can move markets around the world.

A great many market participants will speculate on how a company will report, and its share price often moves significantly in the period leading up to reporting. The reports of the larger cap companies attract a great deal of attention, and are anticipated days and sometimes weeks ahead – surrounded by rumors and leaks. Those expecting a strong report will take a position before the report, in the hope of benefitting from the share price gapping up on opening, rather than miss the rise that holders of the share will enjoy. Vice-versa for short positions. There can be a strong element of speculation in this, and sometimes there will be some insider trading at work.

For the larger cap companies, some analysts will pronounce their assessments before market opening and if you are tuned into one of the television channels, you may hear that particular analysts have called, e.g., Major Inc. up by 2% on opening. Often they are in the right ballpark.

Dividend action

Dividends for the institutions are an important consideration and variances from expectations will move share prices significantly. Where large dividends are involved, there can be substantial movements in share prices before and after the ex-dividend date.

Because most US companies pay dividends four times a year, these movements are not as pronounced as in the UK, where many FTSE 100 company final dividends are around 3% or 4%. Several FTSE 100 companies going ex-dividend on the same day can take several points off the index.

Conference calls

It is common for the CEO on reporting day to hold a telephone conference call for major investors and analysts. This is mainly the domain of the major investors, but any shareholder can register to listen in. Usually, the CEO will focus on highlights of the report and then take questions. Conference calls often produce share price moving information.

You can access many conference call transcripts through <u>Seeking Alpha Earnings Center Transcripts</u> for both US and UK companies.

AGMs

A company will usually hold its AGM to present its full-year results to investors. These are set piece events and rarely produce share price moving information, but there can always be a surprise.

The analysts

July 2013: There is considerable volatility in Easyjet's share price leading up to a trading update, indicating that bad news is already on the streets. An analyst speculates publicly that based on checking out Easyjet flight availability 'to the sun' during August, he expects a poor trading statement. Easyjet's report is strong and the share price gaps up 8% on market opening. Then it is reported that some Easyjet insiders are leaking that summer bookings are down and the share price closes the day flat on heavy trading volume.

The role of the analysts – sell-side and buy-side – have been described in *Chapter 5*. The sell-side people will make their assessments and many will issue their reports as rapidly as possible. Their job is to 'sell' to fund managers who will then invest through their companies and pay commissions. Fund managers will have many analysts' reports landing on their desks soon after reporting, especially for the larger cap companies.

The most important analyst reports will usually be those produced on a company's reporting day or soon afterwards, though an influential analyst report can appear at any time and move a share price up or down sharply. Retail traders will find it a challenge to stay abreast of sell-side analyst output.

Chat rooms and bulletin boards

In 2014, an investment bank accused a trader of improperly sharing client communications with her husband, a trader at a rival bank, on numerous occasions through electronic chat rooms. Information related to mergers and acquisitions, IPOs, and share dealing activities. The trader maintained that it was normal practice for traders to send messages to traders at other banks indicating interest in particular shares.

On 23 April 2013, a fake Associated Press tweet saying that there had been a terror attack on the White House caused the Dow to drop more than 100 points – it had recovered within 5 minutes.

Chat rooms and bulletin boards have been discussed in *Chapter 5.*

Many investment platforms provide a bulletin board facility. They are a useful source of information, in particular for those trading smaller companies.

Unscrupulous traders post false or misleading messages on bulletin boards as they seek to manipulate share prices to their advantage.

Investor activity through the day

The big players

The major market participants include the institutional investors and their fund managers, hedge funds, and investment banks – and the HF traders. They will dominate trading in the larger cap shares with a range of perspectives with respect to investment horizons, EPS projections, dividend forecasts, and risk. Long/short strategies are increasingly used by the big players. Depending on constantly evolving market conditions, they will move funds between markets and asset classes. They will also build up and wind down positions in companies as they execute sector rotation strategies using their trading desks. Institutions building or reducing a position in a company can buy or sell the share heavily for days.

Much information sharing will be going on, some legitimate, and some sailing close to the wind.

There is a constant search for yield and for value.

The traders

A range of trading activities has been described in *Chapter 9* and *Chapter 10* and we have seen that a substantial portion of share trading volume in New York and London is undertaken by high-frequency traders.

Traders work with a range of strategies from front-running institutional investors, competing for alpha, to machine reading important data releases with algorithms, and trading instantly on the data. There will be a mix of long and short strategies. There is a lot at stake and this frenetic and chaotic activity results in the volatility in share prices that makes day trading such a challenge.

Though traders exert a strong influence on the short-term and medium movements of share prices, it is not easy for them to influence long-term movements, as a good company will eventually make its point through its results – and vice versa for a poor company.

The short sellers and bear raiders

Short selling has been discussed in *Chapter 8.*

The amount of short selling taking place ebbs and flows. When markets are strong, the volume of short positions will fall to low levels, but there will always be tactical shorting going on.

The likes of Muddy Waters or Pershing Square Capital can launch a bear raid at any time, with dire consequences for the shares of the target company. Unscrupulous brokers and traders may play pump and dump, and bear squeezes can take the short sellers by surprise, leading to panic buying and sharp share price rises.

Alternative trading venues and dark liquidity

An increasing amount of trading activity occurs in alternative trading venues as well as off-exchange in dark pools where there is a lack of trading transparency.

Trading has become fragmented and it's become problematic for the retail trader to make sense of trading volume on a daily basis. As we have seen earlier, all the significant market participants are doing their best to conceal their intentions or to steal competitive advantage, from a fund manager seeking to wind down a major position to the high-frequency traders looking to front run him.

Alternative trading venues are less well-regulated than the public stock exchanges and so more vulnerable to market abuse.

Fund flows

Institutional money dominates the markets, and there are plenty of organizations tracking flows of money around the globe, between asset classes and between funds. Mutual fund flows are an important indicator of retail investor sentiment and are monitored and regularly reported.

Exchange Traded Funds – ETFs – have become an important tool for both traders and investors. In the short term they are used for responding quickly to changes in sentiment both regionally and globally. They trade as shares on the stock exchanges, so are more suitable for short-term trading than mutual funds.

Market strategists watch ETF flows carefully as an indicator of changing sentiment across asset classes and market sectors, e.g., flows of money between shares and bonds and between emerging markets, Eurozone peripheral countries, and developed economies.

News flow

Information that bears on company fortunes has flowed through the night, and picks up an hour before the markets open when company reports begin to emerge. Important macroeconomic data can move the price of virtually every significant share on the US and London markets. Even companies that have reported well can be dragged down by a sharply falling market. There may have been significant data out of China over the weekend, and there will be data releases that effect regional economies and sectors. Rumors and misinformation will also be flowing through the markets.

The larger the company, the stronger will be the news flow. A regulator may announce action against a bank or a utility company. A company may announce a major project win – or delay. A promising new drug may fail a drug trial, causing a pharmaceutical company share price to fall sharply. There may be a sharp hike in the oil price because of a political flare-up. A takeover rumor may emerge. Analyst reports and rumors of pending analyst's reports will emerge, which can move share prices sharply. The stock exchange news feeds are an important source of news flow.

Professional traders using Bloomberg or Reuter terminals will enjoy a significant advantage over the retail traders and investors.

16 The stock market is not a level playing field

Introduction

In his book 'Broke' (Fourth Estate 2014), David Boyle wrote:

The Financial Sector no longer sees its main function as raising money for productive enterprise run by the middle classes. It buys, sells, and repackages financial assets in a great swirl of useless and corrosive activity, sucking in the money that might play a more useful role. It has become a new kind of landlord, living off rents and charges of a financial system that funnels wealth upwards-while real wages and real salaries have been declining since 1970.

'Wall Street is the only place that people ride to in a Rolls Royce to get advice from those who take the subway.'
Warren Buffett

To develop the metaphor, the playing field is vast and uneven, with playing areas around the world and the game is risky. The aim is to accumulate as many chips as possible and convert them to cash. Surrounding the players are helpers who want to get their hands on as many chips as possible without taking any risk. There are many rule books and the big players find many ways around them. Too few referees struggle to keep up and swap places with players from the big teams on a regular basis. Usually, the referees are not well-supported by their governing bodies around the world. The number of participants is beyond counting. They range from large, well-equipped teams, often working closely together, to a great many individuals with little training and experience.

The value of the chips varies with time and playing area. Sometimes nearly everyone is playing together and winning everywhere. Other times it is a zero-sum gain with both big winners and big losers. Every now and again panic sets in and nearly everyone loses. Some of the individual players always seem to lose, though there are always small areas of the playing field where the most skillful individuals can find some valuable chips.

In this chapter, a number of areas in which the retail investor is at a systematic disadvantage are described.

Disclosure

In January 2014, the New York Attorney General, Eric Schneiderman, announced that BlackRock, the world's largest fund manager, had agreed to stop surveying equity analysts about their views, which was perceived as a means of obtaining share price sensitive information, i.e., analyst re-ratings, early.

In 2015 it is reported that Renishaw co-founder and CEO Sir David McMurtry operates to the principle that share price sensitive information is shared with everyone at the same time. In other words, Renishaw makes no effort to manage analyst forecasts. The Renishaw share price is volatile.

You might say that all market participants are equal but some are more equal than others.

Defenders of the fairness of the markets like to say that everyone has access to the same information about companies at the same time. Companies are barred from making selective disclosure of information that could have a bearing on their share price, but given the interactions between company management and market participants, this is a questionable proposition.

Fortunately for the retail investor, the pressure on publicly traded companies to make prompt disclosure of material information to all investors at the same time is increasing. There has been a long tradition of selective disclosure, in which large institutional investors have received share price sensitive information from companies ahead of smaller investors.

In 2000, the U.S. Securities and Exchange Commission introduced Regulation Fair Disclosure, with the purpose of stamping out these practices. Unsurprisingly, the large institutions mounted a campaign to derail the regulation – arguing that 'fair disclosure' would lead to 'less disclosure.' In the end a grassroots campaign won the day and the regulation came into force – requiring companies to make more timely and frequent communications to investors on a strictly non-selective basis. These are usually made through press releases or in conference calls that all investors have access to and are posted on websites.

The UK now enforces prompt disclosure rules more vigorously to the discomfort of those fund managers who sought unfair advantage.

Has all this solved the problem? You will see from the box at the start of this section, that BlackRock had found a loophole that has now been closed. The search for loopholes will never end!

Access to company management

Early in 2014, billionaire activist investor Carl Icahn had built a US$4bn stake in Apple, and was seeking to persuade the company to undertake a US$50bn share repurchase. On 14 February 2014, Forbes website reported: 'His private meetings with Apple CEO, Tim Cook, has given him more of an insider's insight into what's going on within the company – and in the mind of the Apple chief. The fact that he hasn't sold any of his shares after his meetings with Cook validates the belief that he has gained vital and positive information about Apple.'

The major shareholders in a company, often represented by fund managers, are likely to have direct access to the main board, in particular the chairman, CEO, and other directors, both executive and non-executive. This is difficult to square with the aspiration of non-selective disclosure.

Top investors in large companies, such as fund managers and hedge funds, are increasingly seeking to influence company's management and strategies, and meetings to advance such agendas will inevitably result in a transfer of share price sensitive information.

A further complication is that companies will seek to promote their company with influential analysts for the benefit of their share price. There must be some risk in such situations of price sensitive information leaking to analysts.

The investors in, say, a pension fund represented by a fund manager, should benefit from constructive intervention in a company by the fund manager, but a retail investor could well be wrong-footed by a fund manager who decides to reduce his holding in a company by selling in a dark pool.

Smaller fund managers will not have such ready access and it is common practice in US, UK, Europe, and Asia for fund managers to pay investment bank brokerages for access to their corporate clients' top management. The payments commonly come out of fund managers' commissions, which are meant to be allocated to research, and are made to the brokerages by giving them a prearranged volume of trades. In the UK, the Financial Conduct Authority is endeavoring to stamp out this practice.

In most situations, the retail investor will only be able to access company executives at AGMs and through corporate conference calls.

The influence of analysts

In 2013, the Securities and Exchange Commission was investigating Steve Cohen's hedge fund, SAC Capital Markets. It emerged from interviews that

> *SAC ran according to the doctrine 'get the information faster than anyone else.' SAC's traders were expected to get the first calls from analysts who were upgrading or downgrading a particular share. Their jobs depended on it.*
>
> *In 2014, a major brokerage announced that a UK online retailer had increased third-quarter sales by 45% compared with the same quarter the previous year – three days before the company was due to issue a trading statement. The share price of the retailer rose sharply on the days before and after the announcement.*

The role of analysts in the markets is described in *Chapter 6.*

Sell-side analysts have a substantial influence on share price movements, and churn out their reports with unrelenting energy. The analysts are only meant to have available to them material that has been disclosed to all investors, but this is not a practical proposition. Some analysts, in particular those working for investment banks and major brokerages, will have some degree of access to senior company management for companies that they cover.

Also, companies make presentations to the sales desks of investment banks and brokerages, with the aim of giving their share price a boost. For every major company there are influential analysts that exert significant influence on its share price. Sales desks in their organizations will be first to hear of upgrades and downgrades, quite often through a phone call from the analyst. Next to hear will be well-networked professional traders. Last to hear will be the retail traders and investors.

It is commonplace to read in the financial pages that rumors of an impending analyst report moved a particular share price up or down during a trading day. Analysts' reports are sometimes trailed and even leaked. On a company's reporting day, sell-side analyst recommendations begin to appear before market opening and then emerge during the day. Many professional traders will trade on these reports as soon as they are published.

Analysts will go to extraordinary lengths to gain an edge. There are stories of analysts using Google Maps to count car inventories in China – official figures are difficult to obtain – and counting truck movements in and out of factories, to gauge demand for materials.

The best way to obtain market-beating information from analysts is to build up a strong network of analyst contacts. Most retail investors will not be in a position to do this. The retail investor can conduct his own research on a particular share and decide to buy – only to find that shortly afterwards, the markets are stampeding in the opposite direction, the consequences of a well-trailed analyst report. Many retail investors will not know why a share in their portfolio gained or lost a significant percentage until they read about it in the newspapers or on the Internet the next day.

For a small cap share, it may not be possible to find any cause – perhaps there was just a lot of selling pressure during the day.

Despite all the issues with sell-side analysts, they are producing and disseminating information and views that are helpful to the market in an overall sense, but they make a substantial contribution to the unevenness of the playing field.

Traders

In February 2015, before the UK general election, Britain's Labour party was proposing to hit hedge funds by closing an exemption known as 'intermediaries relief', under which banks can buy shares on their behalf without paying stamp duty reserve tax – stamp duty on electronic transfers.

The big investment banks such as Goldman Sachs, JP Morgan Chase, Morgan Stanley, and Credit Suisse are big traders in both the cash and futures markets. Their revenues from share trading and underwriting new offerings has sometimes approached half of their overall revenues. The hedge funds are also big traders. The trading teams of these large players will have the best possible support in terms of research, news flow, and technology and they will execute both long and short strategies.

Market makers are, by definition, traders and are very good at it! They will 'shake the tree' on a regular basis to get a good price on a block of shares for a client – dropping a share price sharply to induce panic selling.

Then there are the high-frequency trading houses. We have seen in *Chapter 10* that share trading on the major stock exchanges is dominated by high-frequency trading, with less than half the trading volume concerned with normal buying and selling of shares. In addition, about one-third of LSE turnover is conducted through contracts for difference (CFDs), where no stamp duty is paid. The high-frequency traders on the LSE will be trying hard to steal all the 'alpha' without having to pay any stamp duty. They may also watch the world of the day traders on the CFD platforms – seeking to wrong-foot them in a zero-sum game.

The pre-opening auctions are an important opportunity to gain a buy or sell advantage based on the most current information for a company, such as a reporting event. It is possible these days for retail investors to participate in auctions through direct market access. On days where significant news bears on share prices, much of the share price movement occurs in the opening auctions.

After the stock market crashes of 2001 and 2008 with strong recoveries underway, it was not too challenging to make good share selections. All boats floating on a rising tide. Correlation in the S&P 500 peaked at around 85% in 2011. Shares were coming off a low level and were undervalued in the context of improving economic conditions.

When the markets are at a high level and trading sideways, correlation breaks down and good research and rapid response to corporate news becomes crucial. This is when the professional trading teams have a distinct advantage over the retail investor.

So the retail trader is entering an alien robot world – that wants to confuse him and rob him of his hard-earned money. There is a widely held view held that a two-tier market has developed – in the top tier are algorithmic traders with state-of-the-art technology support. And, in the bottom tier, everyone else.

Information and financial information companies

In 2013, it came to light that Thomson Reuters was paying US$1mn to the University of Michigan to receive their Index of Consumer Sentiment two seconds before the general release to the market. Trading activity increased dramatically within milliseconds of the release. This was borderline legal because this is not official government data. Nevertheless, the practice was stopped as a result of regulatory pressure.

The flows of information that move markets and share prices are virtually without limit, and successful trading is critically dependent on them. Processing and interpretation of these flows is big business.

As we have seen, a great deal of information is available on the Internet, much of it free, but it can take valuable time to find key information when decisions have to be made. Relevant, real time information costs time and money and is one of the most significant factors in the unevenness of the playing field.

Market information companies have been mentioned in *Chapter 5*. These are expensive systems beyond the reach of most retail investors and traders. They provide information on a global basis and across asset classes – to those that can afford it. Even the smallest trading teams will have invested in 'trading computers' and a Bloomberg or Reuters screen.

Collaboration, insider trading, and market abuse

In May 2015, Avon stock rose 20% on news of an US$8.2bn bid. PTG Capital Partners had made an SEC filing saying it would pay three times the current share price. It turned out to be a hoax and the share price fell sharply. Hoaxes like this are not uncommon.

In 2014, a former employee of SAC Capital was accused of illegally profiting from insider knowledge on a new Alzheimer's drug. Two doctors had provided SAC Capital with information on an Alzheimer drug trial that had run into difficulties in July 2008. SAC Capital, trading on this information, realised *gains of US$276mn, an unprecedented amount for an insider dealing scam. The employee was jailed for 9 years. The case was prosecuted by Preet Bahara, US Attorney for the Southern District of New York, who had a run of 85 straight convictions for insider trading. His office has prosecuted nearly 100 Wall Street executives.*

Some investment banks have rules prohibiting traders from sending messages containing trading information to competitors.

In 2014, a Chinese investor said, 'Why would you invest in a company when you don't know what's going on?'

An imaginative read of *Chapter 6* will reveal many possibilities for productive collaboration to influence share prices. Much of it will be legal though testing ethical boundaries, and perhaps sailing close to the wind with respect to conflict of interest. Add to the mix the vast network of personal relationships that exist in the financial markets around the globe, and you will begin to recognize the outline of a nightmare for the regulatory community.

The courts are often called upon to decide whether a particular activity or collaboration is illegal, and from time to time dubious activities are given the benefit of the doubt. There is little doubt that professional market participants prepared to sail close the wind will enjoy a significant advantage over most retail investors and traders.

A well-known market abuse is insider dealing or trading which occurs when a party trades on the basis of material (share price moving) information not publicly available. Insider dealing takes money out of the market illegally and therefore affects all market participants. However, definitions of 'insider' and 'material information' are problematic and rules vary between jurisdictions.

2013 saw a record level of insider dealing in the US, with Preet Bahara, again, prosecuting dozens of cases accompanied by an increase in severity of sentencing. However, in December 2014, the US Second Circuit Appeal court ruled that the government was too aggressive in its prosecution of two traders and overturned their insider trading convictions. The Second Circuit has now decided that the motivation of the person passing on the insider information is a key issue. Nevertheless, Bahara's vigorous action is likely to discourage insider trading.

Front running by brokers is probably less commonplace following some successful prosecutions. On receiving a large order from a client to purchase a particular share, a front-running broker would buy some of the shares for his own account, anticipating that the share price would rise.

According to the UK's Financial Conduct Authority, in 2014 there were abnormal price movements leading up to 13.9% of mergers and acquisitions announcements. This was down from 30.6% in 2009 and was at its lowest level in a decade. The FCA puts this down to tough enforcement of market abuse regulations. The US is usually more robust than the UK in seeking to eliminate market abuse.

Some market participants, in particular traders and short sellers, will seek to influence the media to support their positions – in a range of nefarious ways. Pump and dump, mentioned above, is an old trick where unscrupulous brokerages and traders feed rumors into the market that a particular share is hot – pumping the price up. Then they dump it!

Intriguingly some economists, including Milton Friedman, believe that insider trading should be allowed and would benefit markets. You can read an intriguing interview by searching Milton Friedman insider trading.

Dark pools

Dark pool trading should help to protect the value of your pension fund, but frustrates you if you are working as short-term trader because of the impact on price discovery.

Every day the big institutional investors and hedge funds will be building and reducing positions in companies as secretively as possible while the high-frequency trading firms are seeking to anticipate their activities and steal the best alpha. This leads to quite erratic share price movements, which are difficult for the retail trader to anticipate and exploit.

A further problem for the retail trader is that trading volume is less useful as an indicator of share price movements as a result of the fragmentation of trading volume information aggravated by delayed reporting.

IPOs

When a company decides to list on a stock exchange it makes an initial public offering (IPO). The IPO will usually be handled by an investment bank, with the shares offered to institutional investors and hedge funds. The retail investor will not be given the opportunity to participate – he will need to wait until the flotation is complete and then buy the shares on the public stock exchange, if he wants some.

This is a striking example of the uneven of the playing field. However, over the last year or so a great many IPOs have been overpriced, so maybe the retail investor has not been too disadvantaged.

Conclusions

There is little that the retail investor can do about the unevenness of the playing field, but he can look to compete in the less uneven areas. He can undertake sound research of funds and shares, and proactively manage his portfolio as described in *Chapter 18 – Managing your portfolio.* The most uneven area is short-term trading.

17 Using a stockbroker

Introduction

Woody Allen once defined a stockbroker as 'someone who takes all your money and invests it until it's gone.'

Broker-dealers and stockbrokers have been discussed in *Chapter 6.*   Stockbrokers will offer both advisory and discretionary services on a fee or commission basis. With the former, the stockbroker checks with you on all buy and sell decisions; with the latter, you authorize him to trade on your behalf. These are different from the services provided by Investment Advisers (IAs) in the US and Independent Financial Advisors (IFAs) in the UK, which have been described in *Chapter 6.*

This chapter is specifically about advisory stockbroker services for individual shares.

Registered representatives/stockbrokers

There are significant differences between the US and UK.

US

In the US, stockbroker firms, or brokerages, assist clients with share selection, making use of registered representatives (RRs) who are primarily securities sales people who may also describe themselves as stockbrokers/account executives, financial advisors, financial consultants, or investment consultants – all offering a 'full service,' No wonder it's confusing.   RR's may be employed by brokerage firms or act as independent contractors. They owe a duty of care to clients but not a fiduciary duty. They are bound to point out that they are not providing an Investment Adviser service where a fiduciary duty is owed. Whereas IAs stress that they must act solely in the interests of their clients, a broker is less constrained and his interests may not always be strongly aligned with those of his clients. For example, brokerages often employ sell-side analysts to promote – sell – the shares of various companies to institutional investors and fund managers, in the hope of earning a commission. A stockbroker may recommend the same shares to retail clients, to achieve some momentum! Or, he may over-promote a particular product to a client or encourage his client to trade too often.

RRs are licensed to 'sell' securities and have the legal power of an agent. For more information on RRs, search <u>FINRA Registered Representatives Brochure</u>.

In the US, the large brokerages often outsource advisory services, sometimes to thousands of financial advisors around the country. They will provide a range of services to the retail investor, from building a portfolio across a range of asset classes, including shares and bonds, to focusing on shares. The brokerage will provide the execution service.

When you trade through a stockbroker, he either acts as the principal to the trade or as an agent. If you are interested in the fine detail of this, search <u>Investopedia</u> for <u>Principal Trading and Agency Trading</u>.

UK

When you use a brokerage firm for advisory services, you are likely to be allocated to an individual stockbroker who will be in regular touch and responsible for your account. He should be authorized by the Financial Conduct Authority and is under an obligation to exercise reasonable skill and care in providing services to you.

Fees and commissions

The order of the day in selecting a stockbroker is *caveat emptor* – buyer beware. It is essential to establish clearly how much you will be paying for the service and to select a stockbroker that provides value. You don't want your profits to be eaten away by excessive fees and commissions.

US

Stockbrokers are likely to offer to work on an annual fee as a percentage of your portfolio value, perhaps between 1% and 2%, or on a commission basis, charging a percentage of the transaction cost each time you buy or sell some shares. Commission will cover both the cost of the stockbroker for advising you and his brokerage firm's costs for executing the trades.

 In order to assess what will work best for you, you need to take a view on how often you will trade. Cost some typical scenarios to inform which way you go. With a commission basis, your stockbroker may be tempted to 'overtrade' to increase his commissions. If you are on annual fee basis, your stockbroker may lack proactivity.

FINRA advises that in most cases, 5% should be the maximum commission charged, but also suggests that 5% is on the high side – which it definitely is!

If you are a small investor, you may find it difficult to find a good stockbroker to take on your business. It has been reported recently that many brokerages are not taking on portfolios of under US$500,000.

UK

There are some complexities around the matter of fees. You want good value, but you also want your stockbroker to work hard for you.

The stockbroker will present his standard commission structure. It might be based on a flat fee related to trade size or on a percentage basis, possibly in the region of 2% per trade (on both buying and selling), perhaps coming down to 0.5% if you place substantial funds with the firm and trade frequently. In addition, there may be a monthly account fee. Some stockbrokers will have a minimum size of trade, for example £10,000, which may be too high for many retail portfolios.

Also consider that you will be better off paying 2% commission and getting into shares that move up 8% in a month rather than paying 0.5% to get into shares that are down 5% by the end of the day. A stockbroker is likely to pick up the phone first in the morning to someone who is paying a 2% commission than someone who is paying 0.5%.

In addition, where a stockbroker is on 0.5% commission, he is likely to encourage his client to make quite large individual trades or investments in order to boost his commissions. See *Chapter 18*, which discusses size of individual holdings. This is not a recommendation to pay a 2% commission, but a suggestion to negotiate an optimal approach with your stockbroker.

Approach to the market

You will need to select a stockbroker and set up a brokerage account. In the US, this is likely to be an RR stockbroker. In the UK, it's likely to be a stockbroker allocated to you by the brokerage that you have selected. With an advisory service, your stockbroker will always consult you, usually by phone, with trading or investment advice, but you make all the trading decisions.

The proposition here is that you want to proactively invest in individual shares – letting good investments run and easing out of positions that are not working.

To start with, there are a number of considerations that you should discuss with your stockbroker.

Strategy

You need to have a clear and effective strategy based on your needs if you are to work successfully with a stockbroker.

Before you commit to a stockbroker, you should question him on his strategic approach to the market. What sectors does he know best? Does he have any areas of specialization? What is his average holding period? What is his approach to 'special situations' such as recovery plays and takeovers? Does he work with high beta shares, i.e., the most volatile in a particular index? This can be hard on the nerves.

Let him know that you understand the markets and the level of service that you expect. In particular, discuss the size of your portfolio, typical trade size, likely frequency of trading and use of stop-losses. Ask about research, both his own and that by his company's research department. Does he prefer growth or income and how does he go about his share picks? Where does he position himself between Fundamentals and Technicals?

A good 'actively trading' broker should make a decent profit for his client and be satisfied with his commission. However, a buy and hold strategy may suit other investors better, and misunderstandings will be less likely to occur if you agree a strategy with your stockbroker.

Monitoring share prices

You need to be able to access your account so that you can see how your positions are doing. This is likely to come with a 15-minute delay on pricing, which should be good enough for most investors. However, you may be able to get real time prices at an attractive rate, and this is a useful facility to have.

Margin

Will you want to trade on margin? Your stockbroker may be able to facilitate this.

Direct market access

Do you want direct market access (DMA)? Some stockbrokers are now prepared to arrange DMA for retail clients – this enables them to participate in pre-opening auctions, where the experts can pick up the best of the prices, either buying or selling.

Going short

Do you want to be able to go short? Can your stockbroker arrange this for you and at what cost?

Automatic trading

Use of limit and rising buy orders, discussed in *Chapter 3*, can work successfully, but are perhaps more the domain of an investor working by himself rather than one working with a stockbroker. Sentiment in the market and around individual shares can change very quickly and yesterday's good ideas for limit order levels may not look so good the next day when you have picked up a number of shares at prices that no longer look like good value.

Stop-losses

What is your stockbroker's approach to use of stop-losses?

Use of stop-losses has been covered in some detail in *Chapter 10 – Trading* and *Chapter 18 – Managing your portfolio*.

Use of stop-losses is a serious consideration and it's useful to make some specific comment in the context of working with a stockbroker. For many stockbrokers, use of stop-losses is standard operating procedure and your stockbroker is likely to discuss this with you each time you open a position. By recommending the use of a stop-loss, the stockbroker can take the view that he is discharging his duty of care to the investor, and also he reduces the prospects of being sued by investors for large losses.

A further benefit for the stockbroker is that he will earn a sell commission when and if the investor is stopped out and a buy commission when the funds are reinvested.

Size of position

Size of position is a serious consideration, especially where brokerages look for clients with portfolios of over US$500,000. This is a great deal of money to get into the market at reasonable position sizes. Twenty positions at US$25,000 each is a lot of companies to track. And a 20% fall in a share price on market opening will result in a US$5,000 loss, notwithstanding possible use of guaranteed stop-losses

If you employ your stockbroker on a commission basis, he will prefer you to open large positions. This increases your exposure to large falls in individual share prices, which increases the desirability of using a stop-loss – an unvirtuous circle.

Frequency of trading

A stockbroker on a commission basis will probably have a mentality closer to that of a trader than that of an investor. In particular, brokers servicing the smaller end of the market may have a tendency to 'overtrade,' i.e., to trade too frequently, possibly with excessive trade sizes compared with the size of the client's portfolio. This is a good business model for them if they can keep enough clients happy. They should be able to achieve this in a steadily rising bull market and perhaps by specializing in more volatile sectors – effectively swing trading. It will become more difficult when market conditions are 'choppy.' If your preference is to 'buy and hold,' you need to make sure that your stockbroker will fully support you in such an approach.

Taking profits

It is very tempting to simply take a good profit that has appeared on a trade rather than undertake the research that would support a 'continue to hold' judgement. Such judgements take skill and nerve and possibly use of a trailing stop-loss. Many stockbrokers will urge you to take a good profit while it's there – 'leave something for the next man,' goes the old saying, or in other words, don't be greedy. You always have the option to take a proportion of the profit. The better your understanding of a particular share and the state of the market, the better your judgement will be in these circumstances. You may decide to go with your stockbroker's recommendation on each trade. You will soon be able to form a view on how skillful he is in this area.

Cutting losses

There is a saying that your first loss is your best loss. In other words, if one of your holdings suffers a sharp fall, then just sell and move on – don't wait for a bounce or even 'double up' by buying more of the share. However, if you study a number of share price charts, you will see that toughing it out – taking the pain – or even doubling up, can provide a good result. Also, you have the option to sell a proportion of your holding.

Share picking

You may want to rely heavily on your stockbroker's research and 'share picks' and buy and sell decisions as well as his judgement on the state of the market. Or, you may want to undertake quite a bit of research yourself, perhaps along the lines described in *Chapter 14,* and be able to compare notes on companies with your stockbroker – working as a team. An important benefit of having a stockbroker can be for him to keep you in touch with the market if you aren't able – or don't want – to spend a great deal of time on this. He can alert you to significant shifts in sentiment at market level or individual company level.

Execution

Once you have made a buy or sell decision, your stockbroker will execute it for you, seeking the best price across a range of stock markets and market makers. One of the his selling points will be the ability to get the best price in fast-moving systems where bid and offer prices are varying rapidly – minimizing slippage of price between buy or sell decision and making the trade. This is important if you are day trading, but if you are working to longer timeframes it is less critical. The quality of the share picking and timing is much more important.

A typical day

You need to put your tin helmet on.

Your stockbroker is likely to be operating under a great deal of pressure, looking after many clients concurrently. He will try to find time to do his own research in shares as well as talking to colleagues and contacts, and making use of his firm's research department - which may or may not be any good. Good research is essential for success and it is a challenge to keep on top of this as well as managing multiple clients. He will need to be constantly tuned into the overall state of the markets, as well as trying to keep up with a large number of company shares and a large number of different positions. It is tough enough looking after one portfolio of shares – looking after ten or twenty portfolios is a daunting task. Your stockbroker may not be as passionate about your money as you are.

I'll buy you a stiff drink next time you're in town.

Depending on how many portfolios he is managing, he is likely to call you some time after the market opens to tell you 'what he is looking at today.' As share prices tend to move sharply on market opening, quite often he will be recommending a share that has already moved up 2% or 3% or even more. Keep in mind that 3% represents a good dividend yield for a year.

You have to take some pain in order to make money.

During the course of the day, he will look through all his clients' portfolios, looking for where good profits have emerged – and is likely to advise the client to take profit 'while it is there,' especially if he is on a commission basis. He will earn commission on the sale as well as on reinvesting the money. This leads to a tendency to take profit too soon and represents one of the differences between investing and trading. A good investor will think long and hard before taking a profit – letting a good position run can be rewarding. A trader's instinct will be to take a decent profit as soon as it's there. Hindsight is 20/20, but you only have to look at some typical share price charts to see how a share can pull back, pause for breath, and then run up strongly again. The overall state of the marketplace is a crucial backdrop to the decision to take a profit or not – if the judgement is very finely balanced, you could take, say, 50% of the profit instead of all of it. Hindsight is of course a wonderful thing, but experience, hard work, and skill are likely to be rewarded. As Gary Player said, 'The more I practice, the luckier I get.'

> **You got stopped out 8% below your buy price – better luck next time.**

Stockbrokers have to be thick-skinned because they will have to deal with highly disgruntled clients on a regular basis. Even a very good stockbroker is going to make bad trades from time to time and some of his clients will be sufficiently impatient to chew him out. When you lose money, they will be quite good at encouraging you to make the next trade in order to 'get your money back.' He might even tell you to 'double up,' i.e., stick even more money into the share in the hope that there will be a good bounce. Sometimes this works. If your stockbroker is not performing, you need to cut him quickly.

> **This fall is overdone – why don't you double up?**

Many traders and investors will take a position in a company leading up to it issuing a report. You need to know a company very well to do this – or know people that know the company extremely well. If your find a stockbroker with the knowledge and skill to do this well, hang on to him. However, some stockbrokers will persuade you to take such a position based on not much more than a hunch or a rumor. This is getting close to gambling. If a company reports well and significantly beats expectations, the share price may gap up sharply on market opening, but if it disappoints, you could be on the receiving end of a large gap down.

If there's a crash

If the markets go into serious meltdown, you may have difficulty getting through to your stockbroker over the phone. He is likely to be prioritizing his biggest clients.

In serious circumstances and with share price movements amplified by high-frequency trading, share prices can fall very fast. Even online, when trying to sell, the quotes may be moving so fast that it can take some time to realize your sells – especially for smaller cap companies.

However, if you have been reading the state of the market well, you should have already reduced your percent invested (PCI) and the crash will be easier to deal with.

If your stockbroker is not reading the direction of the market well, he can lose you money fast, even with good companies.

Stockbroker regulatory requirements

Stockbroking is a regulated profession in the US and the UK.

US

RRs usually work for or are sponsored by a broker-dealer, which will be licensed by the US Securities and Exchange Commission (SEC) and regulated by the Financial Industry Regulatory Authority (FINRA). They must be certified by FINRA by passing the FINRA-administered Series 7 exam – the General Securities Representative Exam, or equivalent. Some states require the Uniform Securities Agent State Law Exam in addition.

The SEC has prepared a leaflet Protect Your Money: Check Out Brokers and Investment Advisers, which you can find with an Internet search. You should also use the FINRA BrokerCheck web site, again, you can find it with an Internet search.

When you start with a stockbroker, you place your money into a brokerage account, and so you want to be sure that your stockbroker is of good financial standing, so research this aspect carefully.

When you buy a share, this will be recorded electronically on the vast Depository Trust and Clearing Corporation (DTC). Only a 'clearing broker' can directly access the DTC, and most brokers are 'introducing brokers' that must work through a clearing broker. You need to be sure that your stockbroker is covered by the Securities Investor Protection Corporation (SIPC) scheme. Under this, if your brokerage firm goes bankrupt, you will enjoy protection of up to US$500,000. The SIPC will work with the DTC to restore your portfolio. The SIPC's success rate in this is around 99%. You can check out best brokerage practice by searching Charles Schwab SIPC Asset Protection.

If you are unfortunate enough to get involved with a 'rogue broker' you will be unprotected, so you should carry out thorough checks.

UK

In the UK, all stockbrokers must be authorized by the Financial Conduct Authority to do business, so this is the first and most important check to make. Individual brokers have to pass examinations to obtain certification from the Chartered Institute for Securities & Investment (CISI).

Your money and shares will be held in a nominee account with the shares held in your stockbroker's name. This keeps your money and shares separate from the stockbroker's own financial activities, so they should be secure even if the stockbroker gets into difficulty. You should ensure that your stockbroker follows good practice in this area. Because the shares are not in your name, you will not receive material from the company such as annual reports and notices of annual general meetings. Most stockbrokers will be able to set up a CREST nominee account for you, if you want to receive this service. CREST is owned by Euroclear.

Many stockbrokers will be able to accommodate any ISAs and SIPPs that you have, and the custody of your shares and money will be held by a regulated service provider. You will need to give your stockbroker a power of attorney to execute trades in these accounts in accordance with your instructions.

How to find a stockbroker

For the retail investor with perhaps a few tens of thousands of dollars or pounds to work with, finding a good stockbroker is likely to be a challenge. Good advisory stockbroking is a difficult and demanding job. The interests of the investor and the stockbroker are not always particularly well-aligned, but good selection and management of the stockbroker by the investor may overcome this problem.

Many people associate the stockbroking industry with 'churning,' i.e., trading a client's money ineffectively to earn commissions – *in extremis,* trading the client's money entirely away. It would be unfair to tar the whole industry with this brush but the inexperienced retail investor needs to be cautious if engaging a stockbroker. In the UK, many small stockbroking firms run annual recruiting drives, including cold calling, to replenish their client base!

Don't allow your stockbroker to select you through a telephone campaign to get new clients on board, or because they have managed to get hold of your telephone number as someone who might be an investor – or a mug! There are a great many stockbrokers out there that you should avoid.

A good way to find a stockbroker is through personal recommendation but you should still run your own checks. Draw up a shortlist, check them out over the Internet, and then interview them. Prepare a set of questions, as discussed above. If a stockbroker does not engage properly at this stage, then he is unlikely to treat the management of your investments any differently. You need to be very clear on how you will be charged for services.

This regulatory framework is of course a positive, but it does not mean that all stockbrokers have a high level of competence.

In the US, you will probably look to find a RR/stockbroker locally. Make sure he is employed or sponsored by a reputable brokerage.

In the UK, the <u>Investors Chronicle</u> and <u>MoneyWeek</u> magazine websites are a good starting point. The London Stock Exchange has a detailed listing of stockbrokers and the <u>Wealth Management Association</u> (WMA) has a search facility to identify stockbrokers that meet particular criteria.

What you are looking for is a firm that has good research capability and to be assigned to a capable, well-qualified stockbroker. Possibly the larger firms will have the better research facilities, but a smaller firm may have deep knowledge of particular sectors and companies. You will only be able to assess this by visiting the firm and talking to the principals and the stockbroker who will be assigned to you.

Most stockbrokers will have data illustrating how good their share selection is and this is worth looking at closely. However, keep in mind that in a strongly rising market, share selection is not that difficult and with markets continually rising and falling, firms may be selective in the periods they use to illustrate the quality of their share selection – and they may disregard their worst picks.

On the basis that you have determined what proportion of your assets you will commit to the stock market, you should only place a proportion of this – perhaps a third – with your chosen stockbroker, and only increase this if he is making good money for you. Don't worry too much if this means that the commissions are on the high side – if he is any good, he will cover these comfortably. And you will probably be able to enjoy lower commissions as you commit more money – and your portfolio should be growing in value!

Evaluating the performance of your stockbroker

The best benchmarks are the major indices, such as the S&P 500 and S&P Mid Cap 400, and the FTSE 250. You can also benchmark against the performance of a small number of high-performing funds. Something like 70% to 80% of your share selections should beat the index. If not, then you would probably be better off with another stockbroker – or in good funds.

What if my stockbroker performs poorly?

One of the problems is that in a field such as trading and investing, it is very difficult to prove negligence.

Stockbrokers owe their clients a duty of care. If a stockbroker fails to act in his client's best interest, he can face disciplinary action. In the US, regulation is done by the <u>Financial Industry Regulatory Authority</u> (FINRA). In the UK, regulation is done by the <u>Financial Services Authority</u> (FSA), with a first port of call to the <u>Financial Ombudsman</u>, who can make awards to investors of up to £150,000.

However, there are so many factors that can cause a share price to fall (see *Chapter 5*), and many of them can come out of the blue, that even a stockbroker that has given you negligently poor advice will be able to mount a robust defence. This situation has inevitably led there to be many people out there working as stockbrokers – regardless of their qualifications – giving poor advice, who cannot be held to account. A considerable amount of stockbroker performance would not be tolerated in virtually any other profession.

Conclusions

You may well be able to find a very good advisory service stockbroker that will help you to make you money. Many people will like the excitement of developing a synergistic relationship with a stockbroker and speaking with him regularly. However, you should reflect on the realities of working with a stockbroker that have been described. A good way forward may be to place a limited amount of your portfolio with a carefully selected stockbroker and make it clear to him that he is on trial.

18 Managing your portfolio

Introduction

The notion of a blue chip company is one of size and reliability with its products and services in demand through good times and bad; growing steadily, if not dramatically, and with a dividend stream that investors can rely on. Regrettably, in our modern age, there is no such thing as a nice, safe, blue chip company.

We have covered a lot of ground in previous chapters leading up to selection methodologies for funds and shares, covered in some detail in *Chapters 13* and *14*. The present chapter seeks to translate the findings into a practical guide for developing a sound, personal strategy to suit the individual retail investor – taking account of his aspirations, interests, risk appetite and temperament, and how much time and energy he is prepared to spend researching companies and following the markets. It aims to advise him on organizing his portfolio and proactively managing his investments.

The emphasis is on investing – not trading – and on a proactive buy and hold approach, in that you should follow your investments closely, with a view to selling underperforming investments and reducing your exposure to market losses in response to deteriorating market conditions.

Warren Buffett has based his immensely successful investment approach on identifying value and taking a long-term view. Significantly, he is a big enough player to influence the direction of companies that he has invested in. Keep in mind that he is investing huge sums of money at a time, and he does not want to be jumping in and out of shareholdings, though he will if he has to, Tesco being a recent case in point. The retail investor will not be able to influence the management of a company, but will be in a much better position to make judicious adjustments to his portfolio than a major investor such as Warren Buffett.

It is important to recognize that globalization and relentless technological advances have affected the fortunes of many companies. New Internet titans have emerged, some stumble and fall, some stumble and recover, many go from strength to strength. Others have suffered from fierce new competition, sometimes in the form of disruptive technologies such as the digital camera, hit in turn by the camera phone. The PC market has been disrupted by the tablet computer. The Internet has changed the game in the retail market, with many household-name companies suffering from this relatively new form of competition. Data suggests that many fund managers are turning over companies more rapidly than previously, which is consistent with this contemporary dynamic. Against this backdrop, it does not make a great deal of sense to invest in a number of companies and then dig in patiently for years, trusting that over the long run, they will make money for you. If someone offers to get you into some good, low-risk, blue chip shares that pay solid dividends, run a mile. There is no such thing as a low-risk share.

So is the stock market just too risky? You will recollect the advice of Blackrock president Larry Fink in 2014, that about the worst thing that people could do with their money is leave it in cash to be eroded by inflation. The second worst thing that they can do is just stick it in the stock market and fail to manage it proactively. A great many retail investors have an eye to their retirement and should not simply leave this to the vagaries of the stock market. Regrettably, all too frequently, people come into a significant sum of money and take advice to put some or all of it straight into the stock market without regard to the state of the market – only to take a significant loss in a short period of time.

If you want to invest successfully, you need to be proactive, and the power of the Internet puts the retail investor in a better position to succeed in the stock market than ever before. You need to establish a number of Internet sources that work for you, and selective reading of market reports is important. You need to take a view on where you want to get to and how you are going to get there. You may want to build your financial resources – a nest egg – for your retirement; or you may want to invest to enhance your lifestyle – and enjoy developing your investment skills.

Sometimes big winners emerge. You can search for them systematically or just keep a watchful eye out for them.

Don't bother with day trading, unless you have a real passion for it and are prepared to put in a considerable effort. Avoid gambling and only occasionally speculate when you understand a particular opportunity really well.

Prerequisites

Set yourself up to succeed – get organized.

Take the concept of preserving your capital very seriously and make sure you have absorbed the lessons of the major stock market crashes, in particular those of 2001 and 2008, described in *Chapter 7.*

Risk is a poorly understood concept, even by a great many people who work in the financial services industry and its regulators. This can be inferred from the global financial crisis – but then you don't have to worry too much about risk if you are gambling with other people's money. As we have seen earlier, the scientific definition of risk is that it is the product (multiplication) of the probability of an unwelcome event occurring and the consequences if it does occur. You may well have heard of low probability/high consequence events. The concept is that even if the probability of an unwelcome event occurring is low, if the consequences are very severe, such as losing all your money, the risk can still be assessed as high. People should make their own assessment of risk and the level of risk that they are comfortable with.

Carefully assess the amount of your assets that you are prepared to invest in the stock market. Think in terms of at least 50% of your stock market money being in funds. Only increase your activity in individual shares if you can consistently outperform your funds and you have sufficient time to manage a significant portfolio of shares.

Decide your norm for the maximum investment you will make in an individual company share. Have some preference for 'growth' over 'income,' albeit reinvested dividend income can lead to strong growth in the value of a holding. However, keep in mind that if a growth company's earnings stall, its share price can take a hard fall exacerbated by aggressive trading. If a company's earnings fall in half, its share price may well fall in half.

Ignore the people telling you that it's impossible to time the market. All the good professionals buy on pullbacks. Be aware of the state of the market whenever you open a position, either in an individual share or in a fund. Devise sound selection methodologies for both funds and shares, perhaps informed by this book, but also by other sources that make sense to you. Adhere fairly closely to your methodologies. Develop a good understanding of both of Fundamentals and Technicals. Adjust your approach as you go to develop your personal strategy – a very significant factor in this is how much time you are able or willing to put in. It is important to have a plan or strategy – you can always change it.

On the basis that you have taken a view on how much money you are prepared to commit to the stock market – the size of your portfolio including cash – you should then take a view on your appropriate percent invested (PCI) for the pertaining circumstances. This can be thought of as your exposure to the market and is a key parameter for the proactive retail investor.

Tax management

It is important that you understand your tax situation and plan your strategy to be as tax efficient as possible. In other words, pay as little tax on your gains as you can within the law. You should take advice or thoroughly research your tax position, and regard the following as fairly broad guidance which may be incorrect or out of date at your time of reading.

In the US, mutual funds can be held in tax-sheltered accounts, such as <u>Individual Retirement Accounts</u> (IRA), and <u>401(k)</u> and <u>403(b)</u> accounts. Sometimes, individual shares are also held in such accounts.

Dividends and short-term capital gains – less than a year – are taxed at the same rate as ordinary income. Long-term capital gains are taxed at up to 20% with the tax rate increasing with the investor's tax bracket.

In the UK, residents can invest in both individual shares and funds inside an ISA 'wrapper.' ISA stands for <u>Individual Savings Account</u>. Capital gains and dividend income inside a stocks and shares ISA are free of tax. Outside an ISA, there is a tax-free capital gains tax allowance of £11,100 and a tax-free dividend allowance of £5,000 (tax year 2016/17). Currently, a UK investor can place up to £15,240 in an ISA each year.

Tax liability affects risk/reward profile. This is perhaps best illustrated by a UK <u>SIPP</u> – a self-invested pension plan. On retirement in the UK, you can put your pension money into a drawdown plan in which you seek investment returns while drawing income. If you are liable for 40% tax when you draw income, as many people will be, then a 10% gain in effect becomes just a 6% gain and you should take account of this when you are considering investing within the plan, e.g., when the stock markets are expensive – does the potential return, after tax, justify the risk?

Trading or investing?

Perhaps somewhere in between – 'swinging' can work well.

There is a very real difference between trading and investing, though it is probably useful to think in terms of investing and trading being at opposite ends of the spectrum of dealing in shares. Day traders, described in *Chapter 10*, look to open a position early in the day (or sometimes, perhaps, the night before) and close it quickly, usually in the same day. When markets are rising steadily, most traders and investors will make money – though some a little and others a lot. When the markets are highly volatile, investing and trading become more of a zero-sum game – your loss is someone else's gain and vice versa. And the retail trader will be competing with highly organized and well-equipped professional trading teams, many of whom will be using high-frequency trading programs. They will be both working together and competing with each other. The professional teams relieve many hapless individuals of a great deal of money on a regular basis.

Few retail investors will have the resources for successful day trading on an ongoing basis. The odds are stacked heavily against them. You are only likely to succeed as a day trader if you expend considerable time on research, and have set yourself up with extremely good, real time data and information sources. You will need to be prepared to work hard, spending a great deal of the day studying data on computer screens. A quick and agile brain also helps.

Investing is usually understood to take place over a number of years. However, investment timeframes are becoming shorter. Though as a general rule, the investor's intention should be to stay with a position for some time, it will sometimes make sense to close a position quickly, for example if a company seriously disappoints on reporting. These days, it costs very little to close a position. Or, if a share price has risen particularly sharply, it can be a good idea to take some profit – 'leave something for the next man.' This is in effect swing trading, which has been described in *Chapter 10.* The idea is to exploit the swings in share prices, which take place over weeks and months rather than years. For the proactive retail trader prepared to put the effort in, this can be an effective and rewarding approach.

Fundamentals or Technicals?

You need to work with both Fundamentals and Technicals – at both macroeconomic level and individual company level. *Chapter 5* seeks to provide a useful framework.

Awareness of Fundamentals will enable you to take a view on overall market valuations and economic outlook. Fundamental market factors, such as gross domestic product growth, interest rates, and average P/E ratios for countries and sectors are important indicators. You should also look carefully at the Fundamentals of companies you are considering for investment. Technicals can then be used to inform the timing of buy and sell decisions. For example, technical factors such as moving averages, relative strength index (RSI), and the VIX index provide important additional insights into the most likely direction of stock market indices as well as individual share prices.

Investing for income or capital growth?

Capital may keep you warm at night – you can eat and drink income.

In 2014, when a prominent fund manager was asked on CNBC Europe TV for some tips on good, dividend-yielding shares, all he could come up with was the Belgian Post Office – 'BPost yielding 6% on a P/E of around 13.'

The difference between investing for income or growth has been discussed in *Chapters 4* and *12.*

With proactive management, the total return on investment from growth companies will often exceed that for income companies, notwithstanding the powerful effect of compounding dividends.

High-yielding shares are always in demand, particularly during periods of low interest rates. The compounding effect of reinvested dividends is indeed powerful and pension funds need dividends because they have to make monthly pension payments. Because of the strong demand for such shares they tend to be expensive, quite possibly overvalued. The risk you run with excessive focus on yield is that you suffer some capital loss. However, if you can get them at a good price when the markets pull back, they can be a worthwhile component of your portfolio. During a market plunge they may hold up better than growth shares, and the dividends will offset to some degree the fall in capital value.

It will suit many people to invest in companies which have a reliable and progressive dividend policy, paying a dividend of 3% to 4%, and take a long-term view, i.e., not be too concerned if the share price falls as long as the dividends keep coming. This could be regarded as an 'invest and forget' strategy. If the dividend is much greater than 3% or 4%, the company may not have a very strong commitment to growth, though there will always be exceptions, and dividends can always be cut. In general, the upside potential of an income share will be less than for a growth share.

In poor economic times, there tends to be a market preference for defensive shares, such as utilities and consumer staple companies (people always need food and soap), that pay out attractive dividends. However, these companies soon become expensive, causing the percent dividend yield to fall, and when economic growth picks up, they are likely to be sold off in favor of cyclical shares, i.e., shares in companies that are going to benefit the most from a growing economy. These may be, for example, house building companies or consumer discretionary companies such as luxury brands or automobile manufacturers.

Regardless of how you approach the question of income versus growth, you need to select your companies for investment carefully and methodically with a view to identifying companies with good upside potential in both their share price and dividend growth.

Most funds set out their stores as either 'income funds' or 'growth funds.' So whether you are evaluating a share or a fund to invest in, you will need to take a view on the balance between income and growth that you want to have in your portfolio.

People who want a regular income look to achieve this through regular dividend payouts, but you can also achieve income from growth companies by cashing some shares from time to time. However, the more conservative investor may be less comfortable with this approach. Tax may also be a consideration.

Investing for dividend yield is discussed in greater detail below.

Individual shares or funds?

Your stock market strategy needs to change with the times.

If you are prepared to actively manage a portfolio of individual shares, you can achieve very good returns. There is an allure to making a spectacular gain on an individual share in a day or a week. If you invest in, say, half a dozen individual shares, and you select them well (with a little bit of luck) and buy on a sharp market pullback, you could see a very attractive return in a short period of time. However, you need to keep track. Many investors will enjoy a big win from time to time and lose sight of the total picture, that they are not making very much money overall. Once your holdings get above eight or ten shares, sound management of them becomes onerous, and it's better to use a judicious allocation between funds and individual shares. Using this approach, you can check fairly readily, over perhaps 12 months, whether you can beat the best fund managers with your individual share management. You will find it difficult. Regrettably, some of your individual share picks will go wrong, damaging your average performance.

Investing through funds will suit a great many people over their long working lives and also, we hope, through long and happy retirements. The dynamic of investing in funds is different from that of individual share investment. You are hiring a fund manager to manage a portfolio of shares for you. He will be doing the hard work of managing the individual company shares and will be building up and winding down positions in companies. However, it is crucial that you invest your money in the best funds – they will have a track record of beating the index. Funds have been covered in some detail in *Chapter 12* and selection of funds is covered in *Chapter 13*.

Short-term or long-term?

The average holding period of UK shares has fallen from five years in the 1960s to well under one year now.

According to an article in the Harvard Business Review, 87% of large US and global companies experienced a stall after a long period of success: 'most companies accelerate into a stall, experiencing unprecedented progress . . . just before growth rate tumbles.' Olson, van Bever and Verry, March 2008. Available on the Internet.

In 1958, the average age of an S&P 500 company was 61 years; by 2012, it had fallen to 18.

You must keep an open mind with respect to time scale. You should take a longer-term perspective with funds than with individual shares because the fund manager will be trading in and out of companies for you. However, you should watch the markets carefully and be prepared to take money off the table if you believe a serious crisis for the markets is developing. On the other hand, give good runs their head while monitoring the macro-factors carefully and riding out the 'mini crashes.' Proactive investors often take profits too soon.

The ideal situation is to take a long-term 'Warren Buffett' perspective – buy and hold! Select your companies well and always try to buy on a pullback. However, an advantage that you have as a retail investor over Warren Buffett is that you can operate in small areas of value and you can enter and leave a share without moving the price against you. This gives you greater flexibility and, whereas you should avoid frequent jumping in and out of the market either through individual shares or funds, you should monitor your investments and be prepared to exit an underperforming investment.

Increasing globalization and the rise of companies around the world, together with proliferation of disruptive business models and technologies causes many company stars to fade. If you just buy some of the well known 'blue chips' and tuck them away for a few years, whether you make money will be largely a matter of luck and you may well lose money.

Another factor around length of hold is momentum investing, with share prices often trading up to unrealistic levels. If you had bought Asos shares on the AIM market in London at any time during 2012 and 2013, you would have done extremely well – until 2014. No one could possibly make the case that you should not have sold them at 7,000 pence at the outset of 2014. They had plunged to around 4,500 pence by April 2014.

These modern realities of the markets are reflected in the evolving behavior of fund managers who are turning over the companies in their funds increasingly rapidly, 100% per annum being not uncommon, resulting in holding periods often less than a year. This is unsurprising given the rate at which a company's star can fade and another one's can rise. However, keep in mind that we saw in *Chapter 12*, a much lower turnover among a number of top-performing US mutual funds.

You can be sure that the traders in investment banks and hedge funds are not patient for returns.

US and UK or overseas?

There are more than 5,000 listed companies in the US and some 3,500 companies are listed on the London Stock Exchange, though many of them are quite small. Many companies float on the stock market every year as initial public offerings (IPOs). So there are plenty of opportunities for both investors and traders and for both long and short strategies in the US and UK. Consequently, there would need to be a compelling reason to research overseas companies, buy and sell them (often in different time zones), navigate tax liabilities, and quite possibly pay commissions that are not as competitive as those available in the US or UK.

For US investors, the tax treatment of overseas mutual funds is complex. For example, search Why Americans Should Never, Ever Own Shares in a Non-US Mutual Fund (PFIC), Thun financial advisors. Also search the international investor – avoid the tax trap on foreign offshore funds.

The situation for a UK investor investing in overseas OEICs is more straightforward. Any taxes paid on overseas gains are invisible to the UK investor and he is liable for tax on dividends and capital gains in the same way as with an OEIC invested in UK companies. However, any taxes on gains made by a fund manager in an overseas tax jurisdiction will be a drag on fund return.

Investing overseas is discussed later in this chapter.

Preserving your capital

> *23 August 2013, Geoff Cutmore, on CNBC TV said: 'You would have to be nuts to be just in equities.'*

There is no point in investing in the stock market to lose money. Preservation of your capital is the highest priority!

Consider risk properly

You should assess risk from a personal perspective – and not the pseudo version of risk propagated by much of the financial services industry, which conflates risk with volatility. And which is also based on the proposition that many older people are incapable of understanding the markets and managing investment risk.

Standard advice to people approaching retirement is to move into safer, fixed-interest investments. The problem with this is that interest rates are currently low and likely to remain so for some time. When they inevitably rise, rates may struggle to get much above inflation. Even tying your money up for five years in fixed-interest instruments will not achieve much of a return. The risk of staying out of the markets is greater than venturing into the markets – provided you know what you are doing. Remember Larry Fink's words about your money being eaten away by inflation.

A purpose of this book is to assist people who are inexperienced in the markets but prepared to spend the time to develop their investing skills while managing their risk. A good way to start is by investing in funds while monitoring carefully – both the fund performances and the markets. If things go well, then cautiously increase your investments to reflect market conditions. Investing well in individual shares is more demanding.

How bad can it get?

Larry Fink, BlackRock CEO, on the July 2015 Chinese stock market crash: 'We need scary weeks – scary weeks make the stock market more secure. The absence of scary weeks leads to irrational exuberance.'

It is often said that you should only invest what you can afford to lose. This may be too extreme a view, but you must judge that for yourself. The Wall Street Crash occurred between 1929 and 1932 when the Dow lost 89% of its value, but there were many opportunities to get out of the market before the full fall had run its course – though in those days there was no Internet allowing people to stay in close touch with the market. Interestingly, it may well be that if there had been an Internet at the time, the fall would not have been so severe.

Since the Wall Street Crash, there have been only two stock market collapses, getting underway in 2000 and 2007 respectively, where major stock market indices dropped roughly in half and the best strategy had been to sell everything as the falls got underway. These crashes have been described in *Chapter 7.* In both instances, an alert and informed investor should have been able to exit the markets with his losses around 10% or 15%. In terms of the causes of the crashes, history never repeats itself, but it is important to be familiar with the background to these collapses to have the best chance of judging if some sort of situation – geopolitical or otherwise – is developing that would prompt you to 'get out of the market,' i.e., sell just about everything. Perhaps if a third world war was about to start, you would keep your holdings in defence companies – but then again, perhaps you wouldn't. Just about every company share price would fall sharply and then the markets would take a view on which companies are likely to do well out of the war, and then their shares would probably rise again. Provided that stock markets were not suspended.

It follows from this that the risk of investing in the stock market is manageable to some considerable extent – but this will be a function of the expertise that a retail investor is able to develop, coupled with the time he is able and prepared to commit to managing his portfolio.

Asset allocation

'Wide diversification is only required when investors don't know what they are doing.'
Warren Buffett

To start with, the retail investor should have a reasonably good idea of his net worth and, in particular, his liquid assets. He should also take account of his current income and threats to income (for example, job loss) and monthly payment obligations. Against this background he should determine how much to invest in the stock market.

The professional asset managers think in terms of asset allocation, the main asset classes being:

- Property – mainly commercial, but some residential
- Shares/equities
- Fixed interest – bonds
- Commodities such as oil, silver, or copper
- Gold, also a commodity, but unlike silver has little industrial use; regarded by some as a 'safe haven'

A great deal of money these days is just in cash.

Unsurprisingly, this is a useful way of viewing an investment portfolio, and the asset allocation manager will continually review the mix of assets that lie within his brief, taking account of global and local economic factors. Similarly, you need to take a view on what proportion of your assets you are prepared to commit to the stock market.

This book cannot advise you on your asset allocation. You should take a view on this with regard to the attractiveness of other investment opportunities – and the state of the stock market. If you decide to allocate some of your money to the stock market, then the concepts described here should help you to manage your risk and to make some money.

It goes without saying

Fundamental to preserving your capital is to be invested in good companies either directly or by making use of good fund managers. Only invest in individual companies if you have the time and the interest to do it properly.

Market risk

> *'Regard volatility as your friend.'*
> **Warren Buffett**

A serious market crash in the US or the UK will most likely start in the US and drag down the share price of just about every significant company listed in these countries. So it doesn't matter which companies you are invested in, they will be subject to market risk. We have seen that catastrophic collapses are rare, but the consequences are so severe – your portfolio possibly losing 50% of its value or more – that you should never drop your guard.

Take another look at *Chapter 7*, which describes the great stock market crashes of the last 30 years. The first leg of the 2001 crash and the 2008 crash were foreseeable.

When markets are testing new highs on eye-catching multiples, i.e., unrealistically high P/E ratios, the bulls can be heard to say 'this time it's different – the markets will continue to rise.' And often they do, momentum being a powerful force in the markets, sucking in many retail investors who panic that they are missing out on rich returns. In 2000 and 2007, when all stars were aligned for a major crash, a great many people just stayed in the market. When they were down, say, 10%, which was painful enough, they waited and hoped for a bounce that never came – at least not until the market had lost about 50% of its value with a very long recovery road ahead. You need to be prepared to take some modest losses to get out of the market if there are strong signs that a major crash is developing.

However, it's not all or nothing. In nervous or overexuberant times, the experienced and prudent investor will have been taking money out of the markets as a precaution. The concept of exposure to risk or PCI has already been mentioned, and is discussed in some detail below.

In addition to this broad market risk, there is a risk associated with each company share that you invest in – and this can be greater than the market risk.

Borrowing to invest

Borrowing to invest is a high-risk activity. The professionals and a great many retail investors do it all the time, trading on margin, as we have seen in both the cash and futures markets. Risk is enhanced even further in the 'carry trade,' where traders borrow, for example, Japanese Yen when interest rates in Japan are low, convert to, say, US\$ and invest across a range of asset classes including equities. This can work fine until the Yen rises rapidly against the dollar and then they have to move fast to unwind their positions, quite possibly causing turmoil in the markets if this occurs on a large scale. As indeed it did in 2008, doing its bit for the great financial crisis.

Stock market bubbles are invariably inflated by leveraged investments, so when the crash comes, panic sets in and puts wind in the sails of the crash. In recent times, margin lending played a substantial role in the stock market boom and bust in China in 2015. The Shanghai Stock Exchange Composite Index doubled in less than a year and then lost 40% of its value in a little over three months.

You shouldn't borrow to trade or invest unless you have developed a high level of competence in the markets and are confident that you can manage your risk.

If you lose touch

If you are going to be out of touch with the markets for some time, e.g., on a remote holiday or expedition, you should assess the implications of this. One possibility is to sell some or all of your holdings before you go. Or you could authorize someone to manage your investments for you while you are away. The author returned from a remote trip in 2011 to find his portfolio down almost 20%. Events flowing from this led to this book.

Selecting your platform

To invest effectively you should organize yourself on a good investment – brokerage – platform and get to know it. Any good platform will have functionality that enables you to readily bring up charts for funds and shares.

Before putting money into a platform, satisfy yourself with respect to custody issues – will your assets be 100% safe? In the US, you need to check that your platform is covered by the Securities Investor Protection Corporation (SIPC) scheme. You can check out best brokerage practice by searching Charles Schwab SIPC Asset Protection. In the UK, all brokerages must be authorized by the Financial Conduct Authority to do business.

The first situation to look at is where you have a free choice in platform selection. Then we will look briefly at retirement/pension situations where there may be some constraints.

Free choice

The Internet enables the retail investor to manage his investments in the stock market with, if he wishes, little or no input from advisors. However, it would be wrong to say never use an advisor – but you should check their credentials, costs, and way of working very carefully and assess if they really can add value to your investing activities. The most productive fees that you can pay are likely to be the fund management fees in a fund that consistently beats the index.

Whether or not you already have an investment platform, it's worth making a review of platforms available to ensure you have the functionality that you need at costs that are competitive. You need to pay attention to both external costs and internal fund management costs. If you consider switching platforms, check the costs associated with this.

For the investor who wants to work with both funds and individual shares, there are platforms that cater for both. As far as is practical, you should consolidate your holdings into one or two platforms. Many people will have share certificates, perhaps under the bed, from historical activities, and most platforms will take custody of these for you. This will put you in a position to sell them quickly should you need to.

US

The costs around mutual funds in the US can be complex and you should spend some time finding a platform that will give you good flexibility at low cost. Costs associated with investing in mutual funds have been outlined in *Chapter 12.* You should check that the cost of exchanging funds on a fund platform is nil or minimal.

The following platforms have facility for both funds and shares:

- Fidelity
- Vanguard – heavily specialized in tracker funds
- Stifel
- Scottrade
- TD Ameritrade
- Charles Schwab

Stifel offers a virtual portfolio for shares and mutual funds. Scottrade and TD Ameritrade offer a virtual portfolio for shares.

There are a number of companies that just run their own suite of funds. Some examples are:

- BlackRock
- State Street Global Advisors
- JP Morgan Asset Management

Fidelity provides a good benchmark for low external transaction costs. It has established a FundsNetwork for investment in Fidelity funds and 1,400 funds from other companies, all with no-loads or transaction fees on investments. For other funds, it charges a reasonable flat rate transaction fee.

Some share-only platforms are:

- OptionsHouse
- TradeKing
- optionsXpress
- TradeStation

Some platforms offer a flat rate trade fee of as little as US$4.95 on both buying and selling.

UK

The situation in the UK is a little more straightforward than in the US, and there are many good fund supermarket platforms that will allow you to buy and sell funds and switch between them at no cost. The fund managers earn their fees through annual management charges.

Some fund supermarket platforms are:

- Hargreaves Lansdown
- Fidelity
- Charles Stanley
- Halifax
- Interactive Investor
- TD Direct Investing
- Barclays Stockbrokers

Hargreaves Lansdown and Barclays offer virtual portfolios for both funds and shares.

All these platforms will accommodate tax efficient Individual Savings Accounts (ISAs).

The fund supermarkets have negotiated favorable terms with the funds that they make available. For most funds, there will be no initial charge and no charge for switching between funds. You will pay an annual management charge (AMC) and a TER/OCF, as described in *Chapter 12*.

Most fund platforms also offer a share dealing service. A typical cost per trade (paid on buying and on selling) will be between £5 and £12, and discounts are offered for frequent traders. Every time you purchase shares on the London Stock Exchange, you will pay a 0.5% stamp duty – except for AIM shares.

AIM-listed shares have been exempt from stamp duty since 2014; also, there are some companies whose main listing is Ireland and these are exempt, e.g., Kenmare Resources; Smurfit Kappa.

Hargreaves Lansdown has a facility which allows you to manage the monies of family members through power of attorney with just one entry password.

Holding cash

You can hold cash in these platforms. They pay a low level of interest, but of the monies you are prepared to put into the market at any particular time, you should perhaps take the low interest rate 'on the chin' and have the money readily available, as sometimes you will want to put money into the markets quickly.

Choice constrained

You should check out the performance of any private retirement plan/pension holdings that you have, together with the charges levied by the service provider that holds the pension. Your pension will most likely be invested in a number of both equity and bond funds, some or all of which may be funds managed by the service provider.

Check the performance of the equity funds against benchmark indices. Comparing their performance with the S&P 500 in the US and the FTSE 250 in the UK will give you a good idea of the quality of funds that you are in. Check against the total return indices and over various time horizons. Bond fund performance is not a topic of this book, but anything less than 2% or 3% return per annum (after all costs have been deducted) is not all that attractive. You then need to check what other funds are available to you in the plan and the cost of exchanging or switching. It may well be that you can improve the performance of your plan by means of some judicious exchanging or switching, but only do so cautiously and as you are building some confidence in your judgement as a proactive investor. A last resort, if the range of funds available to you is quite poor, is to switch service provider, but this could be expensive, and you should probably seek expert advice.

Information flows

Investment platforms provide a great deal of current information, and you should take a view on this in your selection process and try to pick a platform that will suit your investment style. It's so easy to access information over the Internet, that information flow should not be top of the list for your selection criteria, but other things being equal, it is a consideration.

Establishing your information sources

There are virtually unlimited websites that you can use to support your investing. The following are particularly useful:

- YAHOO! FINANCE – for the main US, UK, and world indices; currency exchange rates; commodity prices.
- Google Finance for a good charting service.
- Morningstar – for funds and shares; there are US and UK websites.
- The Nasdaq website – provides a great deal of information on individual companies including forecasts; covers US and some UK companies.
- CNN Money – ditto.
- DigitalLook – for company reporting dates and summaries of analyst forecasts; screening tools.

- MarketWatch – market information website covering US and UK; analyst upgrades/downgrades; watchlist facility.
- CSIMarket – for detailed information on individual US companies.
- FreeRealTime – for real time share prices.
- ADVFN – for real time share prices – and company reports.
- Seeking Alpha – a very handy US website covering some London-listed companies; a great deal of free information.
- TheStreet – another very handy US website that sells quite a lot of its content.
- Benzinga – market information (US website).
- Stockopedia – subscription market information website, covering US, UK, and Europe.
- shareprices.com – useful UK website for shares.
- Money am – useful UK website for shares.
- Trustnet – for UK funds.
- FundExpert – for UK funds.
- Find.co.uk – UK financial information website.
- Hargreaves Lansdown – for London indices; news and market action; virtual portfolios.
- Interactive Investor – UK website but covers US companies also; good for 'chat' on companies.

If you are not an 'Internet only' person, you should find a newspaper that you like with a good financial section. The Wall Street Journal and Financial Times are useful, if expensive, but more affordable if you take out a subscription. Most upmarket newspapers have good financial coverage, and it's worth finding one that you like.

Virtual portfolios and watchlists

The terms 'virtual portfolio' and 'watchlist' are used somewhat interchangeably. However, the usages that make most sense are that a virtual portfolio allows you to follow the cumulative performance of funds or shares that you have an interest in, whereas a watchlist shows price fluctuations within a trading day.

A watchlist will signal to you any significant price action that is taking place that could raise your interest in a particular share with a view to taking a position or selling a holding. Watchlists are likely to have a 15-minute delay unless you pay for real time data. Virtual portfolios and watchlists are essential tools for both the trader and investor.

Virtual portfolios are most useful in the context of investing in funds, while watchlists are most useful when investing in individual shares. Their use is described in more detail below.

Review your portfolio

'No company can grow forever. Competition hammers them; executives become complacent and hubristic, thinking they walk on water; in the search for growth they move into unfamiliar territory; they make bad acquisitions; they take on too much risk.'

In 2015, against a poor performance backdrop, the CEO of McDonald's said that 'in the last five years the world has moved faster outside the business than inside.'

If you already have investments, you should review them critically and decide if you are happy with them. The best benchmark indices to use are the S&P 500 and S&P Mid Cap 400 in the US and the FTSE 250 in the UK. Take care benchmarking against the FTSE 100, as its long-term performance has been poor. Try to check in terms of total return, as discussed in *Chapter 12*, though this will be difficult for individual shares. If an investment has consistently failed to beat a relevant benchmark index, you should consider switching into another fund or company – but be careful, this can be one of the best ways of making an investment suddenly come to life!

Staying in touch

Tune into the global economy – where are we in the cycle? Which sectors are running out of steam and which are attracting investor interest? Are there tail risks around and how severe are they? And get organized to check the state of the markets every day if you can – it takes less than a minute using mobile Internet devices to check the major indices using a website such as YAHOO! FINANCE. Note how the major indices closed the night before – the New York close being particularly important – and keep an eye on the US index futures. Also check the VIX volatility index. By going into INVESTING/Indices/World, you can see how Asia, in particular Japan and China, is doing. And you can see the state of play between the major currencies as well as some important commodity prices such as copper, oil, gold, and silver.

Read market reports for the previous day, either in the financial pages of a newspaper or on the Internet. On Mondays, the Financial Times carries a useful 'week ahead' section, noting important company reporting dates and key data releases.

If you are actively investing in individual shares, you should try to tune into Bloomberg or CNBC TV before market opening. If you are in the UK, it's also useful to tune in at 2:30 pm when the US markets are opening.

Also, if you can find the time, take a look at an economic calendar – is there key data expected from China over the weekend? Is US nonfarm payrolls out at the end of the week? If you are investing in individual shares, check which company reports are imminent.

There are several good weekly investor magazines, such as <u>Forbes Magazine</u> and <u>Barron's</u> in the US or <u>Investors Chronicle</u> and <u>MoneyWeek</u> in the UK. It's useful to take stock at the weekend when you might have a little more time.

In particular, if you are investing in individual shares, tune into the quarterly US company earnings report cycle.

Timing and exposure/percent invested (PCI)

A 10% fall in the major indices is regarded by the markets as a correction.

Your chances of success as an investor will be enhanced if you pay attention to the timing of your investment decisions. As we have seen, this is not a straightforward matter, but if you are prepared to make the effort to follow and understand the markets, you will almost certainly be rewarded for your efforts. You need to manage your percent investment (PCI) to take account of fluctuating market conditions. There is no point in putting money at risk in the markets unless there is good upside potential and this is an important consideration that the investor should keep under review. The upside potential should always justify the downside risk.

Timing

Every day, thousands of traders around the world attempt to time the market to milliseconds.

Take another look at *Chapter 7*, which bears on the question of timing. This section moves to a finer grain with a minimum of repetition.

The case for timing the markets is compelling. You need to assess where we are in the economic cycle, though this will not always be clear or unambiguous, and within the markets there will always be some sector rotation taking place. If you invest in a declining market, no matter how much research you do, the chances are you will find yourself in a loss position in the short term.

Clearly there have been some very good times to invest and some very bad times – and a great deal in between. It's instructive to study the charts of major indices to see how you would have got on with various entry points along the timeline.

When you look at the performance of the S&P 500 over the Max time period (it has performed much more strongly than the FTSE 100 in recent years), you will see three great bull run phases. The aftermaths of the great crashes of 2001 and 2008 were great investment opportunities. It is fairly clear that selling everything before a major crash and moving back into the market rapidly as recovery got underway would have given a much better return than riding out the crash.

Nevertheless, the received wisdom of most of the fund management industry is that you should stay invested and ride out the crashes – regardless that no one knew how far the markets were going to fall in 2001 and 2008. Remember that in 1929, the US market began a decline that ran to 89% over a period of close to three years. Also, no one knows what would have happened if there had been a different outcome to the Greek election in 2012.

Various arguments are put forward to encourage the retail investor to stay invested through thick and thin. You will hear fund managers say that they are not clever enough to time the market – that it's time in the market and not timing the market that counts; that if you miss the ten best up days in a five-year period, you will actually lose money; that there are more up days than down days, and so on. Studies have been published demonstrating that even if you had invested at each peak, in 2000 and 2007, you would, regardless, be ahead now. Such an outcome arises in large part from the powerful compounding effect of reinvesting dividends, but does not take account of the effect of offsetting management costs or taxes paid on dividends.

In early 2016, a major international fund manager produced a calculation showing that if you had invested £1,000 in the FTSE 350 30 years ago, it would now be worth around £15,000. This is based on reinvesting an average dividend yield of around 3%. What they don't tell you is that if you had avoided the great crashes of 2001 and 2008, your £1,000 would be worth well over £30,000 now. Very few investors would have managed their PCI to perfection during the crashes, but you can conclude that even modestly successful management of PCI would have achieved a great deal more than a £15,000 return.

The 'stay invested' thesis is based on the proposition that you are either 100% in the market or 100% out of the market. You don't have to be either. In fact, it makes much more sense to vary your PCI with market conditions, letting your best investments run, and winding down those that aren't working! The 'stay-in proponents' don't address how much better you would have done if you had proactively managed your investments through these crashes with some understanding of the macroeconomic framework.

Is the execution of such a strategy beyond the capability of the retail investor? *Chapter 7*, which describes the warnings to the two great crashes of the last 15 years, suggests not, but you need to form your own judgement. Very few people would have executed the strategy to perfection, but an alert and informed investor would have done a great deal better than those simply 'riding it out.'

Going forward, it may well be different, and we may not experience crashes of these magnitudes in the next 20 or 30 years. It is possible that better and more coherent government policies and regulation, combined with improving corporate governance, especially of the major banks, can deliver this. This would mean that crashes of up to around 15% or 20% will occur occasionally, though the probability of a crash of around 50% or 60% is certainly not zero. This will result in a very different investment climate. It would be helpful if we get another great bull run in the near future, but we shouldn't count on it.

Where does this leave us? Through late 2014 and 2015, when the S&P 500 was testing all-time highs but grinding up, the constant message from professional investors interviewed on the financial TV channels was 'we continue to be cautiously optimistic about shares – and we are buying on the pullbacks.' This was good advice. Another factor at work is reporting day. If you spend some time observing share price movement on company reporting days, you will see many sharp movements, up and down, that the astute trader and investor should be able to exploit.

One of the more difficult situations to deal with is being 'underinvested' when the markets are perceived to be high. As we have already discussed, markets spend a great deal of the time at or around all-time highs or at their highest level in several years.

Take another look at the S&P 500 long-term chart. You will see that since the 1987 crash, almost 30 years ago, the market has flirted with all-time highs or post-crash highs for around 20 years. During these run-ups, a cautious investor may well have taken the view that the market is 'too high' and just stayed out, missing significant opportunities for gains.

You should also watch the market at sector level. For up to ten-year performance of S&P 500 sectors, search sectorsspdr. For three-year performance of LSE sectors, go to shareprices.com and click on Sectors. Spend a few moments looking at some sector charts.

Also, look at a number of individual share price charts and you will see that there have been many opportunities for good timing of buys, even when market indices are testing highs.

A different perspective between funds and shares is warranted – with funds you are delegating some of the timing responsibility to your fund manager and you should take a longer-term view than if you are heavily invested in individual shares. This is reflected in the discussions below.

If you use an advisory stockbroker, he will attempt to time the market for you – finding value, taking profits, and cutting losses – while earning his commissions. For the retail investor, too much trading can be as bad as too little trading. See *Chapter 17.*

Exposure/percent invested (PCI)

'I'm not going short but don't be too freaking long.'
David Tepper, of hedge fund Appaloosa Holdings, May 2014.

'Preserving your capital,' above, sets out the concept of determining what proportion of your assets you are prepared to commit to the stock market. You should always be aware, to within a few percent, of how much of this is invested in the stock market at any particular point in time. This is your percent invested (PCI). You can think of this as your exposure to potential stock market losses. It's an important variable which should be at the center of your risk-management strategy. You should always keep track of your PCI and try to keep this consistent with the level of risk that you perceive in the market.

There is no point in putting money at risk in the stock market unless there is good upside potential. As already mentioned, the upside potential should always justify the downside risk. For example, if you judge that there is a 30% chance of the market going higher and a 70% chance of it falling, then you should be targeting a PCI of around 30%. In managing your PCI, you need to make an assessment of the state of the markets – in particular, New York and London. Are the markets testing new highs or coming off a significant fall? What tail risks are threatening the markets?

Very often, the markets will move in a sideways trading range. During these movements, the market participants are continually trying to judge whether the market is going to break out to the upside or to the downside, i.e., either move well above the ceiling or well below the floor of the trading range. Another way of framing the question would be 'are the bulls or the bears going to win?' What are the factors in play at any particular point in time that could cause the market to break out of its trading range, either to the upside or to the downside? It is important to tune into the constant commentary and chatter around this and try to get your PCI set at about the right level.

As we have seen, it is quite possible to judge if the stock markets are expensive or cheap, but it's not possible to accurately predict a significant high or a significant low. It would be ideal to move towards zero PCI just before a significant plunge and to ease back towards 100 PCI as the market begins to rise. If we could do this, we would have already made our fortunes. However, what we can do quite effectively is to begin to reduce our PCI if the market is testing recent highs, or indeed all-time highs, and if the market looks vulnerable. If you judge that the market may be about to enter an upwards trend, you should consider increasing your PCI. This is an idealized model and no one will be able to follow it perfectly – sometimes your PCI will be too high and sometimes it will be too low – but it is fundamental to the risk management of a proactive investor.

Keeping some 'lazy cash,' i.e., available cash, which is likely to be earning a low rate of interest, can be a good option. If you have done your research, you should be able to move some cash into the market on a sharp pullback, and quite possibly make a 5% to 10% return on it in a couple of months or even a couple of weeks.

It must be emphasized that even though PCI is an important metric for the proactive investor, it is an imperfect tool in a toolbox that contains many tools. The markets are complex and constantly evolving and there is no easy formula for success.

As we have discussed, the probability of another 50% stock market fall in the foreseeable future is low – but it is certainly not zero. You should always be alert for signs of a substantial crash. Such a crash will wreck the portfolios of those not paying attention to the state of the market and not effectively managing their PCI.

Reducing PCI

In reducing PCI, you should look to exit individual shares or funds that have disappointed, perhaps even taking a loss. Be ruthless, there is no point in taking serious downside risk on a share or fund that is performing poorly; or, take some profit, particularly if the share has had a good run and the upside potential is beginning to look limited. If you believe a share still has some upside potential, you could settle for taking half the profit. You should also take a view on the resilience of each share that you hold. Look at the chart and compare its performance with its index and look at its beta. Is it likely to pull back less than the index? Check the next company reporting date, which will be a moment of truth. Funds tend to be less volatile than individual shares, so if the market is high and looking vulnerable, you might think in terms of selling more, by value, of your individual shareholdings than your funds.

You should also take account of sector strength and weakness in judging which holdings to sell. Sector rotation is discussed below.

Another option is to set some stop-losses, or if you already have some in place, carefully review them. Consider use of trailing stop-losses and guaranteed stop-losses.

Increasing PCI

Equally important is your approach to increasing your PCI. The challenge is to judge the bottom of a fall, and this is easier said than done. 'Don't try to catch a falling knife.' It's less risky to buy when a solid recovery is underway, but then you could miss the best of the upward movement, at least in the short term. Unless you have a long list of shares that you have researched, the best way to quickly increase your PCI is through good funds – then you will be moving rapidly into a number of companies that have been selected by a good fund manager. Markets can move up very quickly.

It's not too productive to build up with regular amounts every month if the market moves up 10% in a month. If things are going well, you could build up to perhaps 75 PCI fairly quickly, holding back the balance to go into the market on any pullback. The market always pulls back – all that is in doubt is when and by how much.

You may never get to 100 PCI invested, though you are more likely to sensibly achieve this by being mainly invested through funds. If you have substantial holdings in individual shares, you are likely to take some profits or cut some losses on a regular basis – giving you cash in your account.

If the market gets into a strong upward trend, you may not have the luxury of waiting for a significant pullback. As we have seen, markets are testing highs a great deal of the time and to avoid missing out on the market rising sharply to a new level, you may have to buy into a rising market. There are a number of ways in which you can manage the extra risk associated with this. These are discussed below under 'Buy and Sell' decisions.

Sector rotation

Sector rotation, discussed in *Chapter 5*, is an important context to managing PCI and you should develop some understanding of this. The retail investor should be seeking to find a good balance between 'buy and hold' and moving out of sectors, companies, or fund categories when they show signs of running out of steam – or they simply haven't performed.

You should avoid jumping in and out of holdings, but there is no point in clinging on to a poor position indefinitely – you should be able to put your money to better use.

Websites for sector charts have been mentioned above. If you go to the <u>Fidelity Learning Center</u>, you will find useful material on sector rotation under <u>An introduction to sector investing</u>.

Managing funds

When you invest in a fund, you are hiring a fund manager to do a great deal of the hard work for you. Depending on his investing style, he may be operating quite proactively, winding down positions in companies if their share price is running out of steam, and moving into new opportunities.

However, no matter how good the fund manager, he suffers one great disadvantage – he can't move into cash to any significant degree. But you can – in a structured way, through management of your PCI.

Virtual portfolios

Some investment platforms provide a virtual portfolio facility as indicated above in 'Selecting your platform.' If your chosen platform does not have a virtual portfolio facility, you can use the Morningstar 'Portfolio Manager.'

Virtual portfolios add a great deal of value to a fund investment strategy. *Chapter 13* describes a methodology for fund selection and you should use this to build a virtual fund portfolio of perhaps 10 or 20 funds. Within a short period of time, you will observe quite a range of performances. You cannot base a successful strategy on simply pushing money into the best-performing funds, but you should apply considerable weighting to real time performance as you develop your portfolio. As you invest, your virtual portfolio will contain a number of real investments that you have made.

The proactive fund investor will try to check his virtual portfolio every few days. You should reset it every one or two months, possibly deleting funds that are underperforming – though they may become a recovery opportunity – and adding some new ones that have caught your interest. You can add a fund anytime you like, but need to keep in mind that it will have a different starting point from the rest of the portfolio. Some websites provide a facility for both individual shares and funds within their virtual portfolio service.

If you include some overseas funds in your virtual portfolio, such as a Japan fund or a Southeast Asia fund, you will most likely see some volatility which can be exploited, but you need to take the trouble to find out what is going on, otherwise you will just be speculating on price momentum.

Monitoring and exchanging/switching

In general, funds are considerably less volatile than individual shares, and good management of a portfolio of funds should also involve a much smaller number of transactions than for a portfolio of individual shares. There will be a fair amount of transactional activity going on within the funds.

Selecting funds that will outperform the index is not an exact science, and it is important to monitor performance of the funds that you are invested in. A virtual portfolio is a handy way to do this. You should give your funds a chance to perform but be prepared to exchange or switch if it becomes clear that a particular fund is underperforming. If the market is not going anywhere, you might just exit and wait for a more propitious time and go into a different fund.

If you have decided that the best approach for you is long-term investment through funds, you still need to be proactive – staying aware of the overall state of the market

– and also monitoring the performance of your funds and making strategic switches from time to time.

Structured investing in funds

It will suit a great many people to invest in a structured way. They will want to invest a fixed amount each month – the rationale is that as time goes by, sometimes they will pay too much for fund units and sometimes they will obtain good value.

Take another look at the long-term chart of the S&P 500. It is evident that a great deal of the time, regular investment would have worked well. However, there are significant periods of market decline, in particular from mid-2000 through 2002 – a two and half year period – and during all of 2008. Regular savings through these periods would not have been productive. You can see that 2010, 2011, and 2012 were years of quite high volatility but without a major crash. As we have discussed, there were significant tail risks hanging over the markets during this time, most notable being the possible financial collapse of the Eurozone during 2012, turning around a Greek election outcome. Nevertheless, regular investing over these years would probably have given a modest return.

Alternatively, the period 2010 through 2012 would have presented good opportunities for refreshing a portfolio, moving out of underperforming funds and shares and into some with more promise. Feeding money into 'resilient' funds on most pullbacks is a useful approach.

Another possibility, if you have the time and the interest, would be to invest 50% of your regular money each month, holding the other 50% back to invest on market pullbacks.

During the great crashes of 2001 and 2008, the ideal situation would have been to be completely out of the markets. It is worth noting from the chart that the recoveries from these crashes were particularly dramatic and the savvy investor prepared to take and manage some risk would have got a good sum of money into the markets fairly quickly during these phases. Investing through funds, as we have mentioned before, is a very effective way of achieving this.

Fund pricing

Mutual funds and OEICs are priced on a forward basis and you should be aware of the price point for the funds in which you have an interest. Funds are priced using rigorous processes allowing little fund manager discretion. In very volatile market conditions, however, the manager may be able to legitimately lower his bid price to discourage investors from selling, i.e., to discourage flight from the fund.

Managing shares

> *Warren Buffett invested heavily in Tesco following its profit warning in January 2012, which caused a fall in share price to 300 pence – close to 25%. Tesco rallied strongly in 2013, but by April 2014 its share price had fallen below 300 pence and Buffett began to bail out. By the end of 2014, Tesco's share price had fallen below 200 pence. A safe assumption would be that Warren Buffett hadn't anticipated the intervention of low-cost operators, Aldi and Lidl, on the UK supermarket scene. Buffett has said that investing in Tesco was a huge mistake. It was reported that several large funds hung in there with Tesco on the basis of being 'long-term value investors.'*

Many people will want the excitement and potential high returns from investing in individual shares. Investing in individual shares, say, more than 10 or 15, is challenging and hard work. It can be very rewarding if you get it right, but you can lose money fast if you get it wrong. If you are going to invest successfully in individual shares, as opposed to funds, you need to drop into a much greater level of detail requiring a well-organized and systematic approach.

As discussed in *Chapter 14,* you should establish your share selection methodology – you can improve it as you go. You should be prepared to take profit – or to cut losses – from time to time with your individual holdings. They will display greater volatility than your funds. As with funds, always try to invest on pullbacks.

Managing your risk

A challenge in investing in individual shares lies in the speed with which a company's fortunes can change, or can be perceived by the markets to have changed. These fortunes are continually assessed by the markets. The great range of factors that can influence share prices have been discussed in *Chapter 5.* Keeping on top of the substantial data flow around share price movements is crucial to proactive investing in individual shares. You don't have a fund manager working for you.

You should be very wary about putting all your eggs in one or two baskets, i.e., having a small number of large holdings relative to the size of your allocated money. If you are fortunate to have, say, US$100,000 or £70,000 that you want to allocate to shares, you should consider limiting your maximum holding in any one company to around 5% of your portfolio – US$5,000 or £3,500 – unless you have very good reason to go higher with one or two shares. For an inexperienced investor, reality will most likely set in quite quickly when one of his holdings gaps down 10% or more on market opening and he does not have a guaranteed stop-loss in place. The situation may then unfold as follows: the share price continues to run down while our investor is hanging in there waiting for the bounce. When the price has fallen by 20% and is accelerating downwards, he decides to cut his losses and sell. A few minutes later, the share price bottoms out, rises sharply and closes the day 12% down. The rapid downwards acceleration has probably been exacerbated by layers of stop-losses – automatic sell orders. Many savvy traders will have made money on the bounce.

If you have limited your maximum investment to 5% of your portfolio, the effect of a 20% fall will not be too painful. However, this would mean that when fully invested, you are managing around 20 shares. Keep in mind that it's quite onerous to do this properly.

Use of stop-losses to manage downside risk is discussed below.

It's probably best to leave the small caps to the fund managers, taking an interest in only one or two of such companies if you believe you have some special knowledge of them. Follow them as closely as you can, and glean information where you can.

Only use an advisory service stockbroker if you can strongly align your interests. Monitor his performance against the most relevant benchmark index. He should beat it comfortably after his commissions. Using a stockbroker has been discussed in *Chapter 17*.

Your watchlist

Using the definitions described above, your watchlist will restart each day to show share price movements during trading hours.

Building and managing a watchlist is indispensable for successful investing in individual shares. Your investment platform should provide this facility. Otherwise, there are many financial websites that provide watchlist capability, for example, YAHOO! FINANCE – in the US, search a company and My Portfolio will come up; in the UK, you will find MY PORTFOLIOS on the Homepage; or CNN Money provides a watchlist capability under Personal Finance. There is likely to be a 15-minute delay with free sites. Alternatively, you can set up a real time watchlist with, for example, FreeRealTime or ADVFN, probably for a subscription.

Real time share prices are essential for successful day trading. Day traders are likely to set up or refresh their watchlists every day. For investing, real time share prices are a 'nice to have,' but not essential.

Many websites provide share price movements during the trading day. Hargreaves Lansdown under Share prices & stock markets provides 'heat maps' for the UK indices, showing individual share price movements with a 15-minute delay.

You should think in terms of a watchlist of 50 to 100 companies – probably 200 maximum. Get to know a number of companies well, perhaps 20 to 30. Learn their tickers, as it will help you to look them up quickly on the Internet.

Your watchlist should include your current holdings and companies that you might invest in – perhaps on a market pullback, a good earnings report, or perhaps an increase in commodity prices for a resource company; or, an overall improvement of sentiment in the market. Whenever you research a company, you should take a view on whether to add it to your watchlist.

If you are not an experienced investor, you may be asking, 'Where do I start?'

Market cap is a good starting point – simply because the larger the market cap, the greater is the number of analysts that will cover the company and the news flow that affects its share price. Where market cap is less than, say, US$750m or £500 million, there may be only one or even no analysts covering the company, and the only substantial news flow may be the quarterly or twice-yearly earnings reports with occasional press releases. So to a very large extent the investor is flying blind. It also means that company reporting day can deliver significant surprises – sometimes nice, sometimes unpleasant, with the share price gapping down sharply on market opening.

There is no shortage of sources for companies to 'run a ruler over.' For example:

- Listed companies are all around us – in the shopping malls and on the high street, flying us around, building our houses and infrastructure, providing our consumer staples and pharmaceuticals and so on. You may be surprised to find that companies you know well are listed companies that you can invest in. If you are impressed with a company, check it out.
- Newspapers and magazines are an excellent source of information. In each edition, there will be news on a number of companies, upgrades and downgrades, and possibly share tips. If a company catches your attention, run it through your selection methodology.
- Follow analyst upgrades and downgrades – you can do this in an *ad hoc* way through newsprint or websites, and you can supplement with a source that provides this information systematically. Nasdaq, under Markets/Analyst Activity//Upgrades/Downgrades, provides data from about 90 major brokerage firms and updates its table three times a day. In the UK, DigitalLook provides a continuous feed of analyst recommendations – upgrades and downgrades – under UK Shares/Broker Views.
- Look for price action. The professionals use computers to search for price action and some companies offer it as a service. The retail investor can scan stock exchange websites for the day's biggest movers. Your investment platform may show the biggest movers or those shares attracting the most interest, as will many market information websites. The first things you should check are if the company has just reported or gone ex-dividend. Then take it from there. You can't base your share selection strategy on daily price movements, but a strong movement could lead you to check out a company further.

- Look at top ten holdings of some of the best-performing funds. Keep in mind that the fund manager may be winding down some positions where he judges further upside to be limited.
- Scan newspapers and magazines for tips.
- Look out for companies where their share price has crashed – they may be a good recovery play at some point.
- Set up your own criteria and use a screening tool. Many websites offer these, for example search Nasdaq screening tool or DigitalLook screening tool. A useful way to screen growth companies is by PEG, perhaps screening for companies with PEG less than one to two.
- See which companies are reporting over the next few weeks. There will be considerable focus on a company when it reports – for a large cap company there will be a number of analysts presenting their views as well as journalists in print and on the Internet. This is an information-rich time, enabling you to make a better assessment than is normally possible.
- If you are in the UK, check out the Hargreaves Lansdown website – it will give you a great deal of information, such as which shares are currently most researched by their clients.
- If you make use of a number of websites in your researches, you will soon find that your email inbox is filling up with hot tips.

There are many websites that provide specialist tools for share selection, for example, BETTERINVESTING.org in the US and ShareScope.co.uk in the UK.

Run companies that catch your interest through your share selection methodology before you put them on your watchlist. You are likely to reject a great many of them – including many of the 'hottest' tips that are out there.

Be wary of big dividend payers – more than 5% or 6%. Don't necessarily rule them out, but look into the reasons for the high dividend before you invest. If a company happens to pay a decent dividend, say 3% to 4%, regard this as a bonus.

If possible, check your watchlist daily. Some investment platforms offer an alert service that will advise you by SMS/text if a share price rises or falls to a level that you specify.

Your virtual portfolio

Your virtual portfolio will show cumulative share price movements.

A virtual portfolio can help you to manage your investments in individual shares, but keep in mind that individual share prices can move up or down very quickly. So to get real value from a virtual portfolio of individual shares, you would need to check it every day.

When the market falls sharply, sectors and companies are re-evaluated for new conditions – so your virtual portfolio may be compromised and you may need to refresh it.

Buy decisions

You need to be a little bit brave to 'buy the red.'

Even if you are thinking long-term, you don't want to buy a share and be down 3% or 4% (plus your costs) by the end of the day, and you can minimize the chances of this by making some important checks. If you think it might be a good day to buy, have regard to both Fundamentals and Technicals, which are covered in some detail in *Chapter 5.*

The further a share price moves up, statistically the less likely it is to go higher, and vice versa – but it's not unusual for a mid or small cap share price to move up by around 20% two days running. This can be very frustrating for a day trader who has been watching the share but is wrong-footed by the size of the move. On balance, the magnitude of rapid share price movements to the downside tend to be greater than those to the upside.

You should have the discipline always to buy from your watchlist. This doesn't mean that you should never be opportunistic, but always apply your share selection methodology, albeit rapidly. As you build your watchlist, it will include a number of shares that you have already checked out, and from time to time you need to assess if anything significant has changed. If a company reports badly, or is downgraded by the analysts, you should probably take it off your watchlist.

Try to judge the state of the markets and sentiment as best you can. Take a global view – greatly facilitated by the 24-hour news culture. Take a look at where the major indices are compared with their moving averages – check out both 50-day and 200-day and take a view. Traders in the US tend to believe that S&P 500 runs into trouble when it gets more than around 6% to 8% ahead of its 200-day moving average. If enough traders believe this, then it will become a self-fulfilling prophecy. The traders will be following these indicators closely and will trade on them. Also check out the RSI of these indices. Keep an eye on the US index futures.

Check the VIX volatility index (type ^VIX into the YAHOO! FINANCE Look Up box) – it could be that the situation with respect to a tail risk hanging over the market is becoming acute and that many traders are wary of a sharp fall. The VIX doesn't usually stay high for too long – 'insurance' is expensive. As we saw in *Chapter 7*, when a black swan appears, the VIX moves up so quickly that it can be of limited use to the retail investor, though the VIX running at over about 15 for a sustained period indicates a stressed market.

Be aware of any key data reports that are imminent, e.g., US nonfarm payrolls, which comes out on the first Friday of each month. If you are in the UK, pay particular attention to the interplay between New York and London. If the US market throws a fit, perhaps due to a bad economic report, the strongest opening movers in London can be thrown into reverse and finish the day in the red.

As well as having a reasonable knowledge of your target company, you should also have some knowledge of its sector and whether it is in or out of favor. For example, house builders may have had a strong run-up with little remaining upside; healthcare shares may be overheating; oilfield services companies may be bombed out by a low oil price, but showing signs of recovery.

Always check for a recent or imminent earnings report. In the UK, also check for interim management statements or trading statements. Check if your target company is about to go ex-dividend. Check 50- and 200-day moving averages and RSI, say over 1 year, for your target share. As an example, take a look at a volatile share price, such as Procter & Gamble (PG) or Arm Holdings (ARM) on YAHOO! FINANCE. Bring up the 1- or 2-year chart, go into Basic Tech. Analysis and add RSI. You will see that it has been a good indicator of the tops and bottoms of the swings. However, significant news will usually override the Technicals.

If all the stars are aligned, then buy the share – probably!

Buying on a pullback

S&P 500 – there have been only three years without a 5% dip since 1960.

In the current investment climate, it is particularly important to buy on market pullbacks to the greatest extent practical.

Markets in regions and countries pull back, sectors pull back, and individual company shares pull back. It is important to understand why a particular market pullback is occurring, and to take a view on whether it represents an immediate buying opportunity or whether it presages a long, sideways or downwards drift in the market.

If a market pullback is occurring, you have to judge the bottom as well as you can. Over the next few weeks or even months, the market might go even lower. Sometimes patience can pay. Look at the stock market indices in terms of RSI and moving averages, and listen to the market commentary. General panicky market selloffs can present attractive buying opportunities for funds and shares. These are often strongly correlated selloffs, with good company share prices falling as much as those of poor companies.

Sectors and companies can pull back in a rising market and often do. They can be traded down aggressively to levels where they represent good value. You should be aware of why a particular share has pulled back. If it has pulled back because of a profit warning or an analyst downgrade, it may not represent good value even if the fall is severe.

Which companies should you invest in on a pullback? You should look to your virtual portfolio and watchlist, which have been discussed above. It's good to be prepared – to know which shares you would like to have in your portfolio. In order to be able to exploit pullbacks, you need a strong watchlist. This will take a little time to build, but it is well worth doing. You should have a fair amount of knowledge about each company on your watchlist and its sector. You should take account of which sectors are moving into favor. For individual shares, Fundamentals are important and you should make an assessment of whether a share is likely to recover with the market in a sustained way, or if it's on a downward trend against a market that is trending up.

Good buying opportunities, especially for individual shares, can be fleeting. In strong selloffs, large imbalances in buy and sell orders can lead to instability in share prices with sharp falls needed to restore stability. A great many market participants will sense value, recovery can be quick, and the opportunity for getting a bargain can be quickly gone.

Remember, you can use limit orders to see if you can pick up a share at a price that you judge to be attractive.

Buying when the market is high

'Look at market fluctuations as your friend; profit from folly rather than participate in it.'
Warren Buffett

As we have seen, a great deal of the time, the markets are moving upwards. Sometimes you just have to be patient and not be panicked into buying high. On the other hand, when you take a look at long-term charts, you will see that a great deal of the time you could buy at a high level and still do well! The only sensible conclusion that you can draw from this is that you should always try to buy on a pullback, but don't be afraid to buy at a high price, perhaps on a small pullback, if your research case is compelling and you believe the market is going higher. An option is to build a position in a share in two or three tranches. If you have set your maximum investment in an individual share at US$3,000, you could consider investing in tranches, say 2xUS$1,500 or 3xUS$1,000. You will pay more in commissions, but you may still come out ahead with a phased approach. You will finish up having paid an average price for the shares. This is often referred to as dollar or pound cost averaging.

All boats float on a rising tide. And they all fall when the tide goes out. There is considerable truth in this – correlation at work! Numerous studies have shown that when the markets rise very strongly, the majority of share price gains – sometimes as much as 85% – result from overall market movements rather than internal company fundamentals. In a strongly rising market, most shares will rise and you will probably not be seriously punished if you make a poor buy. However, many of these rises will be short-lived, with a reversal of fortune when a company reports or some bad news hits the company. In a market trading sideways with high share valuations, poor buy decisions can be punished severely.

History shows that for a great deal of the time market indices in the US and UK are high, and so buy decisions are challenging. Nevertheless, there are many approaches that can enhance your prospects of success – as discussed below.

Monitoring and managing your holdings

Losses feel worse than gains feel good!

You could take the view that you are investing for the long term, so you will just check your portfolio once a month. The problem is that you could well find that some of your companies have issued profit warnings and lost maybe 20% of their value. This will not help the long-term performance of your portfolio.

You need to devise a sound methodology for monitoring your individual share holdings. In particular, you should know when each company in your portfolio is going to report. You can obtain this from each company's website or from a website report calendar. In the US, this will be quarterly earnings reports. In the UK, it will be quarterly or twice-yearly reports, possibly supplemented by interim management reports and trading statements. Keep a close eye on share price movements leading up to and after reporting. You should also know when each company goes ex-dividend, if it pays a significant dividend – quarterly in the US and twice a year for most UK-listed companies. Substantial share price movements often occur around these dates.

In addition to tracking company reports, you should try to achieve the following for each holding:

- Monitor share prices on a daily basis, at least at market opening or close each day.
- Sign up to receive a company's investor alerts, if it provides this service.
- Monitor accumulating gains or losses for each holding.
- Consider taking some profit when a company has had a particularly strong run.
- Consider cutting losses, but have some faith in your share selection methodology – share prices swing strongly on aggressive trading activity and often recover from sharp falls. Perhaps reduce your holding if a share price dips sharply.
- Consider adding to strong holdings, but adhere to your maximum holding size.

- If you can find the time, check which economic data reports will have the most impact on your shares.
- Establish your source for checking market expectations, e.g., Nasdaq, DigitalLook, or CNN Money.
- Get to know how to make a quick assessment of a company report. EPS, dividend payments, and Chairman/CEO statements are particularly important.
- Take a view on how to react to a poor report or even a profit warning; consider use of stop-losses, guaranteed or otherwise.
- Review and manage stop-losses if used.
- Follow the company in the media for news, in particular upgrades and downgrades. Your investment platform may send you research updates on companies in your portfolio.
- Check out analyst views after a company has reported and look for commentary in the newspapers and on the Internet.
- Take a view on reinvesting any dividend on receipt.
- Be alert to factors that will impact share price, such as commodity prices for mining companies; regulation for tobacco companies; drug trial success or failure for pharmaceutical companies, etc.
- Find some bulletin boards or chat sites that cover your shares, especially for the smaller cap shares, which may not have much mainstream news flow.
- Etc.!

Keep in mind that if you are invested through a fund, the fund manager does all this – for a large number of shares!

What should you do if one of your holdings suffers a severe drop? It's hard to say without knowing the company and the cause of the drop. If the fall is because of a secondary factor, such as an economic data release that could impact the fortunes of the company, but won't necessarily, then it might be worth staying with the holding until the impact on the company can be more fully assessed. A subsequent good earnings report from the company could result in a strong recovery in the share price. If the fall was due to a serious profit warning, then the best decision may be just to sell and take the loss on the chin. Hanging on for a recovery, which may not come, could simply result in greater losses.

A brave option is to double up, i.e., invest even more in the hope of a bounce! This is just gambling unless you understand the company well and understand the reasons for the fall.

If the holding that is suffering is in a mid or small cap share, it might take quite some time to discover the reason for the fall. The professionals will know very quickly where the selling pressure is coming from, and be able to manage their losses or even exploit the fall. The retail investor, struggling to find the information that he needs, will be very much on the back foot. Markets move at frightening speed.

The other side of the coin is that a share price can make a spectacular rise during a trading day, possibly because the company has reported well ahead of expectations or because a bid has emerged. Sometimes when a company has reported badly, its share price rises because its results are not as bad as expected and it looks like the share was oversold. This is known as a relief rally.

A good investment platform will display your holdings showing your entry level cost, current value, and percentage movement. It will update continually during the trading day, usually with a 15-minute delay. Some websites will give the option for a subscription for real time prices. This is essential for day traders but not critical for investors.

If you build a position in a share, your platform will show the average performance, which will almost certainly be different from the actual performance of the share which you need to monitor. You can do this readily in a virtual portfolio.

If you have the time and want to be proactive during the trading day, you can sign up for real time share prices using services such as FreeRealTime and ADVFN. This can be a useful facility, e.g., if you are hoping for a market pullback to invest in some of the shares in your watchlist, real time prices can enable you to get into a share at or close to a low point. As mentioned above, the low may not last very long.

Sell decisions

Avoid mistakes – don't chase what is hot; get out of what is running cool.

The sell decision is as important as the buy decision. There are three main reasons for selling a holding – in whole or in part. To take profit, to cut losses, or to reduce percent invested as discussed above. Why take downside risk on an underperforming share if the market is looking vulnerable?

There is some evidence that fund managers are now using much shorter holding periods. They are closing positions when they judge the company to be running out of steam or that it has possibly been impacted by disruptive technology from a competitor. You will be in good company if you decide to take a nice profit after a short holding period. In these circumstances, Technicals can helpfully inform an exit decision, e.g., a share price moving down on strong volume can indicate that the market is losing confidence in the share; or, a very high P/E, which makes the share price vulnerable to even slight bad news.

You should always take a view when a company has reported. Sometimes when a company has reported well and even beaten market expectations, its share price will fall – because the result has been anticipated and now many traders and investors are taking profit, encouraged by analysts. The market may judge that further upside is limited. Quite often the market gets it wrong, and the share price quickly recovers and moves on up. These are difficult calls to make. An option is to sell half your holding in these circumstances. If a company report is disappointing, you should probably sell unless you believe the company is on the mend. Again, an option is to sell half your holding.

From your study of share price charts, you will have seen that it is quite common for share prices to recover nicely from falls of 10% or 15% or more. A significant factor in this is the amount of high-frequency trading taking place – there is increasing evidence that this leads to greater volatility. So don't sell in a panic – have some faith in your ability to assess the real value of a share.

It is very common for a company to have a great run-up, driven by excellent results and strong market sentiment. The share can start to look expensive in terms of P/E and it might be time to take some profit. Some investors will work by rules, e.g., if they are showing a 20% profit on a share, they will sell half their holding. Quite often, after a very strong run-up, there can be a spate of profit taking – with the share price falling and then resuming its upwards trend. If this is what is occurring, then to hold in anticipation of a swift recovery and further advance can work well. A common investment 'mistake' (hindsight is 20/20) is to take profit too early.

Don't necessarily wait for a dividend, especially if a company has reported poorly.

Automatic trading

Many retail investors make use of automatic trading facilities – sometimes because their time is limited and also because a good strategy can be profitable.

Some types of automatic trade have been described in *Chapter 3*. In summary:

- Limit order – buy
- Limit order – sell
- Rising buy order
- Stop-loss
- Guaranteed stop-loss
- Trailing stop-loss

Other types of order are:

- Fill or kill – order to be entirely filled at specified price or 'killed'
- Immediate or cancel at a specified price
- Good till cancelled at a specified price

Some platforms may allow you to keep your automatic orders in place for a day only, i.e., they will expire on market close. You will find some platforms that will keep your orders in place for 30 days. If you work through a stockbroker, you may be able to obtain a 90-day facility.

To use limit orders effectively, you must have good knowledge of the companies on your watchlist or in your portfolio – so that you can take a view on what is a good buy price and what is a good sell price. You should also take into account market conditions. Are they steady or volatile? Are there severe tail risks around? A useful approach is to set buy limit orders on perhaps three or four shares based on a significant fall in the market – you might be pleased if only one or two of these orders get filled. With respect to placing a sell limit order on an existing holding, you may be happy with a profit accrued and feel that further upside is limited, but if the markets are buoyant you could set an optimistic sell limit order, and hope to sell on a spike up.

An overworked market saw is 'don't catch a falling knife,' but you should have looked at enough share price charts by now to know that to catch a share at a low point can be very profitable. However, when a share price is on a downwards path, you should not underestimate its capacity to plumb inconceivably low depths. On the way down, for every seller there is a buyer – people continuously trying to judge 'the bottom' and many of them failing. Many of them will be looking at Technicals, such as RSI and moving averages, but these don't always help. It can be safer to buy when a share price has turned up, perhaps on strong volume, or an influential analyst has turned positive, even if you miss some of the rise. This is where you would use a rising buy order – you would need to watch these closely and reset them regularly.

You can use a stop-loss to cut a loss or you can use a trailing stop-loss to protect a profit. You can set a trailing stop-loss a couple of percentage points below current value and it will follow the share price up – or stop you out if it falls back by the set amount. Keep in mind that unless you have paid for a guaranteed stop-loss, your share could gap down on market opening below your stop, which would then be ineffective. Also keep in mind that if you set the trailing stop-loss too tight, perhaps 2% or 3%, you can easily be stopped out by a bit of volatility and miss out on a good subsequent rise.

There are many ways in which you can make use of automatic trading, and day traders use it extensively, perhaps capturing a sharp upwards movement with both a buy and a sell order. People with a longer-term perspective may use buy limit orders to pick up bargains and then be more thoughtful in determining a good time to sell.

Managing your downside risk on individual shares

One of the most frightening aspects of the stock market is the speed and magnitude of falls in share prices that occur on a daily basis. A fall of 30% – or even a lot more – in an individual share price is not uncommon. The share price may open a lot lower than it closed the day before and then fall like a stone, giving you little or no chance of getting out before you have suffered a serious loss. It is important that you manage your downside risk on individual shares.

The most obvious way to limit losses is to use stop-losses. However, there are some drawbacks with their use, so first we will assume that stop-losses are not routinely used.

If a company reports badly, or due to some other cause, it looks as though the share price is going to open sharply down, you can plan to reduce or eliminate your position as rapidly as possible on market opening. Or, if you have time to monitor, you can hope for a bounce before you sell. To keep control of your investment, you have to find out as quickly as possible what led to the fall. This will be easier with large cap shares, as there will be stronger coverage and news flow. The better your information sources, the quicker you will be able to find out. You then have to take a view on whether the share price is set into a long period of decline, or going nowhere – in which case you should sell and take the loss – or perhaps sell half your holding; or, whether the difficulties are temporary and the current price actually represents a good buy opportunity – in which case you should hold. You could consider adding to your position if you have a good understanding of the company and the reason for the fall.

If the fall is due to an earnings report, then you can review the analyst reaction and see what the financial pages report the next day.

Two 'philosophical' approaches to managing downside risk on individual shares are discussed below.

Limit maximum size of holding

As discussed earlier, an effective way to manage downside risk on an individual share investment is to limit the size of the holding – to perhaps 5% of the money you are prepared to commit to the stock market. And not to use a stop-loss. This leaves you in control of the sell decision. There are plenty of companies to choose from, so this should not disadvantage you. If your portfolio is US$100,000, then your maximum investment in an individual share will be US$5,000. If a US$5,000 holding suddenly loses 20% of its value, i.e., US$1,000, this will represent 1% of your portfolio. Not pleasant, but manageable. By the time you have studied a number of share price charts, you will see that it is not at all uncommon for share prices to recover fairly quickly from quite steep losses, giving you an opportunity to get out if that is what your 'rapid research' suggests.

The point of this approach is that you stay in control of the situation. Depending on the state of the market, if you invest wisely, you won't get too many 20%-plus falls. But almost certainly you will get some.

An alternative view is embodied in the maxim that 'your first loss is your best loss.' However, many share price charts show that this is not always the case.

It is worth being aware that with a small market cap share, you may experience some difficulty in 'getting out,' having to reduce the number of shares you are selling to complete a trade. It is very frustrating to have to sell in, say, three tranches and the share price may fall another 5% or so while you are struggling with this. You can avoid such situations by paying attention to exchange or normal market size, but you may have a holding that has risen above this value.

Use of stop-losses

An alternative approach is to use a stop-loss, where you effectively give up control. Use of stop-losses – not a straightforward matter – is discussed in detail in *Chapter 10.*

Both stockbrokers and derivative trading platforms will usually advise the use of a stop-loss to protect against sharp losses, i.e., you place an instruction to sell the share if the fall reaches a level that you have predetermined – perhaps somewhere between 4% and 8% below your entry price. You could take the view that you will always set a stop-loss at 5% so that you will never take a loss of more than 5%. This may work well in steady – perhaps complacent – markets, but in volatile markets you are likely to get stopped out frequently.

In a trading context when trading on margin – in effect, borrowed money – there is a compelling case for use of stop-losses. Though there is a very big difference between trading with x2 leverage with a stockbroker and trading with much higher leverage in the index futures market or on a CFD platform. In an investment situation, the case is less compelling.

Investing for dividend yield

> *'Chasing yield is crazy.' Warren Buffett on CNBC, May 2013.*

> *The average dividend yield for S&P 500 companies increased by 17.3% in 2014; a lower increase is anticipated in 2015 as many companies are struggling for top-line growth.*

A company's shares are continuously changing hands and it has to be meticulous about who is entitled to each dividend that is paid out. The company will specify in advance the day of record for the dividend payment, and your name has to be on the record on that day if you are to receive the dividend. It takes three days to settle a buy or sell transaction (referred to as T+3) and shares switch from 'cum' (with) dividend to 'ex' (without) dividend two days before the record date. So if the record date is Friday and you buy on Tuesday, you will be entitled to the dividend. If you buy on the Wednesday, the ex-dividend date, you will not get onto the record in time and you will not receive the dividend. If you want to sell the share and still receive the dividend, you can sell as late as Tuesday and you will still be on the shareholder register on Friday, the day of record.

As we have seen in previous chapters, when interest rates are low, there is continuous search for yield by many market participants – usually from share dividends and bond yields. The search for yield in shares can be futile. A company paying a large dividend may be struggling with waning institutional support and the value of a dividend yield can be wiped out in seconds by a sharp fall in share price. The retail investor doesn't have to chase high yield. He can invest in growing companies, perhaps with some yield, and leave the large institutional investors to chase big yields in large cap companies because they have to.

Nevertheless, there are two good reasons for investing for dividend yield. You may want to receive regular income or you may want to benefit from the powerful compounding effect of dividend reinvestment over time. In either case, you should be cautious about investing in a company solely on the basis of a high dividend yield. You also need to take account of your tax situation with respect to dividends. They will not compound so well if heavily taxed, as they can be in the UK.

Companies that are growing strongly, sometimes early stage, reinvest much of their profits to drive their growth. They may pay a small dividend. As companies mature their rate of growth slows, and if they are generating more cash than they need for investment in the business, they may establish dividend programs to support their share price.

Many companies generate strong profits, backed by cash, which enables them to increase their dividend payout year on year by a significant amount - 10% to 15% per annum would not be unusual. Such companies are attractive in particular to institutional investors. Less solid companies may struggle to increase their dividend payouts year on year as a result of pressure on their profit margins or cash flow difficulties, and their dividend cover may become compromised. The markets track dividend cover closely.

Before investing in a company yielding 4% or 5% or more, check out the background to the yield. It may have risen because the share price has fallen sharply. If the company decides to cut its dividend, the share price may fall even further; or, the market could determine that management is getting a grip and the share price could rise. The markets can be perverse!

Markets are likely to game the larger dividend payments. They may trade a share price up as the ex-dividend date approaches, and sell before the ex-dividend date. Or they may capture the dividend and then exit the share very rapidly on the ex-dividend date. The retail investor who has bought a share to pick up a significant dividend may find he is nursing a serious loss. If you judge that a company you hold has lost its luster, then it may be a good move to sell before the ex-dividend date.

Sector rotation comes into play in the search for yield, with investors moving into defensive shares such as utilities and REITs (Real Estate Investment Trusts) in times of economic downturn. These sectors pay a good dividend, but have significantly underperformed the S&P 500 since 2013.

It is quite possible for a share price to be low with a good dividend yield simply because the markets are failing to recognize the value in the share price. This could represent a good buy opportunity. Make sure you check the dividend cover before you buy. The share will pay out its regular dividend and there is a fair chance that over time you will enjoy some capital appreciation.

There is a lot to be said for investing in growth companies paying a dividend of 2% to 3%, even if your main interest is income. If you invest well, you should enjoy some capital gains, which you can use to supplement your dividend income. If you instruct your investment platform to automatically reinvest your dividend, check the commissions that you will be charged. Also keep an eye on the total return on investment. The compounding effect of reinvesting dividends can be seriously offset if the share price is falling away or you are paying significant tax on the dividends.

It's worth checking out the S&P 500 Dividend Aristocrats. These are companies that have increased their dividend payouts for 25 consecutive years. Their dividend yields range from 0.6% to 6%. Currently the average dividend yield of S&P 500 companies is around 1.9%. Despite a recent pickup, the long-term trend is down. Since its inception in May 2005, the ProShares NOBL S&P 500 Dividend Aristocrats ETF has tracked the S&P 500 Total Return Index quite closely.

Search TopYields FTSE 100 for a listing of the highest-yielding UK large cap companies. In the UK, the average dividend yield of FTSE 100 companies is about 3.9%, but many of the sectors comprising the index, such as banks and resource companies, are struggling for growth, and the benefits of dividend reinvestment may be to some extent offset by declining share prices.

Search Association of Investment Companies dividend heroes, for UK investment companies/trusts that have increased dividends year on year for more than 30 years. These companies or trusts are able to hold reserves that they can use to smooth their dividend payments over the years.

Investing overseas

In May 2014, the Russian market was trading on a cyclically adjusted Price/Earnings ratio of 6.1 – only Greece was lower.

During the 2015 China stock market bubble, trading volume by Chinese retail investors reached a third of global share trading volume.

The best way to invest overseas is through funds which will bring other stock market indices into the picture, such as the major European and Asian indices. Keep in mind that tax treatment for US investors is complex.

An alternative to investing through funds is to invest through ETFs, which track an overseas stock exchange index, but an ETF index tracker will 'never beat the index.'

Investing overseas can be rewarding if you get your timing right and don't get wrong-footed by adverse currency movements. There is no hard and fast rule regarding what proportion of your portfolio should be invested overseas, because this will vary with time, but a maximum of between a quarter and a third would seem sensible. If you have the time and the interest, it's worth doing some research to see if you can identify some good opportunities.

Some overseas mutual funds and OEICs hedge against currency risk, using derivatives or short positions, and you will therefore not receive the benefit of an appreciating currency in your investment (nor the reverse). The fund documentation should tell you if the fund hedges. You should take account of this in your fund selection.

Developed economies worth watching are those of Japan, Hong Kong, Western Europe, and Australia. The Japanese market has doubled since 2012, though the gain in US$ terms is more like 50%. The average P/E of Japanese equities was around 17 in February 2016, with the cyclically adjusted price-to-earnings ratio, or CAPE, comparable to the S&P 500 at around 26. Earnings growth rates in Japan are bullish but shares are not currently cheap. Hong Kong's Hang Seng index reached a forward P/E ratio of 12.9 during the market high of May 2015. Subsequently the index fell from over 28,000 to around 22,000. This does not indicate an expensive market. The Australian economy is strongly resource-based.

Emerging markets often offer opportunity, but should not be considered as an amorphous blob. They include China, India, Brazil, Russia, Turkey, and many other countries – all with their own characteristics. All have enjoyed periods of exceptionally strong growth followed by periods of dramatic decline as their fortunes have waned and capital is moved around the globe in a ceaseless search for returns.

Wikipedia provides a useful treatment of emerging markets, defining them as countries with some of the characteristics of a developed market while catching up across a range of factors. Important criteria include per capita income, rate of economic growth, institutional development, and integration into the world economy.

Many funds specialize in emerging markets, and the MSCI Emerging Markets Index is a much-used benchmark. You can check out the MSCI website or just search MSCI Emerging Markets Index chart. If you look at the country profile of various emerging markets funds, you will find a different set of countries in each one.

In recent years it has been possible to make money in the emerging markets using an approach akin to swing trading, i.e., exploiting significant movements taking place over weeks or months. For example, go to YAHOO! FINANCE and take a look at the Brazilian Ibovespa index (^BVSP) over the last five years.

Countries have moved in and out of fashion and capital flows have changed dramatically and erratically. During 2013 and 2014, a great deal of capital flowed out of emerging markets back into the developed world in search of higher returns and lower levels of risk. This flow continued through 2015, which saw considerable weakening of most emerging-market currencies.

The popular expression BRIC was coined in 2001 by Jim O'Neil, formerly of Goldman Sachs Asset Management, to describe the four large emerging markets of Brazil, Russia, India, and China. We have also had CIVETS and MINT:

- CIVETS – Columbia, Indonesia, Vietnam, Egypt, Turkey, South Africa,
- MINT – Mexico, India, Indonesia, Turkey,
- And Europe has had its PIGS – Portugal, Italy, Greece, Spain – the 'peripheral' European economies which have struggled to raise debt at affordable rates of interest.

These acronyms have had mixed success in informing successful investment strategies, to some extent because they have been viewed mistakenly as somewhat homogeneous blocks.

China continues to be more for gamblers than investors. Africa possibly has more promise than anywhere else on the planet, and Mexico is where the smart money is going. We shall see. Russian shares are unbelievably cheap but no one wants them.

A combination of rising share prices and strengthening currency will deliver an attractive return. On the other hand, you don't want to be invested in an overseas stock market that is rising nicely in local currency but going nowhere in US$ or sterling terms because the local currency is weakening.

From early 2013, European shares were judged by most pundits to be undervalued, though stock markets gains were partially offset by a strengthening dollar and pound.

You should select overseas funds for your virtual portfolio using your developed methodology, but paying attention to the relevant stock market valuations. Look at average P/E ratio and average price to book ratio – Search Star Capital Partners Research Stock Market Valuations. This website provides average key metrics for countries with significant stock markets. Metrics include CAPE; P/E; price to cash flow ratio; price to book ratio; dividend yield. Also check out economic growth rates as well as currency exchange rates and trends.

Tune into the market analysts and commentators so that you are in a position to make informed investment decisions. It is possible to follow trends and sentiment and enjoy a good run, but without attention to fundamentals, you will be largely speculating.

Another way to obtain exposure to overseas markets is through the shares of large multinational companies, though sometimes their grand plans for developing in overseas markets run into serious difficulties. Apple in China in 2015 was a glorious success, with the sales of their iPhone going through the roof. There is no doubt that this was due to an exceptionally good product from a world-class brand name.

Ways to even up the odds

There are a number of ways in which the retail trader and investor can even up the odds with the professionals. Some ways are discussed here, but no doubt there are many more.

Recent background

A feature of the market since the 2008 crash has been periods of stability punctuated by periods of high volatility with sharp falls and rises in market indices. This pattern became seen as periods of ´risk on´ and ´risk off,´ with high correlation during the 'risk on' phases. A strongly correlated selloff will drag a lot of good companies down, leading to buying opportunities. If you watch the markets carefully you will be able to recognize periods of high and low correlation.

Early in the bull run which commenced in 2009, stock picking was relatively easy due to high levels of correlation in the major markets. However, at the outset of 2014, correlations were running at a consistently low level, making stock selection much more difficult, with a much greater need to look at both sector and individual company specifics. The macro-factors at play were the gradual recovery in the global economy and the US Federal Reserve having commenced the tapering of its quantitative easing (QE) program. This finally came to an end in October 2014. With less money being pumped into the markets to find its way into a range of assets, including company shares, the emphasis was shifting and creating a challenge to the investment community to allocate capital where it might achieve the greatest returns. Good stock-picking capabilities were at a premium once again. A conventional wisdom is that the better fund managers outperform during periods of low correlation, during which a company´s share price will be more determined by its specifics than by the overall market movements.

Since the middle of 2014, the S&P 500 has moved more or less sideways in a trading range, between 1,850 and 2,100, with occasional sharp pullbacks of up to 20%, providing good buy opportunities. Underlying the index movements have been large individual share price movements, adding to the trading and investing opportunities.

The FTSE 100 has tracked sideways since early 2013, breaking to the downside, below 6,000, at the beginning of 2016 – held back by mining and financial companies. However, during this period a number of FTSE 100 company share prices have done very well. Skillful share picking can be profitable despite the main indices making little headway.

Buy around company reporting

You could opt to make many of your investments around company reporting. Company reporting has been discussed in *Chapter 10* and *Chapter 16*. Make a note of reporting dates for all the companies on your watchlist. By using the great splurge of data and comment that occurs around a company report, the retail investor can get close to being on the same footing as the professionals.

There may well be significant share price movement – up or down – as a company's reporting date is approached. If markets are in a buoyant mood and you are confident that the share price of the reporting company will rerate to a new level, then you might buy on market opening, even if the share price has gapped up sharply. In these circumstances, the ability to make a rapid assessment of the company report is very helpful. Or, you can wait for the price to pull back before buying. If the price doesn't pull back, you might be better off letting it go. This can be a difficult call. Very often, there will be a sharp movement up or down a couple of hours after market opening after major participants have studied the report in detail, or a consensus is building among the analysts. The activities of the high-frequency traders, which have a significant effect on short-term price movements, are a wild card.

Alternatively, you could decide to watch and wait for a couple of days, absorb the market commentary including analyst upgrades and downgrades, and then make a decision. You may miss out on a surge in the share price by biding your time, but this can result in you making a better long-term buy decision. Quite often, you will get the share cheaper by waiting, especially if the markets are volatile. Let the commentators and analysts do most of the work! If you adopt this approach, you may miss some good upside, but over a number of share selections, you could come out ahead. Unexpected bad news in the US can pull back even the most exuberant price rises on reporting, allowing you to get in after all!

If you know a company well and believe that it is going to report well, then you could buy before reporting day in the hope of benefitting from a gap up in the share price. There will often be talk in the market that a company is going to report well – or badly. You can usefully look for large trades late in the day before a company reports.

Look for recovery stories

Search 'Jim Collins, How the mighty fall, 2009.'

413

Regions, countries, sectors, and companies can be recovery plays, and if you follow the markets closely, you will be able to identify recovery prospects.

At a macro-level, the following situations developing during 2015 could become recovery opportunities:

- In 2015, emerging markets crashed.
- China's recovery stalled and cast a shadow over global markets.
- The price of oil, which had begun its sharp fall in the middle of 2014, continued its collapse and was trading between US$28 and US$35 in early 2016. A strong correlation developed between the oil price and major indices. The fall had a dramatic influence on oil company share prices as well as those of supply chain companies. Oil sector share prices will probably be a recovery play at some point.
- Gloom persisted in the mining sector. During 2013, the mining sector made some recovery and then trended down again in 2015. Gold miners were not helped by a collapse in gold price. In early 2016, mining stocks began to make a tentative recovery though with short covering causing considerable volatility.
- All through 2015, analysts said that European shares represented good value – the major indices rose sharply and then fell back, making little progress in the year.
- The Russian stock market is incredibly cheap and should represent a recovery opportunity, but currently no one wants Russian shares.

At a company level, on a profit warning or perhaps some bad sector news, a company's share price can fall dramatically – and then continue to fall, day after day or month after month or even year after year. It can be very tempting to buy into a company share that has fallen a long way. It may still be capable of falling a lot further, sometimes after a bounce, and when it finally bottoms out it could just track sideways. The decline in the mining sector as China's growth slowed is a striking example of long-term decline.

It is particularly important to get your timing right and be sure that conditions for recovery are in place. A company of any significant size that has fallen hard will be heavily shorted and the professional traders will be unrelenting in driving the share price down. Eventually, if the company share price is reaching the bottom of its decline, the short sellers will close their positions, encouraged by bear squeezes along the way. However, if you look back over a number of share price charts, you will see that in many instances the price eventually bottoms out and presents a good entry point. This can be very difficult to judge, but rewarding if you get it right. Sometimes a share price will rally strongly from a low – great for swing traders – and then resume its downwards path.

In the US, Apple (AAPL) and Facebook (FB) share prices have made dramatic recoveries in recent years. In the UK, Thomas Cook Group (TCG), Dixons (now Dixons Carphone – DC), Aviva (AV) and Ocado (OCDO) have all made spectacular recoveries, though in some instances their share prices subsequently fell back significantly. It's worth checking out their share price charts.

In the UK, Thomas Cook Group is worth a look as both a momentum play and a remarkable recovery play getting underway in 2013, with the share price climbing steadily from circa £15 to circa £150. Thomas Cook is not an insubstantial company, with a market cap in the region of £2bn. It has a strong brand and new management has steered the company towards a much stronger online presence. This was a share price rise to die for, but you can be sure that a great many traders missed the big picture.

Changes in senior management, in particular chairman or CEO, can signal a change in the fortunes of a company. If the markets like the change, it is not unusual to see a significant rise in share price. Whether this is sustained will depend on the effectiveness of the new person. In assessing a recovery play, you should check shares out on loan and short interest – see *Chapter 8* for information sources. If you decide that the share is set for recovery, you could hedge your bets by going in cautiously, perhaps buying 1/3 of your selected maximum holding – then monitoring.

Look for momentum plays

Momentum investing has been discussed in *Chapters 4* and *10*. If you look at any number of share price charts, you will see many strong 'momentum' runs that you will wish you had caught. A problem is the very large number of listed shares and the time and energy required to detect strong run-ups in share price. Many spectacular share price performances occur on a regular basis. Since the global financial crisis, many share prices strongly outperformed the recovering indices – this was a period of opportunity for investors and we may not see its like again for quite some time. Some impressive momentum performances by major US companies are shown in Table 18.1.

Company	Ticker	Sector	Since	Share price multiple increase
The Priceline Group	PCLN	Consumer Discretionary	2009	x15
Netflix Inc.	NFLX	Information Technology	2012	x15
Amazon Inc.	AMZN	Consumer Discretionary	2009	x10
Apple Inc.	AAPL	Information Technology	2009	x10
Starbucks Corp	SBUX	Consumer Discretionary	2009	x10
Humana Inc.	HUM	Health Care	2009	x7
Home Depot	HD	Consumer Discretionary	2009	x6
Nike	NKE	Consumer Discretionary	2009	x5

Table 18.1 Momentum performances – by late 2015

The Consumer Discretionary sector stands out strongly.

It's instructive to look at their charts and reflect on what you might have done along the way in terms of taking profit, riding out the dips, or going back in.

Amazon and Netflix also figure in the acronym FANGS – together with Facebook and Google. These put on a spectacular performance in 2015, as can be seen in Table 18.2. 2015 saw a flat performance from the S&P 500.

Company	2015 Gain	P/E Ratio Trailing	P/E Ratio Forward
Facebook (FB)	35%	49	37
Amazon (AMZN)	115%	34	118
Netflix (NFLX)	140%	62	45
Alphabet/Google (GOOG)	50%	27	23

Table 18.2 The FANGS

These were strong momentum runs and the further the share prices rose, the more nervous investors would have been in opening positions. P/E ratios reached, in some instances, extremely high levels. So many conservative investors would have missed these spectacular runs.

Biotech shares, many of them US companies, had a strong momentum run which began to run out of steam at the outset of 2015. Many Internet companies have also enjoyed strong momentum runs.

In the UK, Asos (ASC), touched on above, has been an extraordinary momentum play. Asos (As Seen On Screen) is an online fashion retailer. Its meteoric rise began in 2003. Its share price had fallen to a few pence but it reached around £70 in 2014 before falling back to about £25. At its peak, Asos enjoyed a P/E ratio around 100. A great many analysts who thought that Asos could grow at plus 40% per annum forever finished up with egg on their faces. However, without doubt there are many Asos millionaires. Asos was the darling of the LSE AIM market and one of its few big successes. At its peak market cap, Asos was a contender for the FTSE 100, had it sought a listing there. Again, it's instructive to look at the Asos chart and consider how you might have played it if you had gotten on board early!

Also in the UK, many small and mid cap companies have enjoyed strong runs, as evidenced by the performance of a number of smaller company OEICs.

Clifford Asness, a well-known hedge fund manager, has written on momentum investing. You can check this out on the Internet. In the UK, you can check out The Momentum Investor Newsletter.

Specialize

If you have the time and the inclination, you could specialize in a small number of sectors. Perhaps sectors that do well in different stages of the economic cycle, or sectors that interest you or in which you have some professional knowledge. Get to know these sectors and a number of companies in them.

You will be readily able to establish the most highly rated companies in a sector and assess if these are already fully priced – check out P/E ratios. You may be able to identify that there are some smaller, up-and-coming companies in the sector that may have more potential. The sector may have had a good run, and profit taking may have depressed share prices. You may not have to wait too long for interest in the sector to pick up again, perhaps aided by a change in government policy, or a significant change in a commodity price that can influence revenue or cost.

Alternatively, you could specialize in a small number of companies, researching them deeply, looking for value – try to select shares that have a 10% to 15% upside even in a strong market. Invest before (if you are very confident) or just after companies report. Where you build considerable knowledge of a company you could benefit from swing trading its shares, taking profit on a high and going back in after a dip.

Another possibility is to specialize in small cap shares. Studies have shown that they tend to outperform large cap stocks, but there is plenty of scope for getting it wrong. These studies are looking through a rearview mirror. As we have discussed, the analyst coverage of small cap stocks is invariably low.

Some investing techniques and tactics

Seasonality

There are strong seasonal patterns to stock market movements. They don't always occur, but they should be taken seriously. Some of the most popular are:

- 'As goes January so goes the year.' According to S&P Dow Jones Indices, in the US, a poor January has led to a down year three-quarters of the time since 1929.
- 'Sell in May and go away.' Check out 2012, a clear exception arising due to the disappearance of a strong tail risk. Trading volume tends to fall away in summer months.
- In most Decembers, there is a Santa rally – very true, but occasionally there is an exception.
- The markets rally into the new year – again, often true, but not always.

Doubling up

A tactic of some stockbrokers when they have put a client into a bad trade is to suggest that he 'doubles up,' in order to get his money back (the selloff has been 'overdone'). In other words, if you have invested £1,000 in a particular share and it rapidly falls by maybe 8%, buy another £1,000 worth on the basis that it might bounce back by 8%. This is not a competent approach. In such a circumstance, you need to find out as rapidly as possible the reason for the fall – and decide whether to cut your losses and sell, or watch and wait. The share could become a recovery play, but it may fall quite a bit further before it's worth increasing your holding or 'going back in.' Never say never, but be very cautious about doubling up.

A couple of market aphorisms are 'don't buy a share you have lost money in' and 'never buy more of share that has fallen.' However, given the amount of gaming that takes place in today's market, and given the reality of many share price charts, this advice is perhaps not as sound as it used to be.

Averaging

Share prices are volatile, and no matter how carefully you research a share and judge the timing of your buy, any number of factors can come into play and leave you significantly down in percentage terms by the end of the trading day. You can manage this risk to some extent by buying the share in tranches, say, three times US$1,000. You then finish up with an average price. You pay three commissions instead of one, but you could well finish up with a better average price than investing the US$3,000 in one go. This is known as dollar cost or pound cost averaging.

You can adopt the same approach in selling a share, rather than selling your entire holding in one go and then watching the price put on another 5% or 10%.

Invest in low P/E shares

There is a school of thought that you should simply invest in shares with low P/E ratios and hold them for several years – sometimes described as a 'value investing' approach. There is some value to be found in cheap shares and there are studies that indicate that they 'outperform' in the long term. In modern times, the fortunes of companies are changing so quickly that you should use this approach with caution.

Buying the dogs

A sometimes-advocated strategy is to 'buy the dogs' in an index, defined as the highest-yielding company shares – on the basis that the dividends are high because the share prices have collapsed, and will eventually recover.

You may make money with such an approach, but you should be able to do better by developing a more sophisticated approach to investing.

Rolling and gapping stocks

The website My Rolling Stocks puts you in touch with shares that exhibit a pattern of behavior that can be exploited:

'Rolling stocks, sometimes called Bouncing stocks or Channeling stocks, are stocks that oscillate (roll) between a high price point (ceiling) and a low point (the floor) for a specific time period.'

Working with these shares is akin to swing trading.

The same site identifies stocks that are predicted to gap up on market opening. This is a subscription service.

Using social media

In September 2015, Hillary Clinton tweeted a pledge that she would tackle 'outrageous price manipulation' by US drug companies. This tweet famously took US$15bn off the value of the US pharmaceutical sector. Specialist companies are springing up that track tweets on, for example, mergers and acquisitions and sentiment on individual company shares. They maintain that they can filter out actionable information and give a serious advantage to traders and short-term investors. It is claimed that a team trading on 'twitter sentiment' outperformed the S&P 500 by 80% over the last five years. Companies developing capabilities in this area include Selerity, Marketpsych, Social Market Analytics, and Eagle Alpha Social Sonar. Their services are gaining traction among major market participants and it may not be too long before such services become affordable to the retail trader and investor.

Initial Public Offerings (IPOs)

Market insiders – for example, investment banks and hedge funds – get the best of most initial public offerings (IPOs) before the retail investor gets a look in. During 2014 and 2015, markets were high and new market entrants were pitching their offerings at quite high prices.

In the US towards the end of 2015, against a backdrop of unsettled equity markets, investor appetite for IPOs was waning and several large IPOs were pulled. Others went ahead at prices discounted from earlier expectations. Technology start-ups in particular are facing downwards pressure on their valuations. For more detailed information on US 2015 IPOs, search CNN Money The best and worst IPOs of 2015. Also search MarketWatch IPO Calendar for a useful source of upcoming US IPO activity.

In the UK, 2015 saw a number of successful IPOs. According to Deloitte, the 28 main market IPOs to the end of November had returned an average of about 17%. In the UK, search Hargreaves Lansdown IPOs for a useful source of upcoming IPOs.

You can find an excellent description of the IPO process by searching Initial Public Offering: CNBC Explains.

Finding the big winners

In 2014, Warren Buffett warned that Berkshire Hathaway's size made it hard for him to find worthwhile new investments – although he said he would continue to seek acquisitions in a process he calls 'elephant hunting.'

There have been many big winners in the stock markets, in particular post–financial crisis.

For US big winners, search Barchart.com Stocks – Ranked by 10-Year Percent Change. The list is dominated by pharmaceutical and biotech companies, but with some notable tech companies such as Apple, Netflix, and Amazon. Some of these companies have remarkably high P/E Ratios, sometimes in the region of 200.   Key to the success of these companies has been, a great business model, financial backing, and outstanding management – and, crucially, a buoyant US economy. Arguably, there will be fewer big winners going forward, but there will be some. How do you spot them? By hard work and research, and possibly by following 'smart money.'

Dataroma's website provides the top holdings of superinvestors, for example:

- Warren Buffett of Berkshire Hathaway
- Carl Icahn of Icahn Capital Management
- David Tepper of Appaloosa Holdings
- David Einhorn of Greenlight Capital
- Bill Ackman of Pershing Square Capital Management
- Seth Klarman of Baupost Group

Interestingly, if you check out the holdings of these superinvestors, you will find only a small number of holdings in the Barchart.com top 100 companies. Dataroma indicates movements in holdings, e.g., where the investor has recently increased a position. In a search for future big winners, this is a good starting point. You should pay particular attention to the smaller market cap companies, as these will often have the most upside potential.

Some of these superinvestors use Twitter to talk their books, e.g., Carl Icahn, who has significant holdings in Apple and Netflix, is a regular user of this media platform.

Another approach is to follow sectors to see if you can identify the next hot sector – after an amazingly strong run, the heat came out of pharmaceutical and biotech shares in 2015.

You should put some companies that you like the look of on your watchlist and follow their fortunes and their share prices closely.

The US regularly produces up-and-coming companies that hit US$1bn market cap – known as 'unicorns.'

The ground is less fertile in the smaller UK market. There have been many strong risers since 2009, but mostly in the ranks of small and mid cap companies. Lack of information for these companies renders them a real challenge for the retail investor. Over the last 20 years or so a number of outstanding fund managers in the small and mid cap company space have delivered spectacular returns for investors, and the retail investor specializing in individual shares will struggle to achieve their level of performance.

How much shorting?

Shorting has been discussed in *Chapter 8.* To recap, being long means that you make money when a share price goes up. Being short means that you make money when a share price goes down.

Shorting can play a role in a sophisticated investment strategy. There is a compelling logic in the proposition that your portfolio should always be a combination of 'long' and 'short,' especially when markets are high. You could argue that as you close long positions, you should open short positions – either in individual companies or in an index such as the S&P 500 or the FTSE 100.

Borrowing shares through a stockbroker adds a layer of complexity. Trading futures contracts is a way of going short, but this will draw you into trading on high leverage, and you need to be sure that you want to go there.

In the UK, you can readily take short positions on a CFD platform, again with high leverage.

A great many investors simply don't want to play the shorting game – it goes against the grain and there is some additional risk. If a short goes against you, there is no theoretical limit to your losses, though you can manage this risk using stop-losses. Most of the time there is an inherent upward bias to the markets. There will be a great deal of energy working against you as managers and investors seek to get struggling companies back on track. You don't receive dividends, in fact, you pay them to the lender of a share if it goes ex-dividend while your position is open.

On the other hand, there is no doubt that shorting can be a productive component of a swing trading strategy, for investors and traders with the requisite skill and dedication. Shorting mining companies from around 2011 would have been very rewarding, though there was a very serious short squeeze on these companies in February 2016.

Hedging

Hedging is a complex way to manage your portfolio risk. In the US, you can borrow shares from a stockbroker and sell them short – so you have to research yet more companies; or you can use the futures and options markets, which will involve developing new skills.

It's more straightforward to hedge in the UK using CFDs. You can readily short indices or individual shares on a CFD platform. There will be borrowing costs involved.

A good alternative for the proactive investor wanting to manage his portfolio risk is to manage percent invested (PCI) as described above.

Speculation

Speculation is a skilled activity which involves taking a risk with a plausible, highly desirable outcome that is thought to justify the possibility of a serious loss – and should be informed by some specialist knowledge. If you decide to speculate, you should be able to absorb a worst-case loss.

There is no shortage of ways to speculate in the stock market, and some examples are discussed below.

- Investing in exploration companies – exploring for oil, gas, and other minerals. A good drilling report can move a share price up very sharply. An effective speculator in this area will know the company well and understand to some extent its exploration program and he may have some knowledge of the geology of the areas under exploration. He will also have a view on the quality and track record of the management and its exploration team.
- Taking a position – long or short – in a company shortly before it reports. Some of the sharpest share price movements take place in response to reporting, and the successful speculator will have an informed view of how the company is likely to report.
- Invest in IPOs, which have some good form in rising sharply on flotation. 'Staggers' buy and sell quickly to take a quick gain, often based on nothing more than the euphoria around the offering. With many IPOs, there is not the same level of information available in the IPO prospectus as would be normal for an established company. During 2014 and 2015, with markets at high

levels, there tended to be less 'value' in IPOs than the staggers had come to expect. Many private equity specialists were looking to exit companies that they had paid too much for in the past and were not offering any bargains, and founders of successful companies were looking to realize their fortunes.

- Invest in small cap companies – typically there will be little or no analyst coverage, and possibly the only information available to investors will be the quarterly or twice-yearly reporting. Speculators in these companies should have a view on the value of the product or services that they are looking to back. At the extreme end of this spectrum can be companies that are not yet in profit. Small cap companies generate a lot of 'chat' on bulletin boards, which seems to be a way of life for many retail traders and investors.
- Probably more 'speculative' than speculation is to take a position in a company that you believe may be a takeover target at some point; or in a company that may break up to create more shareholder value. A problem with this is that you may be putting your money in companies that are not really going anywhere – which is why they need attention, but the attention may be some time in coming.
- Following a much-admired investor into a particular share is a form of speculation; as is investing in a company on the recommendation of a tipster with a strong track record.

For people with a strong interest in the markets, it's tempting to have a go at some speculation, but you should resist the temptation unless you are prepared to take some heavy losses in percentage terms.

Bear in mind that buying a share only because it has risen sharply for a couple of days or has fallen to a very low level is not speculation, it is simply gambling.

Using a stockbroker

So should you use a stockbroker?

Only if you can find a good one. This question is addressed in *Chapter 17*. Many stockbrokers will not be interested in helping you with a 'buy and hold' strategy – they need to have a steady stream of commissions. However, in the current climate in which the big gains have occurred after the lows of the financial crisis, swing trading is a viable approach. See *Chapter 10*.

The swing trader seeks to exploit the volatile movements that occur in many share prices; see, for example, the long-term charts for Apple (AAPL), Aviva (AV), or Unilever (ULVR). You may be able to find a stockbroker that can assist you in a successful short-term approach. If you decide to use a stockbroker, it is important that you agree your objectives with him.

Day to day – building your expertise

If you work within a structured framework, you should be able to build your knowledge of the markets and your investment expertise. Proactive investment involves some work, but the Internet makes a very big difference to the prospects of the retail investor and some success should make investing an enjoyable experience. Manage your downside risk and learn from your investment decisions that don't work out. There will inevitably be some of these. The more you practise, the luckier you will get – probably!

Judging your success

You need to judge your success over a period of one to two years, because how you manage your investments through prolonged downturns, should they occur, is important. However, you should review your performance constantly as to how well you have managed your timing and percent invested, and the quality of your selection of funds and shares.

With monies invested, you should aim to beat the total return on the S&P 500 in the US and FTSE 250 in the UK in rising phases of the market.

If you invest in individual shares, you should check your aggregate returns against the best-performing funds. You will inevitably have some shares that you hold because they took a sharp fall, and you have a belief that they will recover, but there shouldn't be too many in this category.

If you read the markets well and select good funds and shares, 70% to 80% of your investments should trend up.

Index

56530094R00252

Made in the USA
Charleston, SC
24 May 2016